DEVELOPMENT and SOCIAL CHANGE

SIXTH EDITION

For Karen, with love and gratitude

DEVELOPMENT and SOCIAL CHANGE

A GLOBAL PERSPECTIVE

SIXTH EDITION

PHILIP McMICHAEL

Cornell University

Los Angeles | London | New Delhi
Singapore | Washington DC

Los Angeles | London | New Delhi
Singapore | Washington DC

FOR INFORMATION:

SAGE Publications, Inc.
2455 Teller Road
Thousand Oaks, California 91320
E-mail: order@sagepub.com

SAGE Publications Ltd.
1 Oliver's Yard
55 City Road
London, EC1Y 1SP
United Kingdom

SAGE Publications India Pvt. Ltd.
B 1/I 1 Mohan Cooperative Industrial Area
Mathura Road, New Delhi 110 044
India

SAGE Publications Asia-Pacific Pte. Ltd.
3 Church Street
#10-04 Samsung Hub
Singapore 049483

Acquisitions Editor: Jeff Lasser
eLearning Editor: Gabrielle Piccininni
Editorial Assistant: Alexandra Croell
Production Editor: Libby Larson
Copy Editor: Amy Harris
Typesetter: Hurix Systems Pvt. Ltd.
Proofreader: Theresa Kay
Indexer: Kathy Paparchontis
Cover Designer: Karine Hovsepian
Marketing Manager: Johanna Swenson

Copyright © 2017 by SAGE Publications, Inc.

Printed in the United States of America

Library of Congress Cataloging-in-Publication Data

Names: McMichael, Philip.

Title: Development and social change : a global perspective / Philip McMichael.

Description: Sixth Edition. | Thousand Oaks : SAGE Publications, Inc., 2016. | Revised edition of the author's Development and social change. | Includes bibliographical references and index.

Identifiers: LCCN 2015039527 | ISBN 9781452275901 (pbk. : alk. paper)

Subjects: LCSH: Economic development projects— History. | Economic development—History. | Competition, International—History.

Classification: LCC HC79.E44 M25 2016 | DDC 306.309—dc23 LC record available at http://lccn.loc .gov/2015039527

This book is printed on acid-free paper.

Certified Chain of Custody
SUSTAINABLE FORESTRY INITIATIVE
Promoting Sustainable Forestry
www.sfiprogram.org
SFI-01268

SFI label applies to text stock

16 17 18 19 20 10 9 8 7 6 5 4 3 2 1

Brief Contents

Detailed Contents

About the Author

Philip McMichael grew up in Adelaide, South Australia, and he completed undergraduate degrees in economics and in political science at the University of Adelaide. After traveling in India, Pakistan, and Afghanistan and doing community work in Papua New Guinea, he pursued his doctorate in sociology at the State University of New York at Binghamton. He has taught at the University of New England (New South Wales), Swarthmore College, and the University of Georgia, and he is presently International Professor of Development Sociology at Cornell University. Other appointments include Visiting Senior Research Scholar in International Development at the University of Oxford (Wolfson College) and Visiting Scholar, School of Political Science and International Relations at the University of Queensland.

His book *Settlers and the Agrarian Question: Foundations of Capitalism in Colonial Australia* (1984) won the Social Science History Association's Allan Sharlin Memorial Award in 1985. In addition to authoring *Food Regimes and Agrarian Questions* (2013), McMichael edited *The Global Restructuring of Agro-Food Systems* (1994), *Food and Agrarian Orders in the World Economy* (1995), *New Directions in the Sociology of Global Development* (2005) with Frederick H. Buttel, *Looking Backward and Looking Forward: Perspectives on Social Science History* (2005) with Harvey Graff and Lesley Page Moch, *Contesting Development: Critical Struggles for Social Change* (2010), and *The Politics of Biofuels, Land and Agrarian Change* (2011) with Jun Borras and Ian Scoones.

He has served twice as chair of his department, as director of Cornell University's International Political Economy Program, as chair of the American Sociological Association's Political Economy of the World-System Section, as president of the Research Committee on Agriculture and Food for the International Sociological Association, and as a board member of Cornell University Press. He has also worked with the Food and Agricultural

Organization of the United Nations (FAO) and the Civil Society Mechanism of the FAO's Committee on World Food Security (CFS), the UN Research Institute for Social Development (UNRISD), the international peasant coalition *Vía Campesina,* and the International Planning Committee for Food Sovereignty.

He and his wife, Karen Schachere, have two children, Rachel and Jonathan.

Preface to the Sixth Edition

The sixth edition of this text updates and refines the narrative. The thread that weaves together this story is that *development* is a concept and practice stemming from the era of expansion of Europe into the Americas, Asia, and Africa, and as such embodies a power relationship. In its most elemental form, it views a very diverse world through a singular lens of cultural evolution, equating civilization with Europe and thereby discounting non-European cultures. At the same time, given the association of development with economic growth, the ecological foundations of human civilization have been seriously discounted. The long arc of development—from colonialism through the development decades to the era of globalization—is now bending toward recognition of the importance of cultural diversity and biodiversity for human and planetary sustainability. As a form of rule, development takes different forms in different historical periods, and these are laid out here as changing sets of political-economic and political-ecological relations, animated by powerful discourses of discipline, opportunity, and sustainability.

While this text may appear to be "one-sided" in its presentation, it may be because development has always been quite one-sided as a ruling discourse and set of practices. As such, it is examined here as a contested historical project, rather than something to take for granted—operating through relationships of power among and within countries and world regions. Modern social thought associates development with human progress, stemming from an Enlightenment ideal. It is, of course, an ideal not necessarily shared by the majority world and yet has become the dominant trope governing international relations via the project of development and its prioritization of the market as a civilizing force. The limits of this secular ideal, as it shaped modern social thought, are becoming increasingly clear today, as the accumulation of environmental uncertainty dramatically reveals development's shortcomings in overlooking the centrality of ecosystems to human life—and, therefore, reveals the illusion of unlimited economic growth. This text may have the appearance of an economic argument, in part because development is generally associated with economic growth. To represent that view, as well as indicate where it comes from, it is necessary to trace its origins and evolution in recent world history. At the same time, it is important to defetishize the economic interpretation and reveal the social processes and ecological consequences of development, as well as the power relations ordering this historic enterprise and thence the world. This account of development focuses on these social and political transformations and the various ways in which development is realized through social and spatial inequalities. It also considers these processes from the perspective of social movements and how their resistances problematize, or question, the dominant vision of economism as a form of rule and as an increasingly evident threat to ecological stability.

The conceptual framework posits development as a political construct, devised by dominant actors such as metropolitan states, multilateral institutions, and political and economic elites to order the world and contain opposition. Development and globalization are presented as projects with coherent organizing principles (e.g., economic nationalism, market liberalization), yet unrealistic in their vision and potential for accomplishment since they are realized through inequality. The theoretical subtext of the development project is organized by extended Polanyian cycles of "market self-regulation" and resistance. In the mid-twentieth century, a form of "embedded liberalism" (market regulation within a maturing nation-state system to contain labor and decolonization movements) informed social–democratic (developmentalist) goals within a Cold War context of economic and military aid to the Third World. This "development era" ended with a "countermobilization" of corporate interests dedicated to instituting a "self-regulating market" on a global scale from the 1970s onward.

The dominant discourse of neoliberalism proposed market liberalization, privatization, freedom of capital movement and access, and so on. This globalization project had a "test run" during the debt regime of the 1980s and was institutionalized with the establishment of the World Trade Organization (WTO) in 1995. A *further* countermobilization—to the deprivations of the globalization project—has gathered momentum through maturing global justice movements in the 1990s, the Latin American and Arab rebellions of the new century, and a growing "legitimacy deficit" for the global development establishment. This is symbolized in the collapse of the Washington Consensus following the 1997 Asian-originating global financial crisis, recovery of the trope of "poverty reduction" in the Millennium Development Goals (MDGs) initiative of 2000, stalemate at the WTO, and growing antipathy toward the World Bank and the International Monetary Fund (IMF) among countries of the global South. Neoliberalism is at a crossroads, complicated by serious security concerns with a social component (in mushrooming slums); an economic dimension (in both financial volatility and the casualization of employment); a political element (in acts of terrorism); and an ecological aspect (in the evidence of global climate change). How the current cycle of opposition and creative development alternatives will unfold is yet to be determined, but we may see a "sustainability project" emerge, including security concerns—largely of those with political and economic power—and grassroots initiatives toward rethinking the values that define development.

The major revision here is threefold. First, Chapter 7 on countermovements refocuses on three key epistemic interventions regarding development's market-centrism: the lack of any systematic accounting for ecosystem degradation and resource depletion, the socially reproductive work performed largely by women, and food insecurity. These are ultimately "externals" to market relations, and as such, they give rise to a series of paradoxes, or contradictions, integral to development. Second, Chapter 8 updates the review of expressions of crisis in the globalization project, focusing on the cumulative social crisis across the world resulting from widespread austerity policies, associated legitimacy questions and initiatives, geopolitical multipolarity as the American century winds down, new developments in India and China, and the public health and ecological crisis. Third, Chapter 9 ("Sustainable Development?") features the climate challenge and three particular forms of response: business as usual, public interventions, and grassroots initiatives; together, these responses reveal an array of disparate attempts to manage the future, pointing toward a future environmental/climate regime.

The subject of development is difficult to teach. Living in relatively affluent surroundings, most university students understandably situate their society on the "high end" of a development continuum—at the pinnacle of human economic and technological achievement. And they often perceive the development continuum and their favorable position on it as "natural"—a well-deserved reward for embracing modernity. It is difficult to put one's world in historical perspective from this vantage point. It is harder still to help students grasp a world perspective that goes beyond framing their experience as an "evolved state"—the inevitable march of "progress."

In my experience, until students go beyond simple evolutionary views, they have difficulty valuing other cultures and social possibilities that do not potentially mirror their own. When they do go beyond the evolutionary perspective, they are better able to evaluate their own culture sociologically and to think reflexively about social change, development, and global inequalities. This is the challenge we face.

A Timeline of Development

WORLD FRAMEWORK	Developmentalism (1940s–1970s)
POLITICAL ECONOMY	State-Regulated Markets (Keynesianism) Public Spending
SOCIAL GOALS	Social Contract and Redistribution National Citizenship
DEVELOPMENT [Model]	Industrial Replication National Economic Sector Complementarity [Brazil, Mexico, India]
MOBILIZING TOOL	Nationalism (Post-Colonialism)
MECHANISMS	Import-Substitution Industrialization (ISI) Public Investment (Infrastructure, Energy) Education Land Reform
VARIANTS	First World (Freedom of Enterprise) Second World (Central Planning) Third World (Modernization via Development Alliance)

MARKERS

Cold War Begins (1946) Korean War (1950–53) Vietnam War (1964–75)

Bretton Woods (1944) Marshall Plan (1946) Alliance for Progress (1961)

United Nations (1943) Non-Aligned Movement Forum (1955) Group of 77 (G-77) (1964) World Economic Forum (1970)

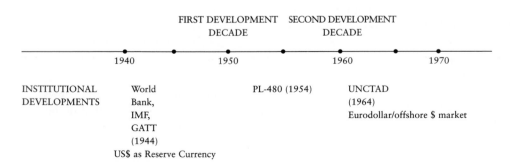

FIRST DEVELOPMENT DECADE   SECOND DEVELOPMENT DECADE

1940   1950   1960   1970

INSTITUTIONAL DEVELOPMENTS

World Bank, IMF, GATT (1944)
US$ as Reserve Currency

PL-480 (1954)

UNCTAD (1964)
Eurodollar/offshore $ market

COMECON (1947)

Globalism (1980s–2000s)

Self-Regulating Markets (Monetarism)
Public Downsizing

Private Initiative and Global Consumerism
Multi-Layered Citizenship and Recognition

Participation in World Market
Global Comparative Advantage
[Chile, South Korea; NAFTA]

Markets and Credit
Financialization

Export-Orientation
Privatization
Entrepreneurialism
Public and Majority-Class Austerity

National Structural Adjustment (Opening Economies)
Regional Free Trade Agreements
Global Governance

Oil Crises (1973, 1979)	Cold War Ends (1989)	"New World Order"	Imperial Wars (2001–)	Islamic State (2013 – ?)
	Debt Regime	WTO Regime	Climate Regime	
New International Economic Order Initiative (1974)		Chiapas Revolt (1994)	World Social Forum (2001)	

Group of 7 (G-7) (1975)	Earth Summit (1992)	Kyoto Protocol (1997)	Group of 20 (G-20) (1999)	MDGs (2000)	Stern Report (2006)	IAASTD Report (2008)	SDGs (2015)

"LOST DECADE"   "GLOBALIZATION DECADE"

1970   1980   1990   2000

GATT Uruguay   NAFTA (1994)
Round (1986–1994)   WTO (1995)
IPCC (1988)
UNFCCC (1988)

Offshore Banking   Structural Adjustment Loans   "Governance"/HIPC Loans   Public Private Partnerships

Glasnost/Perestroika

Acknowledgments

I wish to express my thanks to the people who have helped me along the way, beginning with the late Terence Hopkins (my graduate school mentor), and James Petras and Immanuel Wallerstein. The late Giovanni Arrighi played a critical role in encouraging me to cultivate "analytical nerve." For the first three editions, which include acknowledgment of the various people who were so helpful, special mention still goes to the original editor-in-chief, Steve Rutter, for his remarkable vision and his enthusiasm and faith in this project, as well as friends and colleagues who made significant contributions to improving this project—the late Fred Buttel, Harriet Friedmann, Richard Williams, Michelle Adato, Dale Tomich, Farshad Araghi, Rajeev Patel, Dia Da Costa, Gayatri Menon, Karuna Morarji, and Heloise Weber—and my undergraduate and graduate students (particularly my remarkable teaching assistants) at Cornell.

For this sixth edition, I have been fortunate to have the encouragement and understanding of Jeff Lasser, Publisher for Sociology at SAGE, and the thoughtful guidance of Editorial Assistant Alexandra Croell. Also, special thanks go to senior project editor Libby Larson, to editorial and marketing specialists Theresa Accomazzo and Erica DeLuca for their work behind the scenes, and especially to Amy Harris, my fastidious copyeditor. PhD student Kathleen Sexsmith provided much-needed and thorough research support when I needed it most and turned a critical eye on some of the writing. Great thanks are also due to reviewers of previous editions.

Reviewers for the Sixth Edition

Ozlem Altiok, University of North Texas–Denton

Patricia Campion, Saint Leo University

Cynthia Caron, Clark University

Leif Jensen, Penn State

Alfred T. Kisubi, PhD, BBD-HSP, University of Wisconsin–Oshkosh, College of Education and Human Services

Olena Leipnik, SHSU

Ryan Wishart, Creighton University

Max D. Woodworth, The Ohio State University

Abbreviations

AfDB	African Development Bank
AGRA	Alliance for a Green Revolution in Africa
ALBA	Bolivarian Alternative for the Americas
AoA	Agreement on Agriculture (WTO)
APEC	Asia-Pacific Economic Cooperation
BAIR	bureaucratic-authoritarian industrializing regime
BIP	Border Industrialization Program
BRICS	Brazil, Russia, India, China, and South Africa
CAFTA	Central American Free Trade Agreement
CBD	Convention on Biodiversity
CDM	clean development mechanism
CEDAW	Convention on the Elimination of All Forms of Discrimination Against Women
CGIAR	Consultative Group on International Agricultural Research
COMECON	Council for Mutual Economic Assistance
COP	Conference of the Parties
ECA	export credit agency
ECLA	Economic Commission for Latin America
EOI	export-oriented industrialization
EPZ	export processing zone
EU	European Union

FAO	Food and Agriculture Organization (UN)
FDI	foreign direct investment
FLO	Fairtrade Labelling Organizations International
FTA	free trade agreement
FTAA	Free Trade Area of the Americas
GAD	gender and development
GATS	General Agreement on Trade in Services
GATT	General Agreement on Tariffs and Trade
GDI	Gender Development Index
GDL	global division of labor
GDP	gross domestic product
GEF	Global Environmental Facility
GEM	gender empowerment measure
GHG	greenhouse gas emissions
GlobalGAP	a retailer produce working group on Good Agricultural Practices
GNH	gross national happiness
GNP	gross national product
GPI	genuine progress indicator
HDI	Human Development Index
HIPC	heavily indebted poor countries
HYV	high-yielding variety
IAASTD	International Assessment of Agricultural Science and Technology for Development
ICT	information and communication technologies
IDB	Inter-American Development Bank
IDS	Institute for Development Studies
IEA	International Energy Agency
IFI	international financial institutions

IFPRI	International Food Policy Research Institute
IIED	International Institute for Environment and Development
IMF	International Monetary Fund
IPCC	Inter-Governmental Plan on Climate Change
IPR	intellectual property rights
ISI	import-substitution industrialization
LDC	least developed countries
LDCF	Less Developed Countries Fund
MA	Millennium Ecosystem Assessment
MDGs	Millennium Development Goals
MENA	Middle East North African states
MICs	middle-income countries
NAC	new agricultural country
NAFTA	North American Free Trade Agreement
NAM	Non-Aligned Movement
NAPA	national adaptation programme of action
NEPAD	New Partnership for Africa's Development
NGO	nongovernmental organization
NIC	newly industrializing country
NIDL	new international division of labor
NIEO	New International Economic Order
NTE	nontraditional export
OAU	Organization for African Unity
ODA	overseas development assistance
OECD	Organisation for Economic Co-Operation and Development
PRSP	Poverty Reduction Strategy Papers
RAI	responsible agricultural investment
REDD	Reducing Emissions from Deforestation and Degradation

SAL	structural adjustment loan
SAP	structural adjustment policies
SDG	sustainable development goals
SEZ	special economic zone
TFN	transnational feminist network
TIE	Transnationals Information Exchange
TNB	transnational bank
TNC	transnational corporation
TPN	transnational policy network
TRIMs	trade-related aspects of investment measures
TRIPs	trade-related intellectual property rights
UNASUR	Union of South American Nations
UNCED	United Nations Conference on Environment and Development
UNCTAD	United Nations Conference on Trade and Development
UNDESA	United Nations Department of Economic and Social Affairs
UNDP	United Nations Development Program
UNEP	United Nations Environment Program
UNESCO	United Nations Educational, Scientific and Cultural Organization
UNFCCC	United Nations Convention on Climate Change
WEEE	waste from electrical and electronic equipment
WEF	World Economic Forum
WHO	World Health Organization
WID	Women in Development
WSF	World Social Forum
WTO	World Trade Organization

1

Development

Theory and Reality

Development, today, is increasingly about how we survive the future, rather than how we improve on the past. While ideas of human progress and material improvement still guide theory and policy making, how we manage "energy descent" and adapt to serious ecological deficits, climatic disruption, and social justice effects will define our existence. How will this change our understanding and practice of development?

A central issue is how effectively policy makers (in states and development agencies) recognize the need for wholesale public coordination of planning to minimize and adapt to inevitable climatic changes. Plenty of new ideas, practices, and policies are surfacing, but more as a cacophony rather than a strategic endeavor to reverse our **ecological footprint** (see Glossary/ Index for bolded definitions). For example, while the Chinese government is strategic in promoting green technology, China—the major offshore assembly zone for global commodities—leads in global greenhouse gas emissions (one-third).[1] Climate summits tend to confirm ambivalence of governments held hostage to domestic growth policies—whether these governments are from the **global North** or the **global South**. Across this historic divide, there is now a shared global crisis of unemployment and debt, compounding the challenges of development futures with rising inequalities.

Not only are there increasingly evident biophysical limits to development as we know it, but development is now compromised by public austerity policies across the nation-state system, most recently evident in Greece.

Such policies, introduced to the global South from the 1980s, now shape northern societies and their interrelations. All over, the development ideal of a social contract between governments and citizens is crumbling as hard-won social rights and public entitlements erode, generating despair, disillusionment, or disorder as citizens protest cutbacks. Arguably, "development" is not only in crisis but is also at a significant turning point in its short history as a master concept of (Western-oriented) social science and cultural life.

This book is a guide to the rise and transformation of "development" as a powerful instrument of global social change over the last two centuries. From one (long-term) angle, it appears increasingly cometlike: a brilliant lodestar for ordering the world, but perhaps destined to burn out as its energy-intensive foundations meet their limits. From another (immediate) angle, the energy and inequality dilemma forces renewed critical thinking about how humans might live sustainably and equitably on the planet. These perspectives are the subjects of chapters to come. Here, we are concerned with the source and maturation of development as a master concept—both its promises and its paradoxes.

Development: History and Politics

Development had its origins in the colonial era, as European domination came to be understood as superiority and leadership along a development axis. Global in its origins, the meaning of *development* nevertheless compared European accomplishments with societies increasingly disrupted by imperial ventures. While such accomplishments came with substantial environmental and social—and often violent—upheaval, they have been represented in theory as a set of idealized outcomes to be emulated by other countries. Accordingly, development's ends justify its means, however socially and ecologically disruptive the process may be.

Here, Michael Cowan and Robert Shenton's distinction between development as an unfolding universal social *process* and development as a political *intervention* is useful. In the nineteenth century, development was understood *philosophically* as improving humankind (in the form of knowledge building, technological change, and wealth accumulation). In relation to this, European political elites interpreted development *practically*, as a way to socially engineer emerging national societies. Elites formulated government policy to manage the social transformations attending the rise of capitalism and industrial technologies, so development was identified with *both* industrialization *and* the regulation of its disruptive social impacts. These impacts began with the displacement of rural populations by land enclosures for cash cropping, a process that generated "undesirables," such as menacing paupers, restless proletarians, and unhealthy factory towns.[2] Development, then, meant balancing technological change and the rise of new social classes, fashioning policies to manage wholesale social transformations. At the same time, such transformations became the catalyst of competing political visions—liberal, socialist, conservative—of the ideal society.

In Europe's colonies, the inhabitants appeared undeveloped—by self-referential (evolutionary) European standards. This ideological understanding of development legitimized imperial intervention, whether to plunder or civilize. Either way, the social engineering impulse framed European imperialism. Not only did massive colonial resource extraction facilitate European industrialization, but European colonial administrators also managed subject populations experiencing their own wrenching social transformations. Thus, development assumed an additional, normative meaning, namely, the "white man's burden"—the title of a poem by nineteenth-century English poet Rudyard Kipling—imparting honor to an apparently noble task. The implied racism remains a part of the normative understanding (and global consequence) of development.

Thus, development extended modern social engineering to colonies incorporated into the European orbit. Subject populations were exposed to a variety of new disciplines, including forced labor schemes, schooling, and segregation in native quarters. Forms of colonial subordination differed across time and space, but the overriding object was either to adapt or marginalize colonial subjects to the European presence. In this sense, development involved a relation of power. For example, British colonialism introduced the new English factory-model "Lancaster school" to the (ancient) city of Cairo in 1843 to educate Cairo's emerging civil service. Egyptian students learned the new disciplines of a developing society that was busily displacing peasant culture with plantations of cotton for export to English textile mills and managing an army of migrant labor, which was building an infrastructure of roads, canals, railways, telegraphs, and ports.[3] Through the colonial relation, industrialism transformed both English and Egyptian society, producing new forms of social discipline among working- and middle-class citizen-subjects. And while industrialism produced new class inequalities within each society, colonialism racialized international inequality. In this way, development introduced new class and racial hierarchies within and across societies.

While development informed modern narratives in the age of industrialism and empire, it only became formalized as a *project* in the mid-twentieth century. This period was the high tide of decolonization, as the Western

(British, Italian, German, French, Dutch, Portuguese, and Belgian) and Japanese empires succumbed to the moral force of anticolonial resistance and when a standardizing concept—development as an emancipatory promise—became the new global ontology (a way of seeing/ordering the world).

In 1945, the United Nations, with the intent of expanding membership as colonies gained independence as sovereign states, institutionalized the System of National Accounts. A universal quantifiable measure of development, the gross national product (GNP), was born. At this point, the colonial rule of *subjects* under the guise of civilizing inferior races morphed into the **development project**, based on the ideal of self-governing states composed of *citizens* united by the ideology of nationalism. And by the twenty-first century, the global development project focused on market governance of and by self-maximizing *consumers*. Given this trajectory, *development* is conventionally understood as economic growth and rising consumption.

Development Theory

Identifying development with rising consumption privileges the market as the vehicle of social change. The underlying philosophy—deriving from a popular (but limiting) interpretation of Adam Smith's *The Wealth of Nations*[4] and formalized in neoclassical economic theory—is that markets maximize individual preferences and allocate resources efficiently. Whether this theory reflects reality or not, it is a deeply held belief now institutionalized in much development policy across the world. Why is this the case?

Naturalizing Development

There are two ways to answer this question. First, a belief in markets is a central tenet of liberal Western philosophy. Hungarian philosopher Karl Polanyi noted that modern liberalism rests on a belief in a natural human propensity for self-gain, which translates in economic theory as the market principle—realized as consumer preference.[5] Self-gain, expressed through the market, drives the aspiration for improvement, aggregated as consumption. Second, as Polanyi noted, to naturalize market behavior as an innate propensity discounts other human traits or values—such as cooperation, redistribution, and reciprocity, which are different organizing principles by which human societies have endured for centuries. For Polanyi and other classical social theorists, pursuit of individualism via an economic calculus is quite novel in the history and makeup of human societies and quite specific to modernity, rather than being inherent in human social life.

While cooperative values are clearly evident today in human interactions, the aspiration for improvement, normalized now as a private motivation, informs development. That is, well-being and self-improvement center on access to goods *and* services through the marketplace. Dating from the mid-twentieth century, in an era of powerful anticolonial, labor, and citizenship movements, formulations of development paired private consumption with public provisions—infrastructure, education, health, water supply, commons, clean air, and so forth. The mid-twentieth century was the heyday of the welfare, or development, state. But from the last quarter of the twentieth century, provisioning has increasingly been subjected to **privatization**, as the market, rather than the state, becomes the medium through which society develops.

This outcome was prefigured in one of the most influential theories of development emerging in the post–World War II world. In 1960, economist Walt Rostow published *The Stages of Economic Growth*: *A Non-Communist Manifesto*,[6] outlining a development theory that celebrates the Western model of free enterprise—in contrast to a state-planned economy. The "stages" traverse a linear sequence, beginning with "Traditional Society" (agrarian, limited productivity) and moving through "Preconditions for Take-Off" (state formation, education, science, banking, profit-systematization), "Take-Off" (normalization of growth, with investment rates promoting the expanded reproduction of industry), and "Maturity" (the second industrial revolution that moved from textiles and iron to machine-tools, chemicals, and electrical equipment)—and finally to the "Age of High Mass-Consumption," characterized by the movement from basic to durable goods, urbanization, and a rising level of white-collar versus blue-collar work.

This evolutionary sequence, distilled from the US experience, represents the consumer society as the terminal stage of a complex historical process. Rostow viewed the US model as the goal to which other (i.e., developing) societies should aspire, which partly explains his book's subtitle—expressing the Cold War rivalry between the United States and the Soviet Union at the time. The theorization of development as a series of evolutionary stages naturalizes the process, whether it occurs on a national (development era) or an international (globalization era) stage. Mass consumption was a final goal to be realized through membership of the "free world" at the time, and by implication, US assistance would be available to spur the **Third World** of postcolonial, developing nations into progress along the stages.

However, note that Rostow's "development blueprint" depended on a political context. That is, markets required creating, securing, and protecting (by a **development state**). They could not be natural. And development was neither spontaneous nor inevitable; rather, it was shaped by social struggle, and it required an institutional complex on a world scale (a **development project**) to nurture it along, complete with trade, monetary, and investment rules, aid regimes, and a military umbrella—all of which were supplied through postwar, multilateral institutions and bilateral arrangements led by the United States. In this way, a theory of spontaneous markets diverges from reality. But reality was nonetheless shaped by this theory—informing public discourse and translated into policy implementation via an increasing market calculus. This is a central paradox explored in this book.

Global Context

Reality is more complicated than it first appears. For example, Rostow's prescriptions artificially separated societies from one another. This may have expressed the idealism of mid-twentieth-century nationalism. But to assign stages of growth to societies without accounting for their unequal access to offshore resources discounted a fundamental historic relationship between world regions shaped by colonial and investment patterns. Not only did European powers once depend on their colonies for resources and markets, but these patterns continued in the postcolonial era. Because of continuing **First World** dependence on raw materials from the **Third World,** some societies were more equal than others in their capacity to traverse Rostow's stages, in part because resource extraction was one way, as we shall see in Chapter 4.

It was this reality that stimulated **dependency analysis** and **world-system analysis.** The concept of "dependency" (referring to unequal economic relations between metropolitan societies and non-European peripheries) emerged in the mid-twentieth century from several quarters—an empirical observation by economist Hans Singer that "peripheral" countries were exporting more and more natural resources to pay for increasingly expensive manufactured imports; an argument by Singer's collaborator, Argentinean economist Raúl Prebisch, that Latin American states should therefore industrialize behind protective tariffs on manufactured imports; and earlier Marxist theories of exploitative imperialist relations between the European and the non-European world.[7] Dependency was, then, a relationship accounting for the development of Europe at the expense of the **underdevelopment** of the non-European world. Economist Andre Gunder Frank put it this way:

> [H]istorical research demonstrates that contemporary underdevelopment is in large part the historical product of past and continuing economic and other relations between the satellite underdeveloped and the now-developed metropolitan countries. . . . When we examine this metropolis-satellite structure, we

find that each of the satellites . . . serves as an instrument to suck capital or economic surplus out of its own satellites and to channel part of this surplus to the world metropolis of which all are satellites.[8]

World-system analysis, advanced by sociologist Immanuel Wallerstein, deepened the concept of dependency by elevating the scope of the modern social system to a global scale. States became political units competing for—or surrendering—resources within a **world division of labor**. Here, regional labor forces occupy a skill/technological hierarchy associated with state strength or weakness in the capitalist world economy.[9] From this perspective, the "core" concentrates capital-intensive or intellectual production and the "periphery" is associated with lower-skilled, labor-intensive production, whether plantation labor, assembly of manufactured goods, or routine service work (e.g., call centers). As we shall see, this kind of geographical hierarchy is increasingly complicated by what journalist Thomas Friedman calls "flat world" processes, exemplified, for him, by India's embrace of information technology.[10]

While dependency broadens the analysis of development processes to world-scale relationships, challenging the assumption that societies are aligned along a self-evident spectrum of growth stages, it implies a "development-centrism"—where (idealized Western) development is the term of reference. In this regard, Wallerstein has argued that given the power hierarchy of the world system, (idealized Western) development represents a "lodestar," or master concept, of modern social theory.[11] As such, the privileging of Western-style development denied many other collective/social strategies of sustainability or improvement practiced by non-Western cultures. Nevertheless, while measuring all societies against a conception of (industrial) development may have seemed the appropriate goal for modernization and dependency theory at mid-century, from the vantage point of the *twenty-first century* it is quite problematic. The growing recognition that the planet cannot sustain the current Western-emulating urban-industrial trends in China and India is one dramatic expression of this new reality.

Agrarian Questions

Urbanization is a defining outcome of development and the "stages of growth" metaphor, where "tradition" yields to "modernity" as industrialization deepens and nurtures it. Political scientist Samuel Huntington, writing about the process of modernization in *Political Order and Changing Societies* (1968), claimed, "Agriculture declines in importance compared to commercial, industrial, and other nonagricultural activities, and commercial agriculture replaces subsistence agriculture."[12] While this theoretical sequence is clearly in evidence and has informed policies discounting small-scale farming, there is a further question regarding whether and to what extent this is natural, or inevitable. And this in turn raises questions about the model of separate national development. In fact, the demise of millions of small producers has foreign, or international, origins—in the form of colonialism, foreign aid, and unequal market relations—expressing the global power relations identified by dependency and world-system analysts. How we perceive these changes is the ultimate question: We know, for instance, that agricultural productivity ratios across high- and low-input farming systems have risen from 10:1 before 1940 to 2,000:1 in the twenty-first century,[13] putting small producers (primarily in the global South) at a competitive disadvantage in the global market. Even as social changes occur within nations, does that mean the change is "internally" driven? Thus, if subsistence agriculture declines or disappears, is this because it does not belong on a society's "development ladder"?[14] Or is it because of an expo-sure of smallholders to forces beyond their control, such as unequal world market competition by agribusiness?

Small farming cultures are represented as development "baselines"—in theory and in practice, given modern technology's drive to replace labor and control production (with commercial inputs such as seed, fertilizer, and pes-ticides along with farm machinery). Unrecognized is the superior capacity or potential in surviving agrarian cultures for managing and sustaining their ecosystems compared to industrial agriculture, which attempts to override natural limits with chemicals and other technologies that deplete soil fertil-ity, hydrological cycles, and biodiversity.[15] The current "global land grab" depends on representing land in the global South as "underutilized" and better employed by conversion to commercial agricultural estates producing foods and biofuels largely for export.[16] Such activities raise a fundamental question as to whether and to what extent development—as modeled—is inevitable or intentional, and national or international.

Ecological Questions

This example of conversion of farming into an industrial activity under-scores a significant *ecological blindspot* in development theory. Where the passage from small farming to large-scale (commercial) agriculture is rep-resented as improvement, or development, it is an insufficient measure if it does not take into account the "externals." These are the significant social and environmental impacts, such as disruption of agrarian cultures and ecosystems, the deepening of dependency on fossil fuel, and modern agriculture's responsibility for up to a third of greenhouse gas emissions (GHG). Such consequences challenge the wisdom of replacing a long-standing knowledge-intensive culture/ecology (farming) with an increasingly unsustainable industrialized economic sector (agriculture).

One key example of this ecological blindspot is its reproduction in the **Human Development Index (HDI)**, constructed by the United Nations Development Programme (UNDP) in 1990. The HDI overcame the singular emphasis on economic growth as development, but carried forward the absence of the ecological dimension:

> The concept of human development focuses on the ends rather than the means of development and progress. The real objective of development should be to create an enabling environment for people to enjoy long, healthy and creative lives. Though this may appear to be a simple truth, it is often overlooked as more immediate concerns are given precedence.[17]

While the HDI is known for its more robust measurement of (human) development, its data sources have lacked environmental content. This is particularly so, given that humanity has now overshot the earth's biocapacity (see Figure 1.1). Focusing on the outcomes of development discounts

Figure 1.1   Humanity's Ecological Footprint

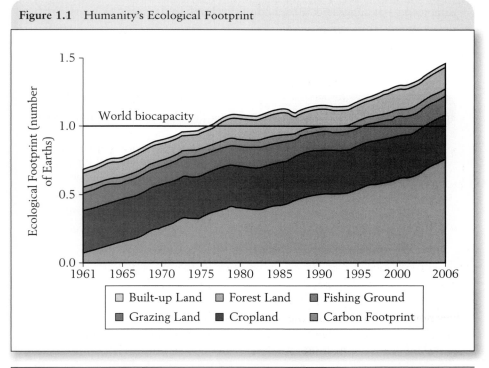

Source: Global Footprint Network, 2010 National Footprint Accounts.

how we live on the earth—that is, measuring what practices are sustainable or not. It was only in 2011 that the UNDP began to embrace an ecological sensibility. Thus, the Human Development Report (2011) is "about the adverse repercussions of environment degradation for people, how the poor and disadvantaged are worst affected, and how greater equity needs to be part of the solution."[18]

Given the UNDP's reputation for questioning conventional wisdom, this new focus complements the *2005 Millennium Ecosystem Assessment,* which noted that the last half century of human action has had the most intensive and extensive negative impact on world ecosystems ever, and yet this has been accompanied by continuing global gains in human well-being.[19] Known as the **"environmentalist's paradox"** (since we might expect ecosystem degradation to negatively affect human well-being), researchers have noted that *average* measures of well-being may reduce the validity of this claim, but perhaps more significantly, "technology has decoupled well-being from nature" and time lags will only tell.[20] In other words, mastery of nature may be effective in the short-term in generating rising consumption patterns, but also in masking the long-term health implications of ecosystem stress. What such research suggests is that development needs a robust sustainability dimension—as suggested at the end of this book in the section on sustainable development approaches.

DEVELOPMENT PARADOXES

The environmentalist's paradox, when inverted, is, in fact, a "development paradox." Former World Bank economist Herman Daly formulated this as an "impossibility theorem"—namely, that the universalization of US-style high mass-consumption economy would require several planet Earths. Either way, the *ultimate paradox here is that the environment is not equipped to absorb its unrelenting exploitation by the current growth model of endless accumulation.* In other words, development as we know it is undermining itself.

Three of the nine designated planetary operational boundaries have been crossed already—climate change, biodiversity, and the nitrogen cycle—while others such as fresh water use and oceanic acidification are at serious tipping points. Meanwhile, the costs of environmental degradation are borne disproportionately by the poor—the very same people targeted by the development industry. This is a key development paradox. Related to these formulations is the notion (advanced by the World Bank in 1992) that economic growth is a condition for sustainable development, which the *UK Stern Review* of 2006 termed a paradox since the cost of climate change adaptation would be far greater if we wait for higher future levels of wealth to address the problem.

Some subsidiary paradoxes include such questions as these: Are low-carbon cultures that live with rather than seek to master nature backward? Are non-Western cultures judged poor in what makes Western cultures rich? Is frugality poverty? Why is malnutrition common to Western and non-Western cultures (see Figure 1.2)? Are non-Western cultures rich in what Western cultures are now poor (nonmonetized items such as open space, leisure, solidarity, ecological knowledge)? Should we measure living standards only in monetary terms?

Sources: Foster (2011); Stern (2006); Daly (1990).

Figure 1.2   Percentage of Population That Is Malnourished and Overweight

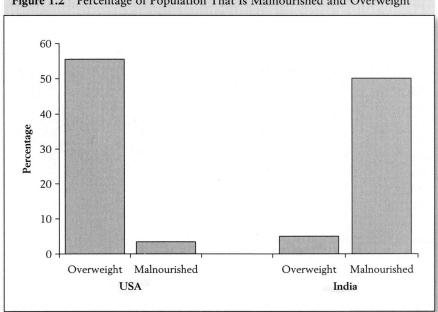

Source: Adapted from *New Internationalist* 353 (2003): 20.

Social Change

As we have seen, development theory provides a blueprint, and justification, for universalizing a European-centered process. European industrialization depended on displacing non-European industry and capturing non-European resources (labor, minerals, raw materials, and foodstuffs). Such colonial intervention was justified as a civilizing mission—asked what he thought of British civilization, the leader of India's independence movement, Mahatma Gandhi, reputedly replied, "It would be a good idea." Of course, colonial subjects resisted—for example, the successful late-eighteenth-century slave uprising in the French colony of Saint Domingue (forming the Haitian free state), but also the unsuccessful Amritsar rebellion, put down savagely by British forces in India in 1919. Such uprisings marked a long-term politics of decolonization, with colonial subjects gaining moral and material power as **countermovements** to European empires, which in turn became increasingly costly to maintain. Resistance to colonial relations—including substantial peasant mobilizations from China to Mexico to Kenya—was matched with labor uprisings and political organization during the late-colonial era. The British faced widespread labor strikes in their West Indian and African colonies in the 1930s, and this pattern continued over the next two decades in Africa as British and French colonial subjects protested conditions in cities, ports, mines, and on the railways.[21]

In other words, large-scale social changes accompanying industrial development involve definitive power struggles. Colonial rule generated a politics of decolonization, including class conflict, identity/cultural claims, and the desire for equality of treatment, including sovereignty. The **colonial project** was certainly anchored in class relations, as empires subordinated colonial labor forces and resources to service imperial needs. But this economic relation was accompanied by fundamental racial politics that both justified subjugation and fueled resistances in the name of human rights across the colonial world. These struggles ushered in a postcolonial era, which informed a mid-twentieth-century global development project, embedded in a system of sovereign nation-states forming the United Nations organization in 1945.

The divisive racial legacy of colonialism certainly did not disappear, but a very diverse world was bound together now by a universal principle: an international governmental structure enshrining the meaning and measurement of development as a *national standard*. This was institutionalized in the UN System of National Accounts, by which monetized economic activity was recorded as gross national product (GNP). Outside of the Communist bloc (also known as the **Second World**), as national economic growth and income levels became the measure of development, so First- and Third-World societies came to be governed by the market (and its metrics), with varying degrees of public regulation.

The "market society" was the product of modern capitalism and commodification of the material world, expressed in monetary exchanges. As Karl Marx pointed out, even human labor power came to be commodified, as villagers lost their means of livelihood and were forced to work for monetary wages.[22] Karl Polanyi extended this observation to land and currency, noting that with the rise of nineteenth-century market society each of these substances came to be traded for a price. He argued that neither labor, land, nor money were *produced for sale,* and so were really "fictitious commodities." When these substances are treated as commodities, workers, farmers, and businesses are exposed to exploitative or uncertain conditions. That is, their labor, farming, or entrepreneurship experience competitive relations beyond their control by a market with seemingly independent authority. Accordingly, social countermovements would inevitably arise and advocate for protection from unregulated markets (a "double movement"). The resulting effect would be to re-embed markets within social/public controls. In Polanyi's account, this explains the origins of the twentieth-century welfare state, which became a model for the **development state**. It arose out of a European-wide social mobilization to protect the rights of workers, farmers, and businesses from the ill effects of unrestrained markets.[23]

The Projects as Historical Framework

Within the terms of this broad social-change theory, then, the postcolonial world order emerged from the combined force of decolonization politics and public initiatives to regulate capitalist markets (as distinct from the Communist model of a state-planned economy). Development as an ideal and as a policy carried forward the social welfare dimension, reinforced by the UN Declaration of Universal Human Rights (1948), by which governments were enjoined to protect civil rights through a **social contract** between state and citizen. This idealistic contract defined the era of the **development project** (1940s–1980), rooted in public regulation of markets as servants of states. The following era of the **globalization project** (1980s through the present) saw markets regain ascendancy—with states as servants—and the incorporation of the "good market, bad state" mantra into public discourse. The tension between these poles continues in what may become a **sustainability project** as the world transitions to a new project governed by environmental stress and climate uncertainty.

Here, we frame the story of development around the three projects: colonial, development, and globalization. This framework stresses that the meaning and practice of development changes with changing political-economic (and environmental) conditions. The transition from the development to the globalization project stemmed from a political reversal "from above" by increasingly powerful business and financial interests and their allies to reduce or eliminate public regulation of corporations and their ability to operate across national borders. Deregulation of markets has been the ultimate goal, legitimized by neoliberal economic theory. And subsequent controversies over the impact of globalization at the turn of the twenty-first century have been generated by social mobilization "from below," driven by economic destabilization and intensification of social inequalities as markets have been disembedded from social controls.[24]

These protests, dramatized in 2011 by the Arab Spring and the Occupy Movement among others, draw attention to the **development paradox,** where poverty accompanies economic growth. This is evidenced in an Oxfam report that 2016 marked the threshold of the top 1 percent of the world's population owning more than 50 percent of global wealth,[25] as well as continuing a food crisis that renders almost a billion people chronically hungry.[26]

The current market malaise and combination of crises—food, energy, climate, social—suggests the world may transition toward another project, which I would term the *sustainability project.* The dynamic that links these projects, and accounts for their succession, can be thought of as a series of Polanyian "double movements": politicization of market rule (for or against) via social mobilization. The colonial project, accompanying the rise of capitalist markets, yielded to the development project, as social and decolonization countermovements challenged the ascendancy of the market in their respective territories. Then the development project yielded to a globalization project installed by a global power-elite to restore market sway and reduce the power of states and citizens to the status of servants and consumers respectively.

Currently, the crisis of the globalization project (addressed in Chapter 8) is stimulating a wide range of sustainability initiatives at all scales, geared to containing or reducing environmental degradation and climate warming. How these may coalesce into some kind of world ordering is not yet clear. Whether we will see or make a more authoritarian world order built on energy and climate security claims or some decentralized, ecologically based social organization are some of the possibilities that are informing debate (see Chapter 9). In the meantime, we can situate our condition via some "development coordinates."

The Development Experience

Development is not an activity that other societies do to catch up to the "developed societies." That nomenclature is unfortunate, since it suggests a condition enjoyed by citizens of the global North that is the goal and envy of the rest of the world. Indeed, some argue that the West is busy "undeveloping," as jobs relocate to growth areas such as China and India, as northern public infrastructure decays, as social services such as education and health care dwindle, and as ecosystems degrade. From this perspective, development does not look like a linear process, nor is there a model outcome since it is an uneven global dynamic.

From a global perspective, development redistributes jobs to lower-wage regions. While transnational firms thereby enhance profitability, northern consumers (at least those with incomes) enjoy access to low-cost products that are produced offshore. In this sense, development has been identified—for its beneficiaries—as consumption. This, of course, corresponds with Rostow's final growth stage, but not as a national characteristic—rather as *a global relationship*. Much of what we consume today has global origins. Even when a product has a domestic "Made in . . ." label, its journey to market probably combines components and labor from production and assembly sites located around the world. Sneakers, or parts thereof, might be produced in China or Indonesia, blue jeans assembled in the Philippines, a cell phone or portable media player put together in Singapore, and a watch made in Hong Kong. The British savor organic vegetables from western China, the Chinese eat pork fed with South American soy, and North Americans consume fast foods that may include chicken diced in Mexico or hamburger beef from cattle raised in Costa Rica. And, depending on taste, our coffee is from Southeast Asia, the Americas, or Africa. We readers may not be *global citizens* yet, but we are certainly *global consumers*.

But global consumers are still a minority. While over three-quarters of the world's population can access television images of the global consumer, only half of that audience has access to sufficient cash or credit to consume. Television commercials depict people everywhere consuming global commodities, but this is just an image. We know that much of the world's population does not have Internet access (despite increasingly ubiquitous mobile phones), and we know that a relative minority of the world's population consumes a vast majority of global goods and services.[27] Distribution of, and access to, the world's material wealth is extraordinarily uneven. Almost half of the ex-colonial world dwells now in slums. Over three billion people cannot, or do not, consume in the Western style. Uruguayan writer Eduardo Galeano makes this observation:

> Advertising enjoins everyone to consume, while the economy prohibits the vast majority of humanity from doing so. . . . This world, which puts on a banquet for all, then slams the door in the noses of so many, is simultaneously equalizing and unequal: equalizing in the ideas and habits it imposes and unequal in the opportunities it offers.[28]

And yet it is important also to note that while readers may be accustomed to a commercial culture and view it as the development "standard," other cultures and peoples are noncommercial, not comfortable with commercial definition, or are simply marginal (by choice or circumstance) to commercial life. Contrary to media images, global consumerism is neither accessible to—nor possible for—a majority of humans, nor is it necessarily a universal aspiration, whether by cultural choice for some peoples, or simply for others needing to make ends meet on a day-to-day basis.

Nevertheless, the global marketplace binds consumers, producers, and even those marginalized by resource consumption. Consumers everywhere are surrounded, and often identified by, world products. One of the most ubiquitous, and yet invisible, world products is coltan, a metallic ore used in consumer electronics, such as computers and cell phones, in addition to nuclear reactors. It comes predominantly from the Congo, where militarized conflict over this valuable resource has caused nearly four million deaths, and mining has negative environmental consequences for forests and wildlife. Such ethical issues, similar to those associated with "blood diamonds," have driven some electronics corporations to mine coltan elsewhere in Africa.[29]

The global economy is a matrix of networks of commodity exchanges. In any one network, there is a sequence of production stages, located in a number of countries at sites that provide inputs of labor and materials contributing to the fabrication of a final product (see Figure 1.3). These networks are called **commodity chains**. The chain metaphor illuminates the interconnections among producing communities dispersed across the world. And it allows us to understand that, when we consume a product, we often participate in a global process that links us to a variety of places, people, and resources. While we may experience consumption individually, it is a fundamentally social—and environmental—act.

Commodity chains enable firms to switch production sites for flexible management of their operations (and costs). Any shopper at The Gap, for

Figure 1.3   A Commodity Chain for Athletic Shoes

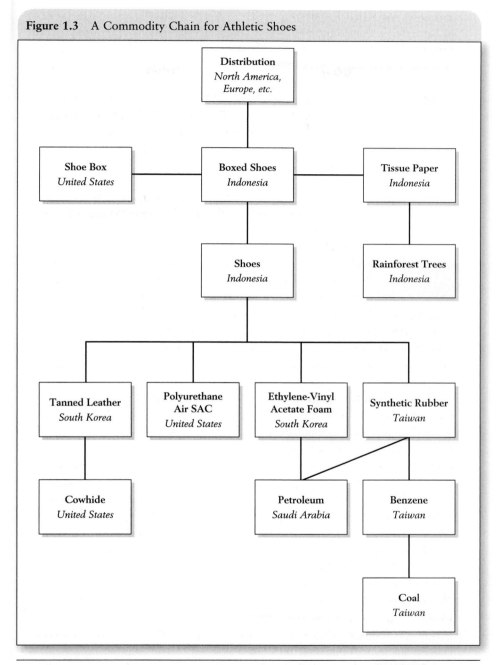

Source: Adapted from Bill Ryan and Alan During, "The Story of a Shoe," *World Watch,* March/ April 1998.

example, knows that this clothing retailer competes by changing its styles on a short-term cycle. Such flexibility requires access through subcontractors to labor forces, increasingly feminized, which can be intensified or let go as orders and fashion changes. Workers for these subcontractors often have little security—or rights—as they are one of the small links in this global commodity chain stretching across an often-unregulated global workplace.

The world was shocked in 2010 when 18 Chinese migrant workers between 17 and 25 years old attempted suicide at Foxconn factories in three Chinese provinces. Foxconn recorded profits that year in excess of some of its corporate customers, such as Microsoft, Dell, and Nokia. Foxconn—responsible for producing the iPhone4, the iPod, and the iPad2—captures 50 percent of the world electronics market share in manufacturing and service.[30]

CASE STUDY   Waste and the Commodity Chain

The disconnect between development theory and the environment is dramatized by the problem of waste, concealed in plain sight. The fact that consumption simultaneously produces waste is neither something consumers want to acknowledge, nor does it feature in measures of economic growth. And yet waste in general, and electronic waste (e-waste) in particular, are huge and problematic by-products of our lifestyle. The household electronics sector is now the fastest growing segment of municipal waste streams, as computing and communication technologies rapidly evolve. The UN estimates the annual global generation of waste from electrical and electronic equipment (WEEE) runs at a rate of between 20 million and 50 million tons. In 2009, the UN Environment Programme (UNEP) reported that e-waste could increase by 500 percent over the next decade in rising middle-income countries. The toxicity of this waste is extraordinary: From 1994 to 2003, for example, disposal of personal computers released 718,000 tons of lead, 287 tons of mercury, and 1,363 tons of cadmium into landfills worldwide.

Cellular, or mobile, phones (1.2 billion sold globally in 2007) leach more than 17 times the US federal threshold for hazardous waste. And yet the noxious ingredients (including silver, copper, platinum, and gold) are valued on second-hand markets, just as discarded e-waste may be recycled for reuse in poorer markets—sometimes by businesses such as Collective Good, which donates a portion of the profits to the Red Cross or the Humane Society. Refurbishing phones occurs from Ghana to India, where labor costs are lower and environmental regulations are less. About 70 percent of the world's discarded e-waste finds its way through informal networks to China, where it is scavenged for usable parts—often by children with no protection—and abandoned to pollute soil and groundwater with toxic metals. Africa is one of the largest markets for discarded phones, while China sells between 200 million and 300 million phones annually to dealers in India, Mongolia, Vietnam, and Thailand, from where they may pass on to buyers in Laos, Cambodia, Bangladesh, and Myanmar. Just as water seeks its own level, unregulated markets enable toxic waste to leach into the global South. While there are regulations regarding hazardous waste, the 170-nation agreement called the Basel Convention is ambiguous on the question of restricting the movement of e-waste from North to South.

Why is the current fixation on the virtual, or "dematerialized," information economy unable to recognize the dependence on offshore manufacturing and disposal of waste—both of which pose social and environmental hazards?

Sources: Schwarzer et al. (2005); Widmer et al. (2005); Mooallem (2008); Leslie (2008); Salehabadi (2011).

Not everything we consume has such global origins, but the trend toward these worldwide supply networks is powerful. Our food, clothing, and shelter, in addition to other consumer comforts, have increasingly long supply chains. Take food, for example. Britain was the first nation to deliberately "outsource" a significant part of its food supply to its empire in the 1840s. In spite of the fact that the British climate is ideal for fruit production, 80 percent of pears and almost 70 percent of apples consumed by Britons now come from Chile, Australia, the United States, South Africa, and throughout the European Union.[31] The Dutch concept of "ghost acres" refers to additional land offshore used to supply a national diet. Britons are estimated to use about 4.1 million hectares of ghost acres to grow mainly animal feed.[32] Ghost acres include "food miles," prompting the remark, "This form of global sourcing . . . is not only energy-inefficient, but it is also doubtful whether it improves global 'equity,' and helps local farmers to meet the goals of sustainable development."[33] In other words, much commercial agriculture today is dedicated to supplying the global consumer rather than improving production for domestic consumers. It is extroverted, rather than introverted as in the Rostow schema.

Half of all [Guatemala's] children under five are malnourished—one of the highest rates of malnutrition in the world. Yet the country has food in abundance.

It is the fifth largest exporter of sugar, coffee, and bananas. Its rural areas are witnessing a palm oil rush as international traders seek to cash in on demand for biofuels created by US and EU mandates and subsidies. But despite being a leading agro-exporter, half of Guatemala's 14 million people live in extreme poverty, on less than $2 a day.[34]

Globalization deepens the paradox of development by virtue of its sheer scale. Integrating the lives of consumers and producers across the world does not necessarily mean sharing the benefits of development globally. The distance between consumers and producers and their environments means it is virtually impossible for consumers to recognize the impact of their consumption on people and environments elsewhere. At the other end, producers experience the social distance in the difficulty in voicing concerns about working conditions or the health of their habitats. Bridging this distance has become the focus of initiatives such as **fair trade**, or brand boycotts organized by activist movements or **nongovernmental organizations** (NGOs), to enhance transparency with information to support more responsible consumption (paradoxically perpetuating dependency on tropical exports versus local food system development).

CASE STUDY   Consuming the Amazon

In a report, *Eating Up the Amazon*, Greenpeace noted, "Europe buys half the soya exported from the Amazon state of Matto Grosso, where 90% of rainforest soya is grown. Meat reared on rainforest soya finds its way on to supermarket shelves and fast food counters across Europe." As the Greenpeace website claimed, "Nuggets of Amazon forest were being served up on a platter at McDonald's restaurants throughout Europe." Following this dramatic report, McDonald's slapped a moratorium on purchasing soya grown in newly deforested regions of the rainforest and entered into an alliance with Greenpeace, and other food retailers, to develop a zero deforestation plan, involving the government in monitoring the integrity of the forest and of its inhabitants, some of whom had been enslaved and subjected to violence. The global soy traders—Cargill, ADM, Bunge, Dreyfus, and Maggi—made a two-year commitment to the alliance.

What is all this about? Like many NGOs, Greenpeace made the unseen relations embodied in chicken nuggets explicit. Documenting the ways in which the Brazilian soy boom—with all its social and environmental consequences—is a product of the fast-food diet, Greenpeace brought to light what is routinely made invisible by the impersonal marketplace. By tracing the soy chain—with the aid of satellite images, aerial surveillance, classified government documents, and on-ground observation—Greenpeace reconstructed the geography of the soy trade, bringing the ethical dimensions of their diet to consumers' notice. While traders can escape the notice of the consuming public, retailers have become "brand sensitive" in an era in which information technology has created a new public space, and consumers have the ability to choose not to consume products that come with baggage.

What is the value of fast food compared with the value of preserving one of the richest and most biologically diverse rainforests on the planet—especially given that the scientific journal *Nature* recently warned that 40 percent of the Amazon rainforest will disappear by 2050 if current trends continue? And what is it about the market that conceals the consequences of our consumer choices?

Source: Greenpeace, *Eating Up the Amazon*, 2006. Available at www.greenpeace.org.

SUMMARY

Development, conventionally associated with economic growth, is a recent phenomenon. With the rise of capitalism, European rulers pursued economic growth to finance their needs for military protection and political legitimacy. But "development," as such, was not yet a universal strategy. It became so only in the mid-twentieth century, as newly independent governments embraced development as an antidote to colonialism, with varying success.

The mid-twentieth-century **development project** (1940s–1970s) was an internationally orchestrated program of *nationally sited* economic growth across the Cold War divide, involving financial, technological, and military assistance from the United States and the Soviet Union. In United Nations terms, development was a timely ideal, as formerly colonized subjects gained political independence, and all governments were enjoined to implement a human rights-based social contract with their citizens, even as this ideal was unevenly practiced. This book traces the implementation of this project, noting its partial successes and ultimate failure, in its own terms, to equalize conditions across the world, and the foreshadowing of its successor, the globalization project, in laying the foundations of a global market that progressively overshadowed the states charged with development in the initial post–World War II era.

The **globalization project** (1970s–2000s) superimposed open markets across national boundaries, liberalizing trade and investment rules and privatizing public goods and services. Corporate rights gained priority over the social contract and redefined development as a private undertaking. The neoliberal doctrine ("market freedoms") underlying the globalization project has been met with growing contention, symbolized by the antineoliberal social revolt in Latin America over the last decade, recent Middle East and southern European rebellions against authoritarianism and austerity, and the growing weight and assertiveness of the more state-regulated economies of China (and India) in the world political economy. Polanyi's double movement is alive and well.

Whether the global market will remain dominant is still to be determined. In the meantime, an incipient **sustainability project,** heavily influenced by the climate change emergency, may be forming, with China leading the green technology race and a myriad of environmental and justice movements across the world, pushing states, business leaders, and citizens toward a new formulation of development as "managing the future" sustainably (in contrast to "improving on the past," as in modernization).

Finally, development, as we know it, is not the same across time, nor is it the same across space. It is uneven within and among societies. It has been, and will continue to be, contentious. This book seeks to make sense of this by emphasizing development paradoxes and providing students with a "birds-eye" (global) perspective on development controversies not easily seen from the ground.

FURTHER READING

Berger, Mark, and Heloise Weber. *Rethinking the Third World*. Houndsmill, Basingstoke: Palgrave Macmillan, 2014.

Crow, Ben, and Suresh K. Lodha. *The Atlas of Global Inequalities*. Berkeley: University of California Press, 2011.

Esteva, Gustavo, Salvatore Babones, and Philipp Babcicky. *The Future of Development: A Radical Manifesto*. Bristol, United Kingdom: Policy Press, 2013.

Galeano, Eduardo. *Upside Down: A Primer for the Looking-Glass World*. New York: Picador, 2000.

Klein, Naomi. *This Changes Everything: Capitalism vs. the Climate*. London: Allen Lane, 2014.

Payne, Anthony, and Nicola Phillips. *Development*. Cambridge, United Kingdom: Polity, 2010.

Perrons, Diane. *Globalization and Social Change: People and Places in a Divided World*. London: Routledge, 2004.

Prashad, Vijay. *The Poorer Nations: A Possible History of the Global South*. London: Verso, 2014.
Sage, Colin. *Environment and Development*. London: Routledge, 2011.
Willis, Katie. *Theories and Practices of Development*. London: Routledge, 2011.

SELECT WEBSITES

Eldis Gateway to Development Information: www.eldis.org
Global Exchange: www.globalexchange.org
New Internationalist: www.newint.org
Raj Patel: www.RajPatel.org
UNDP Human Development Reports: http://hdr.undp.org/en/
World Bank Development Report: http://wdronline.worldbank.org/

PART I

The Development Project (Late 1940s to Early 1970s)

2

Instituting the
Development Project

As we have seen in Chapter 1, "development" emerged as a comparative construct, in context of European colonization of the non-European world. Not only did the extraction of colonial resources facilitate European industrialization, but this process also required colonial administrators to manage subject populations adjusting to the extractive economy and mono-cultures, administering colonial rule for their masters, and experiencing physical as well as psychic displacement. Here, development assumed an additional meaning: the proverbial "white man's burden," underscoring its racial dimension.

Non-European cultures were irrevocably changed through colonialism, and the postcolonial context was founded on inequality. When newly inde-pendent states emerged, political leaders had to negotiate an unequal inter-national framework not of their making, but through which their governments acquired political legitimacy. How that framework emerged is the subject of this chapter. But first we must address the historical context of colonialism.

Colonialism

Our appeal to history begins with a powerful simplification. It concerns the social psychology of European colonialism, built largely around stereo-types that have shaped perceptions and conflict for at least five centuries.

(*Colonialism* is defined and explained in the "What Is Colonialism?" box, and the European colonial empires are depicted in Figure 2.1.) One such perception was the idea among Europeans that non-European native people or colonial subjects were "backward" and trapped in stifling cultural traditions. The experience of colonial rule encouraged this image, as the juxtaposition of European and non-European cultures invited comparison, but through the lens of Europe's missionary and military–industrial engagement. This comparison was interpreted—or misinterpreted—as European cultural superiority. It was easy to take the next step, viewing the difference as "progress"—something colonizers had—to impart to their subjects.

WHAT IS COLONIALISM?

Colonialism is the subjugation by physical and psychological force of one culture by another—a colonizing power—through military and economic conquest of territory and stereotyping the subordinated cultures. It predates the era of European expansion (from the fifteenth century to the twentieth century) and extends to Japanese colonialism in the twentieth century and, most recently, Chinese occupation of Tibet and Israeli occupation of Palestinian territory. Colonialism has two forms: colonies of settlement, which often eliminate indigenous people (such as the Spanish destruction of the Aztec and Inca civilizations in the Americas); and colonies of rule, where colonial administrators reorganize existing cultures by imposing new inequalities to facilitate their exploitation. Examples of the latter were the British creating local landlords, *zamindars*, to rule parts of India; confiscating personal and common land for cash cropping; depriving women of their customary resources; and elevating ethnoracial differences, such as privileging certain castes or tribes in the exercise of colonial rule. Outcomes are, first, the cultural genocide or marginalization of indigenous people; second, the introduction of new tensions around class, gender, race, and caste that shape postcolonial societies; third, the extraction of labor, cultural treasures, and resources to enrich the colonial power, its private interests, and public museums; fourth, the elaboration of ideologies justifying colonial rule, including racism and notions of backwardness; and fifth, responses by colonial subjects, ranging from death to internalization of inferiority to a variety of resistances—from everyday forms to sporadic uprisings to mass political mobilization.

Figure 2.1 European Colonial Empires at the Turn of the Twentieth Century

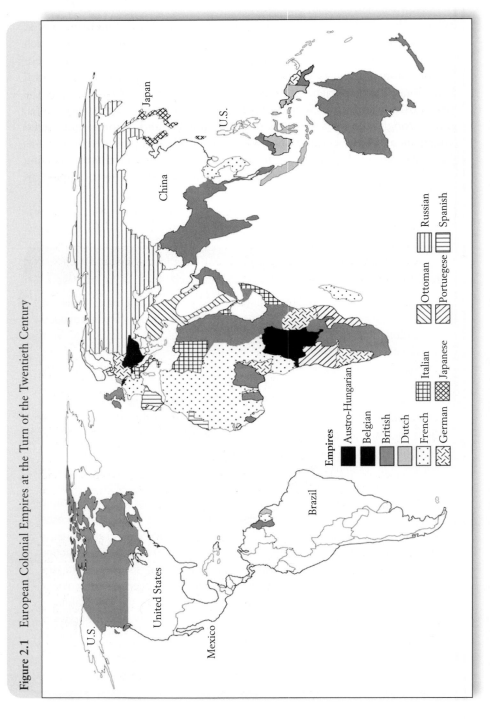

Such a powerful misinterpretation—and devaluing—of other cultures appears frequently in historical accounts. It is reflected in assumptions made by settlers about indigenous people they encountered in the Americas and Australasia. Europeans perceived Native Americans and aboriginal Australians as people who did not "work" the land they inhabited. In other words, the native populations had no right of "property"—a European concept in which property is private and alienable. Their displacement from their ancestral lands is a bloody reminder of the combined military power and moral fervor with which the European powers pursued colonization. It also foreshadowed the modern practice of rupturing the unity of the human and natural world, a unity characterizing some non-European cultures.

In precolonial Africa, communities relied on ancestral ecological knowledge and earth-centered cosmologies to sustain themselves and their environment. These methods were at once conservative and adaptive because, over time, African communities changed their composition, scale, and location in a long process of settlement and migration through the lands south of the equator. European colonists in Africa, however, saw these superstitious cultures as static and as only occupying—rather than improving—the land. This perception ignored the complex social systems adapted first to African ecology and then to European occupation.[1] Under these circumstances, Europeans viewed themselves as bringing civilization to the nonwhite races. French historian Albert Sarraut, ignoring non-European inventions such as gunpowder, the compass, the abacus, moveable type printing, and the saddle, claimed,

> It should not be forgotten that we are centuries ahead of them, long centuries during which—slowly and painfully, through a lengthy effort of research, invention, meditation and intellectual progress aided by the very influence of our temperate climate—a magnificent heritage of science, experience, and moral superiority has taken shape, which makes us eminently entitled to protect and lead the races lagging behind us.[2]

The ensuing colonial exchange was captured in the postcolonial African saying "When the white man came, he had the Bible and we had the land. When the white man left, we had the Bible and he had the land." Under colonialism, when non-Europeans lost control of their land, their spiritual life was compromised insofar as it was connected to their landscapes. It was difficult to sustain material and cultural integrity under these degrading extractive processes and conditions. At the same time, European colonization of natural resources converted land, water, cultivars, and food into economic categories, discounting their complex regenerative capacities and ecological interdependencies.

Development, European-style, thus came to be identified as the destiny of all humankind. The systematic handicapping of non-Europeans in this apparently natural and fulfilling endeavor remained largely unacknowledged, just as non-European scientific, ecological, and moral achievements, and legacies in European culture, were generally ignored.

WHAT ARE SOME CHARACTERISTICS OF PRECOLONIAL CULTURES?

All precolonial cultures had their own ways of satisfying their material and spiritual needs. Cultures varied by the differentiation among their members or households according to their particular ecological endowments and social contact with other cultures. The variety ranged from small communities of subsistence producers, who lived off the land or the forest, to extensive kingdoms or states. Subsistence producers, organized by kin relations, usually subdivided social tasks between men, who hunted and cleared land for cultivation, and women, who cultivated and processed crops, harvested wild fruits and nuts, and performed household tasks. These cultures were highly skilled in resource management and production to satisfy their material needs. They generally did not produce a surplus beyond what was required for their immediate needs, and they organized cooperatively—a practice that often made them vulnerable to intruders because they were not prepared for self-defense. Unlike North American Indians, whose social organization provided leadership for resistance, some aboriginal cultures, such as those of Australia and the Amazon, lacked leadership hierarchies and were more easily wiped out by settlers. By contrast, the Mogul empire in seventeenth-century India had a complex hierarchical organization, based on local chiefdoms in which the chief presided over the village community and ensured that surpluses (monetary taxes and produce) were delivered to a prosperous central court and "high culture." Village and urban artisans produced a range of metal goods, pottery, and crafts, including sophisticated muslins and silks. Caste distinctions, linked to previous invasions, corresponded to divisions of labor, such as trading, weaving, cultivating, ruling, and performing unskilled labor. Colonizers typically adapted such social and political hierarchies to their own ends—alienating indigenous cultures from their natural ecologies and their political systems from their customary social functions, incubating tensions that have been inherited by postcolonial states.

Sources: Bujra (1992); Rowley (1974).

The Colonial Division of Labor

From the sixteenth century, European colonists and traders traveled along African coasts to the New World and across the Indian Ocean and the China seas, seeking fur, precious metals, slave labor, spices, tobacco, cacao, potatoes, sugar, and cotton. The principal European colonial powers—Spain, Portugal, Holland, France, and Britain—and their merchant companies exchanged manufactured goods such as cloth, guns, and implements for these products and for Africans taken into slavery and transported to the Americas. In the process, they reorganized the world.

The basic pattern was to establish in the colonies specialized extraction of raw materials and production of primary products that were unavailable in Europe. In turn, these products fueled European manufacturing as industrial inputs and foodstuffs for its industrial labor force. On a world scale, this specialization between European economies and their colonies came to be termed the **colonial division of labor** (see Figure 2.2).

While the colonial division of labor stimulated European industrialization, it forced non-Europeans into primary commodity production. Specialization at each end of the exchange set in motion a transformation of social and environmental relationships, fueled by a dynamic relocation of resources and energy from colony to metropolis: an unequal ecological exchange.[3] Not only were the colonies converted into exporters of raw materials and foodstuffs, but they also became "exporters of sustainability."[4]

Figure 2.2   Distinguishing Between an International and a National Division of Labor

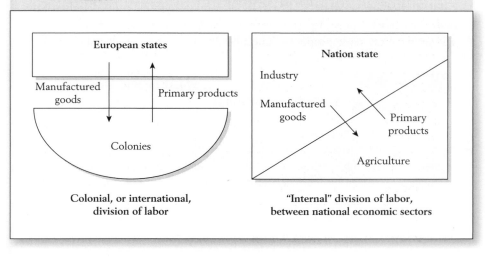

Colonial, or international,   "Internal" division of labor,
division of labor   between national economic sectors

The colonial division of labor, as cause and consequence of economic growth, exposed non-European cultures and ecologies to profound disorganization, as colonies were converted into supply zones of labor and resources. Local crafts and mixed farming systems were undermined, alienating land and forests for commercial exploitation and rupturing the ecological balance. Not only did non-European cultures surrender their handicraft industries in this exchange, but also their agriculture was often reduced to a specialized **export monoculture**, where local farmers produced a single crop, such as peanuts or coffee, for export, or plantations (sugar, cotton, tea, rubber, bananas) were imposed on land appropriated from those who became plantation laborers. Systems of export agriculture interrupted centuries-old patterns of diet and cultivation, creating the all-too-familiar commercial food economy, in which "what was grown became disconnected from what was eaten, and for the first time in history, money determined what people ate and even if they ate."[5]

Handicraft decline was often deliberate and widespread. Perhaps the best-known destruction of native crafts occurred through Britain's conquest of India. Until the nineteenth century, Indian cotton muslins and calicos were luxury imports into Europe (as were Chinese silks and satins). By that time, however, the East India Company (which ruled India for the British Crown until 1858) undermined this Indian craft and, in its own words, "succeeded in converting India from a manufacturing country into a country exporting raw produce."[6] The company had convinced the British government to use tariffs of 70 percent to 80 percent against Indian finished goods and to permit virtually free entry of raw cotton into England. In turn, British traders flooded India with cheap cloth manufactured in Manchester. Industrial technology (textile machinery and the steam engine) combined with political power to impose the colonial division of labor, as British-built railway systems moved Indian raw cotton to coastal ports for shipment to Liverpool and returned across India selling machine-made products—and undermining a time-honored craft.

CASE STUDY   **The Colonial Division of Labor and Unequal Ecological Exchange**

The ecological dimension of the colonial division of labor reminds us that industrialism is premised on transforming nature from a regenerative system to mere "raw material." Prior to industrial society and colonialism, the majority of humans depended on their local ecosystem to supply their various needs via a multiplicity of locally produced materials, harvesting just what was necessary. Overharvesting resources wastes energy, reducing an ecosystem's capacity and thereby threatening the sustainability of the human community. The colonial division of labor depended on overharvesting. Here, trade across ecosystem boundaries focused extractive activities on those few resources profitable to the traders. Stephen Bunker and Paul Ciccantell, in their research on Amazonian ecology, observe the following:

> Extractive economies thus often deplete or seriously reduce plants or animals, and they disrupt and degrade hydrological systems and geological formations [which] serve critical functions for the reproduction of other species and for the conservation of the watercourses and land forms on which they depend. Losses from excessive harvesting of a single species or material form can thus ramify through and reduce the productivity and integrity of an entire ecosystem.

The early Portuguese colonists, enslaving indigenous labor, extracted luxury goods from the Amazon, such as cacao, rosewood, spices, caymans, and turtle eggs—all of which had high value-to-volume ratios in European markets. Wealthy Europeans prized turtle oil for perfume and lighting their lamps, but wasteful harvesting of turtle eggs for the oil severely depleted protein supplies and Amazonian aquatic environments on which populations depended for their material reproduction. English and French colonies of the eighteenth century imposed monocultures of sugar, tobacco, coffee, and tea. Mimi Sheller observes, "In consuming the Caribbean . . . Europe was itself transformed."

By the nineteenth century, European and North American extraction focused on industrial inputs such as rubber, further disrupting Amazonian habitats and ecology and exposing local industry to competition from commodities imported cheaply in the ample cargo space on the return leg of the rubber transport ships. As demand for rubber intensified later in the century, rubber plantations were established in Southeast Asia and Africa, by the British and the Americans respectively—in turn transforming those ecologies by introducing monocultures and also impoverishing the Amazonian economy as feral rubber extraction declined.

What are the consequences of the developmentalist focus on human exchange through trade, ignoring the exchange with nature?

Sources: Bunker and Ciccantell (2005: 34–47); Sheller (2003: 81).

Social Reorganization Under Colonialism

The colonial division of labor devastated producing communities and their craft- and agriculture-based systems. When the British first came to India in the mid-eighteenth century, Robert Clive described the textile city of Dacca as "extensive, populous, and rich as the city of London." By 1840, Sir Charles Trevelyan testified before a British parliamentary committee that the population of Dacca "has fallen from 150,000 to 30,000, and the jungle and malaria are fast encroaching upon the town. . . . Dacca, the Manchester of India, has fallen off from a very flourishing town to a very poor and small town."[7]

While native industries declined under colonial systems, local farming cultures lost their best lands to commercial agriculture supplying European consumers and industries. Plantations and other kinds of cash cropping proliferated across the colonial world, producing specialized tropical exports ranging from bananas to peanuts, depending on local agroecologies (see Table 2.1). Non-European societies were fundamentally transformed through the loss of resources and craft traditions, as colonial subjects were forced to labor in mines, fields, and plantations to produce exports sustaining distant European factories. This was a *global* process, whereby slaves, peasants, and laborers in the colonies provisioned European industrial classes with cheap colonial products, such as sugar, tea, tropical oils, and cotton for clothing. European development was realized through a racialized global relationship, "underdeveloping" colonial cultures. The legacy of this relationship continues today—for example, Mali (ranked 176th out of 187 on the UN Human Development Index) derives half of its export revenues from cotton, with 40 percent of its population depending on this crop for their livelihoods, but the country is in unequal competition with highly subsidized cotton producers in the United States, the European Union, and China.[8]

Colonial systems of rule focused on mobilizing colonial labor. For example, a landed oligarchy (the *hacendados*) ruled South America before the nineteenth century in the name of the Spanish and Portuguese monarchies, using an institution called *encomienda* to create a form of native serfdom. Settler colonialism also spread to the Americas, Australasia, and southern Africa, where settlers used military, legal, and economic force to wrest land from the natives for commercial purposes, using slave, convict, and indentured labor.[9] As the industrial era matured, colonial rule (in Asia and Africa) grew more bureaucratic. By the end of the nineteenth century, colonial administrations were self-financing, depending on military force and the loyalty of local princes and chiefs, tribes, and castes (note that the British presence never exceeded 0.5 percent of the Indian population).[10] Native rulers were bribed with titles, land, or tax-farming privileges to recruit male

Table 2.1 Selected Colonial Export Crops

Colony	Colonial Power	Export Crop
Australia	Britain	Wool, wheat
Brazil	Portugal	Sugar, coffee
Congo	Belgium	Rubber, ivory
Egypt	Britain	Cotton
Ghana	Britain	Cocoa
Haiti	France	Sugar
India	Britain	Cotton, opium, tea
Indochina	France	Rice, rubber
Indonesia	Holland	Rubber, tobacco
Côte d'Ivoire	France	Cocoa
Kenya	Britain	Coffee, tea, sisal
Malaya	Britain	Rubber, palm oil
Senegal	France	Peanuts
South Africa	Britain	Gold, diamonds

peasants to the military and to force them into cash cropping to pay the taxes supporting the colonial state.

Male entry into cash cropping disrupted patriarchal gender divisions, creating new gender inequalities. Women's customary land-user rights were often displaced by new systems of private property, circumscribing food production, traditionally women's responsibility. Thus, British colonialism in Kenya fragmented the Kikuyu culture as peasant land was confiscated and men migrated to work on European estates, reducing women's control over resources and lowering their status, wealth, and authority.

In India, production of commercial crops such as cotton, jute, tea, peanuts, and sugar cane grew by 85 percent between the 1890s and the 1940s. In contrast, in that same period, local food crop production declined by 7 percent while the population grew by 40 percent, a shift that spread hunger, famine, and social unrest.[11] Using tax and irrigation policies to force farmers into export agriculture, Britain came to depend on India for almost 20 percent of its wheat consumption by 1900. Part of the reason that "Londoners were in fact eating India's bread" was the destruction of Indian food security by modern technologies, converting grain into a commodity. New telegraph systems transmitted prices set by London grain merchants, prying grain reserves from villages along railway networks for export to Britain. Thus, new global market technologies undermined the customary system of grain reserves organized at the village level as protection against drought and famine. For example, during the famine of 1899 to 1900, 143,000 peasants in Berar starved to death—as the province exported tens of thousands of cotton bales in addition to 747,000 bushels of grain.[12]

Starvation in the colonies was not simply due to conversion of resources into export commodities. British rule in India, for example, converted the "commons" into private property or state monopolies. Forest and pasture commons were ecological zones of nonmarket resources to which villagers were customarily entitled:

> [Village economy across monsoonal Asia] augmented crops and handicrafts with stores of free goods from common lands: dry grass for fodder, shrub grass for rope, wood and dung for fuel, dung, leaves, and forest debris for fertilizer, clay for plastering houses, and, above all, clean water. All classes utilized these common property resources, but for poorer households they constituted the very margin of survival.[13]

By the end of the 1870s, Britain had enclosed all Indian forests, previously communally managed. Ending communal access to grassland resources ruptured "the ancient ecological interdependence of pastoralists and farmers," and age-old practices of extensive crop rotation and long fallow, to replenish soils, declined with the expansion of cotton and other export monocrops.[14] Export monocultures displaced indigenous irrigation systems with canals, which blocked natural drainage, and thus exacerbated water salinity and pooled water in swamps, the perfect host environment for the dreaded malarial anopheline mosquito. A British engineer reported to the 1901 Irrigation Commission, "Canals may not protect against famines, but they may give an enormous return on your money."[15]

The colonial division of labor developed European capitalist civilization (with food and raw materials) at the same time that it undermined non-European cultures and ecologies. As European industrial society matured, the exploding urban populations demanded ever-increasing imports of sugar, coffee, tea, cocoa, tobacco, and vegetable oils from the colonies, and the expanding factory system demanded ever-increasing inputs of raw materials such as cotton, timber, rubber, and jute, employing forced and slave labor.

As the African slave trade subsided, the Europeans created new schemes of forced, or indentured, labor. Indian and Chinese peasants and handicraftsmen, impoverished by colonial intervention or market competition from cheap textiles, scattered to sugar plantations in the Caribbean, Fiji, Mauritius, and Natal; to rubber plantations in Malaya and Sumatra; and to British East Africa to build the railways that intensified the two-way extraction of African resources and the introduction of cheap manufactured goods. In the third quarter of the nineteenth century alone, more than one million indentured Indians went overseas. Today, Indians still outnumber native Fijians; they also make up 50 percent of the Guyanese population and 40 percent of the residents of Trinidad. In the same period, 90,000 Chinese indentured laborers went to work in the Peruvian guano fields, and 200,000 went to California to work in the fruit industry, on the gold fields, and on the railways.[16] Displacement of colonial subjects from their societies and their dispersion to resolve labor shortages elsewhere in the colonial world have had a lasting global effect—notably in the African, Indian, and Chinese diasporas. This cultural mosaic underlines modern expressions of race, ethnicity, and nationality—generating ethnopolitical tensions that shape national politics across the world today and question the modern ideal of the secular state.

The contradictions of the secular–modernist ideal stem from racialized colonial rule, where industrial and/or military techniques organized labor forces, schooling, and urban and rural surveillance, as well as supervised hygiene and public health.[17] European exercise of power in the colonies revealed the hard edge of power in the modern state, premised on class structuring via racial humiliation.[18] Such methods produced resistances among subject populations, whether laborers, peasants, soldiers, or civil servants. These tensions fed the politics of decolonization, dedicated to molding inchoate resistance to colonial abuses into coherent, nationalist movements striving for independence.

THE COLONIAL PROJECT UNLOCKS A DEVELOPMENT PUZZLE

The **colonial project** was far-reaching and multidimensional in its effects. We focus here on the colonial division of labor because it isolates a key issue in the development puzzle. Unless we see the interdependence created through this division of *world* labor, it is easy to take our unequal world at face value and

(Continued)

(Continued)

view it as a natural continuum, with an advanced European region showing the way for a backward, non-European region. But viewing world inequality as relational (interdependent) rather than as sequential (catch-up) calls the conventional modern understanding of development into question. The conventional understanding is that individual societies experience or pursue development in sequence, on a "development ladder." If, however, industrial growth in Europe depended on agricultural monoculture in the non-European world, then development was more than simply a national process, even if represented as such. What we can conclude from the colonial project is that development historically depended on the unequal relationships of colonialism, which included an unequal division of labor and unequal ecological exchanges—both of which produced a legacy of "underdevelopment" in the colonial and postcolonial worlds.

Decolonization

As Europeans were attempting to "civilize" their colonies, colonial subjects across the Americas, Asia, and Africa engaged the European paradox—a discourse of rights and sovereignty juxtaposed against non-European subjugation. In the French sugar colony of Saint Domingue, the late-eighteenth-century "Black Jacobin" revolt powerfully exposed this double standard. Turning the sovereignty rhetoric of the French Revolution successfully against French colonialism, the rebellious slaves of the sugar plantations became the first to gain their independence in the newly established nation of Haiti, sending tremors throughout the slaveholding lands of the New World.[19]

Resistance to colonialism evolved across the next two centuries, from the early-nineteenth-century independence of the Latin American republics (from Spain and Portugal) to the dismantling of South African apartheid in the early 1990s. Although decolonization has continued into the present day (with the independence of East Timor in 2002 and the Palestinians still struggling for a sovereign homeland), the worldwide decolonization movement peaked as European colonialism collapsed in the mid-twentieth century, when World War II sapped the power of the French, Dutch, British, and Belgian states to withstand anticolonial struggles. Freedom was linked to overcoming the deprivations of colonialism. Its vehicle was the *nation-state*, which offered formal political independence. Substantively, however, the sovereignty of independent states was compromised by the cultural and economic legacies of colonialism.

Colonial Liberation

Freedom included overcoming the social–psychological scars of colonialism. The racist legacy of colonialism penetrated the psyche of the colonist and the colonized and remains with us today. In 1957 at the height of African independence struggles, Tunisian philosopher Albert Memmi wrote *The Colonizer and the Colonized*, dedicating the American edition to the (colonized) American Negro. In this work (published in 1967), he claimed this:

> Racism . . . is the highest expression of the colonial system and one of the most significant features of the colonialist. Not only does it establish a fundamental discrimination between colonizer and colonized, a *sine qua non* of colonial life, but it also lays the foundation for the immutability of this life.[20]

To overcome this apparent immutability, West Indian psychiatrist Frantz Fanon, writing from Algeria, responded with *The Wretched of the Earth*, a manifesto of liberation. It was a searing indictment of European colonialism and a call to people of the former colonies (the Third World) to transcend the mentality of enslavement and forge a new path for humanity. He wrote,

> It is a question of the Third World starting a new history of Man, a history which will have regard to the sometimes prodigious theses which Europe has put forward, but which will also not forget Europe's crimes, of which the most horrible was committed in the heart of man, and consisted of the pathological tearing apart of his functions and the crumbling away of his unity. . . . On the immense scale of humanity, there were racial hatreds, slavery, exploitation and above all the bloodless genocide which consisted in the setting aside of fifteen thousand millions of men. . . . Humanity is waiting for something other from us than such an imitation, which would be almost an obscene caricature.[21]

Decolonization was rooted in a liberatory upsurge, expressed in mass political movements of resistance. In Algeria (as in Palestine today), the independence movement incubated within and struck at the French occupation from the native quarter. The use of terror, on both sides, symbolized the bitter divide between colonizer and colonized (brilliantly portrayed in Gillo Pontecorvo's film, *Battle of Algiers*).

Other forms of resistance included militarized national liberation struggles (e.g., Portuguese African colonies, French Indochina) and widespread colonial labor unrest. British colonialism faced widespread labor strikes in its West Indian and African colonies in the 1930s, and this pattern continued over the next two decades in Africa as British and French colonial subjects protested conditions in cities, ports, mines, and on the railways. In this context, development was interpreted as a pragmatic effort to preserve the colonies by improving material conditions—and there was no doubt that colonial subjects understood this and turned the promise of development back on the colonizers, viewing development as an entitlement. British Colonial Secretary MacDonald observed the following in 1940:

> If we are not now going to do something fairly good for the Colonial Empire, and something which helps them to get proper social services, we shall deserve to lose the colonies and it will only be a matter of time before we get what we deserve.[22]

In these terms, eloquent international appeals to justice in the language of rights and freedom by the representatives of colonized peoples held a mirror up to the colonial powers, in their demands for freedom.

A new world order was in the making. From 1945 to 1981, 105 new states joined the United Nations (UN) as the colonial empires crumbled, swelling UN ranks from 51 to 156 (now 187). The extension of political sovereignty to millions of non-Europeans (more than half of humanity) ushered in the era of development.[23] This era was marked by a sense of almost boundless idealism, as governments and people from the First and Third Worlds joined together in a coordinated effort to stimulate economic growth; bring social improvements through education, public health, family planning, and transport and communication systems to urban and rural populations; and promote political citizenship in the new nations. Just as colonized subjects appropriated the democratic discourse of the colonizers in fueling their independence movements, so leaders of the new nation-states appropriated the idealism of the development era and proclaimed equality as a domestic and international goal, informed by the UN Universal Declaration of Human Rights (1948).

The UN declaration represented a new world paradigm of fundamental human rights of freedom, equality, life, liberty, and security to all, without distinction by race, color, sex, language, religion, political opinion, national or social origin, property, birth, or other status. The declaration also included citizenship rights—that is, citizens' rights to the **social contract:** Everyone was "entitled to realization, through national effort, and international co-operation and in accordance with the organization and resources of each State, of the economic, social and cultural rights indispensable for his dignity and the free development of his personality."[24]

CASE STUDY: The Tensions and Lessons of the Indian Nationalist Revolt

Mahatma Gandhi's model of nonviolent resistance to British colonialism affirmed the simplicity and virtue in the ideal-typical premodern solidarities of Indian village life. Rather than embrace the emerging world of nation-states, Gandhi argued, didactically, that Indians became a subject population, not because of colonial force, but through the seduction of modernity. Gandhi's approach flowed from his philosophy of transcendental (as opposed to scientific or historical) truth, guided by a social morality. Gandhi disdained the violent methods of the modern state and the institutional rationality of the industrial age, regarding machinery as the source of India's impoverishment, not only in destroying handicrafts but in compromising humanity:

> We notice that the mind is a restless bird; the more it gets the more it wants, and still remains unsatisfied. . . . Our ancestors, therefore, set a limit to our indulgences. They saw that happiness is largely a mental condition. . . . We have managed with the same kind of plough as existed thousands of years ago. We have retained the same kind of cottages that we had in former times and our indigenous education remains the same as before. We have had no system of life-corroding competition. . . . It was not that we did not know how to invent machinery, but our forefathers knew that if we set our hearts after such things, we would become slaves and lose our moral fibres.

Gandhi's method of resistance included wearing homespun cloth instead of machine-made goods, foreswearing use of the English language, and mistrusting the European philosophy of self-interest. Gandhi viewed self-interest as undermining community-based ethics and advocated the decentralization of social power, appealing to grassroots notions of self-reliance, proclaiming the following:

> Independence must begin at the bottom. Thus, every village will be a republic or panchayat having full powers. It follows, therefore, that every village has to be self-sustained and capable of managing its affairs even to the extent of defending itself against the whole world.

While Gandhi's politics, anchored in a potentially reactionary Hindu religious imagery, galvanized rural India, Indian nationalism actually rode to power via the Indian National Congress and one of its progressive democratic

(Continued)

(Continued)

socialist leaders, Jawaharlal Nehru. Nehru represented the formative national state, viewing the Gandhian philosophy as inappropriate to the modern world but recognizing its mobilizing power. Infusing the national movement with calls for land reform and agrarian modernization to complement industrial development, Nehru declared this:

> It can hardly be challenged that, in the context of the modern world, no country can be politically and economically independent, even within the framework of international interdependence, unless it is highly industrialized and has developed its power resources to the utmost.

Together, Gandhi and Nehru are revered as fathers of independence and the Indian national state, respectively. Note that the struggle against empire was woven out of two strands: an *idealist* strand looking back and looking forward to a transcendental Hinduism anchored in village-level self-reliance, as well as a *realist* strand looking sideways and asserting that Indian civilization could be rescued, contained, and celebrated in the form of a modern state.

Did Gandhi's and Nehru's opposing visions of development at the time of Indian independence foreshadow today's rising tension between sustainability and maximum economic growth?

Source: Chatterjee (2001: 86, 87, 91, 97, 144, 151).

Decolonization and Development

Decolonization gave development new meaning, linking it to the ideal of sovereignty, the possibility of converting subjects into citizens, and the pursuit of economic development for social justice. Already independent Latin American states adopted similar goals, having been inspired by French and US revolutionary ideologies of liberal-nationalism, which informed nineteenth-century European nation building via national education systems, national languages and currencies, and modern armies and voting citizens. These ideologies also informed the twentieth-century movements in Asia and Africa for decolonization, coinciding with the rise of the United States to global power and prosperity. Eager to reconstruct the post–World War II world to expand markets and the flow of raw materials, the United States led an international project, inspired by a vision of development as a *national* enterprise to be repeated across a world of sovereign states.

US development modeled this vision, being more "inner-directed" than the "outer-directed" British imperial model (as "workshop of the world"). Despite relentless destruction of native American cultures as the continent was claimed (*internal colonialism*), US origins in the revolt of the North American colonies against British colonialism in the late eighteenth century informed an "anticolonial" heritage. Once slavery was abolished, the New South was incorporated into a national economic dynamic, articulating agricultural and industrial sectors. Figure 2.2 depicts the difference between the colonial and the national division between industry and agriculture.

The division of labor between industry and agriculture, defining the global exchange between colonial powers and their colonies, was now *internalized* within the United States. Chicago traders, for instance, purchased Midwestern farm products for processing, in turn selling machinery and goods to those farmers. This mutual prosperity of city and countryside is a *model*—that is, it *prescribes an ideal version*, even as foreign trade and investment continued. But it did industrialize agriculture as a series of specialized crops, requiring endless inputs of chemical fertilizers and hybrid seeds, with corrosive effects on soils and water cycles. The export of this developmental model of capital-intensive industrial farming has defined agricultural modernization, with global ecological consequence.[25]

Postwar Decolonization and the Rise of the Third World

In the era of decolonization, the world subdivided into three geopolitical segments. These subdivisions emerged after World War II (1939–1944) during the Cold War, dividing the capitalist Western (First World) from the Communist Soviet (Second World) blocs. The Third World included the postcolonial bloc of nations. Of course, there was considerable inequality across and within these subdivisions, as well as within their national units. The subdivision of the world is further explained in the "How We Divide the World's Nations" box.

In this era, the United States was the most powerful state economically, militarily, and ideologically. Its high standard of living (with a per capita income three times the West European average), its anticolonial heritage, and its commitment to liberal domestic and international relations lent it the legitimacy of a world leader and the model of a developed society.

HOW WE DIVIDE THE WORLD'S NATIONS

Division of the nations of the world is quite complex and extensive, and it depends on the purpose of the dividing. The basic division made (by French demographer Alfred Sauvy in 1952) was into three worlds: The First World defined the capitalist world (the West plus Japan), the Second World defined the socialist world (the Soviet bloc), and the Third World was the rest—mostly former European colonies. The core of the Third World was the group of non-aligned countries steering an independent path between the First and Second Worlds, especially China, Egypt, Ghana, India, Indonesia, Vietnam, and Yugoslavia. In the 1980s, a Fourth World was named to describe marginalized regions. The United Nations and the development establishment use a different nomenclature: developed countries, developing countries, and least developed countries; this terminology echoes "modernization" theory, which locates countries on a continuum, or "development ladder," ascended as a country develops an industrial economy, rational–legal administrative structures, and a pluralist–representative political system.

Ranged against the United States were the Soviet Union and an assortment of Eastern European Communist states. This Second World was considered the alternative to First World capitalism. The Third World, the remaining half of humanity—most of whom were still food-growing rural dwellers—was represented in economic language as impoverished or, in Fanon's politico-cultural language, as the "wretched of the earth."

Whereas the First World had 65 percent of world income with only 20 percent of the world's population, the Third World accounted for 67 percent of world population but only 18 percent of its income. While some believe the gap in living standards between the First and Third Worlds registers differential rates of growth, others believe that much of it was a result of colonialism.[26] Still others are skeptical of distinguishing cultures via a uniform standard based on income levels, since non-Westernized-cultures value non-cash-generating practices.

Economic disparity between the First and Third Worlds generated the vision of development that would energize political and business elites in each world. Seizing the moment as leader of the First World, President Harry S. Truman included in a key speech on January 20, 1949, the following proclamation:

We must embark on a bold new program for making the benefits of our scientific advances and industrial progress available for the improvement and growth of underdeveloped areas. The old imperialism—exploitation for foreign profit—has no place in our plans. What we envisage is a program of development based on the concepts of democratic fair dealing. . . . Only by helping the least fortunate of its members to help themselves can the human family achieve the decent, satisfying life that is the right of all people. Democracy alone can supply the vitalizing force.[27]

The following year, a Nigerian nationalist echoed these sentiments:

Self-government will not necessarily lead to a paradise overnight. . . . But it will have ended the rule of one race over another, with all the humiliation and exploitation which that implies. It can also pave the way for the internal social revolution that is required within each country.[28]

Despite the power differential between the United States and the African countries, the shared sentiments affirmed the connection between decolonization and development, where sovereign states could pursue national economic growth with First World assistance. The program of development pursued by new nations, "dependence" in independence, marked the postcolonial experience.

President Truman's paternalistic proclamation confirmed this understanding in suggesting a new paradigm for the postwar era: the division of humanity into developed and undeveloped regions. This division of the world projected a singular destiny for all nations. Mexican intellectual Gustavo Esteva commented,

Underdevelopment began, then, on January 20, 1949. On that day, two billion people became underdeveloped. In a real sense, from that time on, they ceased being what they were, in all their diversity, and were transmogrified into an inverted mirror of others' reality: a mirror that defines their identity . . . simply in the terms of a homogenizing and narrow minority.[29]

In other words, the proclamation by President Truman divided the world between those who were modern and those who were not. *Development/modernity* became the discursive benchmark. This was a way of looking at the world, a new paradigm, suggesting that the ex-colonial world was not only backward but could also develop, with help.

This new paradigm inscribed First World power and privilege in the new institutional structure of the postwar international economy. In context of the Cold War between First and Second Worlds (for the hearts and resources of the ex-colonial world), development was simultaneously the restoration of a capitalist world market to sustain First World wealth, through access to strategic natural resources, and the opportunity for Third World countries to emulate First World civilization and living standards. Because development was both a blueprint for the world of nation-states *and* a strategy for world order, I call this enterprise the **development project.** The epithet *project* emphasizes the political content of development, as a global organizing principle. It also underlines the self-referential meaning of development, as defined by those with the means to make the rules.

The power of the new development paradigm arose in part from its ability to present itself as universal, natural, and therefore uncontentious—obliterating its colonial roots. In a postcolonial era, Third World states could not repeat the European experience of developing by exploiting the labor and resources of other societies. Development was modeled as a national process, initiated in European states. Its aura of inevitability devalued non-European cultures and discounted what the West learned from the non-European world. Gilbert Rist observed of postcolonial states, "Their right to self-determination had been acquired in exchange for the right to self-definition,"[30] suggesting that in choosing the Western-centered future for the world, they legitimized (or naturalized) it. Of course, each state imparted its own particular style to this common agenda, drawing on regional cultures such as African socialism, Latin American bureaucratic authoritarianism, or Confucianism in East Asia.

Ingredients of the Development Project

The development project was a political and intellectual response to the condition of the world at the historic moment of decolonization. Here, development assumed a specific meaning. It imposed an essentially economic (reductionist) understanding of social change, universalizing an instrumental form of development across multiple cultures as a single market culture, driven by the nation-state and economic growth.

The Nation-State

The **nation-state** was to be the framework of the development project. Nation-states were territorially defined political systems based on the government–citizen relationship that emerged in nineteenth-century Europe. Colonialism exported this political model (with its military shell), framing the politics of the decolonization movement, even where national boundaries made little sense. The UN Economic Commission for Africa, for example, argued in 1989 that African underdevelopment derived from its arbitrary postcolonial geography, including 14 landlocked states, 23 states with a population below five million, and 13 states with a land mass of fewer than 50,000 hectares each.[31] The following insert illustrates the effects of these arbitrarily drawn boundaries.

HOW WAS AFRICA DIVIDED UNDER COLONIALISM?

The colonial powers inflicted profound damage on that continent, driving frontiers straight through the ancestral territories of nations. For example, we drew a line through Somalia, separating off part of the Somali people and placing them within Kenya. We did the same by splitting the great Masai nation between Kenya and Tanzania. Elsewhere, of course, we created the usual artificial states. Nigeria consists of four principal nations: the Hausa, Igbo, Yoruba, and Fulani peoples. It has already suffered a terrible war which killed hundreds of thousands of people and which settled nothing. Sudan, Chad, Djibouti, Senegal, Mali, Burundi, and of course Rwanda, are among the many other states that are riven by conflict.

Source: Quoted from Goldsmith (1994: 57).

During the 1950s, certain leading African anticolonialists doubted the appropriateness of the nation-state form to postcolonial Africa. They knew that sophisticated systems of rule had evolved in Africa before colonialism. They advocated a pan-African federalism, whose territories would transcend the arbitrary borders drawn across Africa by colonialism. However, decisions about postcolonial political arrangements were made in London and Paris where the colonial powers, looking to sustain spheres of influence, insisted on the nation-state as the only appropriate political outcome of decolonization. Indeed, a British Committee on Colonial Policy advised this to the prime minister in 1957:

> During the period when we can still exercise control in any territory, it is most important to take every step open to us to ensure, as far as we can, that British standards and methods of business and administration permeate the whole life of the territory.[32]

An African elite, expecting gains from decolonization—whether personal or national—prepared to assume power in the newly independent states. The power its members assumed was already mortgaged to the nation-state system: a vehicle of containment of political desires and of extraction of resources via European military and economic aid, investment, and trade—the paradox of sovereignty.

Pan-Africanism was unsuccessful; nevertheless, it did bear witness to an alternative political and territorial logic. Some of Guinea's rural areas were in fact attached as hinterlands to urban centers in other states, such as Dakar in Senegal and Abidjan in the Côte d'Ivoire. Considerable cross-border smuggling today is continuing testimony to these relationships. Fierce civil wars broke out in Nigeria in the 1960s and in Ethiopia in the 1970s, states such as Somalia and Rwanda collapsed in the early 1990s, and, in the twenty-first century, military conflict in the Congo threatened a repartition of Africa, and Sudan subdivided, creating a new state in 2011—South Sudan. Such eruptions all include ethnic dimensions, rooted in social disparities and cross-border realities. In retrospect, they suggest that the pan-African movement had considerable foresight. Ideas about the limits to the nation-state organization resonate today in new macroregional groupings.[33]

Economic Growth

The second ingredient of the development project was economic growth. A mandatory UN System of National Accounts institutionalized a universal quantifiable measure of national development. The UN Charter of 1945 proclaimed "a rising standard of living" as the global objective. This "material well-being" indicator is measured in the commercial output of goods and services within a country: capita gross national product (GNP), or the national average of per capita income. While per capita income was not the sole measure of rising living standards (health, literacy, etc.), the key criterion was measurable progress toward the "good society," popularized by US presidential adviser Walt Rostow's idea of the advanced stage of "high mass consumption."[34]

In the minds of Western economists, development required a jump start in the Third World. Cultural practices of wealth sharing and cooperative labor—dissipating individual wealth, but sustaining the community—were perceived as a *traditional* obstacle to making the transition. The solution was to introduce a market system based on private property and wealth accumulation. A range of modern practices and institutions designed to sustain economic growth, such as banking and accounting systems, education, stock markets, and legal systems, and public infrastructure (transport, power sources) was required.

The use of the *economic growth* yardstick of development, however, is fraught with problems. Average indices such as per capita income obscure inequalities among social groups and classes. Aggregate indices such as rising consumption levels in and of themselves are not accurate records of improvement in quality of life. Running air conditioners are measured as increased consumption, but they also release harmful hydrocarbons into the warming atmosphere. Economic criteria for development have normative assumptions that often marginalize other criteria for evaluating living standards relating to the quality of human interactions, physical and spiritual health, and so on.

The emphasis on converting human interactions into measurable (and taxable) cash relations discounts the social wealth of nonmonetary activities (nature's processes, cooperative labor, people growing their own food, performing unpaid household labor, and community service). Wolfgang Sachs observed this of early 1940s comparative statistical measurement of "economic growth":

> As soon as the scale of incomes had been established, order was imposed on a confused globe: horizontally, such different worlds as those of the Zapotec people of Mexico, the Tuareg of north Africa, and Rajasthanies of India could be classed together, while a vertical comparison to "rich" nations demanded relegating them to a position of almost immeasurable inferiority. In this way, "poverty" was used to define whole peoples, not according to what they are and want to be, but according to what they lack and are expected to become. Economic disdain had thus taken the place of colonial contempt.[35]

Framing the Development Project

Perhaps the most compelling aspect of the development project was a powerful perception by planners, governmental elites, and citizens alike that development was destiny. Both Cold War blocs understood development in these terms, even if their respective paths of development were different. Each bloc took its cue from key nineteenth-century thinkers. The West identified free-enterprise capitalism as the endpoint of development, based in Jeremy Bentham's utilitarian philosophy of the common good arising out of the pursuit of individual self-interest. Communist orthodoxy identified the abolition of private property and **central planning** as the goal of social development, deriving from Karl Marx's collectivist dictum: "From each according to their ability, and to each according to their needs."

Although the two political blocs subscribed to opposing representations of human destiny, they shared the same modernist paradigm. *National industrialization* would be the vehicle of development in each.

National Industrialization: Ideal and Reality

"National industrialization" had two key assumptions. First, it assumed that development involved the displacement of agrarian civilization by an urban-industrial society. For national development policy, this meant a deliberate shrinking of the agricultural population as the manufacturing and service sectors grew. It also meant the transfer of resources such as food, raw materials, and redundant labor from the agrarian sector as peasants disappeared and agricultural productivity grew. Industrial growth would ideally feed back into and technicize agriculture. These two national economic sectors would therefore condition each other's development, as in the US case discussed earlier in this chapter and illustrated in Figure 2.2.

Second, the idea of national industrialization assumed a *linear direction* for development—for example, catching up with the West. Soviet dictator Joseph Stalin articulated this doctrine in the 1930s, proclaiming, "We are fifty or a hundred years behind the advanced countries. We must make good this distance in ten years. Either we do it or they crush us."[36] Stalin's resolve came from the pressures of military (and therefore economic) survival in a hostile world. The Soviet Union industrialized in one generation, "squeezing" the peasantry to finance urban-industrial development with cheap food.

Across the Cold War divide, industrialization symbolized success. Leaders in each bloc pursued industrial development to legitimize their power; the reasoning was that as people consumed more goods and services they would subscribe to the prevailing philosophy delivering the goods and would support their governments. *In this sense, development is not just a goal; it is a method of rule.*

The competitive—and legitimizing—dynamic of industrialization framed the development project across the Cold War divide. Third World states climbed on the bandwagon. The ultimate goal was to achieve Western levels of affluence. If some states chose to mix and match elements from either side of the Cold War divide, well and good. The game was still the same: catch-up. Ghana's first president, Kwame Nkrumah, proclaimed, "We in Ghana will do in ten years what it took others one hundred years to do."[37]

Economic Nationalism

Decolonization involved a universal nationalist upsurge across the Third World, assuming different forms in different countries, depending on the configuration of social forces in each national political system. Third World governments strove to build national development states—whether centralized like South Korea, corporatist like Brazil, or decentralized and populist like Tanzania. The **development state** organizes national economic growth by mobilizing money and people. It uses individual and corporate taxes, along with other government revenues, such as export taxes and sales taxes, to finance public building of transport systems and to finance state enterprises, such as steel works and energy exploration. And it forms coalitions to support its policies. State elites regularly use their power to accumulate wealth and influence in the state—whether through selling rights to public resources to cronies or capturing foreign-aid distribution channels. As Sugata Bose remarked of the Indian state, "Instead of the state being used as an instrument of development, development became an instrument of the state's legitimacy."[38] Either way, the development state was a central pillar of the postwar development era.

Import-Substitution Industrialization

Just as political nationalism pursued sovereignty for Third World populations, so **economic nationalism** sought to reverse the colonial division of labor—as governments encouraged and protected domestic industrialization with tariffs and public subsidies, reducing dependence on primary exports ("resource bondage").

Economic nationalism was associated with Raul Prebisch, an adviser to the Argentine military government in the 1930s. During that decade's world depression, world trade declined and Latin American–landed interests lost political power, as shrinking primary export markets depleted their revenues. Prebisch proposed an industrial protection policy. Import controls reduced dependency on expensive imports of Western manufactured goods and shifted resources into domestic manufacturing.[39] This policy was adopted in the 1950s by the UN Economic Commission for Latin America (ECLA), under Prebisch's lead as executive secretary.

Import-substitution industrialization (ISI) framed initial economic development strategies in the Third World as governments subsidized "infant industries." The goal was a cumulative process of domestic industrialization. For example, a domestic automotive industry would generate parts manufacturing, road building, service stations, and so on, in addition to industries such as steel, rubber, aluminum, cement, and paint. In this way, a local industrial base would emerge. ISI became the new economic orthodoxy in the postwar era.[40]

Development states such as Brazil redistributed private investment from export sectors to domestic production, establishing a development bank to make loans to investors and state corporations in such central industries as petroleum and electric-power generation. When the domestic market was sufficiently large, multinational corporations invested directly in the Brazilian economy—as they did elsewhere in Latin America during this period. Latin America characteristically had relatively urbanized populations with expanding consumer markets.[41]

By contrast, the South Korean state centralized control of national development and the distribution of industrial finance. South Korea relied less on foreign investment than Brazil and more on export markets for the country's growing range of manufactured goods. Comprehensive land reforms equalized wealth among the rural population, and South Korean development depended on strategic public investment decisions that more evenly distributed wealth among urban classes and between urban and rural constituencies.

FOREIGN INVESTMENT AND THE PARADOX OF PROTECTIONISM

When states erected tariffs in the development era, multinational corporations hopped over and invested in local, as well as natural resource, industries. For Brazil in 1956, foreign (chiefly US) capital controlled 50 percent of the iron and rolled-metal industry, 50 percent of the meat industry, 56 percent of the textile industry, 72 percent of electric power production, 80 percent of cigarette manufacturing, 80 percent of pharmaceutical production, 98 percent of the automobile industry, and 100 percent of oil and gasoline distribution. In Peru, a subsidiary of Standard Oil of New Jersey owned the oil that represented 80 percent of national production, and Bell Telephone controlled telephone services. In Venezuela, Standard Oil produced 50 percent of the oil, Shell another 25 percent, and Gulf, one-seventh. In what Peter Evans has called the "triple alliance," states such as Brazil actively brokered relationships between foreign and local firms in an attempt to spur industrial development.

Sources: de Castro (1969: 241–242); Evans (1979).

To secure an expanding industrial base, Third World governments constructed political coalitions among different social groups to support rapid industrialization—such as the Latin American **development alliance**.[42] Its social constituency included commercial farmers, public employees, urban industrialists, merchants, and workers dependent on industrialization, organized into associations and unions. Policy makers used price subsidies and public services such as health and education programs, cheap transport, and food subsidies to complement the earnings of urban dwellers, attract them to the cause of national industrialization, and realize the *social contract*.

The development alliance was also a vehicle of *political patronage*, whereby governments could manipulate electoral support. Mexico's Institutional Revolutionary Party (PRI), which controlled the state for much of the twentieth century, created corporatist institutions such as the Confederation of Popular Organizations, the Confederation of Mexican Workers, and the National Confederation of Peasants to channel patronage "downward" and to massage loyalty "upward." Political elites embraced the development project, mobilizing their national populations around the promise of rising living standards and expecting economic growth to legitimize them in the eyes of their emerging citizenry.

In accounting for and evaluating the development project, this book gives greatest attention to the Western bloc since Western affluence was the universal standard of development and modernity, and this has been extended under the guise of the globalization project to the ex–Second World following the collapse of the Soviet empire in 1989.

SUMMARY

The idea of development emerged during, and within the terms of, the era of the *colonial project*. This global hierarchy informed the understanding of development as a European achievement. Meanwhile, colonialism disorganized non-European societies by reconstructing their labor systems around specialized, ecologically degrading export production and by disorganizing the social psychology of colonial subjects. Exposure of non-European intellectuals, workers, and soldiers to the European liberal discourse on rights fueled anticolonial movements for political independence.

The political independence of the colonial world gave birth to the *development project,* a blueprint for national development as well as a "protection racket," insofar as international aid, trade, and investment flows were calibrated to Western military aid to secure Cold War perimeters and make the "free world" safe for business. Third World states became at once independent, but were collectively defined as "underdeveloped."

The pursuit of rising living standards, via industrialization, inevitably promoted Westernization in political, economic, and cultural terms as the non-European world emulated the European enterprise. Thus, the development project undercut Frantz Fanon's call for a non-European way, qualifying the sovereignty and diversity that often animated the movements for decolonization. It also rejected the pan-African insight into alternative political organization. These ideas are reemerging, and they have a growing audience.

The remainder of this book explores how these ideals have worked out in practice and how they have been reformulated. The next chapter examines the development project in action.

FURTHER READING

Achebe, Chinua. *Things Fall Apart*. London: William Heineman, 1958.

Davis, Mike. *Late Victorian Holocausts: El Niño Famines and the Making of the Third World*. London: Verso, 2001.

Escobar, Arturo. *Encountering Development: The Making and Unmaking of the Third World*. Princeton, NJ: Princeton University Press, 1995.

Evans, Peter. *Dependent Development: The Alliance of Multinational, State, and Local Capital in Brazil*. Princeton, NJ: Princeton University Press, 1979.

Fanon, Frantz. *The Wretched of the Earth*. Harmondsworth, UK: Penguin, 1967.

Leys, Colin. *Underdevelopment in Kenya: The Political Economy of Neo-Colonialism*. Berkeley: University of California Press, 1975.

Memmi, Albert. *The Colonizer and the Colonized*. Boston: Beacon Press, 1967.

Mitchell, Timothy. *Colonizing Egypt*. Berkeley: University of California Press, 1991.

Quinn, Daniel. *Ishmael: An Adventure of the Mind and Spirit*. New York: Bantam, 1993.

3

The Development Project

International Framework

When colonies became independent nation-states, their economies continued to depend on primary exports. But why would political independence be associated with "dependent development"?

- First, the colonial division of labor's legacy of resource extraction was embedded in Third World social structures, where trading classes of landowners and merchants, enriched by the exports of primary goods, would favor continuing this relationship. And, of course, the First World still desired raw materials and agricultural imports and markets for its industrial products.
- Second, as newly independent states industrialized, they purchased First World technology, paying with loans or foreign exchange earned from primary exports.
- Third, nation-states formed within an international framework, with the normative, legal, and financial relationships of the United Nations (UN) and the Bretton Woods institutions integrating states into universal political–economic relations.

National economic growth strategies depended, then, on the stimulus of these new international economic arrangements. The UN declared the 1960s and 1970s to be "Development Decades" to mobilize international development cooperation. In this chapter, we examine the construction of the Bretton Woods system and look at how its multilateral arrangements shaped national development strategies. We then examine the ways in which the development project *reshaped* the international division of labor.

WHAT ARE THE INGREDIENTS OF THE DEVELOPMENT PROJECT?

The development project was an internationally organized strategy for stimulating nationally managed economic growth. As colonialism collapsed, political elites of newly independent states embraced development to pursue growth, revenue generation, and legitimacy. The Western experience offered a (partial) model, and an international institutional complex supplied financial and technical assistance for development across the world, protected by Cold War military relations. Some ingredients were

- an organizing concept with universal claims (e.g., development as rising living standards, rationality, and scientific progress);
- a national framework for economic growth;
- an international framework of aid (military and economic) binding the developing world to the developed world and securing continuing access to its natural and human resources;
- a growth strategy favoring industrialization;
- an agrarian reform strategy encouraging agro-industrialization;
- development-state initiatives to manage investment and mobilize multiclass political coalitions into a development alliance supporting industrial growth; and
- realization of development through new inequalities, embedded in states and markets along regional, class, gender, racial, and ethnic lines.

The International Framework

The pursuit of national economic growth depended on international relations, both material and political–legal. Material supports included foreign aid, technology transfer, stable currency exchange, and international trade. Aid and trade relationships followed well-worn paths between ex-colonial states and their postcolonial regions. Complementing these historic relationships were the Bretton Woods institutions and the political, military, and economic relationships of the new superpower, the United States, as it sought to contain the rival Soviet empire.

Following the severe 1930s depression and the devastation of World War II (1939–1945), the United States spearheaded two initiatives to reconstruct the world economy: the bilateral Marshall Plan and the multilateral **Bretton Woods** program. The development project emerged within the Marshall Plan and was formalized under the Bretton Woods program, but it did not become a full-fledged operation until the 1950s, the peak decade of Third World political independence.

US Bilateralism: The Marshall Plan (Reconstructing the First World)

In the post–World War II years, the United States focused on European reconstruction as the key to stabilizing the Western world and securing capitalism. European grain harvests in 1946 would reach only 60 percent of prewar levels. Scarcity of labor skills and certain goods depleted transport and communication networks, and countless refugees posed enormous problems. There was also a growing popular desire for social reform.[1] Returning from Europe in 1947, US Assistant Secretary of State for Economic Affairs Will Clayton stated,

> Communist movements are threatening established governments in every part of the globe. These movements, directed by Moscow, feed on economic and political weakness. . . . The United States is faced with a world-wide challenge to human freedom. The only way to meet this challenge is by a vast new programme of assistance given directly by the United States itself.[2]

In these political circumstances, the United States hoped to use financial aid to stabilize discontented populations and rekindle economic growth in strategic parts of the world. Central to this strategy was containing communism—primarily in Europe, where the Soviet Union had laid claim to territories east of Berlin, but also in the Far East, where communism had gained ground, first in China and then in North Korea. The United States courted nations' allegiance to the Western free enterprise system with financial assistance. In 1950, Secretary of State Dean Acheson proposed to concentrate assistance in Western Europe in order to counter Soviet rule over Eastern Europe: "We cannot scatter our shots equally all over the world. We just haven't got enough shots to do that. . . . If anything happens in Western Europe the whole business goes to pieces."[3] Hence, the Marshall Plan was a *bilateral* transfer of billions of dollars to Europe (and Japan), serving US geopolitical goals in the Cold War. The plan restored trade and price stability and expanded productive work to undercut socialist movements and labor militancy. Dollar credits, allowing recipients to purchase US goods, and a massive rearmament effort closely integrated these countries' economies with that of the United States, solidifying political loyalty to the Western "free world."

Europeans desired social peace and full employment, to be achieved through closely regulated national economies, but the US government wanted an open world economy. The Marshall Plan solved this dilemma, using bilateral aid to facilitate international trade and encourage US direct investment in European national economies.[4]

Multilateralism: The Bretton Woods System

The idea for an international bank was part of the plan to reconstruct the world economy in the 1940s. Trade was to be restored by disbursing credit to regions devastated by war or colonialism. The famous July 1944 conference of 44 financial ministers at Bretton Woods, New Hampshire, provided the opportunity to create such an international banking system. Here, the US Treasury steered the conference toward chartering the foundation of the "twin sisters": the **World Bank** and the **International Monetary Fund (IMF)**.

Each institution was based on member subscriptions. The World Bank would match these subscriptions by borrowing money in international capital markets to raise money for development. The IMF was to disburse credit where needed to stabilize national currency exchanges. The conference president, Henry Morgenthau, foresaw

> the creation of a dynamic world economy in which the peoples of every nation will be able to realize their potentialities in peace . . . and enjoy, increasingly, the fruits of material progress on an earth infinitely blessed with natural riches. This is the indispensable cornerstone of freedom and security. All else must be built upon this. For freedom of opportunity is the foundation for all other freedoms.[5]

These were the key sentiments of the development project: multinational universalism, viewing nature as an unlimited resource, and a liberal belief in freedom of opportunity as the basis of political development and rising living standards.

The functions of the Bretton Woods agencies were

- to stabilize national finances and revitalize international trade (IMF);
- to underwrite national economic growth by funding Third World imports of First World infrastructural technologies; and
- to expand Third World primary exports to earn foreign currency for purchasing First World exports.

The World Bank's mandate was for large-scale loans to states for national infrastructural projects such as dams, highways, and power plants, complementing smaller scale private and public investments. In its first 20 years, two-thirds of the Bank's loans purchased inputs to build transportation and electric power systems. At the same time, the Bank invested in large-scale cash crop agriculture, such as cacao, rubber, and livestock, deepening the legacy of the colonial division of labor.[6]

The Bretton Woods institutions lubricated the world economy by moving funds to regions that needed purchasing power. Expanded trade stimulated economic growth across the First World–Third World divide. At the same time, these agencies disseminated the technologies of the development project, encouraging Third World states to adopt the capital-intensive methods of the West. Whereas Europe had taken several centuries to industrialize, Third World governments expected to industrialize rapidly with multilateral loans, substituting capital-intensive for labor-intensive production technologies despite substantial populations already displaced from their customary habitats.

The Bretton Woods system was unveiled as a universal and *multilateral* attempt to promote rising living standards on a global scale. Of the 45 nations in attendance at Bretton Woods, 27 were from the Third World. Nevertheless, the institutions had a decided First World imprint. First, the World Bank was, and is, controlled by its five largest First World shareholders. Second, the president of the World Bank is selected by the United States president, and the managing director of the IMF is appointed by the largest European nations (the United Kingdom, France, and Germany).[7] Third, the Bank finances foreign exchange costs of approved projects, encouraging import dependence (in capital-intensive technologies) in development priorities. Finally, the IMF adopted a "conditionality" requirement, requiring applicants to have economic policies that met certain criteria for them to obtain loans. International banks and other lenders inevitably adopted IMF conditionality as their criterion for Third World loans. In this way, Third World development priorities were tailored toward external (i.e., First World) evaluation.[8]

World Bank lending, however effective, reflected First World priorities. The Bank has emphasized "productive" investments, such as energy and export agriculture, rather than "social" investments, such as education, health services, water and sanitation facilities, and housing. In addition, as a global agency, the Bank finds it more convenient to invest in large-scale, capital-intensive projects that might, for example, have common technological inputs and similar appraisal mechanisms.[9] Not only has the Bank sponsored Western **technology transfer**, but it has also established an *institutional presence* in Third World countries. When the Bank finances infrastructural projects, these are often administered through agencies with semiautonomous financial and political power within host countries.

In examining how the development project issued from the Bretton Woods institutions, we have focused on the World Bank as the key multilateral agency responsible for underwriting Third World development. Overall, the World Bank framed development priorities via onsite project agencies and by encouraging large-scale power generation and transport projects, stimulating industrialization on a Western scale. The World Bank also channeled loans into intensive agriculture, requiring fossil fuel, energy-dependent technical inputs such as chemical fertilizers, pesticides, and hybrid seeds. And it created the Economic Development Institute in 1956 to train Third World officials (soon-to-be prime ministers or ministers of planning or finance in their own countries).[10]

In short, multilateralism, World Bank style, characterized the Bretton Woods system—World Bank policy set the parameters for development. Third World elites by and large embraced these parameters, since they were in no position to present an alternative to free enterprise. When governments adopted socialist policies, loan funds would shrink.

Politics of the Postwar World Order

As the realm of free enterprise expanded, the political dynamics of the Cold War deepened. While the United States and the Soviet Union were busy dividing the world, the countries of the Third World came together to assert their own international presence. Here we explore the interplay of all these forces.

Foreign Aid

An examination of the patterns of Western foreign aid shows that patterns of development assistance contradicted the universalism of the development project. All states could not be equal, as some were more strategic than others in the maintenance of order in the world market system. Western aid concentrated on undercutting competition from states or political movements that espoused rival (i.e., socialist) ideologies of development. Economic and military aid and trade to stabilize geopolitical regions prioritized regionally powerful states such as South Korea, Israel, Turkey, and Iran. These states functioned as military outposts in securing the perimeters of the "free world" and in preventing a "domino effect" of defections to the Soviet bloc.

Cold War rivalry governed much of the political geography of the development project. The Soviet Union was expanding economic and political relations with Third World states, especially newly independent states in Asia and Africa. By 1964, the Soviet Union had extended export credits to about 30 states, even though eight received the most aid. Under the Soviet aid system, loans could be repaid in local currencies or in the form of traditional exports, a program that benefited states short of foreign currency. Not only was the Soviet Union offering highly visible aid projects to key states such as Indonesia and India, but aid policies also clearly favored states pursuing policies of **central planning** and public ownership in their development strategies.[11]

For the United States and its First World allies, then, the development project was more than a transmission belt for Western technology and economic institutions. So long as the Third World—a vital source of strategic raw materials and minerals—was under threat from a political alternative, First World security was at stake. In 1956, this view was articulated clearly by Walt Rostow, the influential development economist and presidential adviser: "The location, natural resources, and populations of the underdeveloped areas are such that, should they become effectively attached to the Communist bloc, the United States would become the second power in the world."[12]

The United States' foreign aid patterns between 1945 and 1967 confirm this view of the world. Yugoslavia, for instance, received considerable aid as the regional counterweight to the Soviet Union. Elsewhere, aid to geopolitically strategic states (including Iran, Turkey, Israel, India, Pakistan, South Vietnam, Taiwan, South Korea, the Philippines, Thailand, and Laos) matched the total aid disbursement to all other Third World countries.[13]

The Non-Aligned Movement

Against this world ordering was an emerging Third World perspective that advocated a more independent vision. As decolonization proceeded, the composition of the United Nations shifted toward a majority of non-European member states. In 1955, the growing weight of the Third World in international politics produced the first meeting of "nonaligned" Asian and African states at Bandung, Indonesia, forming the **Non-Aligned Movement (NAM)** by 1961. Key players were the leaders of Yugoslavia (Tito), Indonesia (Sukarno), India (Nehru), Ghana (Nkrumah), North Vietnam (Ho Chi Minh), Egypt (Nasser), and China (Zhou Enlai). The NAM used its collective voice in international fora to forge a philosophy of noninterference in international relations. President Nyerere of Tanzania articulated this position in terms of economic self-reliance:

> By non-alignment we are saying to the Big Powers that we also belong to this planet. We are asserting the right of small, or militarily weaker, nations to determine their own policies in their own interests, and to have an influence

on world affairs. . . . At every point . . . we find our real freedom to make economic, social and political choices is being jeopardized by our need for economic development.[14]

The subtext of this statement, following the final Bandung communiqué, involved questioning the legitimacy of the model of development embedded in the multilateral institutional order. The first bone of contention was the paucity of multilateral loans. By 1959, the World Bank had lent more to the First World ($1.6 billion) than to the Third World ($1.3 billion). Third World members of the UN pressed for expanded loans, with concessions. The First World's response was to channel this demand toward the World Bank, where the International Development Association (IDA) was established to make loans at highly discounted rates (called "soft loans") to low-income countries. In addition, several regional banks were established— including the Inter-American Development Bank (IDB) in 1959, the African Development Bank (AfDB) in 1964, and the Asian Development Bank (ADB) in 1966.[15]

The Group of 77

International trade remained contentious. The **General Agreement on Tariffs and Trade (GATT)**, founded in 1947, enabled states to negotiate reciprocal trade concessions, but without adjusting for the uneven effects of colonialism.[16] In fact, during the 1950s, the Third World's share of world trade fell from one-third to almost one-fifth, with declining rates of export growth and declining terms of trade.[17]

Third World pressure founded the **United Nations Conference on Trade and Development (UNCTAD)** in 1964—the first international forum in which Third World countries, caucusing as the **Group of 77 (G-77)**, collectively demanded world-economic reforms. They demanded stabilized and improved primary commodity prices, opening First World markets to Third World manufactures, and expanding financial flows from the First World.

While UNCTAD had a limited world-economic impact, its scholar/planner members infused international agencies with a "Third Worldist" perspective. Perhaps its most concrete influence was on the World Bank under its president, Robert McNamara (1968–1981), who refocused development (for a time) on quality-of-life issues rather than simply income measures— the idea of "growth with equity."[18]

We now take leave of the institutional side of the development project to examine its impact on the international division of labor.

Remaking the International Division of Labor

If the development project was an initiative to promote Third World industrialization, then it certainly had some success. The result was uneven, however, and in some respects industrialization was quite incomplete. Nevertheless, by 1980 the international division of labor had been remade, if not reversed. Overall, exports from the Third World included more manufactured goods than raw materials, and the First World was exporting 36 percent more primary commodities than the Third World.[19]

The Newly Industrializing Countries (NICs)

The average growth rate for the Third World in the 1960s was 4.6 percent; however, six Third World **newly industrializing countries (NICs)**[20] grew at rates of 7 to 10 percent.[21] These six countries were Hong Kong, Singapore, Taiwan, South Korea, Brazil, and Mexico. The rise of the NICs revealed two sides of the development project. On one hand, NICs fulfilled the expectation of rising living standards and upward mobility in the international system, *legitimizing the development project as showcases*. The other middle-income countries—especially Malaysia, Thailand, Indonesia, Argentina, and Chile—expected to follow the same path (as depicted in Figure 3.1, where Thailand, Malaysia, and Indonesia replace textile exports of the NICs). On the other hand, the NICs also demonstrated the *selectivity* of the development project. They cornered the bulk of private foreign investment and considerable (Cold War–driven) military aid sustaining authoritarian regimes.[22] Much of this was concentrated in developing export production facilities in textiles and electronics in South Korea, Taiwan, Mexico, and Brazil. In 1969, for instance, most of the foreign investment in electronic assembly centered on the Asian NICs—Hong Kong, South Korea, Taiwan, and Singapore.[23] Between 1967 and 1978, the share of manufactured exports from the NICs controlled by transnational corporations (TNCs) was 20 percent in Taiwan, 43 percent in Brazil, and 90 percent in Singapore.[24] Distribution of industrial growth in the Third World was also highly concentrated. Between 1966 and 1975, more than 50 percent of the increase in value of Third World manufacturing occurred in only four countries, while about two-thirds of the increase was accounted for by only eight countries: Brazil, Mexico, Argentina, South Korea, India, Turkey, Iran, and Indonesia.[25]

Across the Third World, countries and regions differed in their levels of industrialization. The manufacturing portion of the gross domestic product (GDP) in 1975 was 5 percent in Africa, 16 percent in Asia, and 25 percent

Figure 3.1   Textiles, Clothing, and Footwear Exports From Newly Industrializing
Countries

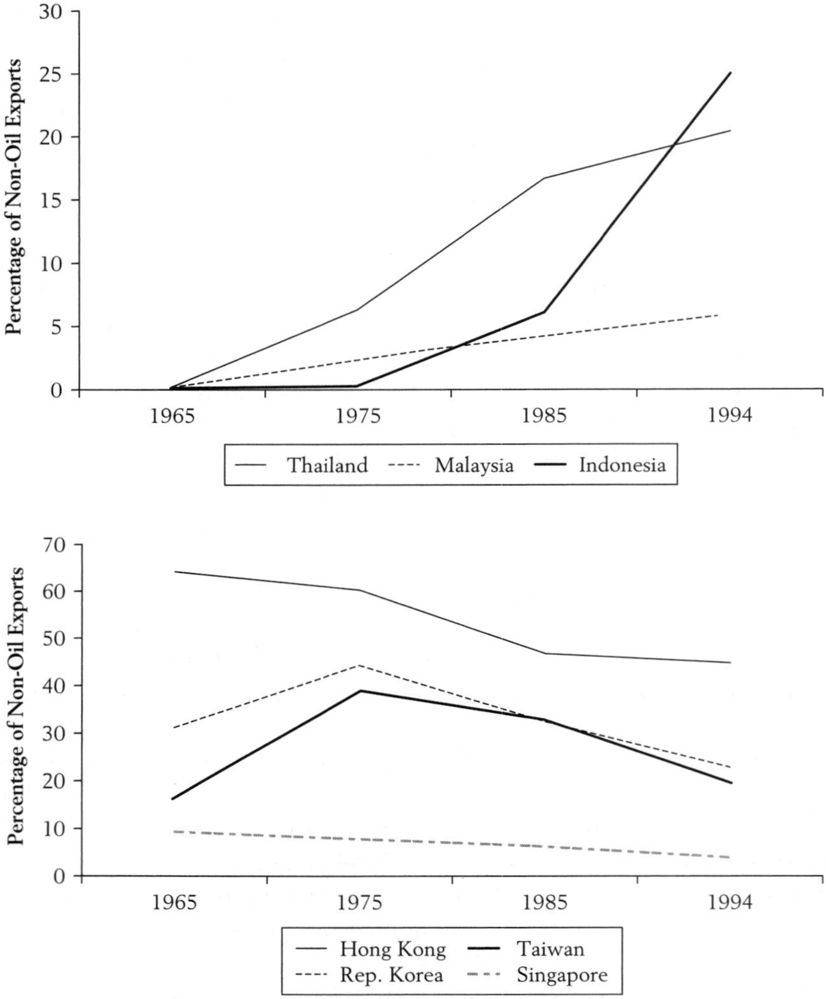

Sources: Adapted from graphs in Ransom (2001b: 103); data retrieved from UNCTAD (1996: 118–119).

in Latin America and the Caribbean.[26] By 1972, the Organisation for Economic Co-operation and Development (OECD) reported that the idea of a universal blueprint was clearly fading:

It has become more and more clear that measures designed to help developing countries as a group have not been effective for [the] least developed countries. They face difficulties of a special kind and intensity; they need help specifically designed to deal with their problems.[27]

The European First World lost its core manufacturing position in this period. Japan and a middle-income group of Third World states improved their share of world manufacturing, from 19 to 37 percent.[28] In agriculture, the Third World's share of world agricultural exports fell from 53 to 31 percent between 1950 and 1980, while the American breadbasket consolidated its critical role in world agricultural trade.[29] By the 1980s, the United States was producing 17 percent of the world's wheat, 63 percent of its corn, and 63 percent of its soybeans; its share of world exports was 36 percent in wheat, 70 percent in corn, and 59 percent in soybeans.[30] On the other side of the globe, between 1961 and 1975 Third World agricultural self-sufficiency declined everywhere except in centrally planned Asian countries (China, North Korea, and Vietnam). In all regions except Latin America, self-sufficiency dropped below 100 percent. Africa's self-sufficiency, for instance, declined from 98 percent in 1961 to 79 percent in 1978.[31]

Two questions arise:

- Why did commercial agriculture concentrate in the First World, while manufacturing dispersed to the Third World?
- Is there a relation between these trends?

The answer lies in the political structures of the development project. While import-substitution industrialization (ISI) protected Third World "infant" industries, farm subsidies protected First World agriculture under the terms of the GATT. These policies complemented one another, whereby American food surplus aid reshaped the international division of labor by subsidizing Third World manufacturing with cheap food for industrial workforces. Central to this process was a "food aid regime," which demonstrated the profoundly international character of the development project as a strategy of ordering the world under the guise of promoting development.

CASE STUDY   **South Korea in the Changing International Division of Labor**

South Korea was arguably the most successful of the middle-income NICs, transforming its economy and society in the space of a generation. In 1953, agriculture generated 47 percent of its gross national product (GNP), whereas

(Continued)

(Continued)

manufacturing generated less than 9 percent. By 1981, these proportions had switched to 16 percent and 30 percent, respectively. At the same time, the contribution of heavy and chemical industries to total industrial output matured from 23 percent in 1953 to 1955 to 42 percent in 1974 to 1976. How did this happen?

South Korea depended on injections of American dollars following the Korean War in the early 1950s, as it pursued the ISI strategy. By 1973, its government's heavy industry and chemicals plan encouraged industrial maturity in shipbuilding, steel, machinery, and petrochemicals and complemented ISI with export-oriented industrialization, beginning with labor-intensive consumer goods such as textiles and garments. From the early 1960s to the early 1980s, manufactured goods rose from 17 to 91 percent of exports, as increasingly sophisticated electronics goods emerged and as Korean manufacturers gained access to foreign markets.

South Korea exemplifies a development state whose success depended on a rare flexibility in policy combined with the unusually repressive political system of military ruler Park Chung Hee (1961–1979). Koreans worked extremely long hours only to find their savings taxed away to support government investment policies. Industrial labor had no rights. Confucianism promoted consensus and the authority of education and the bureaucracy, providing a powerful mobilizing cultural myth. A frontline position in the Cold War helped, as the United States opened its markets to Korean exports.

Meanwhile, cheap US food exports were key. Before 1960, virtually no Western-style bread was consumed in Korea—rice is cherished, and at that time, the country was self-sufficient in food. By 1975, however, South Korea was only 60 percent food self-sufficient, and by 1978, it belonged to what the US Department of Agriculture calls "the billion-dollar club." That is, South Korea was purchasing $2.5 billion worth of American farm commodities, primarily wheat. The government provided free lunch bread to schoolchildren, and thousands of Korean housewives attended sandwich-making classes, financed by US "counterpart funds" from its food aid program.

Since the South Korean "miracle" depended significantly on the subsidy to its industrialization strategy provided by cheap American food (lowering wage costs) and on access to US markets for its manufactured exports, was its development ultimately a domestic or an international process?

Sources: Chung (1990: 43); Evans (1995); Harris (1987: 31–36); Wessel (1983: 172–173).

The Food Aid Regime

In the postwar era, the United States set up a food aid program to channel food surpluses to Third World countries. Surpluses arose out of the US agro-industrial model, protected by tariffs and subsidies (institutionalized in the GATT). Farmers specialized in one or two commodities (such as corn, rice, wheat, and dairy products) and, with technological and subsidy support from the public purse, routinely overproduced. The resulting surpluses were used by the US government to subsidize Third World wage bills with cheap food. It was a substantial transfer of agricultural resources to Third World urban-industrial sectors. This **food aid regime**[32] set in motion the rural–urban dynamic prescribed by development economists, but with a difference: *operating on a global, instead of a national, scale.*

The Public Law 480 Program

To dispose of farm surpluses, the US government instituted the Public Law 480 Program (PL-480) in 1954. It had three components: commercial sales on concessionary terms—discounted prices in local currency (Title I); famine relief (Title II); and food bartered for strategic raw materials (Title III). The stated goal was "to increase the consumption of US agricultural commodities in foreign countries, to improve the foreign relations of the US and for other purposes." In 1967, the US Department of Agriculture reported, "One of the major objectives and an important measure of the success of foreign policy goals is the transition of countries from food aid to commercial trade"[33]—that is, to create new markets for US goods.

Title I sales anchored this food aid regime, accounting for 70 percent of world food aid (mostly wheat) between 1954 and 1977. By the mid-1960s, food aid accounted for one-quarter of world wheat exports, determining the prices of traded foods. Management of food surpluses stabilized prices, and this in turn stabilized two key, interrelated parts of the development project: the American agricultural economy and Third World government industrial plans.

Food Dependency

Under the aid program, wheat imports provisioned rising Third World urban populations. Third World governments established distribution programs to channel aid to reward the so-called development alliance of manufacturers, labor unions, urban professionals, and middle classes. Cheap food thus supported consumer purchasing power and subsidized the cost of labor, stabilizing urban politics and improving the Third World environment for industrial investments.

The impact of food aid varied across the world, depending on the resources of particular countries and their development policies. South Korea was a success story largely because the government centralized management of its rice culture and the supply of labor to the industrial centers. By contrast, urbanization in Colombia followed the collapse of significant parts of its unprotected farm belt under the competitive impact of food aid and commercial imports of wheat. Stimulated by the food aid program, imports of discounted wheat grew tenfold between the early 1950s and 1971, reducing by half the prices obtained by Colombian farmers. Displaced peasants contributed to the characteristic urban underemployment and low-wage economy of Third World countries.[34]

Between 1954 and 1974, major recipients of US food aid were India, South Korea, Brazil, Morocco, Yugoslavia, South Vietnam, Egypt, Tunisia, Israel, Pakistan, Indonesia, Taiwan, and the Philippines (see Figure 3.2). Usually, it was cheaper and easier for governments to import wheat to feed their growing urban populations than to bankroll long-term improvements in the production, transportation, and distribution of local foods.[35] Food aid allowed governments to purchase food without depleting scarce foreign currency, but it built "food dependency."

Shipments of food were paid for in counterpart funds—that is, local currency placed in US local bank accounts as payment; in India, for example, the United States owned over one-third of the rupee supply by the 1970s.[36] These funds could be spent only by US agencies within the recipient country, on a range of activities such as infrastructural projects, supplies for military bases, loans to US companies (especially local agribusiness operations), locally produced goods and services, and trade fairs. Counterpart funds were also used to promote *new diets* among Third World consumers in the form of school lunch programs and the promotion of bread substitutes. US Sen. George McGovern predicted this in 1964:

> The great food markets of the future are the very areas where vast numbers of people are learning through Food for Peace to eat American produce. The people we assist today will become our customers tomorrow. . . . An enormous market for American produce of all kinds will come into being if India can achieve even half the productivity of Canada.[37]

Figure 3.2 Food Shortage Regions and Food Aid Recipients

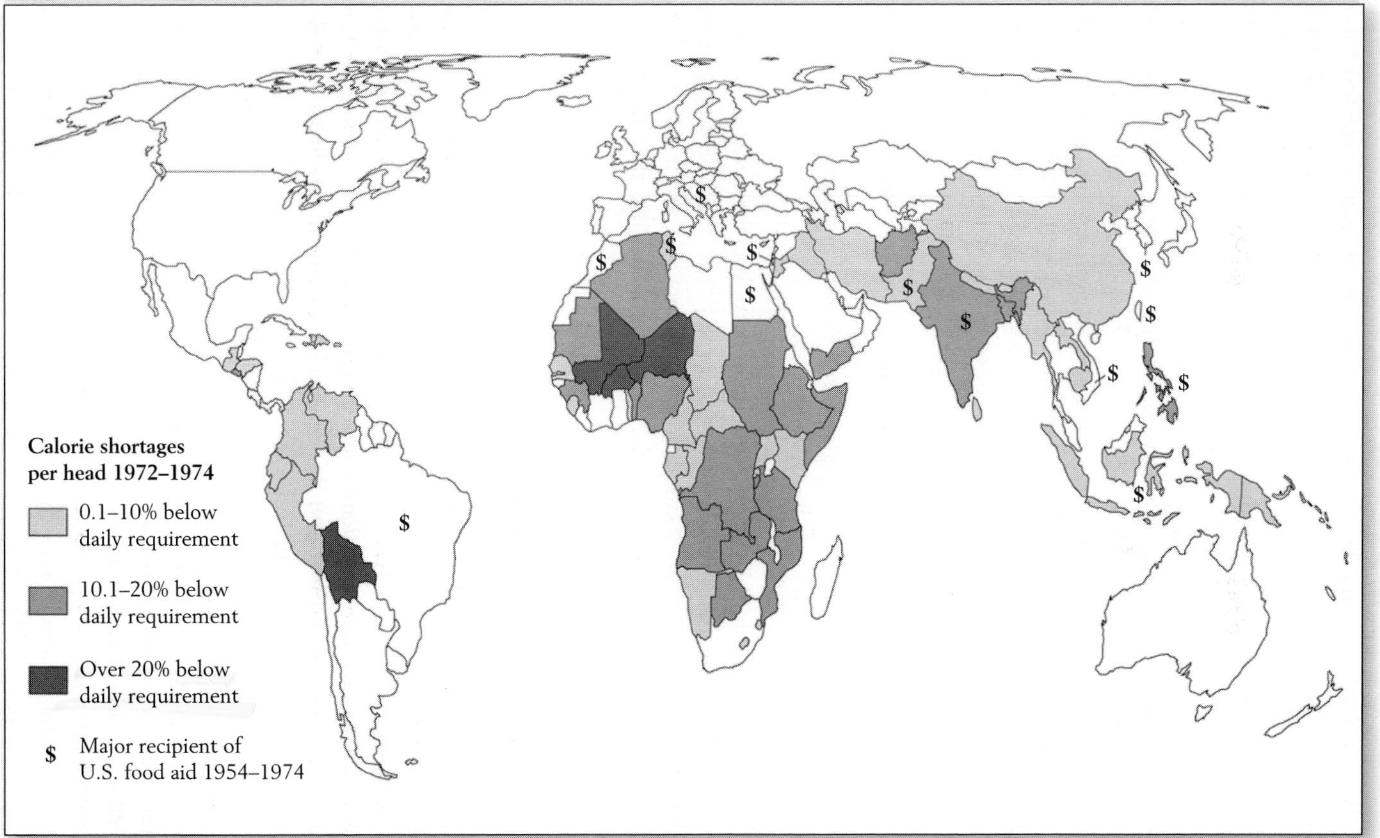

Calorie shortages
per head 1972–1974

☐ 0.1–10% below
daily requirement

☐ 10.1–20% below
daily requirement

☐ Over 20% below
daily requirement

$ Major recipient of
U.S. food aid 1954–1974

Source: Michael Kidron and Ronald Segal, *The State of the World Atlas.* London: Pan, 1981.

By 1978, the Third World was receiving more than three-fourths of American wheat exports. At the same time, Third World per capita consumption of wheat rose by almost two-thirds, and per capita consumption of all cereals except wheat increased 20 percent, while per capita consumption of traditional root crops declined by more than 20 percent.[38] In Asian and Latin American urban diets, wheat progressively replaced rice and corn. Wheat (and rice) imports displaced maize in Central America and parts of the Middle East and millet and sorghum in West Africa. Subsidized grain imports also undercut the prices of traditional starches (potatoes, cassava, yams, and taro). Thus, traditional "peasant foods" were replaced by the new "wage foods" of grains and processed foods consumed by urban workers.[39]

The rising consumption of imported wheat in Third World countries linked two far-reaching changes:

- the erosion of peasant agriculture, as urban food rations enabled subsidized wage foods to outcompete peasant foods; and
- the expansion of an industrial labor force, as small producers left the land for low-wage jobs in the rapidly growing cities.

In the conventional development model, these social trends occur within a national framework. In reality, via the development project, they occurred within an international political–economic framework, as First World farmers supplied Third World industrial workers, remaking the international division of labor.

Remaking Third World Agricultures

The intent of the PL-480 program was to create future markets for commercial sales of US grains as consumers shifted to wheat-based diets. These complemented expanding consumption of other surplus agricultural goods, such as feed grains and agricultural technology. Behind this stood the massive state-sponsored expansion in American agricultural productivity, which outstripped manufacturing from the 1950s to the 1970s. Disposal of surpluses was a matter of government policy. At this point, it is important to reflect on the longer-term consequences of this "food empire" strategy. Such public support of "petro-farming"—where petroleum fuels industrial agriculture via mechanization, inorganic fertilizers, pesticides, herbicides, and seed varnishes, abandoning agriculture's natural biological base—undermines nature's intrinsic ecological qualities over time. In the process, intensive agriculture annually loses two million acres of farmland to erosion, soil salinity, and flooding, in addition to consuming groundwater 160 percent faster than it can be replenished.[40] Presciently, given the recent water crisis in California, Marc Reisner, referring to the American West in *Cadillac Desert,* wrote, "Westerners call what they have established out here a civilization, but it would be more accurate to call it a beachhead. . . . And if history is any guide, the odds that we can sustain it would have to be regarded as low."[41] An unsustainable agribusiness model is one of the key export legacies of the development project.

The Global Livestock Complex

During the food aid regime, surplus grain was sufficiently cheap and plentiful to feed livestock rather than people. Expanding supplies of feed grains stimulated the growth of commodity chains, linking specialized feed producers with specialized animal protein producers across the world. Beyond a wheat-based diet, more affluent consumers shifted up the food chain, from grain to animal protein (beef, poultry, pork, and shrimp). Such "dietary modernization" followed rising incomes, converting rainforest to pasture for cattle in turn converted into hamburger, as a fast-food industry emerged, with environmental consequence. The contributions of beef production to global warming, via carbon dioxide, nitrous oxide, and methane, are significant: "Altered climates, shorter growing seasons, changing rainfall patterns, eroding rangeland, and spreading deserts may well sound the death knell for the cattle complex and the artificial protein ladder that has been erected to support a grain-fed beef culture."[42]

The grain companies that formerly sold and processed wheat diversified into processed feeds (corn, barley, soybeans, alfalfa, oats, and sorghum) for cattle and hog feedlots as well as poultry motels. Consumption of animal protein became identified with "the American way of life," as meat accounted for one-quarter of the food bill by 1965.[43] Beef consumption roughly doubled between the turn of the century and 1976, and poultry consumption more than tripled between the 1930s and 1970.[44] Looking ahead, factory farms in the United States today annually produce well over one billion tons of manure, laden with chemicals, antibiotics, and hormones, which leach into rivers and water tables.[45] The animal protein culture, associated with improved consumption, has disturbing environmental and health consequences and represents a key development paradox.

Through the food aid program, exports of feed grains also flourished as animal protein consumption spread among Third World middle classes. The US Feed Grains Council routinely channeled counterpart funds, via over 400 agribusinesses, into the development of local livestock and poultry industries.[46] In 1969, four South Korean firms entered into joint ventures with US agribusinesses (including Ralston-Purina and Cargill) to acquire technical and marketing expertise. The 1970 PL-480 annual report stated these enterprises would use counterpart funds "to finance construction and operation of modern livestock feed mixing and livestock and poultry production and processing facilities. As these facilities become fully operational, they will substantially expand the market for feedgrain and other feed ingredients."[47]

A global livestock complex formed, with livestock production expanding across the Third World and specialized feed grain supply zones concentrating in the First World and in "middle-income" countries such as Brazil and Argentina. Between the late 1940s and 1988, world production of soybeans increased sixfold. At the same time, maize production was revolutionized as a specialized, capital-intensive agro-industry, outstripping the value of the world wheat trade by a factor of six.[48]

CASE STUDY   Food and Class Relations

The growing feed grains trade traces changing social diets as societies transform.

Animal protein consumption reflects rising affluence as middle-class Third Worlders embraced First World diets beyond those staple (grain, primarily wheat) diets promoted directly through food aid. (Ernst) Engel's law correlated the dietary move from starch to grain to animal protein and fresh vegetables with rising incomes. Rather than reflecting individual choice, however, dietary differentiation reflects who controls production of certain foods and how consumption patterns distribute among social classes.

Consider Egypt, where, between 1974 and 1975, the richest 27 percent of the urban population consumed four times as much animal protein as the poorest 27 percent. Rising incomes, complemented by US and Egyptian government subsidies, fostered a switch from legumes and maize to wheat and meat products. From 1970 to 1987, livestock production outstripped crop production by 10 to 1. Egypt's grain imports exploded as it became the world's largest importer after Japan and China. Timothy Mitchell notes that dependence on imported grain stems from a government-sponsored shift to meat consumption:

> Egypt's food problem is the result not of too many people occupying too little land, but of the power of a certain part of that population, supported by the prevailing domestic and international regime, to shift the country's resources from staple foods to more expensive items of consumption.

Engel's law appears to operate globally, as different classes dine on different parts of the food chain, but the difference is a policy effect. As wealthy consumers dine "up" on animal protein, the working poor dine either on food aid grains or the low end of the food chain: low-protein starchy diets, or little at all.

While it seems *natural* for those with rising incomes to consume animal protein, can we separate meat consumption from the political mechanisms and social inequalities that support such indirect consumption of feed grains at the expense of direct consumption of grains and other staple foods?

Sources: Gardner and Halweil (2000); Mitchell (1991).

The Green Revolution

The other major contribution to the remaking of Third World agriculture was the **green revolution**. This involved a "package" of plant-breeding agricultural technologies originally developed by the Rockefeller Foundation in Mexico—increasing production of corn, wheat, and beans in the two decades after 1943 by 300 percent, and, in a combined venture with the Ford Foundation in the Philippines in the 1960s, in tropical centers in Nigeria and Colombia. In 1971, it culminated in the formation of the Consultative Group on International Agricultural Research (CGIAR), sponsored by the Food and Agricultural Organization (FAO), the United Nations Development Program (UNDP), and the World Bank, with research facilities and gene banks across the world.[49] The green revolution was also the principal medium through which the US model of chemical agriculture was introduced into the Third World—a technology transfer involving specific political choices and consequences.

Green revolution advocacy symbolized the idealized prescriptions of the development project, with its focus on output, despite known social and ecological consequences.[50] In the development narrative, rural population shrinkage is inevitable as agriculture "modernizes." The question is, why shrink huge rural populations where industry is either capital-intensive or not extensive, and slumdwellers comprise 50 percent of Third World populations?

"Productivism" has been a central development theme. It was promoted heavily by the US land-grant university system, with an extension program geared to a model of commodity-specific research, supporting large, capitalized farmers.[51] Within the development project, the "entire argument for increasing yields was framed by the specter of increasing population." This argument lent moral and political legitimacy to a technological solution (despite the consequences); it represented population as an independent variable (we have seen how the case study of Egypt questions this); and, finally, the green revolution program appealed to "economic nationalism," a central ingredient of developmentalism at the time.[52]

Even more compelling were the political implications of the Chinese model where, following the 1949 Communist revolution, about 45 percent of total cultivated land monopolized by landlords was redistributed to small and landless peasants. Collectivization of land mobilized underemployed surplus labor and investment in water management and local enterprises and extended basic health and rural education through a decentralized process supplemented with central government assistance—albeit with a goal of squeezing agriculture to finance industrial growth and the Party.[53] Whether or not this vast social experiment ultimately succeeded, the Chinese model loomed large in countries such as India, where Prime Minister Nehru was determined to match the Chinese.[54] However, Indian national institutional reforms required compliance by state governments, generally dominated by landlords and merchants unfavorable to land reform and labor cooperatives. The revolution would thus change color, from red to a conservative green.

Meanwhile, the United States, with the leverage of its counterpart funds in India, was encouraging India to substitute green revolution technology for land redistribution.[55] Pressure to extend chemical agriculture stemmed from the conversion of wartime nitrogen production (for bombs) to inorganic fertilizer, displacing nitrogen-fixing legumes and manure, and the development of insecticides, stemming from World War I nerve gases, with advances in petroleum refining and organic chemistry.[56]

"Petro-farming"—marrying the chemical industry with the energy sector—both enabled and encouraged proliferation of green revolution technology, with the FAO providing extension services for the disposal of synthetic fertilizer across the Third World, intensifying agricultural dependence on the energy sector.[57] Vandana Shiva suggests, "The Green Revolution seeds were designed to overcome the limits placed on chemically intensive agriculture by the indigenous seeds."[58]

The new high-yielding varieties (HYVs) of hybrid seeds were heavily dependent on disease- and pest-resisting chemical protections in the form of fungicides and pesticides. Intensive irrigation and fertilization were necessary to optimize macronutrient yields, eliminating traditional leafy greens (with micronutrients such as vitamin A) now redefined as "weeds" and targeted by herbicides. The HYVs produced "wage foods" for urban consumers, displacing "peasant foods" produced with methods of crop rotation to maintain soil fertility. In 1984, an Indian farmer commented on the stronger, healthy soils promoted by manure-based fertilizer: "Chemical fertilizer makes the crop shoot up . . . whereas organic manure makes for strength. Without strength, no matter how much fertilizer you put, the field won't give output."[59] The hybrid seed ruptured the ecological cycle of natural regeneration and renewal, replacing it with linear flows of purchased inputs and commodified outputs, and incorporated farmers into the "chemical treadmill."[60] Long-term economic and ecological impacts have been blamed for as many as 100,000 farmer suicides in India between 1993 and 2003.[61]

The expansion of green revolution agriculture embodied the two sides of the development project: the national and the international. From a *national* perspective, governments sought to improve agricultural productivity and the delivery of maize, wheat, and rice to urban centers. In the context of the food aid regime, this *import-substitution* strategy either supplemented food aid or complemented its competitive effects on poorer farmers. The green revolution produced dramatic yields, but highly concentrated in a few ecologically advantaged regions of the Third World. Asia and, to a much lesser degree, Latin America have captured the benefits from the new grain varieties, while Africa—lacking an expansive commercial wheat or rice culture—has charted few gains. The major wheat-producing countries in the Third World—India, Argentina, Pakistan, Turkey, Mexico, and Brazil—planted the bulk of their wheat acreage in the new hybrid varieties, accounting for 86 percent of the total green revolution wheat area by the 1980s. Meanwhile, six Asian countries—India, Indonesia, the Philippines, Bangladesh, Burma, and Vietnam—were cultivating more than 87 percent of the rice acreage attributed to the green revolution by the 1980s.[62]

From an *international* perspective, the food aid program helped to spread green revolution technology. Counterpart funds routinely promoted agribusiness and green revolution technologies, complemented with loans from institutions such as the US Agency for International Development (USAID) and the World Bank.[63] These agencies aimed to weave First World agricultural technologies into Third World commercial farming.

The green revolution was realized through the increase of rural income inequalities. In parts of Latin America, such as Mexico, Argentina, Brazil, and Venezuela, as well as in irrigated regions of India (Punjab and Haryana), this high-input agriculture promoted economic differentiation among—and often within—farming households. Within households, typically women have less commercial opportunity. Hybrid seeds and supporting inputs had to be purchased; to buy them, participants needed a regular supply of money or credit. Women tended to be excluded—not only because of the difficulty of obtaining financing but also because of agricultural extension traditions of transferring technology to male heads of households.[64]

Among farming households, the wealthier ones were more able to afford the package—and the risk—of introducing the new seed varieties. They also prospered from higher grain yields—often with easier access to government services than their poorer neighbors, who lacked the political and economic resources to take full advantage of these technologies. Rising land values often hurt tenant farmers by inflating their rent payments, forcing them to rent their land to their richer neighbors or to foreclose to creditors. Finally, the mechanical and chemical technologies associated with the green revolution either reduce farmhand employment opportunities for poor or landless peasants (where jobs were mechanized) or degrade working conditions where farmhands are exposed to toxic chemicals, such as pesticides and herbicides.[65]

Anti-Rural Biases of the Development Project

Within the framework of the development project, Third World governments strove to feed growing urban populations cheaply, for political support, for lowering wages, and for national security. The term **urban bias** has been coined to refer to the systematic privileging of urban interests, from health and education services through employment schemes to the delivery of food aid.[66] This bias was central to the construction of development alliances based in the cities of the Third World. It also expressed the modernist belief in peasant redundancy.

Urban bias did not go unnoticed in the countryside. Growing rural poverty, rural marginalization, and persistent peasant activism over the question of land distribution put **land reform** on the political agenda in Asia and Latin America. When the Cuban Revolution redistributed land to poor and landless peasants in 1959, land reforms swept Latin America. Between 1960 and 1964, Brazil, Chile, Costa Rica, the Dominican Republic, Ecuador, Guatemala, Nicaragua, Panama, Peru, and Venezuela all enacted land reforms. The Alliance for Progress (1961)—a program of nationally planned agrarian reform coordinated across Latin America—provided an opportunity for the United States to use land reforms to undercut radical insurgents and stabilize rural populations via a US-inspired family farming model.[67]

The land reform movement exempted commercialized farmland, redistributing what was left, including frontier lands. Indeed, considerable "re-peasantization" occurred during this period. In Latin America, two-thirds of the additional food production between 1950 and 1980 came from frontier colonization, and the number of small farmers with an average of two hectares of land grew by 92 percent. Overall, arable land increased by as much as 109 percent in Latin America and 30 percent in Asia but possibly declined in Africa.[68] Resettlement schemes on frontiers, including forests, were typically financed by the World Bank, especially in Indonesia, Brazil, Malaysia, and India, and they usually privileged males as household heads—"one of the principal mechanisms of exclusion of women as direct beneficiaries."[69] These strategies sometimes simply relocated rural poverty. In Brazil between 1960 and 1980, roughly 28 million small farmers were displaced by industrial farming for export to enhance foreign exchange earnings. The displaced farmers spilled into the Amazon region, burning the forest for new and often infertile land.[70]

Persistent rural poverty through the 1960s highlighted the urban bias of the development project. At this point, the World Bank (under Robert McNamara) devised a new poverty alleviation program—a multilateral scheme to channel credit to smallholding peasants and stabilize rural populations where previous agrarian reforms failed, with quite mixed success. Outcomes included leakage of credit funds to more powerful rural operators, displacement of hundreds of millions of peasants, and the incorporation of surviving peasant smallholders via credit into commercial cropping at the expense of basic food farming.[71]

The lesson we may draw from this episode of reform is that neither the resettlement of peasants nor their integration into monetary relations is always a sustainable substitute for supporting agroecological methods that preserve natural cycles of regeneration of land, water, and biodiversity. The assumptions of the development project heavily discriminated against the survival of peasant culture, as materially impoverished as it may have seemed.

Through a combination of food dumping and institutional support of commercial and export agriculture, the long-term assault on peasant agriculture begun in the colonial era intensified. Priority given to import and production of "wage foods"—compromising soil fertility and hydrological cycles—undermines the viability of household food production as a livelihood strategy for peasants and a subsistence base for the rural poor. The result has been a swelling migration of displaced peasants to overcrowded urban centers of Latin America, Asia, and Africa, creating a "planet of slums."[72]

SUMMARY

The development project was multilayered, as national strategies of economic growth dovetailed with international multilateral and bilateral assistance. The Third World *as a whole* was incorporated into a *singular* project, despite national/regional variations in resources, starting point, and ideological orientation.

Military and economic-aid programs shaped the geopolitical contours of the "free world," integrating Third World countries into the Western orbit. They also shaped patterns of development through technological transfer and food subsidies to industrialization programs. Food aid was significant in securing geopolitical alliances, as well as in reshaping the international division of labor via support of Third World manufacturing. As development economists predicted, Third World industrialization depended on the transfer of rural resources. But this transfer was not confined to national arenas, as exports of First World food and agricultural technology constituted a *global* rural–urban exchange.

The international dimension is as critical to our understanding of the development processes during the postwar era. We cannot detail national varieties here, and that is not the point of this story. Rather, the focus is on understanding how the development project set in motion a *global* dynamic, embedding national policies within an international institutional and ideological framework. This framework was theoretically in the service of national economic growth policies, but proved to be ultimately internationalizing. Social changes within Third World countries put a local face on what was ultimately a common global process of development embedded in unequal relations and technology transfer between the First and Third Worlds.

In this chapter, we have examined one such example of these transfers, and we have seen how they condition the rise of new social structures. First World agricultural expansion was linked with the rise of new industrial classes in the Third World. At the same time, the export of green revolution technology to Third World regions stimulated social differentiation among men and women and among rural producers, laborers, and capitalist farmers. Those peasants unable to survive the combined competition of cheap foods and high-tech farming in the countryside migrated to the cities, further depressing wages. Not surprisingly, this scenario stimulated a massive relocation of industrial tasks to the Third World, reshaping the international division of labor. This is the subject of Chapter 4.

FURTHER READING

Chang, Ha-Joon. *Kicking Away the Ladder: Development Strategy in Historical Perspective*. London: Anthem Press, 2002.

Gupta, Akhil. *Postcolonial Developments: Agriculture in the Making of Modern India*. Durham, NC: Duke University Press, 1998.

Kloppenburg, Jack R., Jr. *First the Seed: The Political Economy of Plant Biotechnology, 1492–2000.* Cambridge, UK: Cambridge University Press, 1988.

Rich, Bruce. *Mortgaging the Earth: The World Bank, Environmental Impoverishment and the Crisis of Development.* Boston: Beacon, 1994.

SELECT WEBSITES

Consultative Group on International Agricultural Research (CGIAR): www.cgiar.org
Food and Agriculture Organization (FAO), UN: www.fao.org
International Monetary Fund (IMF): www.imf.org
United Nations Conference on Trade and Development (UNCTAD): www.unctad.org
The World Bank: www.worldbank.org

4

Globalizing Developments

R ecall that the "economic nationalism" of the development project was an ideal, not a guarantee. The conversion of segments of domestic production to export production deepened the impact of the world market in national economies. This chapter focuses on the socioeconomic dimensions of this transformation, anticipating the process and politics of globalization, as the development project gave way to the globalization project.

The development project involved the postwar reconstruction of the world market, within which national governments focused on achieving development. The Cold War marked the rise of a US-centered capitalist world economy in which the US government deployed military and economic largesse to secure an informal empire as colonialism receded. With the West focused on *containing* Soviet and Chinese power, the development project settled on the twin economic foundations of *freedom of enterprise* (multinational corporations) and the US dollar as the *international currency*. Bilateral disbursements of dollars wove together the principal national economies of the West and Japan, and as the dollar source, the US Federal Reserve System led those countries' central banks in regulating an international monetary system.[1]

Within this arrangement, Third World political elites pursued national development targets assisted by substantial military and financial aid packages. Countries differed in their resource endowments and their political regimes—ranging from military dictatorship to one-party states to parliamentary rule. Nonetheless, despite expectations of convergence through development, divergent forces soon appeared. These included a growing, rather than diminishing, gap between First and Third World living standards and a substantial differentiation among states within the Third World, as the newly industrializing countries "took off." *In combination,* these divergent developments signaled a deepening integration of production systems *across,* rather than within, nation-states. The development "fast track" was emerging in the web of economic relations across national borders as a new form of global economy emerged, leaving the national experiment behind.

Third World Industrialization in Context

The rise of the **newly industrializing countries (NICs)** appeared to confirm that the colonial legacy was in retreat and that industrialization would inevitably expand into the Third World. Each of the NICs, with some variation, moved through low-value industries (processed foods, clothing, toys) to higher-value industries (steel, autos, petrochemicals, machinery, electronics). Whereas the Latin American NICs (Mexico and Brazil) began the early phase in the 1930s, graduating to the more mature phase in the 1950s, the Asian NICs (Taiwan and South Korea) began manufacturing basic goods in the 1950s and did not upgrade until the 1970s. The other regional variation was that the Asian NICs financed their import-substitution industrialization (ISI) by exporting labor-intensive products because they lacked the resource base and domestic markets of the Latin NICs.[2]

With the exception of Hong Kong, most of the NICs had strong development states guiding public investment into infrastructure development and industrial ventures with private enterprise. The South Korean development state virtually dictated national investment patterns.[3] Industrialization depended on the size of domestic markets as well as access to foreign exchange for purchasing First World capital equipment technologies. As technological rents rose in limited domestic markets, Latin NICs adopted the **export-oriented industrialization (EOI)** model of the Asian NICs to earn foreign exchange.

Widespread EOI signaled a significant change in strategies of industrialization, increasingly organized by transnational corporation (TNC) investment and marketing networks. For First World firms, EOI became a means of relocating the manufacturing of consumer goods, and then machinery and computers, to the Third World. Third World states welcomed the new investment with corporate concessions and a ready supply of cheap, unorganized labor. At the same time, First World consumption of Third World products intensified with easy credit and a mushrooming of shopping malls and fast food outlets in the 1970s. In this way, the *global consumer* and the *global labor force* became mutually dependent.[4]

Third World manufacturing exports outpaced the growth in world manufacturing trade during this period, increasing their share of world trade from 6 to 10 percent between 1960 and 1979. The NICs accounted for the bulk of this export growth, its composition broadening from textiles, toys, footwear, and clothing in the 1960s to more sophisticated exports of electronics and electrical goods bound for the First World, as well as machinery and transport equipment bound for the Third World, by the 1970s.[5] Asian NIC development was achieved by rooting industrialization in the world economy. Thus,

> Mexico, Brazil, Argentina, and India . . . accounted for over 55% of all Third World industrial production but only about 25% of all Third World manufactured exports (narrowly defined). Hong Kong, Malaysia, Singapore and South Korea . . . were responsible for less than 10% of Third World production but 35% of all Third World manufactured exports (narrowly defined).[6]

The Asian NICs' export orientation was exceptional for geopolitical reasons. First, the East Asian perimeter of the Pacific Ocean was a strategic zone in the Cold War security system. Military alliances opened US markets to exports, often of goods assembled for US corporations. Second, Japan's historic trade and investment links with this region deepened as Japanese firms invested in low-wage assembly production offshore. In each case, the Asian NICs reaped the benefits of access to the near-insatiable markets of the United States and Japan. The global and regional contexts have been as influential in NICs' growth as much as domestic policy measures and national economic cultures.

The World Factory

The expanding belt of export industries in the Third World, led by the NICs, provides a clue to a broader transformation occurring within the world at large. There was a new "fast track" in manufacturing exports, superseding the traditional track of exporting processed resources. It heralded the rise of the **world factory**: proliferating manufacturing export platforms producing world, rather than national, products. Often, production steps are separated and distributed among geographically dispersed sites in assembly-line fashion, producing and assembling a completed product. World products—including automobiles, cell phones, computers, jeans, electronic toys—emerge from a single site or a **global assembly line** of multiple sites (commodity chains) organizing disparate labor forces of varying skill, cost, and function.[7]

The phenomenal growth of export manufacturing using labor-intensive methods in the East Asian region, as well as regions such as Mexico's border-industrial zone, signaled the rise of *a global production system*. In Asia, the stimulus came from the relocation of the Japanese industrial model of hierarchical subcontracting arrangements to sites across the region. The Mexican Border Industrialization Program (BIP) paralleled this "decentralization" of industrial production, importing unfinished components for local assembly as a world market product. In 1965, the Mexican government implemented the BIP to allow entirely foreign-owned corporations to establish labor-intensive assembly plants (known as *maquiladoras*) within a twelve-mile strip south of the border. Concessions to firms employing Mexican labor at a fraction of US wages and paying minimal taxes and import duties to the Mexican government were part of a competitive world factory strategy. In 1967, the Mexican minister of commerce stated, "Our idea is to offer an alternative to Hong Kong, Japan, and Puerto Rico for free enterprise."[8] The *maquiladoras* have earned about one-third of Mexico's scarce foreign currency income.

US firms establishing assembly plants in the BIP concentrated on garments, electronics, and toys. By the early 1970s, 70 percent of the operations were in electronics, following a global trend of US firms relocating electronic assembly operations to southern Europe, South Korea, Taiwan, and Mexico, seeking low-cost labor in response to Japanese penetration of the transistor radio and television market. The 168 electronics plants established by 1973 on the Mexican border belonged to firms such as General Electric, Fairchild, Litton Industries, Texas Instruments, Zenith, RCA, Motorola, Bendix, and National Semiconductor. There were also 108 garment shops, sewing swimsuits, shirts, golf bags, and undergarments; some subsidiaries of large companies such as Levi Strauss; and other small sweatshops (unregulated workplaces) subcontracted by the large retailers.[9]

The cost calculus driving the relocation of manufacturing to the Third World includes avoidance of stringent environmental regulations. Over a quarter of factory operators in the city of Mexicali, close to the California border, cited Mexico's lax environmental enforcement as a condition of relocation. The impact is both physical and environmental. Electronics factories commonly include open and toxic fume-emitting containers of carcinogenic acids and solvents; this results in chronic illness, such as headaches, sore throat, and drowsiness, among the workforce. This is documented in the Mexican film *Maquilopolis,* which depicts resistance led by female workers concerned with protecting community health. Even with more stringent US environmental regulation, California's Silicon Valley includes 29 sites listed on the Environmental Protection Agency's Superfund list of most contaminated toxic dumps—such environmental hazards accompany the proliferation of semiconductor manufacturing. Chemical discharges from *maquiladoras* into open ditches adjacent to shantytowns have been linked to cancer, birth defects, and brain damage, and factories in **export processing zones (EPZs)** have been associated with the dumping of pollutants into local waters, affecting drinking water and fisheries.[10]

The global proliferation of low-wage assembly marked the strategic use of export platforms chiefly in the Third World by competing TNCs from the United States, Europe, and Japan and, later, from some Third World countries. As these companies seek to reduce their production costs to enhance their global competitiveness, so export platforms have spread. Thus, the NICs' strategy of export-oriented industrialization sparked the world factory phenomenon: from sweatshops in Los Angeles to subcontractors in Bangladesh, Ireland, Morocco, and the Caribbean.

CASE STUDY   The Chinese World Factory

Looking ahead, China became the prime location for the "world factory." The government anticipated this development by establishing "special economic zones" (SEZs) in coastal regions in the 1980s to attract foreign investment. By the mid-1990s, when the East Asian NICs had emerged as "middle-income countries" with relatively high-skilled labor forces, China was the preferred site for foreign investors—especially Korean and Taiwanese investors, with rising labor costs at home. In 1995, the ratio of factory wages in China to South Korea/Taiwan to Japan was approximately 1:30:80.

In her investigations of shoe factories (such as Reebok and Nike) in Dongguan City, sociologist Anita Chan notes the vast concrete industrial estates mushrooming on former rice paddies. Local farmers live off the rents from the factories, while tens of thousands of migrants from China's poorer hinterland swell the low-wage workforce. Twelve-hour shifts—with enforced overtime—and seven-day workweeks are common, with managers using militaristic methods to break in and control the migrant labor force—in addition to requiring a deposit of two to four weeks' wages and confiscation of migrant ID cards. Between 1980 and 2001, 380,000 foreign-owned exporting plants were established in China, as the Chinese proportion of world exports from such plants grew from 1 percent to almost 50 percent, and China became synonymous with the "world factory."

Today, China produces about half of the world's shoes and a proliferating array of electronic items, toys, and garments for the global economy. While this may appear to be China's "industrial revolution," to the extent that a substantial portion is export manufacturing, it is also a global industrial revolution.

Since this global industrial revolution depends on a moving belt of world factories (from Hong Kong to Mexico, to China, and now to Vietnam, India, and Bangladesh), including labor and capital-intensive work, how useful is the notion of a national "development ladder"?

Sources: Boyd (2006); Chan (1996: 20); Faison (1997: D4); Greider (2001); Myerson (1997); Perrons (2005); Sachs (2005).

The Strategic Role of Information Technologies

The world factory system is nourished by the technologies of the "information age." Especially important in the latest of these revolutions is the semiconductor industry. Semiconductors—notably the integrated computer chip—are the key to the new information technologies that undergird the globalization of economic relations. Advances in telecommunication technologies enable firms headquartered in global cities such as New York, London, or Tokyo to coordinate production tasks distributed across sites in several countries. Information technologies allow rapid circulation of production design blueprints among subsidiaries, instructing them in retooling their production to accommodate changing fashion or reorganize production methods in their offshore plants. Thus we find **global assembly lines** stretching from California's Silicon Valley or Scotland's Silicon Glen to assembly sites in Taiwan, Singapore, Malaysia, or Sri Lanka. What appears, from a national (accounting) perspective, to be an expansion of industrial exporting is increasingly a global production system. As participants in **global assembly lines,** national economic sites may specialize in producing just airplane wings or automobile dashboards or shoe soles or buttonholes. How has this come about? Microelectronics. This was a leading industry in establishing the world factory, given labor-intensive electronic assembly and the dispersion of electronics *production* to export platforms across the world. In turn, high-tech electronic *products* such as computers and digital telecommunications technology enable the global dispersion and coordination of production and circulation in other industries, from banking to textiles to automobiles. Thus information technology globalizes the production of goods and services, in both senses. In particular, it has enabled the proliferation of EPZs.

The Export Processing Zone

Export processing zones, or free trade zones (FTZs), are specialized manufacturing export estates with minimal customs controls, and they are usually exempt from labor regulations and domestic taxes. EPZs serve firms seeking lower wages and Third World governments seeking capital investment and foreign currency to be earned from exports. The first EPZ appeared at Shannon, Ireland, in 1958; India established the first Third World EPZ in 1965, and as early as the mid-1980s, roughly 1.8 million workers were employed in a total of 173 EPZs around the world. By 2006, there were 3,500 EPZs in 130 countries, employing 66 million workers (40 million of which were in China).[11]

The dynamics of EPZs contradict the economic nationalism of the development project in favoring export markets over domestic market development, based on local production and consumption. Export processing zones typically serve as *enclaves*—in social as well as economic terms. Often physically separate from the rest of the country, walled in with barbed wire, locked gates, and special security guards, EPZs are built to receive imported raw materials or components and to export the output directly by sea or air. Workers are bused in and out daily or live in the EPZ under a short-term labor contract. Inside the EPZ, whatever civil rights and working conditions exist in the society at large are usually denied to the workforce. As noted in 1983, "Free trade zones . . . mean more freedom for business and less freedom for people."[12] It is a workforce assembled under conditions analogous to those of early European industrialization, enhancing the profitability of modern, global corporations. At the same time, resistance by and protection of this workforce spawned a "transnational gender and trade network" (drawing attention to the gendered nature of this workforce), as well as mobilizations of civil society organizations "to monitor and participate in trade policy debates"—recently featured in political contestation over the Trans-Pacific Partnership and the Trans-Atlantic Trade and Investment Partnership.[13]

Export processing zones provided an early portal for Third World women to enter the global workforce, just as English and American farm girls staffed early textile mills. The new "factory girls" earned in one week approximately what their First World counterparts earned in one hour. In the early 1980s, 80 to 90 percent of zone workers were females between 16 and 25 years old. Women were regarded as best suited to the tasks because of their "natural patience" and "manual dexterity"—a personnel manager of a Taiwanese assembly plant claimed, "Young male workers are too restless and impatient to be doing monotonous work with no career value. If displeased, they sabotage the machines and even threaten the foreman. But girls, at most they cry a little."[14] Appealing to Orientalist stereotypes, a Malaysian investment brochure stated the following:

The manual dexterity of the oriental female is famous the world over. Her hands are small and she works fast with extreme care. Who, therefore, could

Figure 4.1   Number of EPZs by Selected Country, 2003

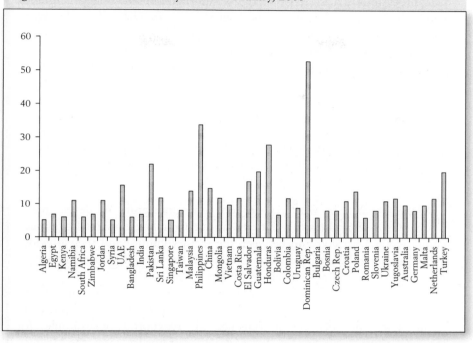

Source: International Labor Organization (ILO, 2003).

be better qualified by nature and inheritance to contribute to the efficiency of a bench-assembly production line than the oriental girl.[15]

Between 1975 and 1995, garment production spawned 1.2 million jobs in Bangladesh, with women taking 80 percent—this imbalance has considerable impact on Islamic culture. In 1998, the International Labor Organization estimated two thousand EPZs employed 27 million workers, 90 percent of whom were female. Seventy percent of the world's now 66-million-strong EPZ labor force are women.[16] In Mexico, young women accounted for roughly 78 percent of the *maquiladora* workforce in 1979, some 85 percent in the mid-1990s, and 54 percent in 2004.[17] The shifting gender proportions of the labor force (here, "defeminization") mark the generalization of the *maquila* system throughout Mexico, at the point when the work upgraded beyond simple assembly; higher proportions of female workers occur in simple assembly zones such as Indonesia, Mauritius, Tunisia, Sri Lanka, and the Philippines.[18] The construction of global assembly work on the foundation of a feminized labor force remains a constant, as sweatshops cycle through countries in search of lower wages and appropriate locations. The absence of rights and regulations renders such labor vulnerable to superexploitation, with employees often being forced to work overtime—sometimes up to 48 hours—to meet rush orders, under debilitating conditions (as in the film *China Blue*). The following description of a worker at an electronics *maquiladora* near Tijuana captures the conditions of sweatshop labor:

> Her job was to wind copper wire on to a spindle by hand. It was very small and there couldn't be any overlap, so she would get these terrible headaches. After a year, some of the companies gave a bonus, but most of the girls didn't last that long, and those that did had to get glasses to help their failing eyes. It's so bad that there is constant turnover.[19]

While sweatshops may register on some indicators of development, Raquel Grossman notes that retirement due to failing eyesight leaves such young women betwixt and between the factory culture and their previous life; many of these are compelled to work in the "entertainment industry," whether in bars and restaurants or the sex trade.[20]

The foreign companies that employ EPZ workers obtain concessions, such as free trade for imports and exports, infrastructural support, tax exemptions, and location convenience for reexport. For example, for *maquila* investment in Sonora, one of the poorest border states, the Mexican government's most favorable offer was 100 percent tax exemption for the first 10 years and 50 percent for the next 10.[21] In short, the EPZ is typically an island in its host country, separated from domestic laws and contributing little to the host economy, other than mostly dead-end jobs and foreign currency earned via export taxes levied by host states. The EPZ belongs instead to an archipelago of production sites across the world—concentrated in Latin America, the Caribbean, and Asia—that serve world markets.

The Rise of the New International Division of Labor (NIDL)

The formation of a global labor force began during the development project. The effects of urban bias, agrarian class polarization accelerated by the green revolution, and cheap food imports combined to expel peasants from the land. From 1950 to 1997, the world's rural population decreased by some 25 percent, and now over half of the world's population dwells in and on the margins of sprawling cities.[22] European "depeasantization" was spread over several centuries, with the pressure on cities relieved through immigration to settlement colonies in the Americas and Australasia. But for

Third World societies, this process has been compressed into a few generations and slightly longer for Latin America. Rural migrants overwhelm the cities, generating what has been termed a "planet of slums."[23]

Depeasantization does not by itself create a global labor force; it simply swells the ranks of displaced people lacking means of subsistence and needing wage work. Wage work for a global labor force stems from the *simplification* of First World manufacturing work and *relocation* of these now separated routine tasks as low-cost jobs to form a **global assembly line** linking sites across the world.

Initially, First World mass production developed around large production runs using assembly lines of work subdivided into such specialized tasks. Simplification *deskills* assembly work, anticipating the **global assembly line.** As the world factory emerged, such tasks as cutting, sewing, and stitching in the garment or footwear industries or assembly, machine tending, or etching in the electrical, automobile, or computer chip industries relocated to cheap labor regions. At the same time, the technologies to coordinate those tasks generated a need for new skilled labor, such as managerial, engineering, or design labor, tasks often retained in the First World. This produced a *bifurcation of the global labor force,* with skilled labor concentrating in the First World and unskilled labor concentrating in the Third World. TNCs coordinated this bifurcation via their "internal" labor hierarchies as early as the 1970s; for example,

> Intel Corporation is located in the heart of California's "Silicon Valley. . . ." When Intel's engineers develop a design for a new electronic circuit or process, technicians in the Santa Clara Valley, California, plant will build, test, and redesign the product. When all is ready for production of the new item, however, it doesn't go to a California factory. Instead, it is air freighted to Intel's plant in Penang, Malaysia. There, Intel's Malaysian workers, almost all young women, assemble the components in a tedious process involving hand soldering of fiber-thin wire leads. Once assembled, the components are flown back to California, this time for final testing and/or integration into a larger end product. And, finally, they're off to market, either in the United States, Europe, or back across the Pacific to Japan.[24]

In the 1970s, the relocation of deskilled tasks to lower-wage regions of the world was so prevalent that the concept of a **new international division of labor (NIDL)** was coined to describe this development. NIDL referred to an apparent *decentralization of industrial production* from the First to the Third World. The requisite conditions were endless supplies of cheap Third World labor, the new technical possibility of separating and relocating deskilled manufacturing tasks offshore, and the rise of transport and informational technologies to allow coordination of global production systems.[25]

With global bifurcation of labor skills, skilled labor concentrated in the First World, extending to enterprising states such as the East Asian NICs (South Korea, Taiwan, Singapore, and Hong Kong), which used public investment to upgrade workforce skills. The upgrading was necessary as their wage levels were rising in relation to other countries hosting export production, such as Malaysia, Indonesia, and the Philippines. In 1975, if the hourly wage for electronics work in the United States was measured at 100, the relative value for equivalent work was 12 in Hong Kong and Singapore, 9 in Malaysia, 7 in Taiwan and South Korea, 6 in the Philippines, and 5 in Indonesia and Thailand.[26]

East Asian countries improved their competitiveness by specializing in more sophisticated export manufacturing for First World markets, using skilled (more male) labor rather than semiskilled and unskilled labor. After upgrading their labor force, the NICs attracted skilled labor inputs as a regional growth strategy. As the skilled work came, these states became headquarters, or cores, of new regional divisions of labor patterned on the production hierarchy between Japan and its East and Southeast Asian neighbors.

By 1985, an East Asian division of labor emerged in the semiconductor industry for US firms through upgrading of the production hierarchy. Final testing of semiconductors (capital-intensive labor involving computers with lasers) and circuit design centers were located in Hong Kong, Singapore, and Taiwan; wafer fabrication in Malaysia; and assembly in Malaysia, Thailand, the Philippines, and Indonesia. In the 1970s, semiconductors were assembled in Southeast Asia and then flown back to the United States for testing and distribution, but by the 1980s, Hong Kong imported semiconductors from South Korea and Malaysia to test them for reexport to the First World and for input in Hong Kong's fabled watch assembly industry.[27]

Patterns of global and regional sourcing have since mushroomed across the world, particularly under the stimulus of informatics. Firms establish subsidiaries offshore or extensive subcontracting arrangements in labor-intensive consumer goods industries such as garments, footwear, toys, household goods, and consumer electronics. The Nike Corporation produces most of its athletic shoes through subcontracting arrangements in South Korea, China, Indonesia, and Thailand; product design and sales promotion are reserved for its US headquarters, where the firm "promotes the symbolic nature of the shoe and appropriates the greater share of the value resulting from its sales."[28] In these senses, the legacy of the world factory revolution has been an initial global bifurcation of labor skills—made increasingly complex by global subcontracting arrangements, as firms have entered into joint ventures to organize their supplies, reduce their costs, and position their final assembly operations for global and/or regional marketing.

CASE STUDY   Gendering the Global Labor Force

Endless supplies of cheap Third World labor needs definition. Much labor-intensive work is feminized, depending on complex patriarchal and subcontracting hierarchies. Labor-intensive export platform industries prefer young, unmarried, and relatively educated women. While employers argue that women are suited to the jobs because of their dexterity and patience, these qualities are required as much by the jobs themselves as by patriarchal assumptions and practices reproduced within the factories, sweatshops, and home work units. Job designation changes with conditions; as Laura Raynolds shows for Dominican Republic plantations, in times of recession unemployed men may displace women via the use of local patronage networks, with work regendered to reward masculine competition.

Women are typically subjected to long workdays and lower wages compared with men. High turnover, lack of union rights, sexual harassment, and poor health characterize the female workforce that has mushroomed across the Asian, Central American, and Middle Eastern regions. Under these conditions, patriarchal states—competing for foreign investment—encourage women to enter the workforce at the same time as the new female workforce may be under official (especially Islamic) scrutiny for loose morals, and governments withhold maternity benefits, child care, and education opportunities on the grounds that they are "secondary workers" in a male-dominated labor market. Rural families propel—and sometimes sell—their teenage girls into labor contracts, viewing their employment as a daughterly duty or a much-needed source of income. Fuentes and Ehrenreich quote Cynthia Enloe:

> The emphasis on family is absolutely crucial to management strategy. Even recruitment is a family process. Women don't just go out independently to find jobs. . . . Discipline becomes a family matter since, in most cases, women turn their paychecks over to their parents. Factory life is, in general, constrained and defined by the family life cycle.

Where young women and children work in family production units (a widespread practice), subcontractors rely on patriarchal pressures to discipline the workers. In the workplace, teenage girls are often forced to take birth control pills to eliminate maternity leave and payments or are forced to have abortions if they get pregnant. Labor contractors and managers routinely demand sexual favors from young women for awarding them jobs, giving rise

(Continued)

(Continued)

to a "factory harem mentality." The endless nature of the supply of female labor comes from their short working life in many of these jobs—because of the eye-hand coordination of girls that peaks at age 16; the physical deterioration from low wages, poor health, and nutrition; the high turnover due to harassment; the steady experience of having the life sucked out of them by long working hours and no advancement in skills; and the steady stream of new cohorts of younger women to follow, whether from the countryside, the children of the working poor, or international traffickers in labor.

Are women working under these conditions better off, empowered, or further devalued?

Sources: Agarwal (1988); Fernandez-Kelly (1983:129); Fuentes and Ehrenreich (1983); Kernaghan (1995); Ong (1997); Pyle (2001); Raynolds (2001).

From the NIDL to a Global Labor Force

The rise of global subcontracting transformed the tidy bifurcation of labor between the First World (skilled) and the Third World (unskilled labor), captured in the NIDL concept, into a *bifurcation of labor everywhere.* Why did this shift take place? First, it occurred because of skill upgrading by firms in the NICs. The second reason is that global subcontracting threatens (by relocation) organized labor in the First World, weakening some unions and casualizing some labor. Bifurcation involves separating a core of relatively stable, well-paid work from a periphery of casual, low-cost labor, irrespective of location. We see it occurring in tertiary education, across and within institutions, where teaching is divided between tenured professors and part-time lecturers. This relationship has no particular geography, although its most dramatic division remains a North–South one.

Bifurcation encourages subcontracting, which often has a dark side in the exploitation commonly experienced by unprotected labor throughout the world. In 1999, the United Nations estimated there were about 20 million bonded laborers worldwide, with half that number in India. Similarly, the International Labor Organization estimates about 80 million children younger than age 14 work across the world in conditions hazardous to their health—in farming, domestic labor, drug trafficking, fireworks manufacturing, fishing, brickmaking, carpet weaving, sex work, stone quarrying, and as soldiers. Many of these children work 14-hour days in crowded and unsafe workplaces.[29] Regardless of whether transnational corporations offer better conditions than local firms, and in spite of campaigns by labor organizations and human rights organizations such as Global Witness, the global subcontracting system weakens and/or eliminates regulation of employment conditions.

As firms restructure and embrace **lean production,** they may trim less skilled jobs and fulfill them through subcontracting arrangements that rely on casual labor, often overseas. The US automobile sector outsourced so much of its components production from the late 1970s that the percentage of its workforce belonging to unions fell from two-thirds to one-quarter by the mid-1990s. Not only did outsourcing bifurcate auto industry labor, but the expansion of this nonunion workforce also eroded wages, such that between 1975 and 1990, the low-wage workforce grew by 142 percent, from 17 to 40 percent of the automobile workforce. And for the US workforce as a whole, industrial restructuring reduced real average weekly earnings by 18 percent from the mid-1970s to the mid-1990s. Meanwhile, union density fell from 25 to 14.5 percent across the period 1980 to 1995.[30]

First World **deindustrialization** occurred from 1970 to 1994: manufacturing employment fell 50 percent in Britain, 12 percent in the United States,

Figure 4.2   Percentage of Workforce Involved in Making Products, Provisions, and Services Exported From Selected EPZ Host Countries, 1994

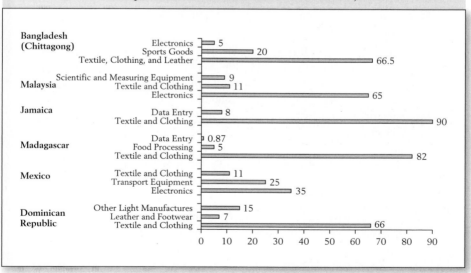

Sources: International Confederation of Free Trade Unions (1995, www.cftu.org); International Labor Organization (1995, www.ilo.org).

18 percent in France, and 17 percent in Germany, with many of these being "low-tech" jobs, such as footwear, textiles, and metals. In 1995 alone, the US apparel industry lost 10 percent of its jobs; jobs lost in the fabrics industry accounted for 40 percent of manufacturing jobs lost that year. More than 50 percent of the US clothing market is accounted for by cheap imports from Asia and Latin America. Around 65,300 US footwear jobs disappeared in the 1980s—for example, Nike ceased making athletic shoes in the United States and relocated most of its production to South Korea and Indonesia. In the early 1990s, a worker—usually female—in the footwear industry in Indonesia earned $1.03 per day, compared with an average wage in the US footwear industry of $6.94 per *hour*.[31] The gap left by the relocation of manufacturing to the Third World has partially been filled by postindustrial work (retailing, health care, security, finance, restaurants), some of which is performed by migrant labor—creating ethnic tensions during economic downturns. Temporary or part-time employment—accounting for 40 percent of US employees in 2015—and multiple jobs have become a common pattern for low-skilled workers. This is hardly a stages-of-growth scenario, or the "development ladder" at work.

CASE STUDY   The Corporatization of World Markets

Export, or world, markets are typically organized by TNCs. UN data reveal that transnational corporations account for two-thirds of world trade. Fifty of the largest 100 economies are run by TNCs—for instance, General Motors and Toyota are larger (by revenue) than Malaysia, Nigeria, Pakistan, Egypt, and Peru. TNCs control most of the world's financial transactions, (bio)technologies, and industrial capacity—including oil and its refining, coal, gas, hydroelectric and nuclear power plants, mineral extraction and processing, home electronics, chemicals, medicines, wood harvesting and processing, and more.

The top five TNCs in each major market (such as jet aircraft, automobiles, microprocessors, and grains) typically account for 40 to 70 percent of all world sales, with the 10 largest corporations in their field controlling 86 percent of telecommunications and 70 percent of the computer industry. The combined annual revenues of the 200 largest corporations exceeded those of the 182 states with 80 percent of the world's population. Corporate tax rates have declined significantly in most northern states—from 30 to 7 percent of US government funds since the early 1950s—shifting tax burdens to lotteries, personal income, and sales.

Most of the largest 350 TNCs are headquartered in the United States, China, Japan, the United Kingdom, France, and Germany, accounting for about 70 percent of all transnational investment and about 50 percent of all the companies themselves. Walmart (with Royal Dutch Shell and Exxon Mobil) is one of the largest corporations in the world and the largest importer of Chinese-made products, with more than one million nonunionized employees, a large proportion of whom are employed part-time with minimal benefits.

Under these circumstances of globalization, has the framework and content of development been redefined—not as governments pursuing social equity for national citizens, but as corporations pursuing choice for the global consumer-citizen?

Sources: Alperovitz (2003: 15); Baird and McCaughan (1979: 135–136); Beams (1999); Brown (1993: 47); Daly and Logan (1989: 67); Ellwood (1993: 5; 2001: 55–63); Hightower (2002); Karliner (1997: 5); Korten (1995: 323); Martin and Schumann (1997: 12); Perrons (2005: 69); *The Economist* (July 16, 1994); Global Policy Forum (2011: http://www.globalpolicy.org/component/content/article/221/47176.html); *Forbes*, Global 2000 (2015).

Manufacturing labor has lost considerable organizational, as well as numerical, power to corporate strategies of restructuring, leading to the qualitative restructuring of work. After a decade of conservative government restructuring of the British labor force (weakening union rights, eliminating minimum wages, reducing jobless benefits), Britain in the 1990s became a new site for offshore investment from Europe—mostly in part-time jobs (electronic assembly, apparel, clerical tasks) undertaken by women at considerably lower wages than would be paid in Europe.[32] Typically, "Third World" working conditions are just as likely to appear in the global North via the practice of lean production. Garment sweatshops are a recurring phenomenon—for example, in New York City—and a range of "Third World" jobs has spread in First World cities over the past two decades. In other words, the *global labor force*—including working conditions—is well entrenched everywhere. What it means is that corporations resort to **global sourcing** (of labor and materials) to secure access to predictable (and cheaper) supplies of inputs to supply continually changing consumer fashion, and they thereby maintain or improve their world market position.

Global integration habitually marginalizes people and their communities, as jobs are automated, shed, or relocated by corporations under global competitive pressures. Competition compels firms not only to go global but also to keep their sourcing flexible, and therefore their suppliers—and their workers—guessing.[33] As the world market has been corporatized, firms that once organized paternalistic "company towns" have shed that responsibility, relying on a more abstract (i.e., flexible and expendable) global labor force.

As corporations shuffle the global employment deck, residents of the global North experience declining real wages (a trend since 1972), rising poverty rates, increased family stress and social disorder, rising public health care costs, and so on. The feminization of work involves lowering wages and job conditions and, in addition to declining social services, has overstressed the work of social reproduction—for which women typically take most responsibility.[34] Proposed retraining schemes to help workers adjust to a shifting employment scene are often ineffectual, as most replacement jobs are low paid and low- or no-benefit service work.[35]

The loss of jobs is not simply an offshoring of production ("global sourcing"); it "hollows out" a nation's economic base and erodes social institutions that stabilize the conditions of employment and habitat associated with those jobs. A century of institution-building in labor markets, in corporate/union relations, and in communities can disappear overnight, when the winds of the market are allowed to blow across uneven national boundaries. Those who have work find they are often working longer hours to make ends meet, despite remarkable technological advances. Development has become a game of snakes and ladders!

CASE STUDY — Global/Regional Strategy of a Southern Transnational Corporation

We tend to think of TNCs as northern in origin. The Charoen Pokphand (CP) Group was formed in Bangkok in 1921 by two Chinese brothers to trade in farm inputs. In the 1960s, CP expanded into animal feed production and then to vertically integrated poultry production, providing inputs (chicks, feed, medicines, credit, extension services) to farmers and in turn processing and marketing poultry regionally in East Asia. In the 1980s, CP entered retailing, acquiring a Kentucky Fried Chicken (KFC) franchise for Thailand, and now controls about one-quarter of the Thai fast-food market as an outlet for its poultry, including 715 7-Eleven convenience stores. By the mid-1990s, CP was Thailand's largest TNC and Asia's largest agro-industrial conglomerate, with 100,000 employees in 20 countries. It was an early investor in China, establishing a feed mill in Shenzhen in 1979 in a joint venture with Continental Grain. In 1995, CP was operating 75 feed mills in 26 of China's 30 provinces; controlled the KFC franchise rights for China, operating in 13 cities; and its

(Continued)

Figure 4.3 Comparison of the World's 25 Largest Corporations With GDPs of Selected Countries (2007)

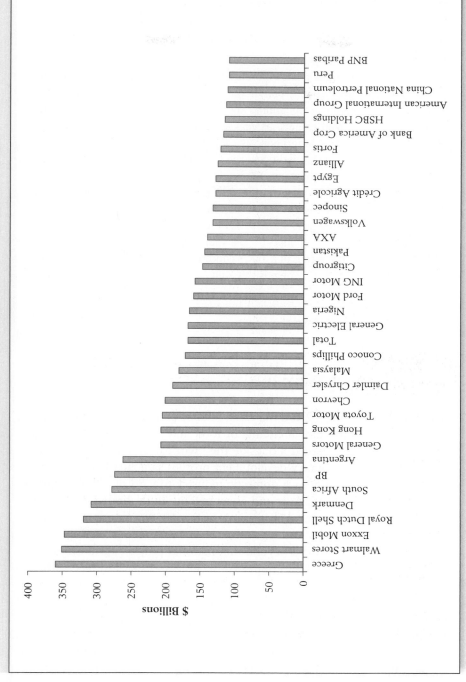

Source: Global Policy Forum (July 20, 2011), http://www.globalpolicy.org/component/content/article/221/47176.html

(Continued)

poultry operations accounted for 10 percent of China's broilers, producing 235 million day-old chicks per annum.

Today, CP has investments in fertilizers, pesticides and agrochemicals, vehicles, tractors, supermarkets, baby foods, livestock operations in poultry and swine, milk processing, crop farming and processing, seed production, aquaculture, and jute-backed carpets, as well as in telecommunications, real estate, retailing, cement, and petrochemicals. CP produces poultry in Turkey, Vietnam, Cambodia, Malaysia, Indonesia, and the United States, as well as animal feed in Indonesia, India, and Vietnam. CP is now involved in shrimp farming, controlling 65 percent of the Thai market, and is the world's largest producer of farmed shrimp, with sites in Indonesia, Vietnam, China, and India, as Thai farms experience ecological stress. A 2014 report linked CP to slave labor used on prawn (shrimp) fishing boats off the Thai coast.

When we see the extent of a TNC's concentration of power over regional or global economic activity, where is this kind of development going, and whose future does it serve?

Sources: Goss et al. (2000); Hodal et al. (2014).

Agricultural Globalization

With the food aid regime and the green revolution both incorporating Third World countries into global circuits of food and agribusiness technologies, the **"world farm"** emerged alongside the "world factory." In this process, many Third World country development profiles switched from a focus on modernizing agriculture as a domestic industry toward developing agriculture as a world industry. A second green revolution facilitated this switch.

As we saw in Chapter 3, beginning in the 1960s, the green revolution encouraged agribusiness in the production of "wage foods" for urban consumers in the Third World. Beyond that *national* project, agribusiness technology has spread from basic grains to other grains—especially feedstuffs—to livestock and to fresh fruit and vegetable horticultures. Further, agribusiness has created feed-grain substitutes such as cassava (corn gluten feed) and citrus pellets, and biotechnology is creating plant-derived "feedstocks" for the chemical industry, as well as an expanding array of biofuels. This kind of industrial agriculture depends on hybrid seeds, chemical fertilizers, pesticides, animal antibiotics and growth-inducing chemicals, specialty feeds, and, most recently, genetically modified plants. It is a specialized, high-input agriculture servicing high-value markets in addition to food processing and agrochemical firms. It has been termed the second **green revolution**.[36] A distinguishing feature is that whereas the first green revolution was a *public* initiative geared to *national* markets (for staples), its successor is a *private* initiative increasingly geared to *global* markets (for higher-value foods).[37]

As global markets have deepened and transport technologies have matured, "cool chains" maintain chilled temperatures for transporting fresh fruit and vegetables grown in the Third World to supermarket outlets across the world. Firms in the United States, such as Dole, Chiquita, and Del Monte, moved beyond their traditional commodities of bananas and pineapples into other fresh fruits and vegetables. By coordinating producers scattered across different climate zones, these firms reduce the seasonality of fresh fruits and vegetables. Year-round produce availability is complemented with exotic fruits, vegetables, and salad greens.[38]

In this new division of world agricultural labor, transnational corporations typically subcontract with or hire smallholders to produce specialty horticultural crops and off-season fruits and vegetables for export processing (canning, freezing, gassing, boxing, juicing, and dicing) to supply expanding consumer markets located primarily in Europe, North America, and the Asia-Pacific. As the conversion of agriculture into a global, increasingly feminized industry proceeds, it impinges on women's livelihoods, their food security, and that of their families. Most food consumed across the world is produced by women, accounting for 30 to 40 percent in Latin America, 50 to 60 percent in Asia, and 80 to 90 percent in Sub-Saharan Africa.[39] Women's lack of security and rights in land means that commercialization easily erodes women's role in and control of food production. As small farming is destabilized, women must work in the agribusiness sector on plantations and in processing plants as planters, pickers, and packers, feminizing the global agricultural labor force and adding to women's workday, despite income benefits and associated "empowerment."

CASE STUDY   Global Labor in Agriculture and the Question of Food Security

The global fruit and vegetable industry depends on flexible contract labor arrangements. Coordination of multiple production sites for a year-round supply of fresh produce is achieved through information technologies. These supply

(Continued)

(Continued)

chains disconnect producers and consumers with interesting consequences: Consumers are ignorant of the conditions under which their goods are produced, while producers increasingly grow food for distant consumers rather than for their own communities.

Deborah Barndt's research retraces the journey of the "corporate tomato" from Mexico to the ubiquitous fast-food and retailing outlets of North America. Naming it "Tomasita" to underline its ethnic and gendered-labor origins, she describes a plant of one of Mexico's largest agro-exporters, Santa Anita Packers, which in peak season employs more than 2,000 pickers and 700 packers. The improved seed varieties need heavy doses of pesticides, but health and safety education and the required protective gear are lacking. Perhaps a more visually striking indicator of monocultural production is the packing plant, employing hundreds of young women whom the company moves from one site to another as a kind of "mobile *maquiladora*":

> The only Mexican inputs are the land, the sun, and the workers. . . . The South has been the source of the seeds, while the North has the biotechnology to alter them. . . . The workers who produce the tomatoes do not benefit. . . . They now travel most of the year—with little time to grow food on their own plots in their home communities. . . . With this loss of control comes a spiritual loss, and a loss of a knowledge of seeds, of organic fertilizers and pesticides, of sustainable practices such as crop rotation or leaving the land fallow for a year—practices that had maintained the land for millennia.

The food security of northern consumers depends on Mexican food *in*security. Displaced *campesinas* (especially indigenous women) work in the *agromaquilas* or in North American orchards or plantations, earning in a day what takes a week to earn in Mexico.

What are the long-term consequence of a global food system that destabilizes peasant communities and exacerbates southern food dependency for private profit and a year-round supply of tasteless tomatoes?

Source: Barndt (1997: 59–62).

The New Agricultural Countries (NACs)

As with manufacturing, agribusiness investments first concentrated in select Third World countries (e.g., Brazil, Mexico, Argentina, Chile, Hungary, and Thailand), known as the **new agricultural countries (NACs)**.[40] They were analogous to the NICs insofar as their governments promoted agro-industrialization for urban and export markets. As the development project has receded,· agro-exporting has intensified. Such agro-exports have been called "nontraditional exports" (NTEs) because they either replace or supplement the traditional tropical exports of the colonial era. Nontraditional exports tend to be high-value foods, such as animal protein products and fruits and vegetables, or low-value feed grains and biofuels.

Thailand's traditional role in the international division of labor as an exporter of rice, sugar, pineapples, and rubber is now complemented with an expanding array of nontraditional primary exports: cassava (feed), canned tuna, shrimp, poultry, processed meats, and fresh and processed fruits and vegetables. Former exports such as corn and sorghum are now mostly consumed domestically in the intensive livestock sector. Raw-agricultural exports, which accounted for 80 percent of Thailand's exports in 1980, now represent 30 percent; processed food makes up 30 percent of manufactured exports. Thailand is a model NAC.[41] Viewed as "Asia's supermarket," Thailand expanded its food-processing industry on a foundation of rural smallholders under contract to food-processing firms. Food companies from Japan, Taiwan, the United States, and Europe use Thailand as a base for regional and global export-oriented production. For example, to promote poultry agro-exporting, the Thai government organized a complex of agri-businesses, farmers, and financial institutions with state ministries in order to promote export contracts, distributing land to landless farmers for contract growing and livestock farming.[42] The feed industry, coupled with low-cost labor, helped Thai poultry producers compete with their US (and now Chinese) counterparts in the Japanese market. Thailand is the world's second-largest producer of farmed shrimp after China.

Just as the NICs served as platforms for global supply chains in manufacturing, so the NACs have served **global sourcing**. Three US agribusiness firms have worldwide meat-packing operations, raising cattle, pigs, and poultry on feedstuffs supplied by their own subsidiaries. Cargill, headquartered in Minnesota, is the largest grain trader in the world, operating in 70 countries with more than eight hundred offices or plants and more than 70,000 employees. It has a joint venture with Nippon Meat Packers of Japan, called Sun Valley Thailand, from which it exports US corn-fed poultry products to the Japanese market. ConAgra, headquartered in Nebraska, owns 56 companies and operates in 26 countries with 58,000 employees. It processes feed and animal protein products in the United States, Canada, Australia, Europe, the Far East, and Latin America. Tyson Foods, headquartered in Arkansas, runs a joint venture with the Japanese agribusiness firm

C. Itoh, which produces poultry in Mexico, supplied with US feedstuffs, for both local consumption and export to Japan.[43]

Second green revolution technologies, and nontraditional exporting, have reorganized agriculture across the world as a "world farm," driving a global process of "supermarketization," led by large retailers such as Walmart, Tesco, Carrefour, and Ahold subcontracting with growers to sell foods across the world. From the early 1990s, the average share of supermarkets in food retailing in much of South America and East Asia (other than China and Japan), northern-central Europe, and South Africa rose from roughly 10 to 20 percent (1990) to 50 to 60 percent by the early 2000s. By comparison, supermarkets had a 70 to 80 percent share in food retail in the United States, United Kingdom, and France in 2005. A "second wave" spread to parts of Southeast Asia, Central America, Mexico, and southern-central Europe, where supermarket shares of food retailing rose from 5 to 10 percent in 1990 to 30 to 50 percent by the early 2000s. A "third wave," reaching 10 to 20 percent of food retailing by 2003, occurred in parts of Africa (especially Kenya), the remaining parts of Central and South America, and Southeast Asia, as well as China, India, and Russia—these last three being the current frontrunner destinations.[44]

As discussed in Chapter 2, New World farmers (in the Caribbean and the Americas) and non-Europeans (Asians and Africans) have been producing specialized agricultural products for export for some time, but the scale and profitability of export food production have expanded greatly in recent decades as the number and concentration of world consumers have grown, carefully nurtured nowadays by global supermarket chains. This means that the producers must meet high and increasingly privatized (i.e., corporate) standards of quality and consistency for marketing purposes. Contract farmers are thus vulnerable to changing standards of competition. On agro-industrial estates, women are considered more reliable and attentive as workers than men, as they are trained to monitor plant health and growth, handle fruit, and work efficiently. Employers presume women are more suited to the seasonal and intermittent employments (e.g., harvesting, processing, and packing) necessary for flexibility.[45]

Global Finance

The globalization of finance enables the deepening of transnational production and consumption relationships. Transnational banks (TNBs) formed in the 1970s via a burgeoning *offshore capital market*. The TNBs were banks with deposits outside the jurisdiction or control of any government, usually in tax havens such as Switzerland, the Bahamas, or the Cayman Islands. TNBs made massive loans from these deposits to Third World governments throughout the 1970s.[46]

Deregulation of the international financial system in the early 1970s introduced an era of uncontrolled—and heightened—capital mobility as currency speculators bought and sold national currencies. Financial markets, rather than trade, began to determine currency values, and speculation on floating currencies destabilized national finances. By the early 1990s, world financial markets traded roughly $1 trillion daily in various currencies, all beyond the control of national governments.[47] The loss of currency control by governments threatens their political-economic sovereignty, meaning financial, rather than social, priorities shape economic policy.

Banking on Development

Fueled by the 1973 spike in oil prices engineered by the Organization of the Petroleum Exporting Countries (OPEC), the offshore capital market grew from $315 billion in 1973 to $2,055 billion in 1982. The seven largest US banks saw their overseas profits climb from 22 to 60 percent of their total profits in the same time period.[48] By the end of the 1970s, trade in foreign exchange was more than 11 times the value of world commodity trade. The instability of currencies, and therefore of profitability conditions, forced TNCs to diversify their global operations to reduce their risk.[49] In this way, the financial revolution, combined with a flood of petrodollars, consolidated a *global production system*. With the First World in an oil price-induced recession, global banks turned to Third World governments, eager to borrow and considered unlikely to default. By encouraging massive borrowing, the banks brokered the 1970s expansion in the middle-income Third World countries, now the world economic-growth engine.

In the early 1970s, bank loans accounted for only 13 percent of Third World debt, while multilateral loans made up more than 33 percent. At the end of the decade, the composition of these figures had reversed, with banks holding about 60 percent of the debt.[50] This represented a significant departure from the original development model, as summarized in the following box.

DEPARTURES FROM THE DEVELOPMENT MODEL IN THE 1970S

The 1970s was a decade of transition, as the development project unwound. First, financial deregulation challenged national sovereignty by opening national markets to cross-border capital flows, destabilizing macroeconomic planning. Second, unregulated private bank lending displaced official, multilateral lending to Third World states, but such debt financing was unsound—too much money was lent on the assumption that countries could not go bankrupt. When the 1980s debt crisis hit, austerity measures undid many of the gains of the development project. Third, TNCs produced more and more manufactured goods and agricultural products for world, rather than domestic, markets. Fourth, by the 1980s, the discourse switched to "world market participation" as the key to development.

Willing private lenders represented a golden opportunity for Third World states to exercise some autonomy from the official financial community. By 1984, all nine of the largest US banks were lending more than 100 percent of their shareholders' equity in loans to Mexico, Brazil, Argentina, and Venezuela, while Lloyds of London lent a staggering 165 percent of its capital to such countries.[51]

Loans typically served several functions. Political elites sought to legitimize rule with grand public development projects represented in nationalist terms, to strengthen their militaries, and to enrich their patronage networks with lucrative contracts resulting from loans. In Brazil between 1964 and 1985, a string of military generals pursued the characteristic Latin American nationalist model, using loans to build the public sector in steel, energy, and raw material production. With debt financing, Brazil transformed itself from a country earning 70 percent of its export revenue from one commodity (coffee) into a major producer and exporter of a multiplicity of industrial goods—including steel, aluminum, petrochemicals, cement, glass, armaments, and aircraft—and processed foodstuffs such as orange juice and soybean meal. As a result, Rio de Janeiro and São Paulo have new subway systems, railroads take ore from huge mines deep in the interior to new ports, and major cities are linked by a modern telecommunications network.[52]

Between 1976 and 1984, the rise in public foreign debt roughly matched a parallel outflow of private capital to banks in New York, the Cayman Islands, and other financial havens.[53] The composition of Latin American borrowing shifted dramatically between the 1960s and the late 1970s, as official loans fell from 40 to 12 percent, private foreign direct investment fell from 34 to 16 percent, and foreign bank and bond financing rose from 7 to 65 percent. Between 1970 and 1982, the average share of gross domestic investment in the public sector of 12 Latin American countries rose from 32 to 50 percent. State managers borrowed heavily to expand public enterprise, sometimes as a counterweight to foreign investor presence. During the 1970s, state enterprises across the Third World enlarged their share of their nation's gross domestic product (GDP) by almost 50 percent.[54] Being uncontrolled, *debt financing inflated the foundations of the development state.* The ensuing debt crisis deepened the vulnerability of Third World development states to banks and multilateral managers, who appeared on the scene in the 1980s (next chapter).

CASE STUDY   Containment and Corruption—Incubating the Debt Crisis

Assigning blame for the debt crisis is complicated. Certainly the old colonial tactic of surrogate rule died hard—for much of the development era, military control was the rule rather than the exception in the Third World, where the West bankrolled dictators as client regimes in the Cold War. Powerful military leaders, such as Ferdinand Marcos of the Philippines, Chile's Augusto Pinochet, and Iraq's Saddam Hussein, ruled through fear as they squandered the national patrimony. An estimated 20 percent of loans by non-oil-exporting countries went to imports of military hardware—in essence, militarizing the development project.

In the Congo, the CIA helped bring President Mobutu to power in 1965 for a rapacious 31-year rule. Mobutu renamed his country Zaire, authenticating his rule in African nationalist terms, but he traded away Zaire's vast natural resources, including a quarter of the world's copper and half its cobalt, for bank loans totaling billions of dollars and half of US aid to sub-Saharan Africa in the late 1970s. From the spoils, by the mid-1980s he stashed $4 billion, in addition to a dozen European estates to which he traveled on chartered Concorde flights. Under his rule, Zaire gained 500 British double-decker buses, the world's largest supermarket, and an unwanted steelworks. After the president was deposed in 1996, Mobutu's family inherited his fortune, and the country inherited his $12 billion debt.

Two years later, when General Suharto was forced to resign, his severance pay was estimated at $15 billion—13 percent of Indonesia's debt—owed mostly

(Continued)

(Continued)

to the World Bank. During Suharto's dictatorship of 30 years, the World Bank loaned more than $30 billion, some of which went into constructive literacy programs, while more than $630 million underwrote the regime's infamous "transmigration" program to colonize the archipelago, including massacres in East Timor. In 1997, a secret World Bank memorandum from Jakarta disclosed a monumental development scandal: that "at least 20 to 30 percent" of the Bank's loans "are diverted through informal payments to GOI [Government of Indonesia] staff and politicians."

If Cold War containment encouraged military rule and corruption was rife, how did it serve development, and why should the burden of debt repayment be borne disproportionately by the citizen-subjects of these Third World states?

Sources: Pilger (2002: 19–20); Roodman (2001: 5–6, 27).

SUMMARY

This chapter has examined the emergence of a global production system. *Specialization* in the world economy, rather than *replication* of economic activities within a national framework, has emerged as the new criterion of "development." NICs and NACs have served increasingly as export platforms for TNCs, which bring technologies of flexible manufacturing and the second green revolution, respectively. As a result, the "world factory" and the "world farm" phenomena have proliferated across the Third World, producing world products for the global consumer class. As jobs have relocated from First World factories to Third World EPZs, a process of labor casualization has occurred, as organized labor in the former has been forced to yield to the competitive low-cost and unorganized labor of the latter, with the aid of information technology by TNCs. The formation of a global labor force has involved political decisions that unravel the social compact with First World labor and cycle Third World labor into sweatshops and plantations. Women predominate in the low-skill, low-paid jobs, but "defeminization" occurs as labor organizes, wages rise, and/or industrial upgrading takes place in the NICs and their immediate followers. This patterning represents a transition between state-managed national economic growth in the development project and the internationalizing market networks anticipating the globalization project.

In effect, a new global economy was emerging, beyond trade among national economies. Global financial reorganization mapped on to global production systems that emerged via Third World export strategies. Offshore money markets redistributed private capital to governments as loans, and transnational corporations invested in export production. A frenzy of development initiatives ensued, as Third World states sought to emulate the NICs. Public investments complemented and underwrote private enterprise, nevertheless rendering states vulnerable to a debt crisis. As we shall see in the following chapter, when credit dried up in the 1980s, the debt crisis reversed the original reliance on the development state, laying the foundations for the globalization project.

FURTHER READING

Bonnano, Alessandro, Lawrence Busch, William Friedland, Lourdes Gouveia, and Enzo Mingione, eds. *From Columbus to ConAgra: The Globalization of Agriculture and Food.* Lawrence: University Press of Kansas, 1994.

Gereffi, Gary, and Miguel Korzeniewicz, eds. *Commodity Chains and Global Capitalism.* Westport, CT: Praeger, 1994.

Hoogvelt, Ankie. *Globalization and the Postcolonial World: The New Political Economy of Development.* London: Macmillan, 1987.

Nash, June, and Maria Patricia Fernández-Kelly, eds. *Women, Men, and the International Division of Labor.* Albany: State University of New York Press, 1983.

Sklair, Leslie. *Assembling for Development: The Maquila Industry in Mexico and the United States.* Boston: Unwin Hyman, 1989.

SELECT WEBSITES

Gender Equality and Development (UNESCO): www.unesco.org/new/en/unesco/themes/gender-equality/

Global Policy Forum: www.globalpolicy.org

Institute for Agriculture and Trade Policy (USA): www.iatp.org

International Labor Organization (UN): www.ilo.org

Multinational Monitor (USA): www.multinationalmonitor.org

PART II

The Globalization Project (1980s to 2000s)

5

Instituting the Globalization Project

The globalization project succeeded the development project—not because development is extinct, but because its coordinates have changed. Development, formerly a public project, was redefined as a private, global project. Why not just "globalization" (without the project)? Isn't globalization inevitable? Maybe so, but as a vehicle of development, it is sobering to realize that, despite the promise of global prosperity with "free markets," material benefits are largely confined to only about two-fifths of the world's population. The remainder toil in highly exploitative work settings or struggle to survive on marginal lands or urban slums, as markets capture resources for the global minority with purchasing power. To call globalization a project emphasizes its political dimensions. Markets are neither natural nor free. They are institutional constructs, managed by powerful players, including international financial institutions, banks, corporations, states, and even nongovernmental organizations (NGOs). The distinctiveness of the globalization project is its political intervention to overcome the limits of the development project.

Intervention involved more than two decades of military and financial disciplining of Third World policies that restricted foreign corporate access to Third World resources and markets, beginning, perhaps, with the installation of General Suharto in Indonesia (1965). Within the Third World, export-oriented industrialization fueled economic growth, legitimizing a new "free market" model of development. Development, which had been defined as nationally managed economic growth, was redefined in the World

Bank's *World Development Report 1980* as "participation in the world market."[1] The redefinition prepared the way for superseding economic nationalism and embracing globalization. *The global economy was emerging as the unit of development.*

Securing the Global Market Empire

In 1965, Indonesian President Sukarno and his brand of economic nationalism were overthrown in a bloody coup led by General Suharto. Declassified documents reveal that a 1964 British Foreign Office file called for the defense of Western interests in Southeast Asia because it is "a major producer of essential commodities. The region produces nearly 85 percent of the world's natural rubber, over 45 percent of the tin, 65 percent of the copra, and 23 percent of the chromium ore." Two years earlier, a CIA memo recorded an agreement between British Prime Minister Harold Macmillan and US President John F. Kennedy to "liquidate president Sukarno, depending on the situation and available opportunities."[2]

Time-Life, Inc., sponsored a 1967 meeting in Geneva between General Suharto, his economic advisers, and corporate leaders representing "the major oil companies and banks, General Motors, Imperial Chemical Industries, British Leyland, British-American Tobacco, American Express, Siemens, Goodyear, the International Paper Corporation, and US Steel." With Ford Foundation help, General Suharto reformulated a development partnership with foreign investment. James Linen, president of Time-Life, Inc., expressed the *birth of this new global order* in the following opening remarks:

> We are here to create a new climate in which private enterprise and developing countries work together . . . for the greater profit of the free world. This world of international enterprise is more than governments. . . . It is the seamless web of enterprise, which has been shaping the global environment at revolutionary speed.[3]

These events marked a turning point, forging a new discourse of *global development partnership* between states and corporations. Intervention was consistent with US President Eisenhower's containment policy articulated for that region in 1959:

> One of Japan's greatest opportunities for increased trade lies in a free and developing Southeast Asia. . . . The great need in one country is for raw materials, in the other country for manufactured goods. The two regions complement each other markedly. By strengthening Vietnam and helping

insure the safety of the South Pacific and Southeast Asia, we gradually develop the great trade potential between this region . . . and highly industrialized Japan to the benefit of both.[4]

The war waged in Vietnam by a US–led coalition during the next decade confirmed this policy, followed by strategic interventions in Chile, El Salvador, Nicaragua, Panama, Granada, and Iraq, as well as disbursements of military and economic aid to secure the perimeter of the "free world" and its resource empire. Militarization was critical, securing and prying open the Third World to an emerging project of global development orchestrated by the United States as the dominant power.

The Third World was unruly during this prelude to the globalization project. Between 1974 and 1980, national liberation forces came to power in 14 different Third World states, perhaps inspired by the Vietnamese resistance. The collusion among the members of the Organization of the Petroleum Exporting Countries (OPEC) in hiking oil prices in 1973 threatened economic stability in the West. Then, in 1974, the Group of 77 (G-77) proposed to the UN a **New International Economic Order (NIEO)** involving reform of the world economic system to improve the position of Third World states in international trade and their access to technological and financial resources. The NIEO initiative offered a "dependency" perspective, namely, that First World structural power stunted Third World development. Despite exceeding the UN growth target of 5 percent growth per annum for the second development decade, economic and social indices showed that most Third World countries had not achieved the rising living standards promised by the development project. In 1974 the World Bank reported,

> It is now clear that more than a decade of rapid growth in underdeveloped countries has been of little or no benefit to perhaps a third of their population. Paradoxically, while growth policies have succeeded beyond the expectations of the first development decade, the very idea of aggregate growth as a social objective has increasingly been called into question.[5]

Algerian president Houari Boumedienne told the UN General Assembly in 1974,

> Inasmuch as [the old order] is maintained and consolidated and, therefore, thrives by virtue of a process which continually impoverishes the poor and enriches the rich, this economic order constitutes the major obstacle standing in the way of any hope of development and progress for all the countries of the Third World.[6]

The NIEO was a charter of economic rights and duties of states, designed to codify global reform along neo-Keynesian lines (public initiatives). Widely perceived as "the revolt of the Third World," the NIEO initiative was a culmination of collectivist politics growing out of the Non-Aligned Movement (NAM). But it was arguably a movement for reform at best, its prime movers being the presidents of Algeria, Iran, Mexico, and Venezuela—all oil-producing nations distinguished by their very recently acquired huge oil rents, as opposed to the impoverished "least developed countries" (LDCs) and the newly industrializing countries (NICs).[7] The Third World united front strategy unraveled—in large part because of growing divergence between middle-income and poorer states.

Coinciding with the NIEO episode was a strengthening of a First World core: the formation of the **Group of Seven (G7)** states. The finance ministers of the United States, the United Kingdom, France, West Germany, Japan, Italy, and Canada held secret meetings annually, performing crisis management, including containing the NIEO and its politics of economic nationalism.[8] The debt regime of the 1980s provided the perfect opportunity.

The Debt Regime

The 1980s debt crisis instituted a new era of *global governance* in which individual national policies were subjected to external, rule-based procedures that strengthened the grip of the First World through the international financial institutions (the IMF and the World Bank). In other words, the debt crisis spawned a **debt regime**. The divisions in the Third World enabled global political and economic elites to argue that a country's debt stress stemmed from failure to copy the NICs' strategy of export diversification in the world market.[9] Although represented as examples of market virtue—to justify neoliberal ideology—the NICs were in fact state-managed economies.

The debt crisis began in 1980 when the US Federal Reserve Board moved to stem the fall in the dollar's value from its overcirculation in the 1970s lending binge—reducing dollar circulation with an aggressive monetarist policy.[10] The contraction of credit raised interest rates as banks competed for dwindling funds. Lending to Third World states slowed, and shorter terms were issued—hastening the day of reckoning on higher-cost loans. Some borrowing continued, nevertheless—partly because of rising oil prices. Higher oil prices actually accounted for more than 25 percent of the total debt of the Third World.[11]

Third World debt totaled $1 trillion by 1986. Even though this amount was only half of the US national debt in that year, it was significant because countries were devoting new loans entirely to servicing previous loans.[12]

Unlike the United States, cushioned by the dollar standard (the *de facto* international reserve currency preferred by countries and traders), Third World countries were unable to continue debt servicing; their dollar reserves lost value as real interest rates spiked, First World recession reduced consumption of Third World products, and Third World export revenues collapsed as primary export prices declined 17 percent relative to First World manufactured exports.[13]

The World Bank estimated the combined average annual negative effect of these "external" shocks in 1981 to 1982 to be 19.1 percent of gross domestic product (GDP) in Kenya, 14.3 percent in Tanzania, 18.9 percent in the Côte d'Ivoire, 8.3 percent in Brazil, 29 percent in Jamaica, and more than 10 percent in the Philippines.[14] Third World countries were suddenly mired in a *debt trap*: debt was choking their economies. To repay the interest (at least), they had to drastically curtail imports and drastically raise exports. But reducing imports of technology jeopardized growth. Expanding exports was problematic, as commodity prices were at the lowest in 40 years—a result of the expansion of commodity exports to reduce debt. The market alone could not solve these problems.

Debt Management

The chosen course of action was debt management. The Bretton Woods institutions were back in the driver's seat, even though 60 percent of Third World debt was with private banks. The IMF assumed a supervisory status, implementing structural adjustment policies (SAPs) in the mid-1980s: a comprehensive restructuring of production priorities and government programs in a debtor country. Working with the World Bank and its structural adjustment loan (SAL), the IMF levied restructuring conditions on borrowers in return for loan rescheduling—demanding *policy restructuring,* whereby debtor states received austere prescriptions for political-economic reforms.

In 1989, the executive director of UNICEF, James P. Grant, observed,

Today, the heaviest burden of a decade of frenzied borrowing is falling not on the military or on those with foreign bank accounts or on those who conceived the years of waste, but on the poor who are having to do without necessities, on the unemployed who are seeing the erosion of all that they have worked for, on the women who do not have enough food to maintain their health, on the infants whose minds and bodies are not growing properly because of untreated illnesses and malnutrition, and on the children who are being denied their only opportunity to go to school. . . . It is hardly too brutal an oversimplification to say that the rich got the loans and the poor got the debts.[15]

Under this regime, debt was defined as an individual liquidity problem (i.e., the shortage of foreign currency) rather than a systemic problem;

that is, the debt managers blamed debtor policies rather than the financial system.

Mexico was the first "ticking bomb" in the global financial structure, with an $80 billion debt in 1982. Over 75 percent of this was owed to private banks. Mexican political forces were divided between a "bankers' alliance" and the "Cárdenas alliance"—representing a nationalist coalition rooted in the labor and peasant classes.[16] The outgoing president, José López Portillo, allied with the latter group, opposed debt management proposals by nationalizing the Mexican banking system and installing exchange controls against capital flight and shocked the international financial community when he declared the following in his outgoing speech:

> The financing plague is wreaking greater and greater havoc throughout the world. As in Medieval times, it is scourging country after country. It is transmitted by rats and its consequences are unemployment and poverty, industrial bankruptcy, and speculative enrichment. The remedy of the witch doctors is to deprive the patient of food and subject him to compulsory rest. Those who protest must be purged, and those who survive bear witness to their virtue before the doctors of obsolete and prepotent dogma and of blind hegemonical egoism.[17]

Portillo's conservative successor, Miguel de la Madrid, agreed to a bailout, in which the IMF put up $1.3 billion, foreign governments $2 billion, and the banks $5 billion in "involuntary loans." In 1986, Mexico was rewarded for resisting a regional effort to form a debtors' club.[18]

The Mexican bailout became a model. In other middle-income nations (e.g., Brazil, Thailand, Turkey) as in Mexico, development alliance constituencies—particularly ruling elites and middle classes benefiting from the original loans—used their power to shift repayment costs on to the working poor via austerity cuts in social services. As World Bank chief economist Stanley Fischer noted in 1989, "Most of the burden has been borne by wage earners in the debtor countries."[19]

Reversing the Development Project

As countries adopted debt regime rules and restructured their social economies, they *reversed the development project*, institutionalizing development as "participation in the world market," focusing on export intensification and "shrinking the state." Social protections evolved from line item subsidies in national policies to the status of "emergency funds"—pioneered by the World Bank as "social funds" to soften the impact of austerity in the Caribbean, Latin America, and Africa. These "social safety nets," such as the Bolivian *Fondo de Emergencia Social* and the Egyptian Social Fund, were administered by NGOs through decentralized feeding and microcredit programs that often bypassed communities with the least resources to propose programs and neglected gender differences.[20] In the meantime, rescheduling bought time for debt repayment, but it came at a heavy cost.

Adjustment measures included

- drastic reduction of public spending (especially social programs and food subsidies);
- currency devaluation (inflating prices of imports and reducing export prices to improve trade balances);
- export intensification (to earn foreign exchange);
- privatization of state enterprises (to "free" the market); and
- reduction of wages to attract foreign investors and reduce export prices.

Most of these measures fell hardest on the poorest and least powerful social classes—those dependent on wages and subsidies. While some businesses and export outfits prospered, poverty rates climbed. Governments saw their development alliances crumble with deindustrialization and shrinking funds for subsidizing urban constituencies.

In Mexico, the debt regime eliminated food subsidies for basic foods such as tortillas, bread, beans, and rehydrated milk. Malnourishment grew. Minimum wages fell 50 percent between 1983 and 1989, and purchasing power fell to two-thirds of the 1970 level. By 1990, the basic needs of 41 million Mexicans were unsatisfied, and 17 million lived in extreme poverty.[21] Meanwhile, manufacturing growth rates plummeted, from 1.9 in 1980 to 1982 to 0.1 in 1985 to 1988, depleting formal employment opportunities.[22] With state financial support, Mexico became a significant agro-exporter—by 1986, exporting to the United States more than $2 billion worth of fresh fruits, vegetables, and beef.[23]

In Africa, the severity of the debt burden meant that Tanzania, Sudan, and Zambia were using more than 100 percent of their export earnings to service debt in 1983. In Zambia, the ratio of debt to gross national product (GNP) increased from 16 to 56 percent in 1985. African economies were particularly vulnerable to falling commodity prices during the 1980s, with individual commodities comprising 40 to 85 percent of export earnings. Thus, African coffee exporters had to produce 30 percent more coffee to pay for one imported tractor and then produce more coffee to pay for the oil to run it.[24]

IMF/World Bank adjustment policies in Africa reduced food subsidies and public services, leading to urban demonstrations and riots in Tanzania, Ghana, Zambia, Morocco, Egypt, Tunisia, and Sudan. In Zambia, for example, the price of cornmeal—a staple—rose 120 percent in the mid-1980s following adjustment. Between 1980 and 1986, average per capita income declined by

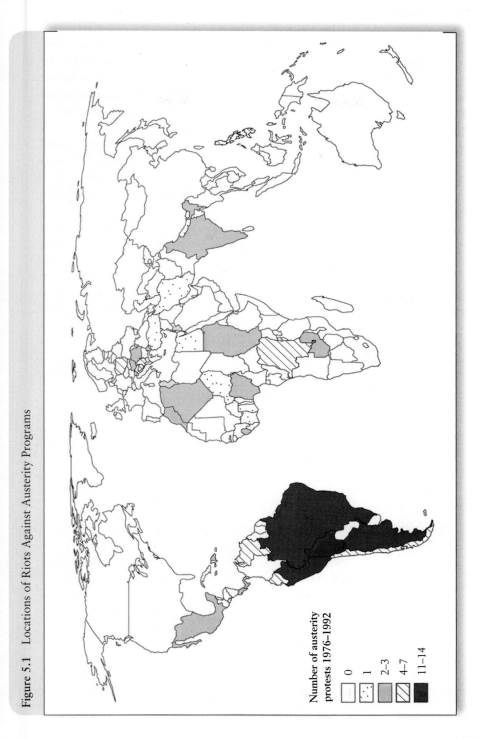

Figure 5.1 Locations of Riots Against Austerity Programs

Number of austerity
protests 1976–1992

0
1
2–3
4–7
11–14

10 percent, and unemployment almost tripled.[25] In effect, all the "development" indicators, including infant mortality, took a downturn under the impact of adjustment policies. The NGO Oxfam reported in 1993 that World Bank adjustment programs in sub-Saharan Africa were largely responsible for reductions in public health spending and a 10 percent decline in primary school enrollment.[26]

During the "lost decade" of the 1980s, the poorer regions of the world economy lost considerable ground. From 1978 to 1992, more than 70 countries undertook 566 stabilization and SAPs to manage their debt.[27] The debtor countries collective entered the 1990s with 61 percent more debt than they held in 1982.[28]

As a consequence of growing debt, many countries found themselves under greater scrutiny by global managers, in addition to surrendering greater amounts of their wealth to global agencies. The turning point was 1984. In that year, the direction of capital flows reversed—that is, the inflow of loan and investment capital into the former Third World was replaced by an *outflow* in the form of debt repayment (see Figure 5.2). The (net)

Figure 5.2   Net Transfers of Long-Term Loans to Third World States

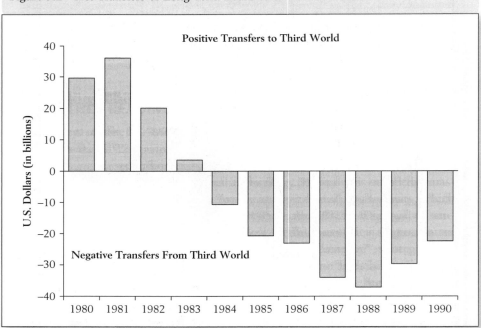

Source: UN, *Human Development Report* (1997: 64).

extraction of financial resources from the Third World during the 1980s exceeded $400 billion.[29] The debt crisis opened up the Third World—now recategorized as the global South[30]—to northern-imposed disciplines, foreign investment, and unsustainable export production to defray debt.

CASE STUDY   **IMF Riots—Citizens Versus Structural Adjustment**

The so-called "IMF riots" swept across the Second and Third Worlds, representing the demise of the development project. Between 1976 and 1992, some 146 riots occurred in 39 of the approximately 80 debtor countries, including Romania, Poland, Yugoslavia, and Hungary. These large-scale, often coordinated, urban uprisings protested the public austerity measures, with rioters often breaking into food banks. The rioters contested the unequal distribution of the means of livelihood, targeting policies that eroded the social contract. Collapsing social entitlements included a range of subsidized services to members of hyperurbanized environments, including food, health care, education, transportation, and housing. Riots sought to restore basic mechanisms of social reproduction. They also targeted the International Monetary Fund (IMF) as the source of policies undermining national public capacity, and therefore, popular sovereignty. Björn Beckman claimed that the logic of the structural adjustment program was to "further weaken the motivation of the state to respond to the popular demands that have been built into the process of postcolonial state formation."

Given the profound transition underway across the structurally adjusted Third World, should this series of protests be understood as being about more than shrinking material resources—such as the shrinking democratic space, or even the demise of the promise of development?

Sources: Beckman (1992: 97); Kagarlitsky (1995: 217); Walton and Seddon (1994).

Challenging the Development State

As neoliberalism consolidated its orthodoxy in the 1980s, debt managers demanded a *shrinking* of Third World states through reductions in social spending and the **privatization** of state enterprises. As a condition of debt rescheduling, governments sold off their public assets. As a result, the average number of privatizations in this region of the world expanded tenfold across the decade. From 1986 to 1992, the proportion of World Bank SALs demanding privatization rose from 13 to 59 percent, and by 1992, over 80 countries privatized 7,000 public enterprises—mostly public services: water, electricity, and telephones.[31]

Although there is no doubt that some development state elites had pursued excessive public financing, privatization accomplished two radical changes:

- It *reduced public capacity* in developmental planning and implementation, thereby privileging the corporate sector.
- It *extended the reach of foreign ownership* of assets in the global South—precisely the condition that governments had tried to overcome in the 1970s (see Figure 5.3).

Rather than losing the money they had loaned in such excessive amounts, banks earned vast profits on the order of 40 percent per annum on Third World investments alone.[32] Foreign investment in the Third World resumed between 1989 and 1992, increasing from $29 billion to $40 billion (especially in Mexico, China, Malaysia, Argentina, and Thailand).[33] The restructured (now) global South was yet quite

Figure 5.3   Select Private Foreign Direct Investment Flows in the 1990s

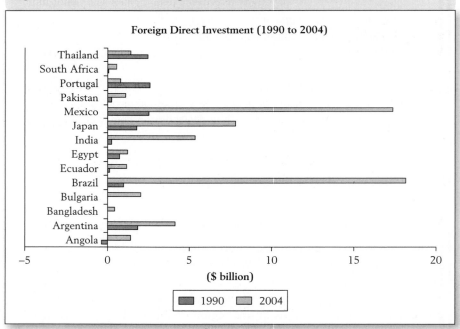

Source: World Bank, *World Development Indicators* (2006).

profitable for private investment: Wages were low, governments were not competing in the private capital markets, and an export boom in raw materials, manufactures, and foodstuffs was underway.

During the debt regime, the World Bank established local agencies (known as *parastatals*) to administer its SAPs. SALs restructure national economies and redistribute power within the state—privileging the central bank and trade/finance ministries over program-oriented ministries (social services, agriculture, education), thus weakening the political coalitions and goals of the national development state.[34] This power shift removes resources from state agencies that support and regulate economic (e.g., import-substitution industrialization [ISI]) and social sectors affecting the majority of the citizenry, especially the poorer classes. These resources are shifted to the agencies more directly connected to global enterprise: Thus, global economic criteria override national social criteria (see Figure 5.4).

Figure 5.4   Government Spending on Foreign Debt and Social Services (Selected Countries, 1995)

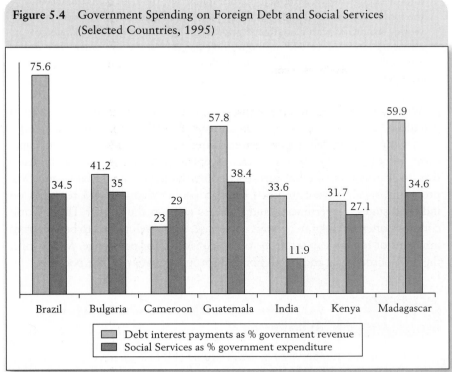

Source: World Bank, *World Development Report* (1998–1999).

Note: Social Services includes health, education, Social Security, welfare, housing, and community services.

The World Bank's premise for the policy shift was that development states were overly bureaucratic and inefficient on one hand, and unresponsive to their citizenry on the other. In the Bank's sub-Saharan Africa report, it reinterpreted "shrinking" the state to mean a reorganization of state administration to encourage popular initiatives. Some of these observations were credible, confirmed by authoritarian government, corruption, and "hollow" development financing—such as Zaire President Mobutu's lavish global, jet-set lifestyle and Côte d'Ivoire President Félix Houphouët-Boigny's construction in his home village of a larger-than-life-size replica of St. Peter's Basilica in the Vatican. Nevertheless, the solutions proposed and imposed by the Bank substituted growing external control of these countries in the name of financial orthodoxy.[35] Noting the revival of "trusteeship" in the 1990s, economist Jeffrey Sachs observed,

> Not unlike the days when the British Empire placed senior officials directly into the Egyptian and Ottoman finance ministries, the IMF is insinuated into the inner sanctums of nearly 75 developing-country governments around the world—countries with a combined population of some 1.4 billion. These governments rarely move without consulting the IMF staff, and when they do, they risk their lifelines to capital markets, foreign aid, and international respectability.[36]

When states become unaccountable, citizens may withdraw into a "shadow" economy and society, as illustrated in the Tanzanian case study.

In summary, the debt regime reformulated the terms of economic management, relocating power within states to open them up to growing influence over their policies by global agencies and markets. The World Bank and IMF programs of adjustment imposed standard rather than tailored remedies on indebted states. Governments and business elites in the former Third World countries often collaborated in this enterprise, being well placed to benefit from infusions of foreign capital, some of which is used for patronage. Meanwhile, the debt burden was and is still borne disproportionately by the poor.

CASE STUDY **Tanzanian Civil Society Absorbs Structural Adjustment**

Political democratization may be one outcome of urban grass roots' resistance to their government's betrayal of the development alliance's social pact by implementing austerity measures. Another may involve depending on the "informal economy" as a survival strategy. Between 1974 and 1988, with real wages falling by 83 percent, Tanzanians intensified their income-generating activities "off the books"—with crop sales on parallel markets in the agricultural sector; sideline incomes for wage workers such as baking, carpentry, or tailoring; schoolchildren absenteeism so that children could work for family income; supplementary tutorials by schoolteachers; moonlighting physicians; and so forth. As Aili Maria Tripp remarks,

> [Austerity] was somewhat softened by the fact that more than 90 percent of household income was coming from informal businesses, primarily operated by women, children, and the elderly. By providing alternatives to the state's diminishing resource base, these strategies diverted demands that otherwise might have overwhelmed the state. . . . In the end, little was demanded of a state that had placed itself at the center of the nation's development agenda and had established itself as the guarantor of society's welfare.

Does this kind of self-organizing activity offer us a glimpse of an alternative, sustainable conception of development, or is it simply an intensified form of feminized social reproduction?

Sources: Rist (1997: 130–132); Tripp (1997: 3–6, 13).

The Globalization Project

Alongside the debt regime, during the 1980s the United States led an attempt to build a free-market global consensus—focusing on breaking down the resistance of the Soviet empire (the Second World) to market capitalism. This was a central geopolitical strategy of the emerging globalization project.

As it happened, Eastern European countries, borrowing from the West to finance consumer items demanded by restive citizens, came under IMF supervision. By 1986, Soviet President Mikhail Gorbachev was formulating plans for *perestroika* (restructuring) in exchange for membership in the Bretton Woods institutions. IMF policies required replacement of **central planning** by "market-responsive" enterprises and reduced food, transport, heating fuel, and housing subsidies (i.e., economic rights of the socialist systems). *Social equality* was redefined as the equality of private opportunity, which was exploited by former public officials who enriched themselves as public property was privatized. Once the Soviet Union and empire fell in 1989, Western shock treatment methods were deployed, leading to a precipitous decline in Russian living standards and an explosion of organized crime. But the world was now unipolar—instead of the bipolarity of the Cold War era—and cleared for the globalization project proper.[37]

The key principle of the globalization project was the implementation of a free world market. The economic nationalism associated with the development project was viewed as limiting development because it obstructed the transnational mobility of goods, money, and firms in the service of efficient (i.e., private) allocation of global resources. As early as 1971, at the inception of the (corporate-based) World Economic Forum, its first publication declared, "Nationalism is economically indefensible."[38] The world market took its place, organized by transnational corporations (TNCs), as opposed to states organizing national markets.

Representing TNCs are institutions such as the World Trade Organization (WTO) that have governed this global project. The founding director-general of the WTO, Renato Ruggiero, expressed this in 2000 in the following way:

> It is a new world. . . . The Cold War is over. Even more significant is the rise of the developing world as a major power in the international economy as a result of the shift to freer markets and open trade—an event that could rank with the industrial revolution in historical significance. All this is taking place against the backdrop of globalization—the linking together of countries at different levels of development by technology, information, and ideas, as well as by economics.

In this vision, the future of development lies with the world market, linked by the rules of neoclassical economic discourse. Ruggiero continued,

> If we want real coherence in global policymaking and a comprehensive international agenda, then coordination has to come from the top, and it must be driven by elected leaders. . . . Progress in resolving the challenge of the new century will hinge on our ability not just to build a coherent global architecture, but to build a political constituency for globalization. . . . Without the WTO, we will go back to a world of national barriers, protectionism, economic nationalism, and conflict.[39]

This was the vision of the globalization project: the implementation of "market rule" via the restructuring of policies and standards across the nation-state system. The globalization project did not begin on any particular date, but it signifies a new way of thinking about development. Global management of capitalism emerged in the 1980s when the Bretton Woods institutions made explicit claims about *managing a global economy*, brought into being via the debt regime. Among the political and economic elites, a consensus emerged, redefining development in private terms as "trade, not aid." Backed with the financial coercion of multilateral institutional debt management, it assumed the name of the **Washington Consensus**. Thus, the globalization project was born.

With the advent of the globalization project, development did not disappear; rather, its meaning changed. Global elites reframed development as the deepening of markets (as resource allocators). The globalization project involved political choices to (re)define the bearings and future of states and their civic responsibilities. If competing in the world market requires policies of cutting public expenditures that may reduce safeguards and standards of employment, health care, and education, then *globalization is a decision, not an inevitability*. And it centers on "governance," which overrides and reformulates government.

Global Governance

In the shift from development to globalization projects, governments faced a world order in which global institutions assumed a more powerful governing role. This role is by no means absolute, and it requires compliance from the states themselves, guaranteed by consensus or coercion (which can backfire, as demonstrated by the Arab Spring of 2011 and the EU/Greek struggle of 2015).

Ultimately, the most effective way of guaranteeing compliance is to institutionalize market rule, where individual governmental functions are recomposed as global governance functions and enforced through multilateral protocols. Indeed, at the first ministerial meeting of the WTO in December 1996, Director-General Ruggiero remarked that preparing a global investment treaty was similar to "writing the constitution of a single global economy." The debt regime was the prelude for this power play, and it had demonstratively political origins, as expressed in 1990 by the newly formed South Commission (representing the global South's contrary position):

> What is abundantly clear is that the North has used the plight of developing countries to strengthen its dominance and its influence over the development paths of the South. . . . While adjustment is pressed on them, countries in the North with massive payments imbalances are immune from any pressure to adjust, and free to follow policies that deepen the South's difficulties. *The most powerful countries in the North have become a de facto board of management for the world economy*, protecting their interests and imposing their will on the South. The governments of the South are then left to face the wrath, even the violence, of their own people, whose standards of living are being depressed for the sake of preserving the present patterns of operation of the world economy.[40]

In other words, the World Bank/IMF partnership in structurally adjusting particular states is a *method of governing* and an attempt to resolve instability in a deregulated global money market. Ongoing management of global financial relations has become a practical necessity to stabilize economies and open or "denationalize" them in the process, with support from the WTO.

Global circuits (of debt, money, investment, and pension funds) are so embedded in national economies (and vice versa) that stabilizing these destabilizing financial relations (as evidenced by domino-like financial crises: Asia in the late 1990s, Europe in the late 2000s) dominated national policy making. While adopted by countries (in varying fashion), governance protocols favoring open markets reflect requirements of, or conditions favored by, the **global managers**—officials of the international financial institutions of the IMF and the World Bank, G7 political elites, executives of TNCs, and global bankers. Indebted states restructure their political-economic priorities to obtain creditworthiness in the eyes of the global financial community. Paradoxically, an agro-export priority, which may negatively affect national food security, nonetheless conforms to the requirements of sound financial policy. It may enhance foreign exchange earnings for a time, but it reorients agriculture to supplying foreign consumers. Thus, global governance essentially deepens global market relations within states, compromising their sovereignty and accountability to citizens.

Under these conditions, the World Bank, now the principal development (financing) agency, has played a definite governing role. It "dictate[s] legal and institutional change through its lending process" since its 1989 report in which it asserted that governance evaluation in debtor countries is within its jurisdiction[41]—in spite of the fact that citizens do not elect the World Bank nor the IMF, nor have they formally consented to WTO protocols, broadly termed "liberalization."

CASE STUDY   **Mexican Soverignty Exposed—From Above and Below**

Mexico's admission into the Organisation for Economic Co-operation and Development (OECD) via its participation in NAFTA precipitated the 1994 *Zapatista* uprising in Chiapas (see Chapter 7), a region of intensive resource extraction by foreign companies. Protesting President Salinas's decision, *Zapatista* spokesperson Subcomandante Marcos claimed it was a "death sentence for indigenous peoples." As Amory Star notes, the *Zapatistas* declared,

> When we rose up against a national government, we found that it did not exist. In reality we were up against great financial capital, against

speculation and investment, which makes all decisions in Mexico, as well as in Europe, Asia, Africa, Oceania, the Americas—everywhere.

Having questioned Mexican sovereignty, the uprising unsettled regional financial markets. The *Zapatistas* suggested that NAFTA was a confidence trick of the globalization project:

> At the end of 1994 the economic farce with which Salinas had deceived the Nation and the international economy exploded. The nation of money called the grand gentlemen of power and arrogance to dinner, and they did not hesitate in betraying the soil and sky in which they prospered with Mexican blood. The economic crisis awoke Mexicans from the sweet and stupefying dream of entry into the first world.

The Mexican peso lost 30 percent of its value in December 1994, generating a negative "tequila effect" throughout Latin American financial markets. International financiers hastily assembled a financial loan package of $18 billion to stabilize the peso: The United States committed over $9 billion, while the European Central Banks provided $5 billion; Canada also contributed $1 billion, and a dozen global banks, including Citibank, added a $3-billion line of credit. Finally, the IMF was called in to lend both money and its stamp of approval to restore investor confidence in the Mexican economy. US president Bill Clinton remarked in 1995, "Mexico is sort of a bellwether for the rest of Latin America *and* developing countries throughout the world." Confidence in NAFTA was also at stake.

If the Mexican bailout was to stabilize the global economy and legitimize the globalization project, the question remains why Chiapas has been occupied by the Mexican federal army ever since. What is it about the globalization project that makes it value foreign investment over human rights?

Sources: Bradsher (1995: D6); Starr (2000: 104).

Liberalization and the Reformulation of Development

Liberalization downgrades the social goals of national development, while upgrading participation in the world economy through such means as tariff reduction, export promotion, financial deregulation, and relaxation of foreign investment rules. Together, these policies reformulate development as a global project—implemented through liberalized states incorporated into a world market constructed by transnational banks and firms, informatics, and multilateral institutions. While liberalization privileges a corporate model of development, its proponents claim it facilitates capital transfer, competition, and trade expansion as methods of increasing economic growth and general well-being. As suggested in the following case study of Chile, liberalization is also realized through new forms of social inequality.

CASE STUDY — Chile—The Original Model of Economic Liberalization

Chile is perhaps the founding model of economic liberalization. A military coup in 1973 eliminated the democratically elected socialist president Salvador Allende, implementing detention, torture, and execution of thousands of Chileans as part of an eight-year period of debilitating authoritarian rule. General Augusto Pinochet pursued a radical free-market reform, otherwise known as "shock treatment," masterminded by economists trained at the University of Chicago, a center of neoclassical economics. Over the next two decades, 600 of the country's state enterprises were sold; foreign investment expanded into strategic sectors such as steel, telecommunications, and airlines; trade protection dwindled; and the dependence of the Chilean GDP on trade grew from 35 percent in 1970 to 57.4 percent in 1990. In other words, *Chile was structurally adjusted before structural adjustment became fashionable.* Sergio Bitar, Allende's minister of mining, remarked that privatization was "the greatest diversion of public funds that has occurred in our history, without the consultation of public opinion or accountability to a congress."

Chile was one of the most democratic of Latin American nations prior to the assault on its parliamentary and civil institutions. Debt restructuring in the 1980s increased social polarization. Social spending continued to fall, wages were frozen, and the peso was seriously devalued. Deindustrialization set in, unemployment levels rose to between 20 and 30 percent, and real wages suffered a 20 percent reduction. Meanwhile, an export boom occurred, retiring debt and earning the Chilean experiment a reputation as a miracle. US president George H. W. Bush declared in Chile in 1990, "You deserve your reputation as an economic model for other countries in the region and in the world. Your commitment to market-based solutions inspires the hemisphere."

By 1990, about 40 percent of the 13 million Chilean people were impoverished in a country once known for its substantial middle class. The pursuit of global efficiency had weakened the domestic fabric of social security and local production. In consequence, a sustained grassroots movement, centered in the *poblaciones* (slums), succeeded in regaining elections in 1988 when Pinochet was defeated.

As the original laboratory for neoliberalization policies, what does the Chilean experience suggest about the construction of the globalization project?

Sources: Bello (1994: 42, 44–45, 59); Collins and Lear (1996: 157, 162); George (1988: 131–132); Schneider, quoted in Chomsky (1994: 184); Schneider (1995: 3, 194, 201).

Theoretical justification for the governing strategy of market opening/ liberalization derives from nineteenth-century English political economist David Ricardo's concept of **comparative advantage**—linking economic growth to optimizing trading advantage through economic specialization, reflecting a nation's relative resource endowments. The theorem stated that when countries exchange their most competitive products on the world market, national and international economic efficiency results.[42] This theorem contradicts the development project's ideal of a series of integrated national economies while affirming the globalization project's focus on the global economy as the unit of development. But the theorem did not allow for capital mobility, which today is central to the construction of a *corporate-based* comparative advantage, so the original *market-based* theorem is no longer operative.

Even here, "capital mobility" is often leveraged by export credit agencies (ECAs), whose loans to southern countries help finance and guarantee foreign investment by northern corporations. The British ECA's goal is to "help exporters of UK goods and services to win business and UK firms to invest overseas by providing guarantees, insurance, and reinsurance against loss."[43] The US ECA favors AT&T, Bechtel, Boeing, General Electric, and McDonnell Douglas. During the 1990s, development loans from ECAs averaged about twice the amount of the world's total development assistance.

Until the 1970s, "comparative advantage" represented a minority strand of economic thought, being out of step with mid-twentieth-century social history. As the welfare state's wage and social program costs ate into profits, a corporate countermovement resuscitated neoclassical market theory, relegating Keynesian ideas of state intervention and public investment to the background. The political form of neoclassical economic theory, **neoliberalism**, took universal shape in welfare reform/reversal, wage erosion, relaxing trade controls, and privatization schemes—the underpinnings of the globalization project.

The doctrine of comparative advantage legitimizes the relationships between liberalization's downward pressure on social rights and its export regime. It is evident in the enlargement of the global labor force at the base of ubiquitous supply chains (foodstuffs, manufactures, services) and in the deepening of natural resource extraction. Where the latter threatens habitats, displaced peasants, fisherfolk, and forest dwellers join the swelling pool of labor, some of whom find work in export production. This doctrine, represented as the new development strategy for countries to find their world market niche, has been interpreted as a *selective development* device, where local and global firms mobilize cheap land and labor for export production to provision distant consumers:

> Millions of acres once used to feed poor families in poor countries are now used to grow kiwis, asparagus, strawberries, and baby carrots for upper-middle-class consumers who can now eat what was once the fare of kings—365 days a year.[44]

The consequence is a *selective* realization of "high mass consumption," an expanding consumer class, and its "insatiable appetite for energy, private automobiles, building materials, household appliances, and other resource-intensive commodities."[45]

Under these circumstances, fueled by "freeing" markets to supply relatively cheap resources, commercial extraction of natural resources has intensified globally, threatening environments and resource regeneration. The close correlation between debt, export liberalization, and high rates of deforestation, as depicted in Figure 5.5, is well known.[46] In Chile, timber exports doubled in the 1980s, reaching beyond industrial plantations to the logging of natural forests. Chile's export boom overexploited the country's natural resources beyond their ability to regenerate.[47] In Ghana—the World Bank's African *model* of structural adjustment—the exports of mining, fishing, and timber products were accelerated to close the widening gap between cocoa exports and severely declining world prices of cocoa. From 1983 to 1988, timber exports increased from $16 million to $99 million, reducing Ghana's tropical forest to 25 percent of its original size.[48] The NGO Development GAP (Group for Alternative Policies) reported that deforestation

> threatens household and national food security now and in the future. Seventy-five percent of Ghanaians depend on wild game to supplement their diet. Stripping the forest has led to sharp increases in malnutrition and disease. For women, the food, fuel, and medicines that they harvest from the forest provide critical resources, especially in the face of decreased food production, lower wages, and other economic shocks that threaten food security.[49]

After 70 countries underwent structural adjustment, the resulting glut of exports produced the lowest commodity prices seen on the world market since the 1930s. The NGO Oxfam calls this the "export-led collapse."[50] Across the world today, 20 million households produce coffee, but the overproduction

Figure 5.5 Debt and Deforestation

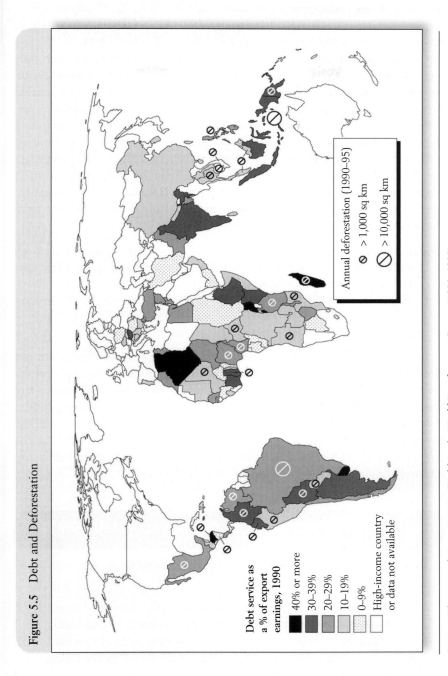

Debt service as
a % of export
earnings, 1990

- 40% or more
- 30–39%
- 20–29%
- 10–19%
- 0–9%
- High-income country
  or data not available

Annual deforestation (1990–95)

⊘ > 1,000 sq km
⊘ > 10,000 sq km

Sources: Thomas and Crow (1994); World Bank, *World Development Report* (1998–1999).

has brought the price of beans to a 30-year low. For a $2.70 cup of coffee, farmers receive on average 2.3 cents, while the transnationals (such as Proctor & Gamble, Philip Morris, and Nestlé) receive around $1.33.[51]

Contrary to the claims of neoclassical theory, export reliance often puts regions in the global South at a *comparative disadvantage*. Liberalization substitutes reliance on the world market for self-reliance as the organizing principle of development. The flow of credit to debt-stressed nations typically depends on renunciation of national development norms, including public investment, protection of local producers, labor forces, communities, environments, the commons, and social entitlements. All of these norms are viewed as impediments to the market, which is why the globalization project begins with market liberalization as the path to "efficiency." The globalization project includes an explicit vision of global order, quite distinct from that of the era of the development project:

- In the development project era, the slogan was "Learn from, and catch up with, the West." Now, under comparative advantage, the slogan is "Find your niche in the global marketplace."
- While the development project held out *replication* as the key to national development, the project of globalization presents *specialization* as the path to economic prosperity.

But specialization in monoculture, or the **global assembly line**, does not alter the reality that the mechanisms of specialization—wage cutting, ecological homogenization, privatization, and reduction of social entitlements—are repeated everywhere, intensifying market competition. Short-term competition/efficiencies are sought at the long-term expense of the social contract and the environment. In theory, this may produce greater productivity—but at the cost of considerable and irreversible economic and social marginalization, impoverishment, environmental stress, and displacement.

NEOLIBERALISM DISPLACES THE DEVELOPMENT STATE

Sociologist Emir Sader (University of Sao Paulo) characterizes the shift from the development state model to neoliberalism:

The state was displaced by the market, workers and citizens by consumers, rights by competition, work and electoral documents by credit cards, public squares by shopping centres, human companionship by television, social policies by private corporate welfare, the national by the global, social integration by social exclusion, equality by discrimination, justice by inequality, solidarity by selfishness, humanism by consumerism, social parties and movements by NGOs and volunteer organizations.

Source: Sader (2009: 171).

The Making of a Free Trade Regime

The debt regime elevated the Bretton Woods institutions to a governance role, targeting the global South. From 1986 to 1994, the whole world became the target of the Uruguay Round of the General Agreement on Trade and Tariffs (GATT). The Uruguay Round was to establish a set of new and binding rules concerning free trade, freedom of investment, and protection of intellectual property rights. Once formulated, these rules framed the WTO.

The United States engineered the creation of the GATT in 1948 as an alternative to the International Trade Organization (which included provisions from the UN Declaration of Human Rights concerning full employment, working conditions, and social security).[52] Through GATT, trade expansion was *delinked from the social contract*. From 1948 through 1980, GATT reduced tariff rates on trade in manufactured goods by more than 75 percent.[53] Agriculture was excluded from the GATT. In the 1980s, at a time of recession and declining industrial leadership, the United States initiated the Uruguay Round, with the aim of liberalizing agriculture and services (such as banking, insurance, telecommunications), in which the North held a competitive advantage. Northern pressure and the promise of open markets for southern products, including agricultural goods, won acceptance from the South.[54]

The liberalization movement was supported by an activist lobby of "free trader" agro-exporting states (the Cairns Group), TNCs such as IBM and American Express, and agribusinesses such as Cargill, Ralston-Purina, General Mills, Continental Grain, RJR Nabisco, and ConAgra, looking to reduce trade barriers, domestic price supports, and supply-management policies restricting demand for farm inputs such as fertilizer and chemicals. Corporations produce and sell farm products across the world—they take advantage of seasonal variation and dietary variation. Alternatively, family farmers are spatially fixed and depend on national farm policy—input and price subsidies, farm credit, risk insurance, and import controls—for their economic viability.

Given the competitive dumping of surplus foods by the United States and Europe, depressing agricultural prices by 39 percent (1975–1989),[55] GATT proposed an "urgent need to bring more discipline and predictability to world agricultural trade."[56] Southern farm sectors were adversely affected by dumping, deepening food import dependency, especially in sub-Saharan Africa. However, while liberalization was expected to stabilize markets, it has not stabilized farming in the global South since markets are controlled by huge agribusiness corporations, which dictate prices at the expense of family farmers. The United States challenged GATT's Article XI food security provisions, arguing for comparative advantage:

> The US has always maintained that self-sufficiency and food security are not one and the same. Food security—the ability to acquire the food you need when you need it—is best provided through a smooth-functioning world market.[57]

In short, the making of a free trade regime reconstructed "food security" as a market relation, privileging and protecting corporate agriculture and placing small farmers at a comparative disadvantage. Food security would now be "governed" through the market by corporate, rather than social, criteria.

The World Trade Organization

The singular achievement of the GATT Uruguay Round was the creation of the World Trade Organization (WTO) on January 1, 1995. The WTO, with over 150 voting members, assumes unprecedented power to enforce GATT provisions. It is unprecedented because the WTO is arguably less about trade rule consistency than about governing member states via liberalization. *Free trade* is a misnomer for the reach of WTO rules. In combination, they challenge national democratic processes, removing decision-making to nontransparent tribunals located in Geneva, Switzerland, using "market logic" to override individual government policy where it interferes with "free trade."

Unlike the GATT (a trade treaty only), the WTO has independent jurisdiction similar to the United Nations. That is, it has the power to enforce its rulings on member states, and these include rulings going beyond simply cross-border trade into the realm of "trade-related" issues. This means setting rules regarding the movement of goods, money, and productive facilities across borders—rules that restrict countries from enacting legislation or policies discriminating against such movement. WTO rules, in advancing trade freedoms, privilege corporate rights to compete internationally. This means ensuring that TNCs receive treatment equal to that received by domestic firms and reducing or removing local restrictions (e.g., labor, health, environmental laws) on trade and investment that might interfere with corporate competitiveness in the global marketplace. The WTO staff are unelected bureaucrats and its proceedings are secret, thus denying citizen participation in making and evaluating policy. In 1994, World Bank economist Herman Daly warned that establishing rules to override national governments' capacity to regulate commerce "is to wound fatally the major unit of community capable of carrying out any policies for the common good."[58]

The WTO has an *integrated dispute settlement* mechanism. If a state is perceived to be distorting trade obligations in one area, such as curbing investments in timber cutting to protect a forest, it can be disciplined through the application of sanctions against another area of economic activity, such as some of its manufactured exports. Member states can lodge complaints through the WTO, whose decision holds automatically unless every member of the WTO votes to reverse it. Should states refuse to comply, the WTO can authorize the plaintiff to take unilateral action. Martin Khor, director of the Third World Network, suggests that, in claiming to reduce "trade-distorting" measures, the WTO becomes "development-distorting."[59] The very *threat* of such challenges has already had the effect of diluting national laws protecting human and environmental health.

The WTO, in enforcing market freedoms, *depoliticizes* their profound social impact. Thus, the 1996 Singapore Ministerial Declaration invites objection to labor rights laws: "We reject the use of labor standards for protectionist purposes, and agree that the comparative advantage of countries, particularly low-wage developing countries, must in no way be put into question."[60] And, as the outgoing director-general of GATT, Peter Sutherland, declared in 1994, "Governments should interfere in the conduct of trade as little as possible."[61] This implies a *general* challenge to national laws and regulations regarding the environment, health, preferential trade relations, social subsidies, labor legislation, and so on. While the challenge does not eliminate all laws, it seeks to *harmonize* regulation internationally, lowering the ceiling on democratic initiatives within the national polity. As we shall see, the goal of depoliticizing the economy can backfire, and this explains in large part the mushrooming global social justice movement.

In this sense, although implementation is uneven, the WTO expresses the essence of the globalization project. That is, global managers assume extraordinary powers to govern the web of global economic relations lying across nation-states, privileging corporate over democratic rights. We now examine four of the principal and mutually reinforcing protocols of the WTO: the Agreement on Agriculture (AoA), Trade-Related Investment

Measures (TRIMs), Trade-Related Aspects of Intellectual Property Rights (TRIPs), and the General Agreement on Trade in Services (GATS).

The Agreement on Agriculture (AoA)

The 1995 Agreement on Agriculture advocated universal reductions in trade protection, farm subsidies, and government intervention. Many southern farmers have been unable to recover the cost of their production in the face of a 30 percent or more collapse of world prices for farm goods in the first half-decade since the AoA was instituted.[62] Countries with the capacity to pay (the United States and European states) retained concealed subsidies at the expense of much larger southern farm populations who are threatened daily with imports (i.e.,"dumping") of cheap farm commodities from the North.

With liberalization, farmers everywhere are under pressure to compete by selling cheap. Corporate farmers survive by subsidized "scale economy." Between 1998 and 1999, UK farm income fell by about 75 percent, driving 20,000 farmers out of business, and US farm income declined by almost 50 percent between 1996 and 1999. In the global South, conservative estimates are that in the 1990s between 20 and 30 million farmers lost their land from the impact of AoA trade liberalization.[63]

Liberalization is evidently less about freeing trade than about consolidating a corporate food regime.[64] Through the AoA, the WTO institutionalized the private form of food security. Under the AoA, states no longer have the right to self-sufficiency as a national strategy. Rather, the minimum market access rule guarantees the "right to export" (therefore the requirement to import), even under conditions of subsidized exports. "Food security," then, is not food self-reliance but rather food import dependency for a large minority of southern states. By the mid-1990s, half of the foreign exchange of the 88 low-income food deficit countries went to food imports.[65]

In the absence of public capacity in the South, unprotected farmers are at a comparative disadvantage. In 2000, Oxfam asked, "How can a farmer earning US$230 a year (the average per capita income in LDCs [least developed countries]) compete with a farmer who enjoys a subsidy of US$20,000 a year (average subsidy in OECD countries)?"[66] In India, Devinder Sharma observes, "Whereas for small farmers the subsidies have been withdrawn, there is a lot of support now for agribusiness industry. . . . The result is that the good area under staple foods is now shifting to export crops, so we'll have to import staple food."[67] Forty percent of Kenya's children work on plantations, which export pineapple, coffee, tea, and sugar. While these foodstuffs supply European markets, four million Kenyans face starvation.[68]

CASE STUDY   **Global Comparative Disadvantage—The End of Farming as We Know It?**

A report from Public Citizen's *Global Trade Watch* documents the elimination of small farmers across the whole North American region as the legacy of NAFTA. While about two million Mexican *campesinos* lost their maize farms to cheap, subsidized corn exports from the North between 1994 and the early 2000s, with about 500 people leaving the countryside daily, some 33,000 US farms with under $100,000 annual income disappeared (six times the decline for 1988–1993). Liberalization policies enhance agribusiness power. Public Citizen notes with respect to US policy,

> Proponents of the legislation contended it would make farming more efficient and responsive to market forces; in reality it essentially handed the production of food to agribusiness. . . . Congress has had to appropriate emergency farm supports—in massive farm bailout bills—every year since the legislation went into effect.

But 56 percent of US emergency taxpayer assistance favored the largest 10 percent of the farms. Once NAFTA opened Mexico to 100 percent foreign investor rights, Pillsbury's Green Giant subsidiary relocated its frozen food processing from California to Mexico to access cheap wages, minimal food safety standards, and zero tariffs on reexport to the United States. Cargill purchased a beef and chicken plant in Saltillo, and Cargill de Mexico invested nearly $200 million in vegetable oil refining and soybean processing in Tula. Anticipating continent-wide liberalization, Tyson Foods has operations in Mexico, Brazil, Argentina, and Venezuela; ConAgra processes oilseed in Argentina; Archer Daniels Midland crushes and refines oilseed, mills corn and flour, and bioengineers feeds in Mexico, Central America, and South America; and Walmart is in Mexico, Argentina, and Brazil. Public Citizen remarks,

> Multinational agribusinesses were positioned uniquely to take advantage of trade rules that force countries to accept agricultural imports regardless of their domestic supplies. The companies utilized their foreign holdings as export platforms to sell imported agriculture goods in the United States, and by thus increasing supply put negative pressures on US agriculture prices.

When liberal policy and northern subsidies enable corporations to *construct* comparative advantages, rendering family/peasant farming "inefficient" and rural populations food insecure, how can "market-based allocation" retain credibility?

Sources: Davis (2006); Jordan and Sullivan (2003: 33); *Public Citizen* (2001: ii–iv, 10, 13, 16, 19–21).

Trade-Related Investment Measures (TRIMs)

The TRIMs effort is an attempt to reduce "performance requirements" imposed on foreign investment by host governments, such as expecting a TNC to invest locally, hire locally, buy locally, and transfer technology as a quid pro quo for access.[69] The WTO uses TRIMs to manage the cross-border movement of goods and services production, especially—the WTO website explains— since trade follows investment, and a third of world trade in 1995 was internal to companies. The point of TRIMs is to secure investor rights, as if they have no political impact. One proponent argues, "The multinational corporate community would then be able to rationalize their regional and global sourcing strategies on the basis of productivity, quality, and cost consider- ations in place of the political dictates that now disrupt their operations."[70]

The argument in favor of TRIMs is that they reduce domestic content requirements that misallocate local resources, raise costs, penalize competitive investment, and burden consumers, in addition to slowing technological adop- tion, reducing quality, and retarding management practices.[71] In other words, the role of TRIMs is to enhance conditions for transnational investment by reducing the friction of local regulations. Greater freedom for investors under TRIMs is justified by evidence of "higher-than-average wages and benefits, advanced technology, and sophisticated managerial and marketing techniques," as well as a stronger "integration effect" with the local economy. It is exemplified in the Mexican auto industry, where parent firms invested in local supply firms for self-interest and not because of local content requirements, resulting in the creation of globally competitive Mexican auto part suppliers. Also, in the Malaysian semiconductor industry, an indigenous machine tool firm matured from supplying parts to foreign investors to supplying high- precision computer-numeric tools and factory automation equipment to inter- national and domestic markets.[72] But the "integration effect" favors integration the other way: of local producers into the world market, rather than foreign investors integrating into a program of domestic industrialization.

CASE STUDY   **Evolving Corporate Property Rights**

TRIMs laid the foundations for corporate property rights, allowing foreign investors to challenge a government for imposing "performance requirements." Under NAFTA's Chapter 11, corporations can bypass domestic courts and directly sue governments when municipal, state, or national legislation threatens their profits. Thus the US Metalclad Corporation successfully sued

Mexico over environmental protection. The municipality of Guadalcázar (San Luís Potosí state) had refused a construction permit to Metalclad to develop a toxic waste landfill in an ecologically protected zone. The company had secured a permit from the federal and state governments, but the municipal government stood firm, as it had with a Mexican owner of the site, and was required to compensate Metalclad to the tune of $16.6 million. Because of these extended rights in regional trade agreements, there is mounting pressure for a new WTO agreement that would extend TRIMs to allow corporations to sue governments for restriction of profits.

Why would states sign protocols that subvert their sovereign power and their citizens' rights?

Sources: McBride (2006); Wallach and Woodall (2004: 270).

Trade-Related Intellectual Property Rights (TRIPs)

The WTO website defines *intellectual property rights* as "rights given to persons over the creations of their minds. They usually give the creator an exclusive right over the use of his/her creation for a certain period of time." The TRIPs protocol was defined by a coalition of 12 major US corporations, a Japanese federation of business organizations, and the agency for European business and industry. Based on a synthesis of European and US patent laws, intellectual property rights protection is to be administered by the WTO. Advocates claim that it simplifies the protection of property rights across national borders and protects and promotes innovation for everyone by guaranteeing profits from technological developments, such as computer software, biotechnological products and processes, and pharmaceuticals. But critics contest this corporate definition of intellectual rights, arguing that biodiverse and generic knowledge should remain available to humankind as a global "commons."[73]

Many commercial drugs these days derive from chemicals found in tropical flora and fauna. The northern lifestyle is directly connected to the extraction of these sorts of resources, such as drugs from the rosy periwinkle of Madagascar to fight childhood leukemia and testicular cancer; Brazzein, a powerful sweetener from a West African berry; biopesticides from the Indian neem tree; and human cell lines to identify genes causing illnesses such as Huntington's disease and cystic fibrosis.[74]

It seems rational that the world's biodiversity should service humankind; for example, this is why so much attention is being paid to preserving the tropical rainforests, given their rich biological variety. At issue is the question of control of resources and the relationship between northern lifestyle and the rights of indigenous peoples in the developing nations, mostly in the global South.

The global South contains 90 percent of global biological wealth, and scientists and corporations of the North hold 97 percent of all patents. Patents on biological wealth give patent holders exclusive control over the use of the genetic materials. Corporations have often patented genetic material obtained from a southern country without payment or obligation, turned it into a commodity such as a medicine, and then charged a fee for use of the genetic resource in local production or high prices for the commodity—even to the country where the material originated, often over centuries. Critics view this appropriation of genetic material by foreigners as **biopiracy**.[75]

The entire living world is up for grabs in this particular vision of commodifying natural endowments and resources. TRIPs grew out of an attempt to stem intellectual property pirating of Western products (watches, CDs, etc.) in the global South, but ironically, it now appears to sanction a reverse biological form of piracy on a disproportionate scale, threatening livelihood rather than commodity rights. About 1.4 billion people in the global South depend primarily on farm-saved seeds and on crop genetic diversity as the basis of cultural and ecological sustainability. Farmers express concern that if firms can patent traditional seed stock, planting of traditional crops may be liable for patent infringement.[76] This concern arises because firms such as I.C. Industries and Pioneer Hi-Bred (now DuPont Pioneer) sought licensing rights to use a gene from an African cowpea. When inserted into crops such as corn and soybeans, the transgene increases pest resistance. As the Rural Advancement Foundation International (RAFI, now ETC) asked, "The question is, who are the inventors? [The scientists] who isolated the gene? Or West African farmers who identified the value of the plant holding the gene and then developed and protected it?"[77] The IPR regime privileges governments and corporations as legal entities, disempowering villagers by disavowing their experimental knowledge rights.[78]

The TRIPs protocol establishes global uniform standards for intellectual property rights protection, allowing exclusion of plants and animals from patent laws, but insisting on intellectual property rights for "inventors" of micro-organisms, microbiological processes and products, and plant varieties, which must be either patentable or subject to an effective sui generis system, which states interpret to mean plant variety protection—as in the 1992 Convention on Biological Diversity, which confirmed national sovereignty over genetic resources and affirmed that nations are entitled to "fair and equitable sharing of the benefits." The significance of the sui generis system is that one premised on collective rights to biodiversity would recognize diverse cultural knowledge and practices—but the extent that it is used in this way is another matter.

| CASE STUDY | Big Pharma and the Question of Intellectual Property Rights |

Perhaps the most visible controversy over IPRs has centered on the question of generic antiretroviral drugs to treat HIV/AIDS patients, of whom there are over 40 million worldwide. Brazil produced generic versions prior to the TRIPs agreement in 1996, sidestepping royalties to the pharmaceutical companies and reducing the price by 80 percent. The government saved about $250 million a year on the drugs and also on hospital care for untreated patients. Government labs, researching the composition of pharmaceutical company drugs to produce lower-cost generics locally, were threatened with a WTO dispute. UNCHR and WHO intervention on the grounds of human rights secured an outcome with the Health Ministry, negotiating price reductions of over 50 percent with the drug companies. Meanwhile, South Africa's Treatment Action Campaign (TAC), spearheading the struggle for affordable medicine for HIV-related illnesses (joined by *Médecins Sans Frontières* and Oxfam), helped to shame 39 pharmaceutical TNCs into settling a suit they brought against the South African government to stop its purchase of generic drugs from third parties (such as Brazil).

The typical antiretroviral AIDS drug cocktail costs US$10,000 to $15,000—fees well beyond the reach of a large proportion of HIV carriers in the global South. Large countries, such as India, Egypt, Thailand, Argentina, and Brazil, manufacture cheap generic drugs (around $600) to reduce public health costs, becoming targets for challenges by the big pharmaceutical companies, citing infringements of the TRIPs protocol's protection of patent rights. A loophole, allowing countries to manufacture or import generic drugs for national health emergencies and challenged for several years by the companies and the United States, was ratified by the WTO in August 2003. The recent Trans-Pacific Partnership (TPP) initiative revived the question of allowing big pharma to limit the sale of generic drugs and "maximize its monopolies."

In times of health crises—or indeed at any time—should intellectual property rights be used to subordinate public rights to corporate rights?

Sources: Ayittey (2002); Becker (2003: 14); Booth (1998); Boseley (2007); Central Intelligence Agency (2000); De Waal (2002: 23); Dugger (2007: 6); Elliott (2001: 12); Flynn (2002); Gevisser (2001: 5–6); Le Carre (2001: 13–13); *Médecins Sans Frontières* website: www.msf.org; Perlez (2001: A12); Stuart (2003: 21); Weisman (2015).

General Agreement on Trade in Services (GATS)

Services, unlike goods, are defined as "anything you cannot drop on your foot."[79] They include public and financial services. The 1994 GATS regime opened markets for trade in services by establishing the rights to corporate "presence" in member countries for the delivery of a service in the areas of finance, telecommunications, and transport. "GATS 2000" is a fundamentally more far-reaching protocol to compel governments to provide unlimited market access to foreign service providers, without regard for social and environmental impacts of the service activities. As Tony Clarke notes, GATS 2000 involves the following:

- Imposing severe constraints on the government's ability to protect environmental, health, consumer, and other public interest standards. A "necessity test" requires government proof that regulations on service provision are the "least trade restrictive," parallel with WTO rules on trade in goods.
- Restricting government funding of public works, municipal services, and social programs. Using WTO "national treatment" protocols on government procurement and subsidies, it would impede the role of government funds for public services, making them equally available to foreign-based private service corporations.
- The guaranteed access of private service corporations to domestic markets in all sectors, including health, education, and water, is accelerated by permitting commercial presence in GATS member countries.
- "Every service imaginable is on the table, including a wide range of public services in sectors that affect the environment, culture, energy and natural resources, plus drinking water, health care, K–12 education, post-secondary education, and social security; along with transportation services, postal delivery, prisons, libraries, and a variety of municipal services."[80]
- Finally, access provisions are more profound, applying to most government measures affecting trade in services, such as labor laws, consumer protection, subsidies, grants, licensing standards and qualifications, market access restrictions, economic needs tests, and local content provisions.

In other words, *GATS threatens the social contract between state and citizen with a private contract between corporation and consumer.* The democratic claims of the citizen-state (expressed in municipal contracts for construction, sewage, garbage disposal, sanitation, and water services) would yield to the private capacities of the consumer-citizen at the expense of the public interest and its development expressions. In this proposal, we see the elimination of all vestiges of the development-state and its replacement by corporate services globally.

CASE STUDY — Water, Water, Everywhere? Unless It's a Commodity . . .

When a service is commodified, it becomes the property of only those who can afford to buy it. Its availability on the market for some makes it scarce for others. Water is understood to be the last infrastructure frontier for private investors. Only 5 percent of water services are in private hands, and expansion opportunities are estimated at a trillion dollars. Water privatization is dominated by two French TNCs: Vivendi SA and Suez Lyonnaise des Eaux. Other TNCs involved include Bechtel, Enron, and General Electric. The GATS protocol favors privatization of this public good, and implementation is anticipated by a provision in NAFTA forbidding a country from discriminating in favor of its own firms in the commercial use of its water resources. Meanwhile, the IMF and the World Bank demand privatization of water services as a funding condition.

A case in point is Ghana, where an IMF loan tranche in 2002 was only released on condition that the government required "full cost recovery" in all public utilities, including water. Vivendi, Suez, and Saur of France and Biwater of Britain used this condition to cherry-pick lucrative contracts, leaving sewerage, sanitation, urban poor, and rural water provision for local authorities and communities. While the national budget is downsized to save money for loan repayment, a public service disappears, and water prices go through the roof. Sammy quotes one community member, exclaiming,

> The rain does not fall only on the roofs of Vivendi, Suez, Saur and Biwater, neither does it fall only on the roofs of the World Bank and the IMF; it falls on everyone's roof. Why are they so greedy?

Should the availability and distribution of a basic and precious resource such as water or food be governed by market forces, which tend to favor only those with purchasing power and compromise human rights?

Sources: www.corpwatchindia.org/issues/PID.jsp?articleid=1603; Amenga-Etego (2003: 20–21); Barlow (1999: 2, 7, 14, 18, 27, 33, 38); Godrej (2003: 12); Sammy (2004: 20); Vidal (2003: 24).

The strategy used by the proponents of GATS 2000 is, to term it appealingly, a *trade agreement*, and it demands openness to "cross-border" provision of services (by TNCs) as a condition for opening EU and US markets in garments, textiles, and agricultural products.[81] Oxfam's Kevin Watkins notes that this is a replay of the Uruguay Round, when the global North offered to open its markets in return for protection of TNC patents (which cost the global South $40 billion in increased technology costs) and suggests that, while the game has changed, the rules are the same: "The West buys your bananas and shirts if you give its banks and insurance companies unrestricted access to your markets."[82] GATS advocates argue that the conversion of public entities into privately owned, profit-making concerns eliminates bureaucratic inefficiency and government debt, providing superior services on a user-pays basis.

WHAT ARE THE INGREDIENTS OF THE GLOBALIZATION PROJECT?

The globalization project combines several strands:

- a (Washington-based) consensus among global managers/policymakers favoring market-based rather than state-managed development strategies;
- centralized management of global market rules by the G7 states;
- implementation of these rules through multilateral agencies (World Bank, IMF, and WTO);
- concentration of market power in the hands of TNCs and financial power in TNBs;
- subjection of all states to economic disciplines (trade, financial), varying by geopolitical position, position in global currency hierarchy, debt load, resource endowments, and so forth;
- realization of global development via new class, gender, race, and ethnic inequalities; and
- resistance at all levels, from marginalized communities to state managers to factions even within multilateral institutions, contesting unbridled market rule.

SUMMARY

The development project incubated an economic nationalism that became increasingly limiting to TNCs. At the same time, a rising debt crisis enabled new direction in world ordering via the debt regime. The new direction was the globalization project, an alternative way of organizing economic growth, corresponding to the growing scale and power of the transnational banks and corporations. The increasing volume of economic exchanges and the greater mobility of money and firms required forms of regulation beyond the reach of the nation-state even if imposed through the system of nation-states. The WTO represents one such form of interstate-system regulation.

The new global regulatory system subordinated states' social protections to liberalization. Overall, despite differences among states, they became surrogate managers of the global economy (or "market states"). The standardized prescriptions for liberalization reorganize regions and locales: from the removal of Mexican *campesinos* from long-held public lands to the rapid dismantling of public ownership of the economies of Eastern Europe to the proliferation of export processing zones and agro-export platforms. Many of these mushrooming export sites suffer the instability of flexible strategies of "footloose" firms as they pick and choose their way among global sourcing sites, enlarging their market reach and reducing their costs. Social protections decline as communities lose their resource bases (declining social subsidies, dwindling forests) or their employment bases (as firms downsize or move offshore).

Under these conditions, globalization is everything but universalist in its consequences. It assigns communities, regions, and nation-states new niches or specialized roles (including marginalization) in the global economy. The development project proposed social integration through national economic growth under individual state supervision and according to a social contract between government and citizenry. Alternatively, the globalization project offers new forms of authority and discipline governed by the market.

FURTHER READING

George, Susan. *The Debt Boomerang: How Third World Debt Harms Us All*. Boulder, CO: Westview Press, 1992.

Mgbeoji, Ikechi. *Global Biopiracy: Patents, Plants, and Indigenous Knowledge*. Ithaca, NY: Cornell University Press, 2006.

Payne, Anthony. *The Global Politics of Unequal Development*. New York: Palgrave Macmillan, 2005.

Rosset, Peter M. *Food Is Different: Why We Must Get the WTO Out of Agriculture*. Halifax, NS: Fernwood, 2006.

Soederberg, Susanne. *Global Governance in Question: Empire, Class, and the New Common Sense in Managing North–South Relations*. London: Pluto, 2006.

Wallach, Lori, and Patrick Woodall, eds. *Whose Trade Organization? A Comprehensive Guide to the WTO*. London: New Press, 2004.

Woods, Ngaire. *The Globalizers: The IMF, the World Bank and Their Borrowers*. Ithaca, NY: Cornell University Press, 2006.

SELECT WEBSITES

Bretton Woods Project (USA): www.brettonwoodsproject.org
International Forum on Globalization (USA): www.ifg.org
Millennium Development Goals (MDGs): www.un.org/millenniumgoals
Public Citizen Global Trade Watch (USA): www.citizen.org/trade
Structural Adjustment Participatory Review International Network: www.saprin.org
UN Capital Development Fund: www.uncdf.org
World Health Organization (WHO): www.who.int/en
World Trade Organization (WTO): www.wto.org

6

The Globalization
Project in Practice

The globalization project in practice has been about deepening market reach and disciplines and managing the inevitable fallout across an uneven world. At the turn of the twenty-first century, the United Nations reported that the richest 20 percent of the world's population enjoyed 30 times the income of the poorest 20 percent in 1960, but by 1997, the difference was of the order of 74.[1] The exacerbation of global inequality via market integration made *legitimacy management* a priority for the development establishment to justify staying the course with liberalization and the corporate agenda.

Food riots, poverty stabilization schemes, and a dramatic uprising in the Chiapas province of southern Mexico underscored the 1994 statement by the Inter-American Development Bank (IDB) on the eve of the World Trade Organization (WTO)'s formation: "The resumption of economic growth has been bought at a very high social price, which includes poverty, increased unemployment, and income inequality, and this is leading to social problems."[2] One telling example is that of the Indian growth "miracle," where two-thirds of the poorest fifth of Indian children nevertheless remained underweight in 2009, just as in 1995.[3] Then in 1999, the WTO Seattle Ministerial registered a threshold in "antiglobalization" protest, as a variety of social justice movements from across the world blocked the proceedings, giving voice to a widespread discontent with the neoliberal model of global development. The following year, the United Nations offered the world "globalization with a human face" in the **Millennium Development Goals (MDGs)**, dedicated to

147

addressing the key challenges of the new century: persistent poverty, pandemic disease, environmental damage, gender inequality, and southern debt. And all this occurred during an explosion of the "fast world," driven by the Internet boom, corporate mergers, and healthy-looking national accounts, as rates of foreign investment and trade ballooned. As we shall see in Chapter 8, this economic expansion did not last.

The globalization project has two faces: the face of unprecedented prosperity for the world's minority of investors and consumers; and the face of poverty, displacement, job and food insecurity, health crises (AIDS), and a widening band of informal activity (over one billion slumdwellers) as people make do in lieu of stable jobs, government supports, and sustainable habitats. *This paradox is the subject matter of this chapter.*

Here, we consider some key practices of globalization as a project. These are poverty governance, outsourcing, displacement, informalization, and recolonization. They provide part of the stimulus to the global countermovements to be examined in Chapter 8.

Poverty Governance

Consistent with the projectlike nature of global development, the World Bank and International Monetary Fund (IMF) have played a central role in global governance. This takes the form of "market rule" (where states are enjoined to serve the market). Structural adjustment policies (SAPs) spawned in the 1980s preceded the universal adoption of liberalization policies through the WTO from the mid-1990s. But the international financial institutions (IFIs), recognizing that SAPs increased the poor's vulnerability (and eroded IFI legitimacy), were compelled to create a Social Emergency Fund (World Bank) and a new Compensatory and Contingency Financing Facility (IMF) in 1988 to target those who fell through the cracks. In the 1990s, the IFIs created "humanizing" global policies, starting with the Heavily Indebted Poor Countries (HIPC) Initiative of 1996, to provide exceptional assistance to countries with unsustainable debt burdens. The IFIs' goal was to stave off a legitimacy crisis by elaborating "governance" mechanisms that continue to this day, as poverty elimination remains unfulfilled. And legitimacy is crucial since both institutions depend increasingly on loan repayment by borrowing countries to bankroll their operations, as northern countries have significantly reduced their contributions.

Securing legitimacy involved "democratizing" SAPs, encouraging countries and nongovernmental organizations (NGOs) to take "ownership" of policy formation and implementation. By 1999, an enhanced HIPC was created with African debtor states in mind, defining "conditionality" by a broad, participatory poverty reduction strategy.[4] The Bank director spoke of a "civil society revolution," basing development on "inclusion and participation, bringing together civil society, local competition, NGOs, the private sector, and the poor themselves . . . in order to foster trust and sustainability."[5] In this context, the World Bank commissioned a *Voices of the Poor* project by gathering testimony from 60,000 poor women and men in 50 countries, who overall expressed deep dissatisfaction with government corruption and a preference for World Bank involvement—although participating researchers suggested this was largely a legitimacy exercise.[6] While this exercise was underway, the hard truth was that from 1996 to 1999, HIPC-eligible country debt had quadrupled—from $59 billion to $205 billion—mobilizing northern activists, in particular the Jubilee 2000 organization dedicated to debt forgiveness.[7]

Under these controversial circumstances, the IFIs, still committed to debt repayment, repackaged neoliberal policies in participatory rhetoric and incorporated NGO leaders into the World Bank's networks. Unpopular SAPs were refashioned as "partnerships," with states required to author their own development plans, subject to IFI approval, on which loans, debt rescheduling, and debt forgiveness can be made. These plans, known as **Poverty Reduction Strategy Papers (PRSPs)**, are compiled as "performances" in order "to meet the charge that imposing conditions is undemocratic, the IFIs now insist that other stakeholders, such as NGOs, churches, unions, and business, rather than just governments, are involved in writing the plans."[8] The PRSPs are a form of crisis management, marking a new phase of IFI management of the global South. The Bank's initial Bretton Woods focus on *project* loans for public infrastructure shifted to *policy* loans geared to structural adjustment in the global South during the 1980s, as market reforms redefined IFI development philosophy. Now PRSPs focus on new *process* conditions.[9]

The World Bank and the IMF characterized the PRSP program in 2002 as "a new approach to the challenge of reducing poverty in low-income countries based on country-owned poverty reduction strategies."[10] These procedures, in holding states accountable for poverty reduction, embed public priorities in market relationships—in effect fashioning "governance states."[11] Here, private commercial law adopted as public policy at the national level embraces WTO prescriptions for countries to "trade themselves out of poverty." At the global level, the project of poverty reduction— paralleling the 2000 MDGs—entails policy coordination between the WTO, the IMF, and the World Bank.[12]

Poverty governance also involves coordinating international NGOs with access to information and resources, enabling them to leverage initiatives within states. Thus World Vision International and *Médicins sans Frontières* are pervasive in Africa today, organizing local schools and clinics in lieu of failed states, respectively.[13] As Oxfam, for example, observes, "PRSPs offer Oxfam and other NGOs major opportunities to influence policy and practice at local, national, and international levels, both at the formulation and implementation stage."[14] The privatization of states is also shaped by transnational policy networks (TPNs)—in Africa through the African Policy Institutes Forum, created by the World Bank to serve as professional training program centers and serving as sites for preparation of PRSPs.[15] Privatization no longer means simply selling off public assets, but integrating states into TPNs as global market intermediaries—with the IFIs and the international NGO community acting as "surrogate representative(s) of . . . civil society in the state–donor partnership."[16]

Promoting market access substantially reconstructs the state–civil society relation. Here, public authority serves market principles, where IFI "budget monitoring" secures conditionality, establishing "a surveillance architecture capable of disciplining democracy"[17]—that is, policy is driven by a financial rather than a social/civic logic. Further, instead of states being responsible for social safety nets, surveillance includes providing microloans through NGO intermediaries to the poor.[18] The rationale is that microlending will redirect existing survival networks, viewed by the World Bank as "social capital," into entrepreneurial activities.[19] Poverty governance enhances institutional legitimacy at the same time it subjects societies to the market calculus and erodes the social contract. This has been the central impact of the neoliberal globalization project.

Outsourcing

Outsourcing relocates the production of goods and services as a cost-reduction strategy and a means to increase operational flexibility of an organization. It includes offshoring, as firms shift production overseas.[20] Outsourcing has become significant for two reasons: (1) the hypermobility of capital in an era of deregulation and expanding access to cheap/flexible labor and (2) the privatization of states. Under neoliberalism, in addition to corporate outsourcing, governments outsource service contracts to reduce public expenditure and/or privilege the private sector. GATS and IFIs promote such outsourcing, often with the effect of transferring monopoly power over the management of utilities to corporations and outsourcing "governance" functions to NGOs, sometimes at the expense of the underprivileged.

Thus, when the South African government outsourced Telkom, the state telephone company, in 2003, it completed the privatization of this essential service, which already had increased tariffs for poor households while slashing rates for rich families and firms, and cut 80 percent of new land lines because of the inability of poor subscribers to pay.[21] Meanwhile, in health care, the World Bank has made loans to outsource public health to private managed care initiatives in the name of reducing public sector inefficiencies. In Latin America, TNCs such as Aetna, CIGNA, the American International Group (AIG), and Prudential have invested heavily in Argentina, Chile, Brazil, and Ecuador. As a result, neoliberal policy brings about these three characteristic effects:

1. Access to health care for the poor shrinks while investments grow—"between 1996 and 1999, revenues of multinational health care corporations grew much faster in Latin America than in the United States."
2. Outsourcing and cutbacks in public sector budgets reduce preventative programs, allowing banished diseases such as cholera, dengue fever, and typhus to reemerge as epidemics.
3. As has happened in a dozen states in the United States, after profiting through the privatization of public health care systems, managed care organizations and health insurance companies move on when profit margins fall.[22]

Corporate outsourcing has become virtually synonymous with globalization. We have seen how the "world factory" emerged on a foundation of the new international division of labor (NIDL), as a forerunner of the era of global integration. This pattern, amplified by trade-related aspects of investment measures (TRIMs), has consolidated as the **"global division of labor,"** now extending to high- and low-paid services and perishable agricultural commodities. Outsourcing of production has depended on the deepening of information and communication technologies (ICTs), especially microprocessing power and developments in fiber optics—for example, "e-mailing a 40-page document from Chile to Kenya costs less than 10 cents, faxing it about $10 and sending it by courier $50." By the twenty-first century, "more information was sent over a single cable in a second than over the entire Internet in a month in 1997."[23] This compression of space by time enhances the ability of firms to manage far-flung and fragmented outsourcing operations—coordinating movement of components through the supply chain and of foods shipped across seasonal and time zones.

On top of a steady movement offshore of manufacturing jobs from the 1970s, *service jobs* began migrating from North to South in the 1990s. For instance, between 1996 and 2000, US corporate outsourcing grew from $100 billion to $345 billion, concentrating in call centers, graphic design, computer programming, and accountancy.[24] Many of the new jobs in the Caribbean, for example, are data processing positions that large US insurance, health industry, magazine subscription renewal, consumer credit, and retailing firms have shifted offshore at a lower cost. Swissair, British Airways, and Lufthansa relocated much of their reservations operations to Indian subcontractors in Bangalore, where "the staff are well educated at English-speaking universities, yet cost only a fraction of what their counterparts are paid in the North." Swissair claims, "We can hire three Indians for the price of one Swiss." The relocation of revenue accounts preparation saved eight million francs and 120 jobs in Zurich. Eastern Europe has become an increasingly competitive site for labor-intensive computer programming, as well as "virtual sweatshops" where Romanians provide computer gaming services for wealthy Western players.[25] The Delhi telecomputing firm Selectronic receives doctors' dictation from a US toll-free number, transcribing and transmitting transcriptions as texts to an American HMO, while America Online employs 600 Filipinos to answer over 10,000 technical and billing inquiries per day, mainly from the United States (80 percent of AOL's customer e-mail)—paying its customer service representatives a daily rate equivalent to an hour's pay for an unskilled American worker. With outsourcing upgrades in India into product research and development, financial analysis, and handling insurance claims and payrolls, call center employee wages increased by 50 percent, providing an opportunity for the Philippines, where call center jobs rose 100 percent over five years to 200,000 in late 2006.[26] India now outsources outsourcing in order to capture an expanding back-office industry as Indian wages rise, and China, Morocco, and Mexico challenge India's successful model. Tata Consultancy Service has offices in Mexico, Brazil, Chile, and Uruguay. Cognizant Technology Solutions is in Phoenix and Shanghai, and Infosys even subcontracts outsourcing to the Philippines, Thailand, Poland, China, and Mexico.[27]

Information technology (IT) services have expanded in India at a rate of between 30 and 60 percent annually (contributing to 60 percent of Indian GDP now), with new frontiers of "virtual services" beyond customer service centers beckoning to TNCs—"health care, where a scan may be carried out in one country, processed in another, and sent to a third for another opinion before being sent back home again, is one example."[28] The economics profession may be another mobile "virtual service." Thomas Friedman refers to this as the "democratization of technology," a conceptual forerunner of his "flat world," implying that technological capability enables the South to participate on a leveled global playing field.

Barbados, with a literacy rate of 98 percent and a reputation for order and polite service, used its English-speaking tradition to turn itself into a haven for offshore information-based data processing work, globally sourced by subsidiaries of British and US telecommunication corporations. On a typical shift, between about 50 and 100 Barbadian women sit in partitioned computer cubicles of a given production floor from 7:30 a.m. until 3:30 p.m., taking a half-hour break for lunch and sometimes a 15-minute stretch in between. Their keystrokes per hour are monitored electronically as they enter data from airline ticket stubs, consumer warranty cards, or the text of a potboiler novel for top US airlines, appliance houses, and publishers.

While such work is unskilled and gendered, Carla Freeman found that, despite better pay in the sugar cane fields, these women find "pink-collar" jobs attractive because of the identification with office work and informatics technology, because the Barbados Development Plan—development via information-based exports—includes guarantees of basic employment benefits such as maternity and sick leave and paid vacations, and because differentiation from field and factory work through dress codes and consumption styles enables them to "experience class as gendered Afro-Caribbean subjects within a distinctly feminized arena."[29]

India, in particular, is "blessed" with an English-speaking tradition, and, as with parts of the Caribbean, South Africa, Pakistan, and the Philippines, language has become a "comparative advantage" for this kind of service outsourcing. At the Spectramind call center in Delhi, in addition to a two-hour seminar on the royal family, one set of "recruits receive a 20-hour crash course in British culture. They watch videos of British soap operas to accustom them to regional accents. They learn about Yorkshire pudding. And they are taught about Britain's unfailingly miserable climate." Another set of recruits, exposed to American TV shows and sporting slang, are "trained in the nuances of baseball, and Blue 'Tennessee Titans' pennants fly above their desks."[30]

Following liberalization in 1991, foreign corporations established subsidiaries in India to outsource jobs in IT, financial services, business processes, pharmaceuticals, and automotive components, generating thousands of new jobs and annual rates of growth that are twice those in the North. Bangalore, Hyderabad, Delhi, and Mumbai displayed their newfound wealth as emerging "global cities."[31] While one-third of Bangalore's population are slumdwellers, half "lack piped water, much less cappuccino, and there are more ragpickers and street children (90,000) than software geeks (about 60,000)."[32] Not only are two-thirds of the populace (230 million) still residing in publicly neglected and deteriorating rural habitats, but the IT sector generates less than 2 percent of national income and employs one million in an economy where eight million join the labor force annually.[33] Outsourcing generates clusters of prosperity networked more often across national borders than within them.

Rural land appropriation for outsourcing industries is routine (though not without resistance). In China in Dongguan City (site of Reebok and Nike shoe manufacturers), local farmers now live off factory rents while tens of thousands of migrants from the hinterland swell the workforce.[34] Datang, a rice-farming village in the late 1970s, with a cottage industry in socks, now produces nine billion socks annually:

> Signs of Datang's rise as a socks capital are everywhere. The center of town is filled with a huge government-financed marketplace for socks. The rice paddies have given way to rows of paved streets lined with cookie-cutter factories. Banners promoting socks are draped across buildings.[35]

Renamed "Socks City," Datang is one of many new coastal cities: southeast is Shenzhou, the world's necktie capital; west is Sweater City and Kids' Clothing City; and to the south, in the low-rent district, is Underwear City.[36] In one of these cities, *China Blue* (2006) was filmed in a blue jeans factory—portraying the manufacturer's reliance on labor of teenage girls fresh from the rural hinterland. With an ethnographic approach, the film documents how pressures to cut costs are passed down from the English buyer through the factory owner to his vulnerable workforce, who are also forced to work shifts lasting sometimes more than 40 hours to meet "just in time" orders. Buyers, under pressure to ensure ethical brands, send inspectors who focus on product quality and turn a blind eye to the duplicate time cards and employee coaching organized by factory owners.

The global supermarket revolution is founded on an outsourcing model of "buyer-driven commodity chains," linking contract farmers with centralized food processing and retailing operations.[37] Transnational firms such as Ahold, Carrefour, and Walmart comprise 70 to 80 percent of the top five supermarket chains in Latin America, centralizing procurement from farmers across the region (and their own processing plants) and, together with Nestlé and Quaker, supplying regional consumer markets throughout the Mercosur trading bloc in the eastern part of Latin America. In Guatemala, where supermarkets control 35 percent of food retailing, "their sudden appearance has brought unanticipated and daunting challenges to millions of struggling, small farmers," lacking binding contractual agreements, rewarded only if they consistently meet new quality standards, and facing declining prices as they constitute a virtually unlimited source for retailers.[38]

"Standards" are critical to the outsourcing revolution, especially with perishables. WTO regulation of trade relations is complemented by extensive private regulation of production standards regarding quality, safety, packaging, and convenience. The new "audit culture" generates certification schemes such as GlobalGAP (Good Agricultural Practices), an association of European supermarket chains concerned with regulating quality, safety, environment, and labor standards (in crop, livestock, and aquaculture production), surpassing publicly required standards.[39] Risk management encourages production consolidation—UK supermarkets are doing this to reduce their exposure to risk by expanding control over production and distribution.[40] In Kenya, where about 90 percent of horticulture is destined for Europe (especially the United Kingdom), the shift from smallholder-contract production to centralized employment on estates and in packing houses in the mid-1990s has in turn transformed farming women into a migrant labor force, as a household survival strategy.[41] Likewise, in Brazil's São Francisco Valley, "new agricultural districts" exporting mangoes, grapes, tomatoes, and acerola must meet specific quality controls and design, as well as setting parameters for labor and environmental conditions.[42]

Global Labor-Sourcing Politics

While outsourcing is typically associated with firms "going global," there are growing migrant circuits across the world contributing to the sourcing of labor on a global scale and serving all facets of industry (manufacturing, agriculture, and services). Ironically, as northern manufacturing has moved offshore, southern labor has found its way north in the form of farmworkers and food workers. In Europe, the "great turnaround" describes the reversal of patterns of migration, where southern European states formerly supplied migrant labor to industrialized centers of northern Europe, but now southern Europe is the destination for inflows of North African migrant labor, where a growing proportion of farm labor in Italy is foreign.[43] In the United States, by contrast, 70 percent of farmworkers are foreign, mostly from Mexico (and southern Mexico now hosts migrant labor from neighboring Guatemala). Migrant labor conditions are always precarious because of issues of documentation, exploitation, racism, sexism, and employment uncertainty (not to mention separation from family and community back home).

A landmark case of pushback against such precarious conditions was the 2014 success of the Coalition of Immokalee Workers in the tomato fields of Florida, which produces 90 percent of US winter tomatoes. After decades of abusive practices (e.g., 95-degree heat, no rest breaks for women, crew leader abuses including sexual predation, poverty wages), the Coalition developed partnerships with fast-food companies (McDonalds, Taco Bell, Pizza Hut, KFC, and eventually Walmart) to buy only from growers who increased wages (for 30,000 workers) and followed strict standards, mandating rest breaks and the end of sexual harassment and verbal abuse. It is expected that such standards may spread to other farm states. Meanwhile, this single case is underscored by the fact that Immokalee, "30 miles inland from several wealthy Gulf resorts, is a town of taco joints and backyard chicken coops where many farmworkers still live in rotting shacks or dilapidated, rat-infested trailers."[44]

Outsourcing not only allows global firms and employers to access new forces of labor from southern (and eastern European) regions characterized by new workers leaving the land and/or weak labor laws, but it also weakens traditional blue-collar industries (textiles, automobiles, household appliances) in the global North as jobs disappear, threatening remaining northern workers with capital flight. By 2002, the new working class of China was twice the size of industrial labor in all G7 countries together, attracting corporate investment from all parts of the global North.[45] The microelectronics revolution has become the new industrial core (including transforming all other production systems with the semiconductor)—its labor force centered in a new (and distinctly feminized) labor force in the South. Sociologist Beverley Silver notes, "As a result of these combined processes, the mass-production industrial proletariat has continued to grow rapidly in size and centrality in many lower-wage countries," arguing that the geographical relocation of production, from North to South, "has not created a simple race to the bottom" as labor movements (particularly in the NICs) have nonetheless played a key role in politicizing working conditions and in political democracy movements.[46] China in particular has seen more frequent strikes (often localized), rising wages, and government legislation in the form of a Labour Contract Law (2008)—which has increased job security for some migrant and other low-wage workers, as well as expanding social insurance schemes—presaging an extension of the rule of law to China's labor market.[47]

Meanwhile, an incipient labor internationalism has emerged to present a combined front to global and/or footloose firms that divide labor forces across national borders and to states that sign antilabor free trade agreements (FTAs). NAFTA politics in the 1990s provided a model example of cross-border unionism to protect labor on either side. It was in the interest of American labor to support Mexican labor rights in order to reduce the recursive effect of job loss to Mexico in search of cheaper labor. The American Federation of Labor and Congress of Industrial Organizations (AFL-CIO) sought alliances with independent Mexican (and Central American) unions, including supporting independent labor organizing in the *maquiladoras*.[48]

Sociologist Peter Evans calls this outcome "reverse whipsawing," whereby solidarity networks allow stronger labor organizations to champion the rights of weaker ones as pushback against exploitative firms. A case in point was a mobilization in 2010, led by apparel organizers from the Honduran Central General de Trabajadores (CGT) and supported by a cross-regional network of labor NGOs and US unions, to organize the Honduran *maquila* industry for living wages by forcing US-based Russell Athletics to negotiate a contract. Recent attacks on national labor in the North have stimulated interest in cross-border alliances, and southern labor movements, confronted with TNCs, are complementing these alliances where they are enabled by national political conditions, with Brazilian labor in the forefront. These alliances adopt European models of Global Union Federations (GUFs) and develop global framework agreements as instruments of global governance—labor-style—to address conditions in factories, mines, and plantations across the world.[49]

This development mirrors movements elsewhere in the global South where independent unions respond to global integration. For instance, the Transnationals Information Exchange (TIE) forged networks of labor organization across the world, targeting the production of the "world car," and formed the Cocoa-Chocolate Network, based on the global commodity chain, whereby TIE linked European industrial workers with Asian and Latin American plantation workers and peasants, linking chocolate factories to the cacao bean fields. Communication technologies enable such organization, encouraging alliance building via NGOs joining with labor organizations to mobilize consumers around fair-trade and production norms.[50]

The idea of **fair trade** paralleled the intensification of global integration, with aid agencies sponsoring links between craftspeople from the global South and northern consumers with a taste for "ethnic" products. Fair trade has now blossomed as a method of transcending abuses in the free trade system and rendering more visible the conditions of production of globally traded commodities to establish just prices, environmentally sound practices, healthy consumption, and direct understanding between producers and consumers of their respective needs. Fair-trade exchanges have an annual market value of $400 million, and the market for fair-trade products (organic products such as coffee, bananas, cocoa, honey, tea, and orange juice—representing about 60 percent of the fair-trade market, alongside organic cotton jeans and an array of handicrafts) expands at between 10 and 25 percent a year. Three fair-trade labels—Transfair, Max Havelaar, and Fairtrade Mark—broke into European markets in the late 1980s and are now united under the Fairtrade Labelling Organizations International (FLO), an umbrella NGO that harmonizes different standards and organizes a single fair-trade market (in the absence of national regulations). Producing communities must undergo certification, requiring democratic representation of producers and/or workers, with labor conditions upholding basic ILO conventions regarding labor rights. Above-world market prices are guaranteed. In Costa Rica, for instance, a cooperative (Coopetrabasur) achieved Fairtrade registration to supply bananas and in so doing eliminated herbicide use, reduced chemical fertilizers, built democratic union procedures, raised wages, and established a "social premium" set aside for community projects such as housing improvement, electrification, and environmental monitoring.[51]

Displacement

In the shadow of globalization lurks a rising dilemma: the casualization of labor and the redundancy of people.[52] Despite, and perhaps because of, an expanding global economy, numbers of unemployed (including hard-to-count long-term unemployed) in the global North rose from 10 million to almost 50 million between 1973 and the early twenty-first century.[53] This is the dilemma of structural unemployment, where automation and/or outsourcing of work sheds stable jobs and where redundant workers cease rotating into new jobs. It is matched across the world by other forms of displacement, including SAP-mandated dismantling of ISI sectors and privatization of public enterprise, forced resettlement by infrastructural projects (e.g., 1.2 million peasants resettled in China's Three Gorges Dam project),[54] civil wars, and the destabilization of rural communities by market forces (dumping of cheap food, land concentration, and decline of farm subsidies). At the turn of the twenty-first century, one billion workers (one-third of the world's labor force, mainly southern) were either unemployed or underemployed.[55]

Displacement begins with depeasantization, even though agriculture is the main source of food and income for the majority of the world's poor. While about 3.4 billion people across the world directly depend on the agricultural sector, more than half of the South's population is agrarian, rising to 85 percent in some of the poorest countries. The UN Food and Agriculture Organization (FAO) notes the following:

> Agriculture is also of great social, cultural, and environmental significance for rural communities. It tends to be particularly important for women, who have the main responsibilities for feeding their families and are estimated to produce 60–80% of food grown in most developing countries.[56]

Long-term food security depends on diversity of crop species, in contrast to industrial agriculture's dependence on 15 crop species for 90 percent of its food calories;[57] nevertheless, the subordination of agriculture everywhere to agribusiness and global retailing is steadily driving peasants into an exploding global slum in an era characterized by "jobless growth."

As we saw in Chapter 5, the neoliberal vision of food security means privileging food importing over local farming for many southern states. Meanwhile the transnational peasant coalition *Vía Campesina* notes, "The massive movement of food around the world is forcing the increased movement of people."[58] Under the WTO's Agreement on Agriculture (AoA), decoupling of (northern) subsidies from prices removes the price floor, establishing a *low* "world price" for agricultural commodities and undercutting small/family farmers everywhere, which results in displacement.

Liberalization policies are rooted in IMF–World Bank structural adjustment measures, which have routinely required "free markets" in grain—for example, in formerly self-sufficient countries such as Malawi, Zimbabwe, Kenya, Rwanda, and Somalia. Following a decade of neoliberalism in India, its Ministry of Agriculture stated in 2000, "The growth in agriculture has slackened during the 1990s. Agriculture has become a relatively unrewarding profession due to an unfavorable price regime and low value addition, causing abandoning of farming and migration from rural areas."[59]

Global economic integration intensifies displacement as the global economy stratifies populations across, rather than simply within, national borders. At the same time, failing states, war, and persecution have expelled 60 million people, half of whom are children.[60] With provocative imagery, in 1991 Jacques Attali distinguished *rich nomads* ("consumer-citizens of the privileged regions") from *poor nomads* ("boat people on a planetary scale"):

> With no future of their own in an age of air travel and telecommunications, the terminally impoverished will look for one in the North. . . . The movement of peoples has already begun; only the scale will grow: Turks in Berlin, Moroccans in Madrid, Indians in London, Mexicans in Los Angeles, Puerto Ricans and Haitians in New York, Vietnamese in Hong Kong.[61]

Such fears founded in latent stereotypes, as well as fears of associations with terrorism, underlie the concern of global elites and many northern consumer-citizens to stem the tide of global labor migration. Consequences range from the spread of "gated communities" to a rollback of civil rights in the global North and outbreaks of racist violence toward "guest workers." This attitude has spread in Europe, where millions of "illegal" migrants (from Eastern Europe, Turkey, Central Asia, China, and Francophone West Africa) work in restaurants, construction, and farming—they "enjoy none of the workers' rights and protections or social benefits of the state . . . are paid less than the legal wage, and are often paid late, with no legal recourse." Advocates argue that legalizing the status of the "*sans papiers*" would reduce xenophobia.[62]

In the global North, continuing immigration is in the interests of firms that need cheap labor and of the privileged who require servants. But such organized migration has led to the *displacement of love* via the feminization and export of care workers from the South to care for children of working women in the North; it has been termed the *global heart transplant* and linked to the "care drain" from the South via "chains of love," whereby migrant women work as "global nannies" at considerable emotional cost to their own children, who in turn are cared for by relatives or teenage girls at home.[63]

MIGRANT LABOR IN THE GLOBAL ECONOMY: ECONOMIC AND ENVIRONMENTAL REFUGEES

As the twenty-first century proceeds, as many as 232 million people are estimated to be living as expatriate laborers around the world. Asian women are the fastest growing group of foreign workers, increasing by about one million each year.

Environmental migration is increasingly significant, with reports that one billion people could be displaced by climate change by 2050:

- 135 million people whose land is being transformed into deserts (desertification);
- 900 million of the world's poorest, existing on less than a dollar a day and living in areas vulnerable to soil erosion, droughts, desertification, and floods;
- 200 million people facing rising sea levels due to climate change;
- 50 million people in famine-vulnerable areas subject to climate change; and
- 550 million people already suffering from chronic water shortage.

Sources: Baird (2002: 10); Boyd (1998: 17); Perrons (2005: 211); Swing (2015); Vidal (2007a).

Labor: The New Export

The mobility rights for capital guaranteed by neoliberalism do not extend to labor. Nevertheless, labor increasingly circulates, seeking employment opportunities—whether "legal," "illegal," or slave/bonded labor. Migration is not new to this century. The separation of people from the land is etched into the making of the modern world. Colonialism propelled migrations of free and unfree people. Between 1810 and 1921, 34 million people, mainly Europeans, emigrated to the United States alone. The difference today is the feminization of global migration: 75 percent of refugees and displaced persons are women and children.[64]

During the 1980s, spurred by debt regime restructurings, there was an internal migration in the former Third World of between 300 and 400 million people.[65] This pool of labor has contributed to global migration from over-burdened cities to northern regions as migrants seek to earn money for families back home. In excess of 100 million kinfolk depend on remittances of the global labor force. In the 1990s, for example, two-thirds of Turkey's trade deficit was financed by remittances from Turks working abroad.[66] The World Bank estimated remittances to the South in 2009 of US$316 billion from some 192 million migrants—or 3 percent of the world population. In fact, in 2013 remittances were over three times larger than Overseas Development Assistance, as depicted in Figure 6.1. Estimates show those remittances rising to US$454 billion by 2015:

> For some individual recipient countries, remittances can be as high as a third of GDP. Remittances also now account for about a third of total global external finance; moreover, the flow of remittances seems to be significantly more stable than other forms of external finance.[67]

The influx of foreign exchange not only supplies much-needed hard currency, but in an era of structural adjustment and privatization, remittance money also supplements or subsidizes public ventures. Thus in Indonesian villages, remittances finance schools, roads, and housing in lieu of public funding. Migrants invested $6 million in new roads, schools, churches,

Figure 6.1   Remittance Flows Are Large and Growing

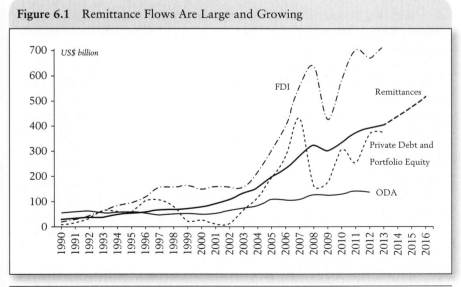

Source: World Bank. http://siteresources.worldbank.org/INTPROSPECTS/Resources/334934-1288990760745/MigrationandDevelopmentBrief23.pdf

water systems, and parks in Zacatecas, Mexico, and President Vicente Fox (2002) commented, "The families that receive the money use it to buy shoes or beans, clothes, or books for their children. Now we want to channel part of that money for production for projects that generate jobs," matching, peso for peso, money remitted by migrant workers for public works projects in their home communities.[68] Then there is Kerala, an exceptionally socially progressive state in southern India and recognized by the UN in 1975 as having an impressive record of health and education expenditure, with life expectancy and literacy rates considerably higher than the Indian average. The "Kerala model," with its social priorities trumping the market-driven development model, nevertheless depends for 25 percent of its revenues on remittances from its almost two million expatriate workers in the Persian Gulf.[69]

Spurred by debt, labor export has become a significant foreign currency earner: Filipino overseas earnings are estimated to amount to $5.7 billion, for example. About six million Filipinos—increasingly from rural areas—work overseas in 130 countries as contract workers (seamen, carpenters, masons, mechanics, or maids).[70] The government of the Philippines includes labor in its export-led development strategy.[71] In addition to products, labor is exported—mainly to the oil-rich Middle East, where contractors organize the ebb and flow of foreign labor. One contractor, Northwest Placement, a privately run recruiting agency, receives 5,000 pesos ($181)—the maximum allowed by the Labor Department—from Filipino applicants on assurance of a job; this covers the costs of a medical check, visas, and government clearance fees. Not surprisingly, there are also plenty of unlicensed agencies operating.[72]

International labor circulation combines formal policies with decidedly informal working conditions. Migrant workers routinely lack human rights. Workers in the Gulf States, for example, are indentured, with no civic rights, no choice of alternative jobs, and no recourse against poor employment conditions and low wages—which are determined by the income levels of the country of origin. Migrant workers must surrender their passports on arrival; they reportedly work 12 to 16 hours a day, seven days a week. Governments in the migrant workers' home countries in Asia, dependent on foreign currency earnings, are reportedly resigned to the exploitation of their nationals. International labor union organizations have been ineffectual, especially as Middle Eastern states have united to suppress discussion in international forums of working conditions inside their countries.[73]

Labor migrates from all over the world into the United States. The scale is such that immigrants retain their cultural and linguistic traditions rather than assimilate. The juxtaposition of distinct cultures in countries to which labor migrates creates a *multicultural* effect—not necessarily benign, as a New York City Labor Department Official noted: "In the underground economies of the ethnic enclaves of Vietnamese, Cuban, Dominican, Central American, and Chinese, it is a case of immigrants exploiting immigrants."[74] Neoliberal restructuring and rising economic uncertainty have amplified "ethnicism," including "nativism" in a backlash against immigration. US political discourse, for example, is polarized around the issue of undocumented Mexican workers, forgetting about the two million *campesinos* displaced by corn imports from the United States and withdrawal of rural credit under the terms of NAFTA.[75] The "race to the bottom" is not just about wage erosion; it is also about tensions regarding difference.

Informalization

The globalization project is Janus-faced. It exaggerates the market culture at the same time as it intensifies its opposite—a growing culture of informal, or marginal, activity. This culture involves people working on the fringes of the market, performing casual and unregulated (often outsourced) labor, working in cooperative arrangements, street vending, or pursuing what are deemed illegal economic activities. Those who are bypassed or marginalized by development often form a culture parallel to the market culture. The question of whether informal culture is a real alternative or simply an unrecognized or impoverished margin of the formal culture depends on the context. For example, revival of subsistence farming may improve living standards over working as a rural laborer or existing on the urban fringe, as long as land is available. Marginalization is closely associated with forms of displacement—for example, cycles of expansion and contraction of formal economic activity or the concentration of resources in fewer corporate hands generate informalization, producing the idea of a **"precariat"**: an unstable class of casual proletarians.[76]

Informalization is a politico–cultural process. With the rise of market societies, the boundaries of the formal economy were identified and regulated by the state for tax purposes, but they have always been incomplete and fluid, often by design and certainly by custom. An army of servants and housecleaners, for example, routinely works "off the books." Casual labor has always accompanied small-scale enterprise and even large-scale harvesting operations where labor use is cyclical. Also, a substantial portion of labor performed across the world every day is unpaid labor—such as house-work and family farm labor.

Distinguishing between a formal economy (with its legal/moral connotations) and an informal sector (with its illegal or immoral connotations) is either artificial or political. We make the distinction here as it reveals the limits of official, formal development strategy and identifies alternative, informal livelihood strategies—often intimately connected and mutually conditioning. Economists and governments make the distinction because national accounting measures legal cash transactions. By ignoring informal activity, development policy discounts and marginalizes substantial mechanisms of social reproduction, on which the formal "productive economy" depends. The consequences of this artificial distinction illuminate the crisis of structural adjustment, spotlighting the gendered foundations of material life. Bharati Sadasivam notes that the language of SAPs focuses

> overwhelmingly on the "productive economy," on making profits and covering costs. In the process, it takes for granted the "reproductive economy," which meets needs and sustains human beings. Macro models of mainstream economics assume that the process of reproduction and the maintenance of human resources will continue regardless of the way resources are reallocated. These models conceal the large contribution to the economy provided by the production and maintenance of the labor supply through childbirth and child-care, shopping, cooking, and housework. Economic reforms such as structural adjustment policies that call for cutbacks in state services and the free play of market forces fail to consider how such changes affect the relation between the "productive economy" and the "reproductive economy." Because the latter is sustained by unpaid nonmarket work mostly undertaken by women, macro-economics also assumes an unlimited supply of female labor.[77]

The "informal economy" comprises two related domains: forms of social reproduction complementing production (as above); and informal "productive" activity off the books. For example, one of the world's largest slums, Dharavi, has an "informal" output of $1.25 billion a year, largely from the work of 250,000 people recycling the discarded waste of Mumbai's 16 million citizens. Before celebrating such ingenious microentrepreneurship among Dharavi's one million slumdwellers, note the following:

> [Most] workshops are constructed illegally on government land, power is routinely stolen, and commercial licenses are rarely sought. There is just one lavatory for every 1,500 residents, not a single public hospital, and only a dozen municipal schools. Throughout the slum, chicken and mutton stalls dump viscera into open drains thick with human and industrial waste; cholera, typhoid, and malaria are common. Taps run dry most of the time.[78]

Slumdwellers now comprise *a third* of the global urban population, and 50 percent of the population of the global South. UN-Habitat, an agency for human settlement and sustainable urban development, estimates that the world's highest percentages of slumdwellers are in Ethiopia (99.4 percent of the urban population), Chad (99.4 percent), Afghanistan (98.5 percent), and Nepal (92 percent). Mumbai is the global slumdwellers' capital, with 10 to 12 million, Mexico City and Dhaka (9–10 million each), followed by Lagos, Cairo, Karachi, Kinshasa-Brazzaville, São Paulo, Shanghai, and Delhi (6–8 million each).[79]

In effect, neoliberal development and the generation of a "planet of slums" go together. Of course, these *peri-urban* communities, as they are known, have been expanding throughout the twentieth century, as the world's urban population surpassed that of the countryside in 2006:

> Cities will account for virtually all future world population growth, which is expected to peak at about 10 billion in 2050. Ninety-five percent of this final buildout of humanity will occur in the urban areas of developing countries. . . . Indeed, the combined urban population of China, India, and Brazil already roughly equals that of Europe and North America.[80]

With global integration, the lines are drawn even more clearly, on a larger scale, and possibly more rapidly. There are professional and managerial classes—the Fast World elite—who participate in global circuits (involved with products, money, electronic communications, high-speed transport) that link enclaves of producers/consumers across state borders. Many of these people increasingly live and work within corporate domains connected to the commercial and recreational centers, which are, in turn, delinked from national domains.[81] And there are those whom these circuits bypass or indeed displace. These are the redundant labor forces, the structurally unemployed, and the precariat, who live in shantytowns or urban ghettos or circulate the world.

Informalization as a process has two related *aspects:* the casualization of labor via corporate restructuring and new forms of individual and collective livelihood strategies. The distinctive feature of corporate globalization is the active informalization of labor cascading across the world, as it is flexible, cheap, and depresses wages everywhere. Beginning with export processing zones (EPZs), labor has been progressively *dis*organized via weakening and dismantling of labor regulations, incorporating vulnerable first-generation labor forces as depeasantization has proceeded. International Labour Organization (ILO) estimates show some variation in the percentage of informalization of nonagricultural employment: 48 percent in North Africa, 51 in Latin America, 65 in Asia, and 72 in sub-Saharan Africa.[82]

Figure 6.2   Growth of World's Largest Cities, 1950 and 2007

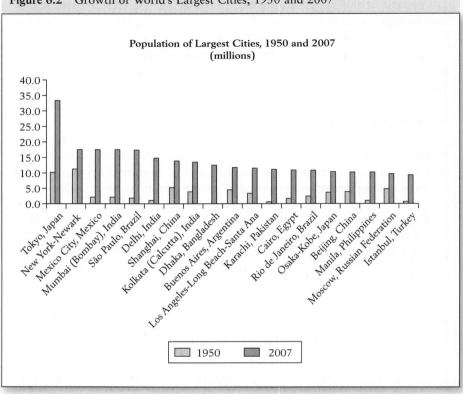

Source: Earth Policy Institute, 2008. Available at www.earth-policy.org.

China shows an interesting variation on labor informalization. Given the draconian agricultural tax system in China and an urban/rural differential greater than anywhere else, between 1996 and 2000 over 176 million peasants migrated to cities for work, but they went without the social benefits extended to urban residents. This itinerant labor force works mainly in newly zoned export factories and cost foreign corporations one-third the wage (itself a fraction of northern wage costs) of city-born workers. During this migration, the female percentage of informal workers rose from 45 percent to over 65 percent.[83] Li Quiang's study of Beijing migrants (2002) revealed that one quarter were unpaid, almost two-thirds worked over 10 hours a day—with a sizable percentage working over 16 hours a day (over and above rush order episodes)—and health care was nonexistent.[84]

Meanwhile, in export agriculture from the global South, millions of women, comprising between 50 and 90 percent of workers employed in producing, processing, and retailing high-value horticultural crops (roses, apples, snow peas, green beans, and avocados), experience informalization. TNCs organize these global supply chains, using their market power to pass business costs and risk on to suppliers, who in turn displace these onto their workforce. The ILO reports that rights violations of agricultural workers are "legion" and that women suffer weak labor rights, casualization, low wages, long hours, lax health and safety practices, gender stereotyping, and sexual harassment. Human rights violations of informal agricultural labor extend to child labor—for example, in 2003 to 2004, almost 83,000 children worked on cotton seed farms in India's Andhra Pradesh state, some supplying subsidiaries of TNCs such as Advanta, Bayer, Monsanto, Syngenta, and Unilever. NGOs report that many of these workers are under 10 years old, 85 percent are girls, and many are migrants from low castes, sold into debt bondage to pay off family loans: The "children's job is usually to cross-pollinate cotton flowers by hand for up to 13 hours a day; in the process they are exposed to toxic pesticides . . . and complain of headaches, nausea, and convulsions."[85]

The other face of informalization is the expanding range of activities of production and social reproduction occurring in the "shadow economy," comprising over 50 percent of the population of the global South. Commercial agriculture and habitat degradation routinely expel peasants and laborers from rural livelihoods; they migrate to urban centers where—as they hear on the radio and through migrant networks—jobs and amenities may be available. As Hernando de Soto observes for Peru, peasant migrants "discovered that they were excluded from the facilities and benefits offered by the law . . . that they must compete not only against people but also against the system. Thus it was, that in order to survive, the migrants became informals."[86]

Complementing that image, Kalpana Sharma's *Rediscovering Dharavi* (the Mumbai slum) observes,

> It is a story of ingenuity and enterprise; it is a story of survival without subsidies or welfare; it is a story that illustrates how limited is the term "slum" to describe a place that produces everything from suitcases to leather goods, Indian sweets, papads, and gold jewelry.
>
> Every square inch of Dharavi is being used for some productive activity. This is "enterprise" personified, an island of free enterprise not assisted or restricted by the state, or any law. It brandishes its illegality. Child labor, hazardous industries, adulteration, recycling, popular products from cold drinks to toothpaste produced in Dharavi—it is all there for anyone to see.[87]

While such positive accounts restore perspective on life in "informal" areas, slumdwellers face recurring violence through demolition of their shacks. Sociologist Gayatri Menon's research on Dharavi notes, "Despite their careful selection of sites, because they live on public thoroughfares, pavement dwellers are routinely subjected to violent evictions and demolitions of their homes."[88] Reframing the notion of "invisibility," Fantu Cheru represents the active withdrawal of African peasants from a failing formal economy, including paying taxes, as a "silent revolution": "The resuscitation of rural cooperatives, traditional caravan trade across borders, catering services and other activities that had once fallen into disuse, depriving the state of the revenue that traditionally financed its anti-people and anti-peasant development policies."[89] Here, exit is a strategic solution for producers and workers consistently bypassed by state policies. Serge LaTouche views the informal as

> comprehensive strategies of response to the challenges that life poses for displaced and uprooted populations in peri-urban areas. These are people torn between lost tradition and impossible modernity. The sphere of the informal has, incontestably, a major economic significance. It is characterized by a neo-artisanal activity that generates a lot of employment and produces incomes comparable to those of the modern sector.[90]

The "lost decade" intensified pressures to consolidate new livelihood strategies in already overburdened cities. Among Mexico's urban poor, collective pooling of resources to acquire land, shelter, and basic public services (water, electricity) was one widespread strategy for establishing networks among friends and neighbors to build their own cheap housing.[91] In 1992, Gustavo Esteva observed of the culture of the "new commons":

> Peasants and grassroots groups in the cities are now sharing with people forced to leave the economic center the ten thousand tricks they have learned to limit the economy, to mock the economic creed, or to refunctionalize and reformulate modern technology.[92]

The lesson here is that, again, development is a contradictory process on the one hand, and on the other, disadvantaged populations are not simply passive—that is, they not only develop ingenuity under such circumstances, but exhibit what it is to be human (rather than "developed").

This culture, embedded in dense social networks among informals, has emerged as a new "safety valve" for the development establishment. An expanding sector of socially excluded people became embarrassing to the agents of structural adjustment since traditional/collective forms of mutual aid and livelihood strategies among informals were considered modern anachronisms. To address this legitimacy crisis and stabilize the poor (through the market, beyond the state), the culture of informality, serving as a survival mechanism for the poor, was redefined by the World Bank as an economic resource, as **social capital** to be targeted by microlending.[93] While microcredit has had some success in supporting low-income women, research in Nepal shows that it can also reinforce gender hierarchies, where women's work burden intensifies and husbands gain control of their business income—which means individual empowerment needs complementing with gender relations transformation.[94]

On top of the privations of structural adjustment, microcredit schemes also deplete mutual aid networks essential to survival of the poorest: women and children. Mercedes de la Rocha warns that, in Mexico, "persistent poverty over two decades has effectively brought the poor to their knees," and an NGO worker in Haiti claims the "tradition of mutual giving that allowed us to help each other and survive—this is all being lost."[95] Under these conditions, regions of informality may become anomic, deepening human exploitation such as child prostitution and organ selling, with Chennai (India) having become world renowned for its "kidney farms."[96]

According to UN-Habitat, slum populations now expand annually by 25 million. Consequently, countries such as India are developing secondary cities to absorb informals; as India's chief economic planner, Montek Singh Ahluwalia, observes, "One hundred million people are moving to cities in the next 10 years, and it's important that these 100 million are absorbed into second-tier cities instead of showing up in Delhi or Mumbai."[97] *Planet of Slums* author Mike Davis notes that with "high-tech border enforcement blocking large-scale migration to the rich countries, only the slum remains as a fully franchised solution to the problem of warehousing this century's surplus humanity."[98]

Global Recolonization

The globalization project is realized through quite selective mechanisms of accumulation, dispossession, and neglect within a global field of power that retains the colonial imprint.[99] In Africa, postcolonial states, overly centralized and militarized, have generally served as instruments of wealth extraction.[100] Urban bias was amplified in Africa by state patronage systems constructed during colonialism on the basis of artificial tribal hierarchies.[101] The African one-party state arose out of the difficulties of securing power in and administering nation-states with artificial political boundaries. Such bifurcated power, between the centralized modern state and a "tribal authority which dispensed customary law to those living within the territory of the tribe," conditioned the current debility of African states.[102] This structure of power has facilitated the exploitation of rural areas by urban elites, enriched by foreign investment in resource extraction.[103]

Nobel laureate Wangari Maathai observes that the "modern African state is a superficial creation: a loose collection of ethnic communities or micro-nations" lumped together into a nation-state by the colonial powers:

> Some countries include hundreds of micro-nations within their borders; others only a few. Kenya has forty-two, Nigeria, two hundred and fifty . . . Zimbabwe, fewer than ten, and Burundi and Rwanda, three. . . . Most Africans didn't understand or relate to the nation-states created for them by the colonial powers; they understood, related to, and remained attached to the physical and psychological boundaries of their micro-nations.[104]

Access to power and wealth operates through these filters, often at the expense of national coherence. The neoliberal era, combining austerity with extractive policies, has exacerbated these internal tensions. Either states serve as transmission belts between their hinterlands and an extractive global economy, or subnational (ethnic) forces exploit political divisions and incapacities for similar purposes.

In the twenty-first century, anthropologist James Ferguson observes that deepening inequality stems from the condition where "capital 'hops' over 'unusable Africa,' alighting in mineral-rich enclaves that are starkly disconnected from their national societies." He continues, "It is worth asking whether Africa's combination of privately secured mineral-extraction enclaves and weakly governed humanitarian hinterlands might constitute not a lamentably immature form of globalization, but a quite 'advanced' and sophisticated mutation of it."[105] The model, restoring a colonial division of labor at the expense of coherent national institutions and societies, represents a form of "recolonization."

The contrast between Zambia's formerly paternalistic copper mining industry—with extensive social investment in housing, schools, hospitals, social workers, and sports clubs—and contemporary oil mining in Angola is instructive. Whereas the former industry shed its social amenities under the glare of neoliberal reforms, the Angolan oil industry has been private from the start:

> [Where] nearly all of the production occurs offshore . . . and very little of the oil wealth even enters the wider society. In spite of some 25 years of booming

oil production, Angolans today are among the most desperately poor people on the planet.[106]

The dominant model emerging across the African oil states, similar to that of Angola, is characterized by

> enclaved mineral-rich patches efficiently exploited by flexible private firms, with security provided on an "as needed" basis by specialized corporations while the elite cliques who are nominal holders of sovereignty certify the industry's legality and international legitimacy in exchange for a piece of the action.[107]

John Le Carré's 2006 novel *The Mission Song* fictionalizes this pattern. African inequality expresses the selectivity of neoliberal development. Debates about Africa's marginality to the globalization project forget that sub-Saharan Africa's foreign trade accounted for 52.7 percent of GDP in 2003, compared with a global average of 41.5 percent—one might argue that these countries' general "wealth is inversely proportional to their integration."[108] The 20 lowest-ranked countries in a 2004 United Nations Development Program (UNDP) ranking of "human poverty" (economic and well-being measures) are in Africa, which accounts for 39 of the 50 lowest-ranked countries.[109] The augmentation of the HIPC initiative in 2005 reinforced neoliberal conditionalities of macroeconomic austerity and privatization of services, despite acknowledgment by the Bank that the objectives of financial liberalization were not met, as billions of dollars a year flow offshore into private accounts.[110] According to the Chief Economist of the African Development Bank (ADB): "Close to $1.4 trillion were drained out of Africa" during the era of neoliberalism, far in excess of the total inflow of foreign aid, investments, and remittances.[111]

The New Partnership for Africa's Development (NEPAD), an African initiative agreed to by the G8 (anticipating the formation of the African Union in 2002), continues this policy, urging African leaders to promote "democracy and human rights in their respective countries . . . [while simultaneously] instituting transparent legal and regulatory frameworks for financial markets."[112] In consequence, capital flight from every African country to open up its financial markets is endemic: "Africa's continued poverty ('marginalization') is a direct outcome of excess globalization, not of insufficient globalization, because of the drain from ever declining prices of raw materials (Africa's main exports), crippling debt repayments and profit repatriation to transnational corporations."[113] The drain includes a serious "brain drain," with three million Africans with tertiary education living in the European Union, labor migration from displacement, and a general desire for exodus, where "fantasies of migration have replaced dreams of development."[114] Charles Piot makes these claims:

> It would not be exaggerating too much to say that everyone in Togo is trying to leave—by playing the lottery, by trying to get into European or American universities, by arranging fictitious marriages with foreigners, by joining churches that might take them abroad, by hoping to be signed by a European soccer team, by joining the fan club that accompanies the national soccer team overseas.[115]

An optimistic report in 2010 by consultants McKinsey and Company, titled *Lions on the Move*, portrayed a continent with growing national economies, an expanding middle class of consumers (who accounted for 316 million mobile phone purchases since 2000), and the prospect of the highest rates of return in the global South for foreign investors. It noted the changing economic landscape, with China providing more financing of roads, power, railways, and other infrastructure than the World Bank.[116] Here, it appears Africa is designated as an "extractive resource."

Governance reforms enable the "resource grab" in Africa, where natural resource exports accounted for almost 80 percent of all exports in 2000, compared with 31 percent for the global South and 16 percent for the North. The United Nations Conference on Trade and Development (UNCTAD) noted in 2003 that 12 African countries depended on a single export commodity: crude petroleum (Angola, 92 percent; Congo, 57; Gabon, 70; Nigeria, 96; and Equatorial Guinea, 91), copper (Zambia, 52 percent), diamonds (Botswana, 91 percent), coffee (Burundi, 76 percent; Ethiopia, 62; Uganda 83), tobacco (Malawi, 59 percent), and uranium (Niger, 59 percent).[117] In 2004, foreign direct investment in Africa was $15 billion (up from $2 billion in 1986), with most new investment concentrated in mineral extraction, especially in Angola, Equatorial Guinea, Nigeria, and Sudan, and in deepwater oilfields off the West African coast—from which 25 percent of North American oil imports will come by 2015.[118]

In an era of Chinese ascendancy, the resource grab intensifies. Once self-sufficient in oil (1990), China was the second largest importer of oil after the United States by 2003, accounting for 40 percent of rising demand for oil between 2001 and 2005.[119] One-third of its oil is African. The Chinese National Petroleum Corporation (which overtook Shell in 2006 as the world's sixth largest oil company) and two other large Chinese oil firms operate in 17 African countries, including Sudan (Darfur notwithstanding), where a Chinese state-owned company owns 40 percent of the oil concession in the South (with 4,000 Chinese troops protecting Beijing's oil interests).[120] In 2006, China made a $1.4-billion deal to develop new oilfields in Angola, which became the largest supplier to China ahead of Saudi Arabia. The deal includes China rebuilding Angola's railway and bridges, inland roads, irrigation systems, hospitals, and schools.[121]

For controversial anti-foreign aid economist Dambisa Moyo, the "explosive development of infrastructure" is a "transformational moment for Africa," leading to a maturing civil society as the middle class expands. But such "resource for infrastructure" development, while boosting economic growth statistics (and a middle class linked to state patronage), raises questions about an infrastructure of dependency. A Congolese lawyer remarked, "Six billion dollars in infrastructure is not development. . . . China is taking the place of the West. . . . Our cobalt goes off to China in the form of dusty ore and returns here in the form of expensive batteries." And a Congolese law school dean commented,

> The Chinese are not even making use of Congolese talent. They hire laborers, and that's it. When they pack up and go, the Congo will be left with nothing, not even an upgrade in our human resources. Our earth will be dug up, emptied, and left that way.[122]

China's relation to Africa resembles colonization, but with a twenty-first century twist. Between 2001 and 2006, China's trade with Africa rose fivefold, to $50 billion, exceeding its trade with the European Union and positioning it as Africa's third-largest trading partner. It has almost 700 state companies with investments in 800 joint projects in Africa.[123] The Council on Foreign Relations reported in 2006, "China is acquiring control of natural resource assets, outbidding Western contractors on major infrastructural projects and providing soft loans and other incentives to bolster its competitive advantage."[124] That same year, exploiting a "South-South" rhetoric, China claimed its growing interests as a "strategic partnership with Africa, featuring political equality and mutual trust, economic win-win cooperation"—implying that China does not require governance reforms and anticorruption initiatives as a condition for aid and trade, as do the IFIs, "which some see as a way to justify links with abusive regimes, such as those in Zimbabwe and Sudan."[125] Sociologist Ching Kwan Lee cautions that these relations are not monolithic and the Chinese impact depends on local political conditions and the learning curve of Chinese firms. Thus she finds Zambian copper miners, with an organizing tradition, able to leverage concessions from the new Chinese owner of the Chambishi mine in the name of resource nationalism and in the context of rising world copper prices, compared with the unchecked casualization of textile workers in the Tanzania–China Friendship Mills in Dar es Salaam. She remarks, "China has become a compelling and effective conduit of capitalism in Africa. Its unparalleled rise . . . achieved largely independent of international financial institutions, [has] lent it enormous credential as a model of development for many African countries."[126]

In the wake of debilitating neoliberal reforms, endless debt servicing, and NEPAD, African countries now have access to a superwealthy southern state, lacking northern colonial baggage. Yet neocolonial relations obtain. South Africa, where 86 percent of clothing imports are from China, has lost 300,000 textile jobs since 2002. Since 2000, Nigeria lost 350,000 jobs directly and 1.5 million indirectly due to Chinese competition.[127] Cheap imports of Chinese manufactured goods are matched by Chinese investment in the sectors such as commercial aviation, agricultural machinery, urban transportation, and telecommunications.[128] Human Rights Watch claims Chinese policies in Africa (following the historic lead of the West) have "propped up some of the continent's worst human-rights abusers." Ethiopia has pioneered the "Chinese model of development," its late prime minister Meles Zenawi proclaiming, "There is no connection between democracy and development," and implementing an "authoritarian developmentalism" devoid of civil rights.[129] Exploitation of natural resources reproduces the colonial pattern of "export of sustainability," and concerns have been raised over "the environmental impact of various Chinese-run mining operations in Africa, including copper mines in Zambia and Congo and titanium sands projects in ecologically sensitive parts of Mozambique, Kenya, Tanzania, and Madagascar."[130]

Loss of resource sovereignty accompanies compromised political authority:

> Particularly in Sub-Saharan Africa, government forces are in decay and private security organizations are on the rise, including forces loyal to regional warlords, citizens' self-defense groups, corporate-sponsored forces, foreign mercenaries, and criminal gangs. In fact, it is becoming more difficult to make clear-cut distinctions between legitimate and illegitimate, and between public and private, security forces.[131]

One dramatic manifestation of the loss of political cohesion of some African states is an exploding refugee population, consisting of "international refugees" and "internally displaced persons," underlining the civilian casualty in the militarization of the continent, which has deep roots linking the colonial era to an era of recolonization. The nineteenth-century scramble for Africa, symbolized by the Berlin Conference of 1884, is on again—with the United States, France, Britain, India, and China competing for oil, gas, timber, bauxite, copper, diamonds, gold, and coltan.

The Global Land Grab

Another form of "recolonization" is the "global land grab." Land enclosing is a time-honored process, from the imperial age to the present. In the twenty-first century, enclosure by "land grabbing" has intensified as investors and companies and states acquire land for profit and/or access to new food and fuel supplies. In its 2010 report, *Rising Global Interest in Farmland*, the World Bank noted that global investors acquired 111 million hectares of agricultural lands over four years, 75 percent of which were in Africa.[132] China and the Middle Eastern countries were the first players in the land rush. Since 2008, China, Saudi Arabia, Egypt, Bahrain, the Gulf countries, Jordan, Kuwait, Libya, Qatar, United Arab Emirates, India, Malaysia, Japan, and South Korea have been on a land rush to Africa, South and Southeast Asia, Central Asia, Australia, and South America.

Aside from these food-insecure states, other investors include agribusiness firms, investment houses, private equity funds, and fund managers. They work either through local private partners, host governments, or their own governments in joint ventures with target countries. Host governments, with Bank assistance, alter national laws, policies, and land-owning practices to facilitate foreign acquisition for food or biofuels, usually leasing or selling land at low prices. The Japanese firm Mitsui, for example, has purchased 100,000 hectares of land in Brazil for soybean production. In Ukraine, overriding local community voice, an agribusiness empire that commands 450,000 hectares and is supported by hundreds of millions of dollars of financing from the World Bank is developing the Vinnytsia poultry farm to transform the country from "Europe's breadbasket" into its "meat basket."[133] Meanwhile, Chinese firms are shifting their focus from mining to financing agricultural infrastructure in Western Australia to develop grain and beef lands as offshore farms for Chinese consumers.[134] And in 2015, a report by Mozambique's National Farmers Union (UNAC) and GRAIN (Genetic Resources Action International), titled *Land Grabbers of the Nacala Corridor,* details how the government of Mozambique has attracted foreign investment from Japan and Brazil for a program called ProSavanna, "which aims to transform 14 million hectares of lands currently cultivated by peasant farmers serving local markets in this area into massive farming operations run by foreign companies to produce cheap commodities for export."[135]

Not only have the food and energy crises propelled and justified investment in land offshore in the name of addressing food shortages and alternative energy, but also investment in agriculture offers a new profit frontier for investors at a time of jobless growth, when investors also may prefer speculative versus real investments. Land grabbing pushes up prices—and over time and for large investment houses, it is a relatively safe investment haven for the mid- to long-term. Susan Payne, founder and CEO of the UK firm Emergent Asset Management (EAM), raising $450 million to $750 million for investment to consolidate and industrialize farmland in sub-Saharan Africa for food and biofuels, stated the following:

> Farmland in Sub-Saharan Africa is giving 25% returns a year and new technology can treble crop yields in short time frames. . . . Agricultural development is not only sustainable, it is our future. If we do not pay great care and attention now to increase food production by over 50% before 2050, we will face serious food shortages globally.[136]

The cost of land may be low for investors, but not to the locals. And governments are typically classifying lands, whether common lands or privately used, as "idle" or "unproductive." Ethiopia's "land lease project," intended to develop large-scale commercial farming (mainly for export of food and fuel), allocated three million hectares of "idle land" (about 20 percent of currently cultivated land). An indigenous Anuak from the fertile Gambella region of Ethiopia observed, "All the land 'round my family village of Illia has been taken over and is being cleared. People now have to work for an Indian company. Their land has been compulsorily taken and they have been given no compensation."[137]

This "modernizing" perspective obscures the intrinsic cultural and survival value of such land to its inhabitants; instead, it is viewed as an opportunity for capitalization, usually for export production of food or biofuels. In this way, the globalization project has morphed into a new form of colonization of land, largely to supply affluent appetites elsewhere, and at the expense of land users, their lands, and their food security.

SUMMARY

The globalization project has had many social and political dimensions. We have examined several of its vectors: poverty governance, outsourcing, displacement, informalization, recolonization, and land grabbing. None of these is unique to the globalization project. They have all appeared in previous eras in different forms, but not on the scale found today. They are linked—indeed, they are mutually conditioning processes, being dimensions of a single process of global restructuring affecting all countries, although with local variation. The social and environmental consequences are substantial.

Poverty governance shifts responsibility by embedding impoverishing policies in states themselves. These are supplemented by the technological shedding of labor and the downsizing and stagnation produced by structural adjustment programs, in turn expanding the informal sector, as more and more wage labor is casualized. Corporate strategies of flexibility contribute to this informalization as much as the displacement of populations from their land and livelihood. Some observers see informalization as an alternative to the official economy and to state regulation—asserting a culture of the "new commons." Informalization is a by-product of neglect, exclusion, and resource dispossession—processes endemic in Africa today, where the resource race is being played out via a recolonization process, as well as a concentration of contemporary land grabbing. The globalization project may have a universal vision, but it is often unequal in its outcomes.

FURTHER READING

Boo, Katherine. *Behind the Beautiful Forevers: Life, Death and Hope in a Mumbai Undercity*. New York: Random House, 2012.

Caraway, Teri L. *Assembling Women: The Feminization of Global Manufacturing*. Ithaca, NY: Cornell University Press, 2007.

Davis, Mike. *Planet of Slums*. London: Verso, 2006.

Elyachar, Julia. *Markets of Dispossession: NGOs, Economic Development, and the State in Cairo*. Durham, NC: Duke University Press, 2005.

Ferguson, James. *Global Shadows: Africa in the Neoliberal World Order*. Durham, NC: Duke University Press, 2006.

Guerrero, Dorothy-Grace, and Firoze Manji, eds. *China's New Role in Africa and the South*. Capetown: Fahamu & Bangkok: Focus on the Global South, 2008.

Hall, Derek. *Land*. Cambridge: Polity Press, 2013.

McCallum, Jamie. *Global Unions, Local Power: The New Spirit of Transnational Labor Organizing*. Ithaca: Cornell University Press, 2013.

Raynolds, Laura T., Douglas Murray, and John Wilkinson, eds. *Fair Trade: The Challenges of Transforming Globalization*. Abingdon, UK: Routledge, 2007.

Standing, Guy. *The Precariat: The New Dangerous Class*. London: Bloomsbury Academic, 2011.

SELECT WEBSITES

China Labor Watch: www.chinalaborwatch.org
Farmlandgrab.org
FoodFirst Information and Action Network: www.fian.org
Grameen Bank: www.grameen-info.org
International Labor Rights Forum: www.laborrights.org
International Labour Organization (ILO): www.ilo.org
Maquila Solidarity Network (Canada): www.maquilasolidarity.org
Migrant Rights International (Switzerland): www.migrantwatch.org
TransAfrica Forum (USA): www.transafricaforum.org
Transparency International: www.transparency.org
UNI Global Union: www.uniglobalunion.org
United Nations High Commissioner for Refugees (UNHCR): www.unhcr.ch

7

Global Countermovements

The globalization project has been a relatively coherent perspective advanced by a powerful set of northern (and southern) states, agencies, and corporations working on its behalf. Nevertheless, its market-based claims and rules are always in contention precisely because this project generates cultural and material insecurities in imposing a "one-size-fits-all" program across a very diverse world. As with the development project, the globalization project attempts to fashion the world around a central principle (the free market) through powerful political and financial institutions. Framed as a discourse of rights and freedom, the power of the organizing principle ultimately depends on the interpretation, legitimacy, and effect of these ideals. Diane Perrons puts it this way:

> Neoliberalism is a powerful ideology and appeals to people's self-interest. It implies that free markets are somehow a natural and inevitable state of affairs in which individual endeavor will be rewarded, and perhaps because of this the poor accept growing inequalities because they think they have a chance of becoming rich themselves as society appears to be freer and more open.[1]

Of course this is an illusion, as decades of development have not ended hunger and malnutrition, and now material inequality (wealth, health, resource access) is more entrenched than ever across the world.[2] Further, self-interest and monetary wealth alone are not universal goals, as evidenced by the social and political struggles of global countermovements.

As noted in the opening chapter, Karl Polanyi characterized market society as a "double movement." That is, as nationwide markets were instituted in the nineteenth century, social classes deprived of livelihoods on the land, of rights in the workplace, and of stable business conditions formed protective **countermovements** against attempts to rule through free-market principles. He referred to this dynamic as a double movement, where countermovements focused on bringing markets under social control.[3]

Polanyi's legacy is to have reminded us that markets are neither natural nor necessarily neutral in their origin and operation. They are social constructs—the most far-reaching being the creation of markets in human labor, as farming communities and village artisans are displaced (onto the labor market) by land enclosure and cheap manufactures mass-produced in factories. This general process, understood as "industrial revolution," fundamentally alters livelihood possibilities as land and labor are treated as commodities to be bought and sold, accumulated, and disposed of. Overall, markets govern society with a singular financial calculus, devaluing non-monetized contributions to social life and disregarding various forms of discrimination and environmental degradation.

What are the consequences of understanding and prescribing the market as the site and vehicle of development? For one thing, it reinforces the belief that well-being depends on increasing GNP—a correlation increasingly questioned by recent studies, including the series of Human Development Indexes.[4] For another thing, it reinforces the association of nonmonetized activity with poverty. If what is productive (and therefore key) to development is only that which can be measured in monetary terms, then, for example, women's unpaid labor is discounted, as are the myriad activities through which people share common resources and construct livelihood networks. Small-scale farmers customarily experiment with seed-sharing and crop rotations as risk-averse activity in variable environments to sustain communities and ecosystems—activities not valued in monetary terms. Within the development paradigm, then, these practices become targets for displacement or commercialization in order to record increasing gross domestic product (GDP). This is expressed, for example, in the following way:

> When such non-market spheres are brought into the market, GDP grows. So when a peasant changes from growing her own food and giving the surplus to neighbours to growing commercial crops for sale on the market, GDP rises. When a peasant is displaced by a commercial farm and has to go and live in a nearby city shantytown, working . . . to pay for food and housing, GDP increases even more.[5]

As we shall see in this chapter, countermovement politics challenge the easy association of markets with development, offering alternative prescriptions.

Of course, there are always resistances of one kind or another (e.g., anti-GMO, fair trade, labor union rights), but here we examine *systemic* countermovements. Systemic alternatives are not about simply *reforming* the system; rather, they offer the possibility of *transforming* the system—by questioning its key assumptions. Examining each movement offers a particular angle on the shortcomings of the development project.

It is necessary to point out here that social movements are an integral part of the landscape of modern capitalist development, which is realized through various forms of unequal or uneven market relationships, especially those of gender, ethnicity/race, and property. As we have seen, the development project itself emerged through a long-drawn-out struggle for racial justice led by anticolonial movements over the last two centuries. While formal sovereignty for new states in the non-European world was the outcome, racial injustice continues in multiple forms: from the perception of developers that indigenous lands are "empty" or "unimproved," through Israeli subjugation of Palestinians, Han Chinese repression of Tibetan and Uighur cultures, and racial legacies in other settler states (United States, Canada, Australia, New Zealand, South Africa, and Southern Cone states) to exploitation of migrant labor streams across the world. These continuing forms of injustice are infused with gender, cultural, and class inequalities.

Our focus here is on three substantive critiques of the epistemic foundations of development in the form of environmentalism, feminism, and sovereignty movements. These movements are hardly homogeneous; this chapter attempts to extract coherent threads from each to capture the essence of the Polanyian concept of the "countermovement"—that is, more as a historic intervention than an everyday resistance.

Environmentalism

In a sense, environmentalism is as old as the hills. Indigenous communities have survived millennia by practicing forms of environmentalism—that is, developing ways to sustain themselves by working *with* natural cycles and processes, modifying them to be sure (for domesticated agriculture), but attending to different ways of restoring or maintaining natural habitat. Swidden agriculture is one example of this, involving land clearing for farming, followed by periods of fallow and renewal of grassland or forestland. Pastoralists have practiced transhumance, moving their livestock herds through landscapes to sustain them and their animals. Such practices are inherently environmental, even if they were not conceived as such. "Environmentalism" as an episteme (a way of thinking) is very much a modern concept.

As a countermovement, environmentalism challenges the artificial separation of the social from the natural world in the development enterprise. Not only do we depend on nature, we exploit it *unaccountably* through the market model. And we exploit it at our peril, with greatest impact on the most vulnerable populations. Pope Francis made this connection in his influential climate change encyclical of June 2015, when he referred to the "ecological debt" of the global North with respect to southern resources—an unequal exchange effected through the market as "development" in either region: "Developing countries, where the most important reserves of the biosphere are found, continue to fuel the development of richer countries at the cost of their own present and future."[6] The significance of this encyclical was to draw attention to the short-term focus on accumulation of wealth at long-term environmental expense, particularly in the global South as zone of extraction.

A key inspiration for the environmental countermovement in the global North was the 1962 publication of Rachel Carson's *Silent Spring*. This pathbreaking work documented the disruption in the earth's ecosystems caused by agricultural chemicals. Its title refers to the absence of birdsong in the spring. Carson's metaphor dramatized the dependence of human life on environmental systems. At the same time, it emphasized modernity's rationalized perception of nature as "external" to society, a perception encouraging the belief that nature is an infinitely exploitable domain.[7]

Such research addressed the health consequences of industrial pollution, underscoring the fact that our lifestyle has direct impact on our habitat (and that of other species). The role of the environmental countermovement, then, has been to raise social consciousness of this relationship and to focus attention on the artificiality of a development paradigm that takes nature for granted. The outcome of this kind of movement is to explore and generate ways to re-embed economy in ecology. There is no shortage of such initiatives across the world, North and South, as citizens become aware of the importance of repairing and sustaining ecosystems, the significance of public health effects of toxic pollution, and the urgency of mitigating climate change effects.

Following Rachel Carson and Francis Moore Lappé's *Diet for a Small Planet* (1971), environmentalist sentiment evolved with a growing awareness of the limits of "spaceship earth"—depicted in photographs from space of planet earth, dramatizing the biophysical finiteness of our world. The paradox of economic growth and ecological damage was articulated by the Brundtland Commission's call in 1987 for "sustainable development," as it observed, "We all depend on one biosphere for sustaining our lives."[8] It was this kind of sentiment to which the Amazonian Kayapo Indians in the 1980s were able to appeal internationally for protection of their ecological practices in the rain forest against the threat of dams, logging, mining, and cattle ranching. The efficacy of this protest, in pressuring the government to include indigenous rights in the Brazilian Constitution and to legally recognize their territory, stemmed from the support they cultivated from the global community through enlisting the help of conservation organizations and celebrities (e.g., Sting) in protecting "the lungs of the earth."[9]

The Kayapo Indian protest was an example of what ecological economist Juan Martinez-Alier terms the "environmentalism of the poor" and characterizes such movements of minorities in the name of "environmental justice" to protect their habitat and community health. His point is that their material needs and cultural identities are embedded in their biophysical environments. Despite the questionable use of the term *poor* to describe such indigenous cultures practicing low-input ways of life, the point here is these communities are under threat from developers depleting their ecosystems. Accordingly, in order to protect their "life-worlds" from market society, they must resort, opportunistically, to modern environmental politics to be heard—representing their claims in a language of environmental protections. Martinez-Alier argues that his use of the term *environmentalism of the poor* explains the conflicts

> in which poor people defend the environment (in rural situations, but also in cities) against the state or the market. Well-known instances are the Ogoni, the Ijaw, and other groups in the Niger Delta against the damage from oil extraction by Shell. Also, the complaints against eucalyptus in Thailand and elsewhere because plantations are not forests. Or the movements of oustees from dams as in the Narmada River in India or in the movement of *atingidos por barragens* in Brazil. Or some new peasant movements, such as Via Campesina against seed multinationals and biopiracy. . . . The words *ecology* and *environment* were not used politically at the time. Until recently, the actors of such conflicts rarely saw themselves as environmentalists.[10]

The "recently" here refers to the growing acknowledgment of environmental degradation or habitats associated with resource extraction and its impact on contiguous communities and of the environmental blind spot of contemporary markets. While monetary incomes may expand with extraction of resources (and cleanup), the social and ecological impact (including waste) is usually not counted—leaving affected communities to pursue environmentalism to protect their habitat and livelihoods. Environmental claims have increasing resonance today as citizens beyond the affected areas recognize the more general threat to public health, as articulated in the 2015 encyclical by Pope Francis:

> Account must also be taken of the pollution produced by residue, including dangerous waste present in different areas. Each year hundreds of millions of

tons of waste are generated, much of it non-biodegradable, highly toxic and radioactive, from homes and businesses, from construction and demolition sites, from clinical, electronic and industrial sources. The earth, our home, is beginning to look more and more like an immense pile of filth. . . . Frequently no measures are taken until after people's health has been irreversibly affected.[11]

Historically, local farming, grazing, fishing, or forest-dwelling communities have always had to protect their habitats from encroachment by colonial or commercial forces intent on enclosing their lands or commons as state or private property—and thereby compromising livelihoods dependent on nature. Such early forms of (modern) environmentalism include eighteenth-century English peasants protesting enclosure of the commons for the wool industry, Native Americans and Australian Aborigines resisting the takeover of their habitats, and Indians struggling against British colonial forestry practices. In the late twentieth century, forest dwellers across the tropics caught the world's attention as they attempted to preserve tropical rainforests from extensive timber cutting, resource mining, and river damming to the overuse of natural resources, resulting in desertification, excessive water salinity, and chemical contamination associated with the green revolution. And in the twenty-first century, environmentalism has extended to antifracking alliances (of land users and urban supporters) as some states and energy companies seek to capitalize on new technologies of extracting shale oil and natural gas to expand energy supplies.

Valuing Environments

As a general countermovement, environmentalism underscores that natural resources are not infinitely renewable. The finiteness of nature has been a global preoccupation, from the neo-Malthusian specter of population growth overwhelming land and the food grown on it to anxiety about the dwindling supplies of raw materials, such as the fossil fuels and timber that sustain modern economies.

Lately, however, this rather linear perspective has yielded to a more dynamic one that sees a serious threat to natural processes such as the atmosphere, climates, and biodiversity. Trees may be renewable through appropriate replanting schemes (not eucalyptus plantations, for example), but the atmospheric conditions that nurture them may not be so easily replenished. The world has moved to a new threshold of risk to its sustainability:

It used to be feared that we would run out of non-renewable resources—things like oil, or gold. Yet these, it seems, are the ones we need worry least about. It is the renewables—the ones we thought would last forever—that are being destroyed at an accelerating rate. They are all living things, or dynamic parts of living ecosystems.[12]

The problem is that such renewables, not being identified as "resources" in economic accounting, are easily exploited as disposables (biodiversity) or waste sinks (oceans) because they do not command a price and are therefore made invisible by development metrics. Such renewables are casualties of the extractive model of contemporary capitalism.[13] One response is to price "ecosystem services" via what is called **ecological accounting**. At the turn of the twenty-first century, the world's ecosystem services were estimated at around $33 trillion a year, exceeding the global gross national product (GNP) of $25 trillion at the time.[14]

Ecological accounting seeks to internalize environmental "externalities" to approximate the real social and ecological costs of repairing or restoring a natural world subjected, for example, to industrial agriculture, mining, and the absorption of waste and greenhouse gases. Natural processes are not commodities in themselves, calculations may be made in relation to the costs of preservation or replenishment costs. Thus, the Costa Rica government began paying landowners $42 per hectare per year to preserve forest when deforestation for expanding pastures to supply beef to the North American fast food industry was at its peak in the 1980s. And in the 1990s, New York City paid over $1 billion to landowners in its upstate watershed to alter farming practices to prevent animal waste and fertilizer from leaching into streams and rivers: "In doing so, the city avoided spending $6 billion to $8 billion on a new water filtration plant and $300 million to $500 million annually to run it—the replacement cost of the natural filtration provided by waterways."[15]

However, ecological economics is no panacea, nor is it automatic, given unequal power structures. Martinez-Alier's take on this reads in the following way:

> The strength necessary to incorporate negative local externalities is often lacking in the South. Poverty and powerlessness result in the local environment and health being sold cheaply. This does not indicate a lack of environmental awareness but simply reflects a lack of power to defend both health and environment. Anticipating Pope Francis's charge of "ecological debt," Martinez-Alier continued, "As the North has profited from an ecologically unequal trade, it is in a debtor position."[16]

Furthermore, pricing ecosystem services fixes a market value to (fractionated) ecological processes that are by nature systemic and indivisible. If ecological value is reduced to a unitary price, it may, paradoxically, promote consumption of the environment. A case in point is the indigenous Yasuní region in Amazonian Ecuador, where oil reserves were offset by environmental values as President Correa unsuccessfully explored the possibility, through a UN Program of Reducing Emissions from Deforestation and Degradation (REDD), of selling carbon credits (to northern governments and investors) to preserve the forest. Adam Ma'anit noted this point:

> The real danger is that once a dollar value has been assigned to something as arguably incalculable as a tree, a forest, or yes, even a human life, it allows the bean counters to start comparing costs and benefits. Economists can start to ask, when the price of oil hits $200 a barrel: Does the benefit of extracting a billion barrels of oil outweigh the cost of destroying the Yasuní National Park and the communities of people that live there?[17]

This question underscores the dangers of imposing a standard cost/benefit metric across a diverse world, insofar as dollar values are incommensurate with the life worlds of particular communities (and their contributions to low-input, sustainable living). Monetizing (and thereby segregating and subdividing) the environment is an extension of the development paradigm's promise of a singular future to a variety of cultures that have, or had, their own time horizons, not necessarily involving high-mass consumption. "Had," because the force of development has sometimes reduced choice in communities and regions where habitats are compromised by extractive industries. For example, investigations suggest the following:

> In virtually every community on the front lines of extractive battles, some faction invariably makes the argument that it's not up to Indigenous people to sacrifice to save the rest of the world from climate change, that they should concentrate on getting better deals from the mining companies so that they can pay for base services and train their young people in marketable skills.[18]

Nevertheless, there are many powerful examples of indigenous mobilizations as ecological countermovements, intent on asserting their cultural and environmental rights against top-down colonization of their territories in the name of development.[19] Resistance to the Narmada Dam is a case in point. Since the 1980s, the Indian government has been implementing a huge dam project in the Narmada River valley with assistance from the

World Bank. More than two million people were originally targeted for displacement. In 1992, at the time of the Rio Earth Summit, there was an embarrassing release of an independent review (the first ever) of the World Bank's Sardar Sarovar dam project in India. The review claimed "gross delinquency" on the part of the World Bank and the Indian government in both the engineering and the forcible resettlement of indigenous peoples. These revelations and the growing resistance movement, the Narmada Bachao Andolan (movement to save the Narmada), forced the World Bank to withdraw its support for this project. Grassroots opponents to the dam argue that the resistance

> articulates . . . the critical legacy of Mahatma Gandhi . . . of the struggles all over the country that continue to challenge both the growing centralization and authoritarianism of the state and the extractive character of the dominant economic process—a process which not only erodes and destroys the subsistence economies of these areas, but also the diversity of their systems. . . . The movement is therefore representative of growing assertions of marginal populations for greater economic and political control over their lives.[20]

The Supreme Court of India ruled in 2000 that

> the argument in favor of the Sardar Sarovar Project is that the benefits are so large that they substantially outweigh the costs of the immediate human and environmental disruption. . . . Set against the future of about 70,000 project affected people, even without the multiplier effect, the ratio of beneficiaries to affected persons is well over 100:1.[21]

Award-winning Indian author Arundhati Roy contested this estimate, showing the ripple effects of displacement beyond tribal people of the river valleys. She also situated dam building as a symbol of a deeper separation of humans from their ecological foundations embedded within the global development project, referring to them as

> malignant indications of civilisation turning upon itself. They represent the severing of the link, not just the link—the understanding—between human beings and the planet they live on. They scramble the intelligence that connects eggs to hens, milk to cows, food to forests, water to rivers, air to life and the earth to human existence.[22]

Even though indigenous people around the world have had their rights to land and self-determination enshrined in the International Labour Organization Convention, they are routinely viewed as marginal (in spite of their light ecological footprint). The World Bank, in adopting the term *indigenous* in its documents, stated this in 1990:

> The term *indigenous* covers indigenous, tribal, low caste, and ethnic minority groups. Despite their historical and cultural differences, they often have a limited capacity to participate in the national development process because of cultural barriers or low social and political status.[23]

Viewed through the development lens, this perspective carries a significant implication. On the one hand, it perpetuates the unexamined (and often racist) assumption that these cultural minorities need guidance. On the other hand, it often subordinates minorities to national development initiatives, such as commercial logging or government forestry projects or dam building, as mentioned. In 2007, the United Nations General Assembly passed a Declaration on the Rights of Indigenous Peoples. Not only does it proclaim the rights of indigenous peoples to "the protection of the environment and the productive capacity of their lands," but also it provides "the right to redress" for confiscated, occupied, or damaged lands "without their free, prior and informed consent." Redress rights are to be claimed against their state. Ironically, governments such as those of Bolivia and Ecuador, elected with indigenous support and legalizing indigenous rights, still sanction extractive mining, forestry, and plantation projects to enhance export revenues.[24]

Generally, indigenous peoples do not have the resources and political influence to protect their rights. In Indonesia, where the Forestry Department controls more than two-thirds of the national territory, a Minister for Forestry claimed, "The forest belongs to the state and not to the people. . . . They have no right of compensation," when their habitats fall to logging concessions.[25]

Under these conditions, environmentalism takes two forms: active resistance, which seeks to curb invasion of habitats by states and markets, and adaptation—renewing habitats in the face of environmental deterioration. One dramatic form of resistance was the 1970s Chipko movement in the central Himalaya region of India, adopting a Gandhian strategy of nonviolence, symbolized in the primarily women-led tree-hugging protests against commercial logging. Similar protests spread across northern India in a move to protect forest habitats for tribal peoples. Emulating a Chipko (adaptive) practice of tree planting to restore forests and soils, the movement developed a "pluck-and-plant" tactic. Its members uprooted eucalyptus seedlings—the tree of choice in official social forestry, even though it does not provide shade and ravishes aquifers—and replaced them with indigenous species of trees that yield products useful to the locals.[26] Environmental activism proliferates across the South. In Thailand, where the state promotes eucalyptus plantations that displace forest dwellers, there has been sustained rural activism in the name of community rights to local forests versus eucalyptus monoculture.[27]

CASE STUDY   Las Gaviotas—Tropical Sustainability

In the early 1970s, Paulo Lugari and collaborators (engineers, artists, students, Indians, and even street children) built a sustainable village in the remote plains of Colombia, 500 kilometers from the capital, Bogotá. Despite continuous violence within the country around the coca economy, Las Gaviotas has survived, supported by ingenious renewable energy technology (water systems, distillers, solar-powered cookers, windmills, and pumps), hydroponic farming, and a project of regenerating surrounding rainforest from the barren savannah soil. Knowing the savannah was once part of the Amazon forest, Lugari managed to introduce Caribbean pine seedlings to provide shade, increase soil moisture, and promote biodiversity. The regenerated forest yields drinking water, with valuable resins, oils, and fragrances from the forest supporting this experiment in self-sufficiency. The village supports 200 workers with piece rate wages and room, board, and medical care; 50 resident families and approximately 500 children from the region have accessed its school. Adults rotate among jobs in the village (construction, planting, gardening, and cooking).

Aside from providing a haven from civil strife, social collaboration involves all in the project of sustainability: "The success of Las Gaviotas in sustainably supporting the community from the products of the regenerated rainforest has prompted new dreams of expanding the forest across the savannah, with both environmental and social benefits." In 2004, the government endorsed plans to achieve this extraordinary environmental and social transformation, "beginning with a tenfold expansion of the forest around Las Gaviotas." Further plans for developing the carbon sequestration system, production of potable water, and ecotourism have obtained financial support from a socially responsible corporation from Belgium, Zero Emissions Research and Initiatives (ZERI).

In what sense might this project be a countermovement?

Source: White and Marino (2007: 22).

As environmentalism mushrooms across the South, community control gains credibility by example. At the same time, the institutional aspects of technology transfer associated with the development project come under question. An ex-director of forestry at the Food and Agricultural Organization commented,

> Only very much later did it dawn on the development establishment that the very act of establishing new institutions often meant the weakening, even the destruction of existing indigenous institutions which ought to have served as the basis for sane and durable development: the family, the clans, the tribe, the village, sundry mutual aid organizations, peasant associations, rural trade unions, marketing and distribution systems and so on.[28]

Forest dwellers have always managed their environment. From the perspective of colonial rule and developers, these communities did not appear to be involved in management because their practices were alien to the specialized pursuit of commercial wealth characterizing Western ways that began under colonialism. Local practices were therefore either suppressed or ignored, with consequence. An example of this is the condition of the Australian landscape, which Aboriginal people managed via a complex system of combining fire and native plant life cycles to secure yearlong supplies of plant foods and wildlife. Destruction of this system by white settlers has left the Australian bush vulnerable to deadly bushfires. Now, where colonial forestry practices erased local knowledge and eroded natural resources, recent grassroots mobilization, such as the Green Belt Movement in Kenya organized by women, has reestablished intercropping to replenish soils and tree planting to sustain forests. Where development planners have attempted to impose irrigated cash cropping, such as in eastern Senegal, movements such as the Senegalese Federation of Sarakolle Villages have collectively resisted in the interests of sustainable peasant farming.[29]

The challenge for environmental movements in the South is twofold: to create alternatives to the capital- and energy-intensive forms of specialized agriculture and agroforestry appropriate to the goal of restoring and sustaining local ecologies; and to build alternative models to the bureaucratic, top-down development plans that have typically subordinated natural resource use to commercial, rather than sustainable, social ends. Perhaps the fundamental challenge to southern environmentalism is the perspective that has defined World Bank programming: "Promoting development is the best way to protect the environment."[30] The question is whether development, from the World Bank's perspective, can respect environmental limits.

Environmental Countermovement Principles

The protective impulse of these various movements is often twofold: first, to guarantee territorial rights, and second, to repair and restore damaged environments. The latter has generated a growing interest in protecting the "rights of nature"—for example, they are now enshrined in the national constitutions of Bolivia and Ecuador as the "rights of Mother Earth" (*Pachamama*), but more as a principle than a practice at this stage. A related effort in Europe to declare ecocide a crime under international law is indicative of the progress of the environmental countermovement at large. It represents a reformulation of a code of life based on regenerative ecological principles, as distinct from the linear economic vision of the development paradigm.

In addition to critiquing the ecological blindspot of the conventional development paradigm, the key to the contemporary environmental countermovement is how it embodies a self-organizing ethos among its participants. This generally takes the form of community building around alternative material practices, geared toward regeneration of habitats rather than endless extraction of resources to maintain or attain levels of high-mass consumption. In other words, such environmentalism turns development on its head. The mushrooming of local experimentation, based on identifying human scale projects to sustain community life and replenish ecosystems and watersheds, is the proof of this pudding. The **Transition Town** movement, begun in England in 2006, exemplifies this (see Chapter 10). It is a movement, or network, by and across communities anticipating peak oil and climate change, focusing on building local social and ecological resiliences. As of 2010, there were over 300 official towns from the United Kingdom, Ireland, Canada, the United States, Australia, New Zealand, Chile, and Italy engaged in processes to manage "energy descent."[31]

Alongside Transition Towns, there is a global proliferation of local farmers' markets, seed sharing, and community-supported agricultures (CSAs) dedicated to shortening supply chains and reducing the social distance between producers and consumers to encourage an ecological ethic:

> Linear, one-way relationships of pure extraction are being replaced with systems that are circular and reciprocal. Seeds are saved instead of purchased. Water is recycled. Animal manure, not chemicals, is used as fertilizer, and so on. There are no hard-and-fast formulas, since the guiding principle is that every geography is different.[32]

Central to these developments is the recognition of the integrity of place—something the market does not recognize, except as an economic resource.

This is abundantly clear in the current "push into ever more extreme and high-risk forms of fossil fuel," at a time of energy uncertainty.[33] The resulting global antifracking coalitions embody the environmental countermovement principle for the twenty-first century—a century juggling energy needs with the need to drastically reduce greenhouse gas emissions to avert catastrophic climate uncertainty and to preserve fresh water supplies. Much of the wastewater from fracking is toxic and radioactive, and accordingly, "extreme energy demands that we destroy a whole lot of the essential substance we need to survive—water—just to keep extracting more of the very substances threatening our survival and that we can power our lives without."[34]

Energy companies are ranging the world for new sources of such "extreme energy," including the global North. The difference now is that all places are potential sites: The privileged class in England is now finding their country estates threatened by fracking pollution, France has banned fracking outright, and the more exploration conducted by energy companies across previously untouched landscapes, the more intense the pushback, such as in US areas threatened by the Keystone pipeline from the infamous tar sands of Alberta; according to a Texan rancher, "I just don't believe that a Canadian organization that appears to be building a pipeline for their financial gain has more right to my land than I do." This refrain is repeated across the US landscape, as a New York state resident and former corporate lawyer who lent her talents to towns adopting antifracking ordinances proclaimed what others are most likely thinking:

> Are you kidding me? You think you can just come into my town and tell me you're going to do whatever you want, wherever you want, whenever you want it, and I'm going to have no say? Who do you think you are?[35]

The point is that energy development is no longer simply threatening the environments of the poor; it is now "putting many people who thought they were safe at risk,"[36] potentially implicating all environments, water sources, and, of course, threatening planetary viability. Naomi Klein observes,

> We know that we are trapped within an economic system that has it backward: It behaves as if there is no end to what is actually finite (clean water, fossil fuels, and the atmospheric space to absorb their emissions) while insisting that there are strict and immovable limits to what is actually quite flexible: the financial resources that human institutions manufacture, and that, if imagined differently, could build the kind of caring society we need.[37]

This is the essence of the countermovement claim—namely, that a financial calculus overrides two fundamental human reproductive needs: a healthy environment and the capacity for self-determination. As environmental movements have discovered, allowing the market to decide concentrates power in the hands of investors with no allegiance to place—at a time when place is becoming more precious precisely as fossil fuel-based conventional development threatens all places, regardless of class. This has both rural and urban consequence: For example, China is confronted with this dilemma, with pollution now trumping land disputes as the major source of social unrest, with air quality decline causing over a million premature deaths annually. Li Bo, a leader of China's oldest environmental organization, Friends of Nature, noted that the former Chinese rhetoric of "We get rich first, we deal with the environmental problems second" is now a vision "suffocated in the smog."[38]

Feminism

Where southern environmental movements entail protection of local resources and community, women often play a defining role. This has always been so, but one consequence of colonialism is that this activity has become almost exclusively a women's preserve. As private property in land emerged, women's work tended to specialize in use of the commons for livestock grazing, firewood collection, game hunting, and seed gathering for medicinal purposes. These activities allowed women to supplement the incomes earned by men in the commercial sector. Women assumed a role as environmental managers, often forced to adapt to deteriorating conditions as commercial extractions increased over time.

The establishment of individual rights to property under colonialism typically privileged men, consolidating patriarchy as an anchor of modern capitalism. The result has been to fragment social systems built on the complementarity of male and female work. Men's work became specialized: In national statistics, it is routinely counted as contributing to the commercial sector. Conversely, the specialization of women's labor as "nonincome-earning" work means that women's work remains outside the commercial sector, leaving much of it invisible. The domain of invisible work includes maintaining the commons, and farming and producing food. It is not, however, sufficient to assume—as some ecofeminists do—that women constitute a "natural" constituency for environmental stewardship. Rather, women's role in social reproduction includes their relationship to nature: "Women relate to natural resources as part of their livelihood strategies, which reflect multiple objectives, powerful wider political forces, and, crucially, gender relations (i.e., social relations which systematically differentiate men and women) in processes of production and reproduction."[39]

At the practical level, women engage in multifaceted activity. Across the world, women's organizations empower poor women and communities and pressure governments and international agencies on behalf of women's rights. Countless activities of resource management undertaken by women form the basis of these practices. Perhaps most basic is the preservation of biodiversity in market and kitchen gardens. In Peru, the Aguarun Jivaro women nurture more than 100 varieties of manioc, the local staple root crop. Women have devised ingenious ways of household provisioning beside the cash-cropping systems managed by men.[40] Forest products (game, medicinal plants, condiments) are cultivated and harvested routinely by women.

In Kenya, the Kikuyu women in Laikipia have formed 354 women's groups to help them coordinate community decisions about access to and use of resources. Groups vary in size from 20 to 100 neighbors, both squatters and peasants; members contribute cash, products, and/or labor to the group, which in turn distributes resources equally among them. The groups have been able to pool funds to purchase land and establish small enterprises for the members. One such group, the Mwenda-Niire, was formed among landless squatters. Through saving funds, by growing maize and potatoes among the owner's crops, and through political negotiation, the group purchased the 567-hectare farm, allowing 130 landless families to become farmers. Group dynamics continue through labor-sharing schemes, collective infrastructure projects, and collective marketing. Collective movements such as this go beyond remedying development failures. They restore women's access to resources denied them under colonial and postcolonial developments.[41]

"Modern" Feminism

As with "environmentalism," empowerment initiatives such as these are not necessarily named, but they nevertheless are consistent with the modern feminist countermovement. The term *féminisme* first appeared in France in the 1880s, referring to a European movement for women's rights. It reappeared in the 1970s as "second-wave feminism" in the midst of the women's liberation movement for gender equality, taking on multiple meanings for women in the Third World, women of color, lesbians, and working women.[42] It is important here to underscore the diversity of this movement. Like environmentalism, feminism comes in different political shades—for example, from liberal to Marxist to ecofeminists. Our intent here is to extract key threads from feminisms.

With respect to development, the feminist countermovement has served to transform our understanding of the meaning and implications of development, as well as to institutionalize policy agendas committed to broad gender equality in a transformed concept of human development—"supporting the development of peoples' potential to lead creative, useful, and fulfilling lives."[43] Thus, in 1999, the Women's International Coalition for Economic Justice issued a Declaration for Economic Justice and Women's Empowerment, which demanded the following:

> [M]acro-policies designed to defend the rights of women and poor people and protect the environment, rather than expand growth, trade, and corporate profits exclusively. . . .[r]edefining economic efficiency to include measuring and valuing women's unpaid as well as paid work. Economic efficiency needs to be reoriented towards the effective realization of human development and human rights rather than growth, trade, and corporate profits.[44]

Embedded within this statement are three feminist threads that weave an alternative development agenda: assigning equal value to productive work, valuing the work of social reproduction, and reorienting social values from economism to humanism. These threads have informed successive phases of feminist influence on development thinking—in particular, issues concerning economic justice in the workplace, social policy supporting unpaid labor, and identification of the threat to human sustainability embodied in the mutual reinforcement of patriarchy and the market system. Thus, the "Advocacy Guide to Women's World Demands," arising from the 2000 World March of Women, declared,

> We live in a world whose dominant economic system, neoliberal capitalism, is fundamentally inhuman. It is a system governed by unbridled competition that strives for privatization, liberalization, and deregulation. It is a system entirely driven by the dictates of the market and where full enjoyment of basic human rights ranks below the laws of the marketplace. The result: the crushing social exclusion of large segments of the population, threatening world peace and the future of the planet. . . .
> Neoliberalism and patriarchy feed off each other and reinforce each other in order to maintain the vast majority of women in a situation of cultural inferiority, social devaluation, economic marginalization, "invisibility" of their existence and labor, and the marketing and commercialization of their bodies. All these situations closely resemble apartheid.[45]

The trajectory of feminist influence on development began with the first UN World Conference on Women, held in Mexico City in 1975, focused on extending existing development programs to include women—especially regarding equality in employment and education, political participation, and health services. This movement was known as Women in Development

(WID) and framed the UN Decade for Women (1976–1985). Since then, the movement has changed gears, shifting from remedies to alternatives,[46] meaning an "integrationist" approach to an "agenda-setting" approach, which challenges conventional development thinking with a feminist perspective.[47] The goal includes involving women as decision-makers concerned with empowering all women in their various life situations and championing opposition to all forms of gender discrimination (e.g., gendered divisions of labor). This has come to be known as Gender and Development (GAD), which refocuses on the different development priorities and needs of women and men without segregating gender issues into separate projects. The WID/GAD initiatives have focused on influencing development discourse and practice, especially through policy making in the development agencies.

An important resource in this project has been the Convention on the Elimination of All Forms of Discrimination Against Women (CEDAW), adopted by the United Nations Assembly in 1979, Article 5 of which imposes the responsibility on states to transform customs, attitudes, and practices that discriminate against women. This convention was the culmination of 30 years' work by the UN Commission on the Status of Women, instrumental in documenting discrimination against women.

Feminist Formulations

The WID position redresses the absence of gender issues in development theory and practice, in particular "women's inequality of access to and participation in the definition of economic structures and policies and the productive process itself."[48] In the development debate, WID feminists identified problems and formulated remedies in the following ways:

- Women have always been *de facto* producers, but technological and vocational supports have been minimal because development focuses on male cash-earning activity. Planners should therefore recognize women's contributions, especially as food producers for rural households and even urban markets.
- Women bear children, and a more robust understanding of development would include education, reproductive health care, family planning, and nutrition as social supports.
- Since women perform unpaid household/farm labor in addition to any paid labor development, planners should pursue ameliorative measures. Findings reveal that where women can be incorporated into income-earning activities, a net benefit accrues to community welfare since male income is often dissipated in consumer/urban markets.
- Thus, in addition to claiming what women need from development, *WID advocates what development needs from women.*[49]

In contrast, GAD feminism has offered new development agendas as follows:

- Since gender is socially constructed, it is important to address gender inequality not simply on the basis of who is doing what and whether it is valued, but also by asking how activities come to be valued, by whom, and in whose interest. The goal is to not simply identify women's discrimination but also to understand the structuring of gender discrimination.
- Households are differentiated social units, with conflictive and/or cooperative gendered divisions of labor. It is important to understand the nature of relations between productive and reproductive work, as well as the impact of development on household relations and vice versa.
- By shifting the focus to gender relations, or roles, and making visible the work of social reproduction (sustaining families and communities), GAD enables policy makers to see the benefits of delivering resources to women.

The WID/GAD project has served as a platform for reforming development initiatives, with the World Bank initiating WID projects in 1987 and shifting toward the GAD approach in the mid-1990s. This approach, for instance, seeks to substitute "gender mainstreaming" for individual women's projects, to avoid singling women out and to emphasize overall transformative programming for gender equality, taking male and female needs and experiences into account. WID projects were largely supplemental and left unchallenged the questions of differential access to services, resources, and opportunities between women and men—and the social and development consequences. Since the 1995 Beijing Conference on Women, the World Bank has attempted to "mainstream" gender issues, with variable results.[50]

Outside of such "policy-feminism" (mainstreaming gender issues in development programs), feminist countermovements have proliferated into a matrix of transnational feminist networks or TFNs (see the list of websites at the end of this chapter), working in national organizations, multilateral, and intergovernmental organizations and with local organizations to advocate for particular questions such as human rights, demilitarization, labor standards, and so on. Sociologist Valentine Moghadam notes that global communication technology allows these TFNs a fluid constituency and flexibility, which combines with nonhierarchical feminist principles and both formal and informal ways of operating. Some TFNs include

- DAWN (Development Alternatives with Women for a New Era): gender and economic justice, IFI policy, reproductive rights, and health—especially for poor southern women, redistribution of global wealth;

- WIDE (Women in Development Europe): enhanced European aid to ACP (African, Caribbean, and Pacific) countries, feminist alternatives to economic theory and development policies of the North, the IFIs, and the WTO;
- WEDO (Women's Environment and Development Organization): equal participation of women in policy making, formulation of alternative and sustainable solutions to global problems, democratization of the WTO; and
- WLUML (Women Living Under Muslim Laws): promotes human rights of women in Muslim states, exposes fundamentalist and state collusion, implementation of CEDAW in all Muslim states.[51]

Reflecting the development countermovement principle, DAWN, for example, argues, "Women should not depend on government but develop autonomously through self-organization," and its manifesto spells out its humanistic vision:

> Each person will have the opportunity to develop her or his full potential and creativity, and values of nurturance and solidarity will characterize human relationships. In such a world women's reproductive role will be redefined: men will be responsible for their sexual behavior, fertility and the well-being of both partners. Child care will be shared by men, women, and society as a whole.[52]

Such humanism evolved from an initial identification of "male bias" in social attitudes and thought and in public policy, as laid out in Diane Elson's *Male Bias in the Development Process* (1991). Elson notes that structural adjustment policies assume an infinite capacity of women to perform the work of social reproduction, given austerity cutbacks in social services: "The hidden 'equilibrating factor' is the household's, and particularly women's, ability to absorb the shocks of stabilization programs, through more work and 'making do' on limited incomes."[53] Male bias that ignores unpaid labor uses terms such as *efficiency* so that streamlining costs for a public hospital, for example, achieves efficiency by "transferring costs from the productive to the reproductive economy," where women's additional and unpaid work in caring for convalescing patients at home compensates for the shortfall in hospital care.[54] And WIDE, for example, extended this to a general critique of the free-market thesis, arguing that women must "reclaim the market in a global system where every part of life—even a person's kidney—is increasingly peddled as a commodity, and which sees people as consumers rather than citizens."[55]

Thus, a feminist paradigm has emerged that is not simply about adding women to the equation. Rather, from the standpoint of women's experience, feminists have gained a unique perspective on the limits, silences, and violence of an economic model that accounts only for certain definitions of what constitutes "productive" work via an unsustainable system of accounting that has no debit side (for what economists term *externalities*). It stems from the UN System of National Accounts, which records additions to GNP, but not "costs" such as discrimination (in schooling, nutrition, employment), environmental degradation, the invisible work of social reproduction in the home, and so forth. As Marilyn Waring notes in *If Women Counted: A New Feminist Economics* (1988), economics serves as a "tool of people in power," insofar as value is imputed to a narrow band of cash-generating activity: Women, assigned to the household, are discounted, and "informals"—indigenous peasants, nomads, and forest dwellers—are marginalized or displaced as "unproductive," along with disregard for "nature's economy." Thus, economic theory conditions the possibility of a predatory relationship toward women and nature through development practices. The conventional development paradigm, in positing a rationalist (Eurocentric) approach, discounts diverse non-European knowledges governed by ecological and cultural practices, where stewardship of nature is cultural, rather than a program.[56]

The Question of Empowerment

Broadly, the feminist paradigm stresses that development is a relational, not a universal, process, and we should be aware of how our ideals shape assumptions about other societies and their needs. Concerns for the empowerment of women in Third World settings should refer to those circumstances, not to abstract ideals of individual emancipation. Consider the "feminization of global labor." As Jeffrey Sachs argues regarding the garment factory expansion in Bangladesh, "Sweatshops are the first rung on the ladder out of extreme poverty" for the female workers who have "grown up in the countryside, extraordinarily poor, illiterate and unschooled, and vulnerable to chronic hunger and hardship in a domineering patriarchal society."[57] Far from an unproblematic gain for women, sweatshop jobs are constructed for women as repetitive, dead-end, and often debilitating so that their introduction to the global economy is on unequal terms. Cynthia Enloe's research, guided by the question of what makes labor cheap, argues that women are not simply acted on by globalization; rather, corporate strategies depend on local constructions of femininity.[58] And, while Asian women have experienced wage gains (until "defeminization" through industrial upgrading in the Asian regional division of labor), research on Mexican *maquiladoras* reveals a different experience where wages stagnate.[59] Political economist Lourdes Benería notes, for contextualization, "Evaluation of the effects of employment for women needs to take into consideration what happens at the level of gender socialization and power relations."[60] As it happens, women's organizations in the *maquiladoras* have gone beyond traditional male concerns with wages—considering health, reproduction freedom, and environmental concerns—and challenge "the idea that what happens in the factory is separate from what happens in the community and that the company's responsibility does not extend beyond the factory gate."[61]

Gender, Poverty, and Fertility

Women's resource management can be ingenious, but often poverty subverts their ingenuity. For example, where women have no secure rights to land, they are less able to engage in sustainable resource extraction. Environmental deterioration may follow. When we see women stripping forests and overworking fragile land, we see just the tip of the iceberg. Many of these women have been displaced from lands converted for export cropping, or they have lost common land on which to subsist.

Environmental damage stemming from resource impoverishment has fueled the debate surrounding population growth in the former Third World. Population control has typically been directed at women—ranging from female infanticide to forced sterilization (as in India and Peru) to family planning interventions by development agencies.[62] Feminists entered this debate to protect women from such biological manipulation and to underscore that fertility control of southern women overlooks excessive northern consumption of global resources.

Feminists advocate enabling women to take control of their fertility without targeting women as the source of population growth. On a global scale, the current world population of about 7.5 billion is likely to peak at 9 billion, but could possibly double by 2050 unless more aggressive intervention occurs. Studies suggest that female education and health services reduce birthrates. A World Bank report noted that women without secondary education, on average, have seven children; if almost half these women receive secondary education, the average declines to three children per woman.[63] Sub-Saharan Africa is currently the region of greatest population growth. Declining African fertility rates in the 1980s have reversed because of the failure to meet needs for contraception and preference for large families related to women's continuing unequal access to education.[64] As Diakhoumba Gassama, of the Senegalese Council of Women, stated the following:

> The lack of investment in rights-based comprehensive sex education means very few young women use sexual and reproduction health services before the age of 18, less than a third of those aged 15 to 24 have profound knowledge on HIV, and many single women have unsatisfied contraceptive needs.[65]

Enabling equal education for women may also reduce patriarchal practices of marrying daughters off once they reach puberty, associating status with large families (rural Latin America), and selling farm girls to contractors for factory work and/or the sex trade (East and Southeast Asia).

Evidence based on the results of contraceptive use in Bangladesh has been cited as superseding conventional theories of "demographic transition." Demographic theory extrapolates from the Western experience a pattern of demographic transition whereby birthrates decline significantly as economic growth proceeds. The threshold is the shift from preindustrial to industrial society, in which education and health technologies spread. Children are viewed increasingly as an economic liability rather than as necessary hands in the household economy or as a response to high childhood mortality rates. Evidence from Bangladesh showed a 21 percent decline in fertility rates during the decade and a half (1975–1991) in which a national family planning program was in effect. The study's authors claimed that these findings "dispute the notion that 'development is the best contraceptive,'" adding, "Contraceptives are the best contraceptive."[66]

Feminist groups argue that family planning and contraception need to be rooted in the broader context of women's rights. Almost twice as many women as men are illiterate, and that difference is growing, often rendering women vulnerable to males who do not allow them to make "contraceptive choices." Nzira Deus of Movfemme (Mozambique) claims,

> Often sexual and reproductive programmes in Mozambique ignore the social and cultural factors that prevent young women and girls from making health decisions, thus making them vulnerable to undesired pregnancy, sexual violence and debilitating health conditions such as obstetric fistulas.[67]

The International Women's Health Coalition identified the Bangladesh Women's Health Coalition, serving 110,000 women at 10 clinics around the country, as a model for future UN planning. This group began in 1980 to offer abortions. With suggestions from the women it served, the coalition has expanded into family planning, basic health care services, child immunizations, legal aid, and training in literacy and employment skills.[68]

The correlation between women's rights and low fertility rates has ample confirmation. In Tunisia, the 1956 Code of Individual Rights guaranteed women political equality, backed with family planning and other social programs that included free, legal abortions. Tunisia is a leader in Africa, with a population growth rate of only 1.9 percent. The director-general of Tunisia's National Office of Family and Population, Nebiha Gueddana, claims that successful family planning can occur in a Muslim society: "We have 30 years of experience with the equality of women and . . . none of it has come at the expense of family values."[69] And in Kerala, where the literacy rate for women is two-and-a-half times the average for India and where the status of women has long been high relative to the rest of the country, land reforms and comprehensive social welfare programs were instrumental in achieving a 40 percent reduction in the fertility rate between 1960 and 1985, reducing the population growth rate to 1.8 percent in the 1980s.[70]

With supportive social conditions, fertility decisions can have both individual and social benefits. Fertility decisions usually occur within patriarchal settings—households or societies. Recent population debates incorporate elements of the feminist perspective, emphasizing women's reproductive rights and health in the context of their need for secure livelihoods and political participation.[71] This view was embedded in the document from the 1994 UN Conference on Population and Development. Although contested by the Vatican and some Muslim nations (particularly Iran), the document states that women have the right to reproductive and sexual health, defined as "a state of complete physical, mental, and social well-being" in all matters relating to reproduction.[72]

In relation to the post-2015 Sustainable Development Goals (SDGs) deliberations, Mariana Mancilla of Mexico's feminist organization, Balance, implores,

> As our governments negotiate . . . it's important to remind them that young people should not only be valued for their role in reducing poverty. All of our human rights must be recognized. Young people, especially young women, have a right to a quality education and access to youth-friendly sexual and reproductive health services that comply with our needs to control all aspects of our sexual lives. Only then will we achieve truly sustainable development.[73]

Women's Rights Trajectory

The feminist countermovement has clearly made an impact on the development agenda since the days of WID's inception. However, the improvement of women's material condition and social status across the world has not followed in step. In 2005, UNESCO sponsored a 10-year anniversary "stock-taking" of the condition of women, including proposals for measuring women's empowerment—a timely complement to CEDAW. The core of this report was twofold: first, that the 2000 Millennium Development Goals (MDGs), in producing gender-neutral development indicators (other than primary education), remained silent regarding women's unpaid care work, reproductive and sexual rights, subjection to violence, and empowerment needs (for example, emphasizing secondary school opportunities which in turn would increase marriage age, reduce fertility, improve employment prospects, and reduce child malnutrition); and second, that in developing empowerment measures, "It is as important to determine women's participation and rights *across* social groups as it is to understand women's access and rights in relation to men's access and rights."[74] Recent negotiations regarding gender issues in the Sustainable Development Goals (SDGs) include a more holistic treatment of gender equality and empowerment (see Chapter 9), transcending the MDG focus on parity in female access to primary education and employment—essentially a WID-style approach.[75]

In 2011, the first report of the new agency UN Women claimed more than half of working women in the world—600 million—have insecure jobs without legal protection, and justice remains out of reach for many: "In Cambodia, for example, the forensic test necessary to lay a rape charge costs two weeks' wages. In Kenya, a land claim in an inheritance case can cost $800."[76] In 2013, UN Women launched a database examining national constitutions through a gender lens:

> Expected to be of great use to gender equality and human rights activists and experts, the innovative searchable database, to be updated annually, provides a comprehensive overview of the current status of provisions relevant to women's rights and gender equality across the world, including comparison of the data across various countries. The resource covers 195 countries.[77]

The question of women's rights also concerns how different cultures regulate women's private lifestyles. In some Muslim states, with considerable cultural variation, women's rights generally remain subordinated to Islamic law or, as Muslim feminists claim, to a male interpretation of the Koran. In Morocco, for example, women require the permission of male relatives to marry, name their children, or work. In most Islamic states, the gender division of labor is the cultural foundation, with women having the additional right to seek higher education and work/volunteer outside the home. A female Pakistani journalist notes Muslim women's roles "in the overall scheme of things are foundational, and contribute significantly, if not crucially, towards making human society function productively and optimally as a whole."[78] An orthodox interpretation would claim Muslim women "prefer to be respected for their intelligence and character rather than being chased after for their looks, and would like to pursue personal and spiritual fulfillment at a human pace without having to neglect their families."[79] Some Islamic women's groups mobilize against "Muslim apartheid," or gender segregation and forms of oppression of women (e.g., restrictions on mobility, dress codes, sexual freedom, property rights)—some of which were imposed by the West in the colonial era.[80]

In short, different cultures have their own trajectory of mobilization around women's rights, depending on political opportunity rather than simply advocating individual women's rights on a Western model.[81] This is analogous to the environmental countermovement that has different place-based needs and opportunities, even as it may share common principles of challenging development's environmental "externalities," or, in the case of feminism, gender silences, deficits, or inequalities.

In 2015, the UN convened a post-2015 Sustainable Development Agenda conference focusing on women's rights in relation to climate change. According to the UN, women are the most vulnerable to climate change since they have a disproportionate role in farming and the agricultural workforce and within households are responsible for food and water provisioning. Land access rights and recognition of women's unique local ecosystem knowledge are central to addressing and overcoming such vulnerabilities. On average, "63 percent of rural households depend on women to obtain drinking water . . . [and] women in Sub-Saharan Africa spend an average of about 40 billion hours a year collecting water." But on the positive front, from 2008 to 2014, "Women delegates representing nations at the United Nations Framework Convention on Climate Change rose from 33 percent to 38 percent, while women's participation as Heads of Delegations increased from 18 percent to 26 percent."[82] This suggests a greater likelihood of a more explicit gendered understanding of the implications of climate change as policy choices are made.

Food Sovereignty

Food sovereignty has emerged as a powerful global countermovement in the twenty-first century, engaging both rural and urban constituencies. The term *food sovereignty* refers, ultimately, to community self-determination in producing and consuming food equitably and sustainably. It embodies the values of environmentalism, gender rights, collective democracy, and restoring the centrality of farming to the human life-world. As a countermovement, food sovereignty appeared publicly in 1996, but its roots are in the 1980s in Central America, where, for example, peasant mobilization in Costa Rica and organized initiatives in Panama and Nicaragua espoused the goal of food autonomy. [83]

When the Mexican government instituted its National Food Program (Programa Nacional de Alimentación) in 1983, its stated objective was "to achieve food sovereignty"—implying not simply food self-sufficiency but also reducing food dependency and imports of agrotechnologies, and strengthening national control of the food chain.[84] During the next decade, a neoliberal Mexican government entered into negotiations to eliminate this program and its foundations in its distinctive *ejido* (collective lands) system as it signed on to the North American Free Trade Agreement (NAFTA). Meanwhile, peasant producers in the southern state of Chiapas, denied the promise of land reforms, were squeezed by expanding cattle ranches and coffee plantations and displaced into the Lacandon rainforest to fend for themselves laying groundwork for a dramatic rebellion.

On New Year's Day 1994, hundreds of impoverished peasants rose up against what they perceived to be the Mexican state's continued violation of local rights, in the name of the Mexican revolutionary Emilio Zapata. Not coincidentally, the revolt fell on the day NAFTA was implemented. To the Zapatista rebels, NAFTA symbolized the undermining of the revolutionary heritage in the Mexican Constitution of 1917, by which communal lands were protected from alienation. In 1992, under the pretext of structural adjustment policies and the promise of NAFTA, the Mexican government opened these lands for sale to Mexican and foreign agribusinesses. In addition, NAFTA included a provision to deregulate commodity markets— especially the market for corn, the staple peasant food, and to enable its import from the American Midwest. The rebel organization, Ejército Zapatista de Liberación Nacional (EZLN), recognizing the new government had sold out the possibility of "food sovereignty," proclaimed the following:

> What we see is our country being governed by neoliberals . . . our leaders are destroying our nation, our Mexican Patria. . . . For example, they make laws like the Free Trade Agreement, which end up leaving many Mexicans destitute, like campesinos and small producers, because they are "gobbled up" by the big agro-industrial companies . . . because food is no longer being produced in our countryside, just what the big capitalists sell, and the good lands are being stolen through trickery and with the help of the politicians.[85]

In this way, the Zapatistas inspired disadvantaged communities throughout Mexico and the world to seek self-determination, with their uprising against NAFTA providing a powerful and symbolic critique of the politics of globalization. As it happened, NAFTA flooded Mexico with cheap (subsidized) corn from Iowa, undercutting local maize prices for campesinos, and driving almost two million producers off the land during the 1990s.[86] NAFTA was indeed a dress rehearsal for the impact of the WTO's Agreement on Agriculture. The WTO universalized the exposure of small-scale producers to dumping of subsidized grains from the United States and Europe by a handful of food corporations that manage 85 percent of the world grain trade and contribute to the centralized control of the global food chain—from gene to supermarket shelf. In the name of globalization, this agro-industrial model (including risks associated with factory farming and food scares) is adopted across the world as the solution to food insecurity, displacing northern and southern farmers. Canadian farmer Nettie Wiebe remarks, "The difficulty for us, as farming people, is that we are rooted in the places where we live and grow our food. The other side, the corporate world, is globally mobile."[87]

Resistances to this global conception of "food security" are mushrooming—framed by the alternative conception of food sovereignty. Emerging in the context of universal liberalization of farm sectors across the state system in the 1990s, it has inspired the largest social movement in the world,[88] appeared as a legal norm or in the constitutions of several states—notably Venezuela, Ecuador, Bolivia, Senegal, Mali, Nicaragua, and Nepal, helped to frame a growing civil society presence in the United Nations Committee on World Food Security,[89] and stimulated a mushrooming of local food system politics.[90] Perhaps most of all, food sovereignty's arrival marks a threshold moment in humanity's relationship to Earth, given the centrality of agriculture to the health of both humans and the environment. Its vision is fundamentally at odds with conventional development priorities that privilege urbanism and industrial agricultures. In 2008, the comprehensive UN and World Bank–sponsored International Assessment of Agricultural Science and Technology for Development (IAASTD) observed that "agriculture is at a crossroads," referring to the problem of expanding an unsustainable form of industrial agriculture at the expense of farming livelihoods and practices that could ensure local, domestic food security and ecological and public health.[91]

The food sovereignty countermovement emerged through the experience of a global agrarian crisis accompanying the neoliberal era (1980s to the present), as structural adjustment policies (SAPs) dismantled farm sector supports across the global South and small producers were forced, under a "free trade" regime, to compete unfairly with imported foodstuffs from the world's granaries (the United States and the EU). At the 1996 FAO World Food Summit in Rome, an NGO Forum declared that "food sovereignty" should take "precedence over macro-economic policies and trade liberalization," drawing attention to the shortcomings of the neoliberal conception of "food security"—where food dumping by northern agribusiness amplified southern food dependency as well as a farmer exodus from the land.[92] Vía Campesina (VC), the international peasant coalition comprising over 150 organizations from more than 70 countries and representing over 200 million small producers and landless peasants, declared, "The neo-liberal agricultural policies have led to the destruction of our family farm economies and to a profound crisis in our societies."[93] In this way, the food sovereignty countermovement politicized the existing global "food security" policy by challenging the corporate-centered trade architecture, its anti-rural population prejudice, its discounting of women's rights (even as they are ubiquitous as farmers and farmworkers), and its disregard for soil and water health. The urban bias and ecological blindspot of conventional development was linked to social crisis.

The programmatic element of food sovereignty concerns the struggle for food policy autonomy (against the WTO trade regime), alongside revaluing rural communities and their landscapes. Vía Campesina's 1996 definition of food sovereignty emphasized "the right of each nation to maintain and develop its own capacity to produce its basic foods respective of cultural and productive diversity."[94] Later, European VC leader Paul Nicholson summarized, "We propose local food markets, the right of any country to protect its borders from imported food, sustainable agriculture and the defence of biodiversity, healthy food, jobs and strong livelihood in rural areas."[95] Vía Campesina makes the following claim:

> Biodiversity has as a fundamental base the recognition of human diversity, the acceptance that we are different and that every people and each individual has the freedom to think and to be. Seen in this way, biodiversity is not only flora, fauna, earth, water, and ecosystems; it is also cultures, systems of production, human and economic relations, forms of government; in essence it is freedom.[96]

In addition to defending biodiversity and developing agroecology, Vía Campesina claims small producers to be the principle agent to "feed the world and cool the planet," insofar as stabilizing diverse small-scale farm systems addresses the global prominence of undernutrition in the countryside and supports a low-input agriculture. Current estimates are that small producers feed up to 70 percent of the world and have the capacity (if adequately supported) to produce as much if not more food than large monocultures of industrial agriculture.[97]

As a Polanyian countermovement, food sovereignty establishes that the global market is instituted in such a way that states serve private interests, reducing food to the status of a commodity. It offers an ethical challenge concerning material and practical applications: By what right does the global market displace people, knowledge, and cultures at the risk of food insecurity? The coordinator of the coalition of agrarian movements and progressive NGOs—the International Planning Committee on Food Sovereignty (IPC)—Henry Saragih noted, "By reducing the meaning of food to a commodity only those who have money will be able to have access to food."[98]

In shifting the emphasis from market value to social need, Vía Campesina observes that "food is first and foremost a source of nutrition and only secondarily an item of trade."[99] Of course, nation-states are by no means endowed with similar natural and economic "resources," and some are ex-colonies established historically as food exporters, so some food circulation remains necessary for populations currently dependent on food/exporting.[100] Here, the right to food is at once universal but not universally available, given the diversity of landscapes and of effects of empire. At the same time, the food sovereignty movement posits a substantive, rather than formal, conception of rights to food "whose content is not necessarily preordained by the state. . . . The right is a right to self-determination, for communities to redefine for themselves the substance of the food relations appropriate to their geographies [and ecologies]."[101] And women's rights have become a key element of the food sovereignty countermovement in the twenty-first century, particularly insofar as women are central to production, procurement, and household food security.[102] In 2006, Vía Campesina issued this declaration:

> We recognize the fundamental role of women in agriculture and fishing and in the use and management of natural resources. There can be no genuine agrarian reform without gender equity. Therefore we demand and we commit ourselves to ensuring that women receive full equality of opportunities and rights to land and natural resources.[103]

The claim is that states and/or other international institutions should guarantee, but not necessarily author, the content of these rights, which include collective rights to be realized in community-supported agricultures. Thus, the movement represents both an umbrella of resistance to corporate-led agriculture and a strategic vision transcending the conventional categories of neoliberal economic development discourse. A key thread, of course, is the claim to respect and value small-scale producers, rejecting the development narrative that consigns people of the land to the historical dustbin and overcoming economistic assumptions of human separateness from nature:

> No agrarian reform is acceptable that is based only on land distribution. We believe that the new agrarian reform must include a cosmic vision of the territories of communities of peasants, the landless, indigenous peoples, rural workers, fisherfolk, nomadic pastoralists, tribes, afro-descendents, ethnic minorities, and displaced peoples, who base their work on the production of food and who maintain a relationship of respect and harmony with Mother Earth and the oceans.[104]

Put another way, Brazilian Landless-Workers Movement leader João Pedro Stedile observes, "We want an agrarian practice that transforms farmers into guardians of the land, and a different way of farming, that ensures an ecological equilibrium and also guarantees that land is not seen as private property."[105]

While the meaning of food sovereignty is anchored in the struggles of the small producer coalition, the term has traveled beyond its identification with the countryside, being adopted in the United States also by "advocacy groups associated with the turn to sustainable/organic/local food systems, as well as development NGOs, faith-based charities, Native American rights organizations, and environmental groups," and across Australia through the medium of community-supported agricultures, culminating in the Brisbane-based social enterprise, Food Connect, which emerged in 2004.[106] While not disengaging food sovereignty from its producer origins, the term itself includes political alliances with urban labor and urban consumers. And it seeks to restore urban/rural balance:

> In the context of food sovereignty, agrarian reform benefits all of society, providing healthy, accessible and culturally appropriate food, and social justice. Agrarian reform can put an end to the massive and forced rural exodus from the countryside to the city, which has made cities grow at unsustainable rates and under inhuman conditions.[107]

Stabilizing the word's small-producer population is a vision of urban/rural balance, as well as of environmental stewardship, and here, in addition to the right to food, the movement claims the right to *produce* food. Here, land is key, and Vía Campesina declares,

> Access to the land by peasants has to be understood as a guarantee for survival and the valorization of their culture, the autonomy of their communities and a new vision of the preservation of natural resources for humanity and future generations. Land is a good of nature that needs to be used for the welfare of all. Land is not, and cannot be, a marketable good that can be obtained in whatever quantity by those that have the financial means.[108]

This concluding comment is *apropos* of the current "global land grab," by which a variety of investors, including states, are acquiring land as a speculative or productive financial asset. The food sovereignty countermovement represents, then, the voice of citizens across the world concerned with the insecurities of a development model premised on commodifying land and food.

SUMMARY

This chapter has introduced the concept of the countermovement, stemming from Karl Polanyi's treatise on the contradictions of market society. While Polanyi viewed the "double movement" (markets stimulating protective responses) as initially resolved in the institution of the twentieth-century welfare state, global conditions are now different. The public sphere has been progressively sold off, and states now serve the market, rather than the other way around. While governments are under pressure to play by the global rules of a free trade and investment regime, citizens do not always share their outlook and resist in countless ways.

In this chapter, we have focused on how countermovements both resist and challenge the priority given to the market calculus in the name of development. While they are an integral dimension of development, such historic countermovements can express a fundamental desire to transcend the homogenizing and disempowering dynamics of the global development project and to establish sustainable and diversified social life based on new forms of associative politics. Whether one supports them or not, their responses reveal problematic aspects of development as such. As the new century unfolds, it is clear that the assumptions and content of the global development project are in (cumulative) question. Indeed, the crisis of the globalization project is the subject of the following chapter.

FURTHER READING

Baviskar, Amita. *In the Belly of the River: Tribal Conflicts Over the Development in the Narmada Valley.* New York: Oxford University Press, 2005.

Claeys, Priscilla. *Human Rights and the Food Sovereignty Movement. Reclaiming Control.* London: Routledge, 2015.

Desmarais, Annette Aurélie. *La Vía Campesina: Globalization and the Power of Peasants.* Halifax, NS: Fernwood, 2007.

George, Susan. *Another World Is Possible If. . . .* London: Verso, 2004.

Harcourt, Wendy. *Body Politics in Development: Critical Debates in Gender and Development.* London: Zed Books, 2009.

Hawken, Paul. *Blessed Unrest.* New York: Penguin, 2008.

Martinez-Alier, Joan. *The Environmentalism of the Poor: A Study of Ecological Conflicts and Valuation.* London: Edward Elgar, 2002.

Starr, Amory. *Naming the Enemy: Anti-Corporate Movements Confront Globalization.* London: Zed Books, 2000.

Wolford, Wendy. *This Land Is Ours Now: Social Mobilization and the Meanings of Land in Brazil.* Durham, NC: Duke University Press, 2010.

SELECT WEBSITES

Amnesty International: www.amnesty.org
Corporate Watch (USA): www.corpwatch.org
Development Alternatives with Women for a New Era (DAWN): www.dawnnet.org
Equal Exchange: www.equalexchange.com
Erosion, Technology, and Concentration: www.etcgroup.org
Fairtrade Labelling Organizations International (FLO, Germany): www.fairtrade.net
Focus on the Global South (Thailand): www.focusweb.org
Food First (USA): www.foodfirst.org
Friends of the Earth International (Netherlands): www.foei.org
Genetic Resources Action International (GRAIN): www.grain.org
Global Environment Facility (USA): www.gefweb.org
Global Exchange (USA): www.globalexchange.org
Greenpeace International (Netherlands): www.greenpeace.org/international/
International Forum on Globalization (USA): www.ifg.org
Jubilee South: www.jubileesouth.org
Médecins Sans Frontières: www.msf.org
Oxfam International (UK): www.oxfam.org
Public Citizen Global Trade Watch (USA): www.citizen.org/trade
Rainforest Action Network (USA): www.ran.org
Survival International (UK: tribal peoples' rights): www.survival-international.org
Third World Network (Malaysia): www.twnside.org.sg
Transnational Institute (Netherlands): www.tni.org
UN Women: www.unwomen.org
United Students Against Sweatshops (USA): www.studentsagainstsweatshops.org
Via Campesina (Honduras): www.viacampesina.org

PART III

Millennial Reckonings (2000s to Present)

8

The Globalization
Project in Crisis

While the globalization project still shapes development initiatives and policies, there are signs that its tensions and contradictions are coming to a head. Just as the development project unraveled as corporations and banks went global, precipitating a debt crisis and "lost decade" in the South and a trade regime to undo "economic nationalism," so the globalization project is unraveling in its own way. The world is in a process of transition toward a reformulation of development from various angles, goaded by (among other forces) Pope Francis's 2015 encyclical, *Laduato Si'*—an astonishing papal pronouncement linking social and environmental justice. As the editor of *The Guardian Weekly* commented,

> For Francis, there is a vital distinction between human needs, limited but non-negotiable, and appetites, which are potentially unlimited. The poor, he says, have their needs denied, while the rich have their appetites indulged. The environmental crisis links these two aspects of the problem.[1]

In this contentious conjuncture, different responses converge on the rather overused nomenclature of *sustainable development*. This chapter examines some of these tensions, anticipating sustainable development initiatives outlined in the following chapter.

In the autumn of the globalization project, neoliberal economic policies have exposed citizens to greater uncertainty with increasingly volatile financial markets and precarious employment. In May 2015, the British newspaper *The*

Guardian Weekly's article "Has Globalisation Hit the Wall?" argued that "failure to shield workers from foreign competition has . . . undermined faith in globalisation," that "the impact of the [2008] financial crisis has led the public to feel they need protection from the ravages of the markets," and suggested this desire contributed to "the resurgence of Scottish nationalism, rising support for the Front National in France, and the election of the radical Syriza government in Greece"—all anti-*status quo* developments.[2]

A month earlier, *The New York Times* article "At Global Economic Gathering, US Primacy Is Seen as Ebbing" reported that at the annual meetings of the International Monetary Fund (IMF) and the World Bank, the chief economic advisor to the Indian government observed that because of "tight budgets and competing financial demands, the United States is less able to maintain its economic power, and because of political infighting, it has been unable to formally share it either"—propelling China to create the Asian Infrastructure Investment Bank, which Lawrence Summers (top economic advisor to Presidents Clinton and Obama) suggested signaled "the moment the United States lost its role as underwriter of the global economic system."[3]

The unpopularity of a casino-like global economy, in which unrelenting competition is the name of the game, with firms restructuring and outsourcing jobs in order to survive, rendering employment everywhere precarious with drastic *human* consequence, is one signal of crisis. The other is the erosion of the network of international rules and institutions first established by the US-orchestrated "development project" in the post–World War II era. This has led to a growing multipolarity as new regional and trade alliances fill a vacuum left by a retreating United States. President Obama's sponsorship of the Trans-Pacific Partnership (TPP) in 2015 exemplified this hiatus, insofar as this regional trade agreement was not about development (as it excluded "poorer" countries); rather, it was about creating a political-economic counterweight to a rising China in a US-orchestrated Pacific Rim market.[4] Development ideals no longer shape such discourse, now framed more explicitly in "market rule" terms—as if the market is now the only legitimate pathway to the future.

Much of this chapter suggests a cumulative crisis of vision—in other words, the problem is recycled as the solution, which, in turn, deepens the actual crisis. This is evident, for example, in the recycling of austerity policy in the South and now the global North and in the "booming business of global warming," revealing the inertia of political and economic structures and mindsets. In detailing how the catastrophe of global warming is viewed as a market opportunity, one commentator observes:

It should not be surprising that the ideologies that led us here, those that have guided the postindustrial age—techno-lust and hyper-individualism, conflation of growth with progress, unflagging faith in unfettered markets—are the same ones many now rely on as we try to find a way out. Nowhere is humankind's mix of vision and tunnel vision more apparent than in how we're planning for a warmed world.[5]

Just as the big energy companies and countries such as the United States and China expect to release almost 3,000 more gigatons of CO_2 into the atmosphere (five times more than would keep global warming manageable), in part because these reserves represent investments worth \$27 trillion,[6] so there is a discursive inertia supporting powerful political and economic interests. This chapter examines various dimensions of the crisis of the globalization project, expressed in a growing groundswell of resistance and revision of development.

Social Crisis

A straightforward way of understanding the source of social crisis in the globalization project is to recognize that this project changed the conditions of development drastically by creating a global labor force. It is commonplace that the rise of the so-called First World was fueled by the extraction of material resources in the non-European world, and this gave rise to the claim that Europe and its settler societies pioneered "development." Evidently, *now that the global development project's commodification of resources has extended to labor in the global South, development has lost its luster as northern citizens experience increasingly uncertain livelihood opportunities.* Between 1980 and 2000, the *global* labor supply trebled as the ex-Soviet bloc was incorporated into the global economy alongside China's and India's rising workforce. The newcomers came with very low wages, *weakening the bargaining position of workers elsewhere*, and since 2000, "other emerging market countries have added to the supply, including Vietnam, Indonesia, Cambodia and Thailand, with Bangladesh and others entering the picture."[7] Under these circumstances, transnational corporations (TNCs) have been able to extract concessions from northern labor with the threat of offshoring jobs. Job insecurity has become the new normal, with labor flexibility policies advocated by the IMF and the World Bank as necessary to the competition for foreign capital, intensifying a process of weakening employment protections. Economist Guy Standing points out the following:

> In the 1960s, a typical worker entering the labour market of an industrialized country could have anticipated having four employers by the time he retired. In those circumstances, it made sense to identify with the firm in which he was

employed. Today a worker would be foolish to do so. Now, a typical worker—more likely to be a woman—can anticipate having nine employers before reaching the age of 30.[8]

While Rostow's "age of high mass consumption" may serve a global minority, it is hardly a trajectory now for national citizenries, many of whom experience increasingly unstable livelihood possibilities.

The social crisis, then, is twofold. On the one hand, it is a crisis of the development promise. For the global North, instead of leading the way as a stable region of relatively prosperous citizenries, its foundation of steady employment is steadily eroding. Those jobs not offshored have lost considerable ground, with US-based firms reducing health care benefits, for example, and cutting pension obligations and other social entitlements won by organized labor in the development project:

> In 1980, US employers paid 89 percent of contributions towards retirement benefits; by 2006, that had fallen to 52 percent. By 2009, only a fifth of US employees had company-based pensions. . . . In 2009, Ford's workers gave up cost-of-living allowances and lost holiday pay and college scholarships for their children as well as tuition assistance.[9]

Northern citizens' expectations of improvement as members of the advanced industrial countries have foundered on a trade regime that has exposed their employment security to relative labor costs across an uneven world. For those in the global South, while jobs are incoming with transnational investments, the highly competitive global labor market has a similar effect—working against a national development scenario. The social crisis is truly global, as the global South has experienced a declining wage share of 10 to 20 percentage points since 1994, while the wage share in the North has fallen by 9 percentage points since 1990. And alongside 12 million stateless people, the "rights of a huge proportion of the world's 214 million migrants remained unprotected in 2012, both at home and in the host state."[10]

On the other hand, northern economies are now hosting the very same structural adjustments visited upon the global South from the 1980s. Public debt is endemic. This recalls the 1980s debt regime, in which southern governments were required by the international financial institutions (IFIs) to privatize their public assets to stabilize the financial sector. The antistate syndrome spread to the North, where during the 1990s corporate tax reduction in the name of promoting productive investment eroded public finance without growth—leaving states (other than in Scandinavia) living beyond their means.[11] When the debt crisis hit the global North in the first decade of the twenty-first century, privatization and new financial disciplines rolled back northern public services, and public employees faced retrenchment as public sector downgrading became "part of the post-2008 adjustment across all industrialized countries."[12]

Public spending cuts exacerbated already weakened economies following two decades of industry offshoring. The decline in stable employment has reduced tax bases and public capacity to provide social safety nets: In the United States, for instance, with one in nine Americans living on food stamps in 2010, more than half of the unemployed are now ineligible for unemployment benefits.[13] Policy responses have uniformly focused on reducing government spending in the name of debt reduction. The argument for public austerity is market based, with neoliberal policy claiming that a retreat of the state allows the private sector to fill the gap, which has not happened significantly—because there is more money to be made in financial instruments and speculation, rather than productive investments.[14] As a result, a growing proportion of the working population "whose jobs are insecure, who have limited access to secure housing, and who juggle jobs and child-rearing in a frantic effort to keep up" represent, in Standing's terms, a new "**precariat**." He estimates 40 percent of the UK population now belongs to the precariat, a more significant destination than the "middle class," and increasingly evident in a politics of frustration, expressed in the mushrooming of the Occupy Movement in 2011 and rising ethnic tensions across the North.[15]

Unemployment has become the great leveler across the North/South divide. By the end of the twenty-first century's first decade, global unemployment was running at around 200 million, in addition to 1.4 billion working poor. The International Labour Organization (ILO) reports that by 2019 more than 212 million will be out of work, with youth unemployment rates running three times higher than for their adult counterparts.[16] About half of the world's workforce holds casual jobs—which means that around 90 percent of the global workforce is poor, vulnerable, or unemployed. The European Union has about 50 million "vulnerable" workers and 72 million working poor. Most dramatic of all was the approximately 9 percent unemployment rate following the 2008 financial crisis in the "developed economies and the EU"—higher than any other global region, including central and southeastern Europe, Latin America, and the Caribbean.[17]

Two related processes are at work: first, a hollowing-out of northern economies—in part, because "companies themselves have become commodities, to be bought and sold through mergers and acquisitions," reducing loyalty to employees (skilled and unskilled) as shareholders (often foreign pension and private equity funds) assume ownership;[18] and also because of the relocation of goods and services production to the global South. The consequence is a distinctive (and potentially politicizing) bifurcation between a global consumer class and a large casual and unemployed labor force across both world regions.

One palpable example of this bifurcation is that of Spain, where 85 percent of the jobs lost in the 2008 financial crash were temporary. That is, "flexible labor" enabled adjustment to the downturn:

> Government and trades unions had reacted to earlier pressure for flexibility by preserving securities for regular workers and creating a buffer of temporaries. This not only led to a multi-tier labour force but resentment by the precariat towards the unions that looked after their own members at its expense.[19]

While some of this precariat were migrant laborers from northern Africa and Ecuador, labor flexibility is a strategy by which corporations and governments divide and rule labor. Manipulating labor is exacerbated by an undemocratic EU financial architecture associated with the Euro currency union—with its structural adjustment-inspired deflationary policies overriding sovereignty on the southern Europe perimeter in the wake of the 2008 crisis. As sociologist Boaventura de Sousa Santos characterizes it,

> In broad terms, this amounts to chaining these countries to their peripheral position within the continent, subjecting them to unfairly disproportionate indebtedness, actively disabling the state apparatus and public services, pushing the middle classes into abrupt impoverishment, forcing young people to emigrate and cutting investment in education and research. . . . Spain, Greece and Portugal are paradigmatic tragedies.[20]

Such austerity policies deepened Greece's depression, with its gross domestic product (GDP) declining 26 percent (compared with 7 percent decline in Spain, Portugal, and Ireland), an unemployment rate of 26 percent, and youth unemployment running at 50 percent, with 40.5 percent of minors impoverished. *The Wall Street Journal* and other European media editorialized that punitive measures for Greece were necessary to prevent antiausterity political contagion in Spain, Portugal, and Italy. Robert Savio of the Society for International Development remarked, "The European project has radically changed. It is not based on solidarity and union, but on money and markets."[21] And Joseph Stiglitz, former chief World Bank economist, noted the role of special interests in "using the troika to get what they could not have obtained by more democratic processes"; for instance, the IMF, the European Central Bank, and the European Commission "forced Greece to drop the label 'fresh' on its truly fresh milk and extend allowable shelf life" to allow Dutch and other European milk producers access to the Greek market.[22]

In consequence is the rise of new political parties: Podemos (in the "Spanish Spring") and Syriza in Greece have challenged the institutional unaccountability of the EU, whereby the European Central Bank has centralized power to make decisions regarding debt repayment and associated domestic policies in member states, producing "unprecedented constraints on social expenditure."[23] At the same time, the austerity regime has precipitated mobilizations to restore social rights (on a scale far exceeding traditional leftist party agitation). Pablo Iglesias, general secretary of Spain's Podemos, observes the following:

> The emergency policies to "save the euro" imposed—and soon normalized—by the German-led bloc have had disastrous effects in Portugal, Ireland, Italy, Greece and Spain, where millions have lost their jobs, tens of thousands have been evicted from their homes and the dismantling and privatization of public health and education systems has sharply accelerated, as the debt burden was shifted from banks to citizens. The EU has been split along north–south lines, a division of labour that mandates a low-wage workforce and cheap goods and services for the Mediterranean countries, while the young and better-trained are forced to migrate.[24]

The "Latin Americanization" of southern Europe has stimulated new forms of political mobilization: in Spain, combining an anti-eviction network to support mortgage victims, the *Marca Blanca* movement to preserve health services, and the *Marca Verde* to defend public education.[25] Podemos is a new kind of "party movement"; unlike Syriza in Greece its genetic code is non-ideological, taking its bearings from southern experiments in participatory democracy during the era of the rise of the World Social Forum (2000s):[26]

> The movement has studiously avoided engaging with ideological agendas, unions and, most importantly, professional politicians. It has filled city squares, coordinated online actions and targeted specific topics like banking and electoral reform. It has experimented with bottom-up networked approaches to challenge the rigid, top-down, party driven system that has dominated Spanish political life since 1978. City square by city square, individual meeting by individual meeting, thousands of citizens have come together in a networked approach to politics that is fresh and engaging because it defies, above anything else, the hierarchical approach favoured by vested interests.[27]

The turmoil in southern Europe mirrors the wave of popular antiauthoritarian/anticorruption struggles in the global South—in Brazil, Bolivia, Ecuador, Venezuela, Chile, Colombia, Mexico, Guatemala, Turkey, South

Africa, and elsewhere. In 2015 in Honduras, a journalist said, "The peak of corruption has reached its limit. Citizens are just fed up."[28] Earlier, in 2012, India's new "common man's party," Aam Aadmi, targeted corruption via a participatory democracy mobilization against the political establishment, gaining the second largest vote in Delhi's Legislative Assembly and modeling the new "counterpower" movements in India, Brazil, and South Africa, which reject "the increasing nexus of political and economic power and the subordination of democracy to money."[29]

Santos describes the spirit of the mobilization wave, remarking that citizens have lost faith in liberal representative democracy and its unholy alliance with financial and corporate oligarchies corrupting the state and the entire political system, with the provocative comment, "Never before has it become so clear that we live in societies that are politically democratic but socially fascist." For the United States, the turning point was the Supreme Court's *Citizens United* decision, allowing corporate political expenditure in election campaigns. Santos has this conclusion:

> From then on, the agendas of the big corporations have had complete control over the political agenda, from the absolute commodification of life to the closing down of the few quality public services still in existence; from the termination of environmental and consumer protection to the neutralization of workers' union opposition; from the major overhaul that turned universities into business services for hire to making precarious workers out of university professors and changing students into consumers indebted for life; from the unheard-of submission of foreign policy to the interests of global financial capital.[30]

The bottom line is that the globalization project, intent on clearing the social underbrush for private capital's maximum competitive advantage, has enabled occupation of development institutions and national states by financial interests, reversing the consolidation of social contracts in both North and South. In consequence, there are countless mobilizations for social rights and public integrity across the globe. As one commentator observed,

> In 2011 the world all of a sudden experienced protests that far superseded anything that had happened in the previous years in scale and intensity. From Tunis to Cairo, from Madrid to Athens and London and onwards to New York, people took to the streets and rejected the inequality of neoliberal capitalism.[31]

Southern Europe captured the world's attention in 2015, but the social crisis of the globalization project has universal reach and contentious impact. All of these struggles are strands of what Polanyi would describe as a new countermovement against "market rule."

Legitimacy Crisis

If the development project started with the aim of poverty alleviation, then by the end of the twentieth century it became clear that development was not working and faced a legitimacy crisis. World Bank president James Wolfensohn said, "We have yet to solve old problems—above all, that of the yawning gulf between the haves and the have-nots of the world."[32] The United Nations coordinated a response in the form of the **Millennium Development Goals** (2000), with the key goal of halving world hunger by 2015, as well as halting the spread of HIV/AIDS, addressing gender inequality, and providing universal primary education. A decade later the 2010 *MDGs Report* stated that despite gains in reducing malnutrition in the 1990s, since 2000 such progress stalled. The 817 million undernourished in 1990 to 1992 approached one billion in 2010, following the food price and financial crises of 2008.[33]

The "gulf" was "yawning" wider. Despite a general reduction in the proportion of the world's population living in absolute poverty (the "China effect"), there has been a widely observed expansion of global inequalities between and within countries: "The world's rich benefited disproportionately from global growth over the 1990s and the per capita consumption of the poor increased at only half the average global rate."[34] In 2012, the richest 10 percent of people accounted for 86 percent of the world's wealth, and in 2014, just 0.7 percent of the global population owned 41 percent of the world's wealth.[35] A 2014 Pew Research Center survey in 44 nations found that majorities perceive inequality as a big problem, and majorities in 28 nations consider it a *very* big problem. Pew reported that "elites are worried about this issue, too"—though most likely from the perspective of a crisis in their legitimacy. As the Pope might claim, "This is a moral problem, which demands a moral solution, a turn away from the . . . problem of unrestrained appetite."[36]

The legitimacy crisis is doubly expressed in the refusal, or inability, of the development agencies (as in the MDGs) to address global *inequality,* to refocus on how neoliberal development aids the rich more than—or at the expense of—the poor. Thus, "the object of concern is not global inequality but global poverty, the instrument of analysis is economic data processing, and the bottom-line remedy is freeing up market forces, now with a human face."[37] In consequence, there remains a fixation on the "bottom billion"— those on the bottom rung of a (staged) development ladder. Of course, some are poor in standard metric terms (but often simply practicing low-input lifestyles), while others are genuinely destitute (lacking adequate means to live). Such a focus on "the poor" not only collapses this distinction, favoring a single, artificial standard (as depicted in Figure 8.1), but it also removes from view and contention structural inequality. From here, it is easy to blame the poor for their condition, rather than examine the disproportionate access of the rich to world resources. In neoliberal terms, then, unemployment is a matter of individual responsibility: "People came to be regarded as more or less 'employable' and the answer was to make them more employable, upgrading their 'skills' or reforming their 'habits' and 'attitudes'."[38]

In 2015, the World Bank's *World Development Report*, titled "Mind, Society and Behaviour," formalized this approach to poverty alleviation, shifting responsibility from public policy to the "poor." To change the behavior of the poor requires first understanding it, which is difficult for World Bank economists who might be prone to cognitive bias. As an Indian commentator noted, the poor have no influence on economic destiny, so a refocus on billionaire investors' behavior is necessary:

Figure 8.1   The Global Wealth Pyramid

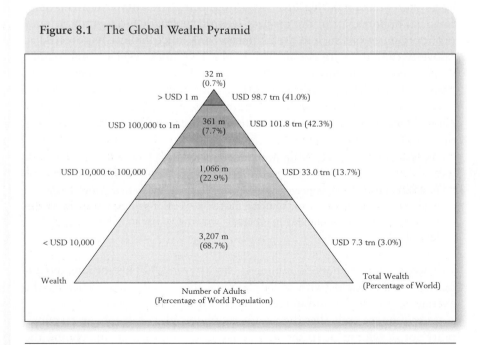

Source: Davies, Lluberas, and Shorrocks, *Credit Suisse Global Wealth Databook*, 2013.

For instance, manipulating them into deploying their billions on productive rather than speculative investments could generate more beneficial, and more effective, outcomes than micro-manipulating the financial decisions of a poor peasant. . . . As democratic nation states reorient themselves to being account-able to global financial markets, non-democratic bodies such as the World Trade Organization, and trade agreements such as Trade in Services Agree-ment, they will necessarily become less responsive to the aspirations of their own citizens. With overt repression not always the most felicitous or cost-effective policy option, it has become imperative to find ways and means to ideologically tame the economically excluded. Hence the new focus on the minds and behavior of the poor.[39]

Anticipating this formalization of control and surveillance of "the poor," the microcredit phenomenon has targeted the poor with instruments of the rich, which "discipline the poor."

Taming the Poor? Microfinance or Poverty Capital

Microfinance performs three tasks at once: providing credit to the poor as an entrepreneurial "leg up," deepening market relations, and enlarging financial opportunity in the form of *legitimacy repair*. Originating in non-profit organizations such as the Grameen Bank, microfinance has evolved as "poverty capital," with commercial banks, investment vehicles, and money markets now embracing it.[40] In the words of the governor of Israel's central bank, Stanley Fischer (formerly IMF deputy managing director), microfi-nance provides "bankers with a profitable business opportunity" and "poor people a stake in the economic future of their countries."[41] These poor are the so-called "bottom billion."

As Nobel Prizewinner Muhammad Yunus of Bangladesh wrote,

In 1983, I founded Grameen Bank to provide small loans that people, espe-cially poor women, could use to bring themselves out of poverty. At that time, I never imagined that one day microcredit would give rise to its own breed of loan sharks.[42]

There are now about 650 million clients at over 3,000 institutions spread-ing across the world (with India claiming about 180 million clients), the average loan is $250, and interest rates often exceed 20 percent.[43]

Microfinance embodies the neoliberal philosophy of devolving responsi-bility for development to the individual as self-maximizer. In echoing the "bad state/good market" axiom, it reproduces the ideology of the globaliza-tion project. As political scientist Heloise Weber underscores, microcredit and microfinance schemes simultaneously facilitated and legitimized financial liberalization, serving as a "counter-response to reinforce the supremacy of 'the market' in light of potential social and political challenges."[44] Working through the NGO community in dispensing and monitoring credit and its repayment, microfinance simultaneously empowers and disciplines its recipients—an ideal form of development as rule (financial opportunity by financial dependency). Where it valorizes the poor as consumers of credit, it realizes Yunus's questionable claim that "credit is a fundamental human right."

Microfinance has various criteria of success—empowerment of marginalized women, stabilization of the poor, extension of frontiers of bank profits, reduction of the informal economy, expansion of microenterprise, enhancement of World Bank legitimacy, the NGO-ization of development, or new development "rents." But perhaps its fundamental significance is the renewal of the legitimacy of neoliberal development via "bankrolling the poor." Anthropologist Julia Elyachar's research in Cairo suggests microcredit appropriates alternative values and visions of social life. Replacing social networks of survival with "empowerment debt" has proven to be a double-edged sword, incorporating "informal" workers and craftspeople into credit relations that may create both new microenterprises and/or new individual dependencies (infused with class/gender inequalities), with the loans often being used to meet daily consumption needs.[45] Sometimes debt has intergenerational effects, such as taking children—especially girls—out of school in order to make loan payments.[46] A report by the World Bank–based Consultative Group to Assist the Poor on the microfinance portfolios of the UN and the Bank concluded, "Less than a quarter of the projects that funded microlending were judged successful."[47] In 2014, the Centre for the Study of Financial Innovation questioned the microfinance industry's ability to meet new challenges of web-based technologies accelerating loans via ubiquitous mobile phone links, noting a rise in "over-indebtedness."[48]

By classifying informal practices as "poverty," thereby targeting them with "empowerment debt," the development establishment potentially disempowers informal cultural networks. At the same time, it seeks to renew its legitimacy by redefining development on a "human scale." But it is one thing to bring credit to the grass roots, creating dependencies, and another for people at the grass roots to self-organize. For example, there are many examples of community-managed microfinance via local cooperative banks and financial institutions with accountability to local savers and the wider community—the principle being that enabling savings within poor communities is more effective than credit provision that is followed by debt.[49]

Such grassroots self-organization is prevalent in European communities responding to debt issues.

Greek or European Tragedy?

Unlike the profile of the Third World debt crisis of the 1980s, the northern debt crisis morphed from unsustainable private debt encouraged by deregulation into "an alleged sovereign debt crisis."[50] In the neoliberal lexicon, this crisis is represented as a crisis of the state, rather than as a consequence of unregulated capitalism.

In Europe the so-called **sovereign debt crisis** is exacerbated by membership in the European Union (EU). States are required to use the euro, a currency they do not issue, which forces them to borrow to cover their deficits. The financial crisis exposed the vulnerability of the weaker states (Portugal, Ireland, Greece, and Spain), subjecting them to austere loan conditions imposed by the European Central Bank and the IMF to preserve the value of the euro and the viability of the eurozone. From 2010, EU authorities agreed to Greek bailouts, but in return, they demanded massive public-sector cuts such as layoffs, salaries, pensions, and other benefits. In the absence of having its own currency, the Greek government was unable to offset fiscal austerity with easy monetary policy (reducing interest rates, expanding exports with currency devaluation) to enable economic growth. Neoclassical economist Milton Friedman predicted earlier that the euro was an "economic liability" with divisive political consequences, and this came to pass in the Greece/Germany showdown of 2015, with the European financial institutions intensifying Greek austerity in the face of popular opposition via election of the leftist Syriza government in 2015.[51]

The Greek bailout exposed the limitations of the EU, lacking European-wide institutions "with sufficient powers to coordinate the economic policies of the member states effectively," thereby amplifying taxpayer "liability for the budgetary risks of each of the other member states."[52] Taxpayer resentment in the stronger states (Germany, France) at paying for the (perceived) profligacy of the (citizens of the) weaker states expresses the dilemma of a union of states with different levels of economic development. But this hardly matches taxpayer vulnerability and resentment in the weaker states subject to draconian cutbacks. The Bretton Woods Project reported in 2011 that conditionalities imposed on Portugal "mirror those the IMF typically imposed in Africa during the structural adjustment era," such as privatization, wage cuts, layoffs, increased health service user fees—in addition to "reducing: incentives for renewable energy; the number of municipalities; social security contributions paid by employers," and private bank bailouts. Portugal's largest trade union confederation, the CGTP, described the package as "an attack against democracy and national sovereignty, a clear capitulation to foreign interference, a denial of the country's development, and a genuine assault on workers and the people."[53]

Austerity policies were viewed as a result of excessive eurozone bank lending. Huge citizen protests in Greece in May and June 2011—turning Athens' main square into a semipermanent encampment—targeted debt regime politics and privileging of the banks:

> Aided by the rating agencies, the announcements of the insolvency or financial fragility of the eurozone's deficit members—Greece, Portugal, Ireland, Spain, and Italy—enabled [the big European banks] to amass enormous profits based on (highly inflated) debt-bond interest rates.[54]

Greece's debt was amplified by first, concealment of prior debt loads (enabled by Wall Street banks), and second, irresponsible lending reminiscent of bank loans to Third World states in the 1970s.[55] Similar and durable mass mobilizations through 2014 and 2015 protested the undemocratic procedures of the EU and its effecting of a "deep crisis in entire party systems, incapable by now of representing their citizens and at the same time incapable of pursuing effective policies."[56] This created a tidal wave of support for the Syriza coalition (commanding only 4 percent of the national vote a decade earlier), elected on an explicit promise to challenge austerity policies but ultimately forced to retreat. Nevertheless, this infamous episode of sovereignty override put down strong roots regarding a need for social policy in Greece—exposing the legitimacy crisis of the EU political union and its financialized power structure, as implied in an interview with one of the new young Syriza politicians:

> Rena Dourou, whom I first met as a bedraggled protester in the Occupy camp at Athens' Syntagma Square four years earlier, can't contain her smile as she waves a hand at the streets, crammed with supporters: "Nobody listened to us for years," she says. "Now everybody is listening. And this is not just about Greece. It's about Europe, and especially the young."[57]

Sociologist Della Porta suggests this episode is symptomatic of EU unaccountability:

> Policies oriented toward the free market against measures for social protection have furthermore been imposed with the explicit refusal for fair negotiations between social partners. . . . In the process, the decision making power of the European institutions extended further, from monetary to financial policies, and then on to social policies. . . . Whereas the structural adjustment programs in the global South were presented as being temporary, the shift toward an EU

ever more oriented on the market, and less and less toward the rights of its citizens, has been accomplished through decision-making procedures and institutions designed to last.[58]

From another angle, the depth, and terms, of the financial crisis suggest a double edge. The legitimacy claims of the globalization project for universal prosperity are deeply contradicted by the universal reach of austerity politics. Now in question is whether this version of "globalization" is sustainable, given the social unrest generated by the subordination of the "public" to private interest, the principal contradiction of the globalization project.

The Latin Rebellion

The legitimacy crisis of neoliberal development originated in Latin America. At the start of the twenty-first century, a democratic revolution swept the continent, with the pendulum swinging back from market rule to the restoration of social rights and the role of the development state (the "pink wave"). New social-democratic presidents were elected in 11 countries—Venezuela, Brazil, Argentina, Uruguay, Bolivia, Chile, Ecuador, Nicaragua, Guatemala, Paraguay, and El Salvador—alongside Cuban socialism. More pragmatic and populist than ideological, these governments have espoused a social egalitarianism, drawing on the deepening frustration of poor and indigenous citizens with the deprivations of the globalization project. This has been accomplished, particularly in Bolivia, Ecuador and Peru, on the ruins of traditional party systems, unable to resolve domestic tensions stemming from neoliberal capitalism.

Latin America has the highest levels of inequality in the world.[59] After three decades of neoliberalism, three-fourths of Latin Americans remain poor, and social movements have mobilized against privatization, low-wage labor, alienation of habitat, crippling foreign debt inherited from previous dictatorships, and the erosion of national sovereignty. But only in three countries (Venezuela, Bolivia, and Ecuador) has "postneoliberalism" gained some traction in regulating capital—in particular, substituting productive for speculative investment, supporting labor rights, and encouraging fair rather than "free" trade.[60]

In addition to the electoral shift, distinctive political initiatives emerged in the crucible of the Latin American rebellion. In Argentina, for example, workers occupied almost 200 empty factories and workplaces, organizing production themselves via cooperative models.[61] And Bolivian indigenous peoples institutionalized their newfound voice in the Movement for Socialism (MAS) party, powering the electoral victory of the first indigenous president, Evo Morales.[62] Venezuela adopted a new constitution (1999) centered on the theme of human development, with a vision of citizens empowering themselves through the political (participation in communal councils) and economic (establishment of cooperatives) spheres.[63]

Controversial Venezuelan president, Hugo Chávez, blessed—or cursed, as resource economists might say—with oil wealth, poured billions of dollars into his "Bolivarian Revolution," expanding health care and education (Venezuela is now an "illiteracy-free territory" by UN criteria), subsidizing food and fuel, providing cash benefits for single mothers and low-interest loans for small businesses, and encouraging farm worker-owned cooperatives on ranches and sugar plantations seized by the state.[64]

To finance this revolution, Chávez instigated a new wave of **resource nationalism** in Latin America in 2002, demanding that foreign oil companies enter into joint ventures, with the Venezuelan state holding at least 60 percent of the capital. Ecuador (expropriating Occidental Petroleum), Peru, and Bolivia followed, "where foreign companies, in particular the Brazilian Petrobras, accepted the nationalization of gas fields without a fight."[65] The drawback, at least in Venezuela, was that oil money corrupted the state bureaucracy. Nevertheless, the resource nationalism taps into a historic antipathy toward foreign control, with the populist dimension rooted deeply in indigenous suspicion of the "[European] white-settler elite that has dominated the continent for so many centuries."[66] At the same time, mining and extractive industries threaten indigenous rights, with Bolivia driving a road through the Tipnis National Park and Ecuador extending oil drilling in the Yasuni National Park, contradicting regional claims to protect Pachamama ("mother earth").

Drawing on the anticolonial heritage of Simón Bolívar (leader of nineteenth-century Latin independence movements), contemporary movements demand a second independence—from foreign corporations, banks, and US military involvement across the continent—forming the South American Community of Nations. This community evolved into the **Union of South American Nations (UNASUR)** in 2007, moving the region closer to independence from the United States via economic integration around a single currency (the *sucre*), destined to be an international reserve currency. By 2009, the Bank of the South (*Banc del Sur*) was established as an alternative to the IMF.

A radical offshoot of the integration initiative is an alternative regional economic bloc named the **Bolivarian Alternative for the Americas (ALBA)**, based on the concept of "cooperative advantage"—fostering mutual cultural and economic exchanges, such as cheap oil from Venezuela for Cuban doctors and teachers, and building a form of cooperative development to encourage collective interest in sharing material goods and social services.[67]

How these various confrontations with global neoliberalism evolve depends on the viability (and integrity) of the new governments and on the durability of the continental alliances. But they have served as counterweights to the globalization project.

Arab Spring?

In 2011, the African Development Bank (AfDB) claimed that the revolution in Tunisia reinserted "social inclusion" into the center of the development debate. Ironically, Tunisia (a North African country of 10 million) was regarded by the development agencies as a macroeconomic success, with record growth of 6.7 percent in 2007—despite the persistence of long-standing social and spatial inequalities characterizing the North African region at large. With President Zine al-Abidine Ben Ali stepping down, the **Arab Spring** stepped up, spreading to Egypt, Libya, Bahrain, Yemen, Syria, and even Palestine. With regard to Tunisia, the AfDB noted in its now soft loan proposal, "The revolution and the ensuing social protest demonstrate the urgency of addressing the issues of unemployment, especially among the youth in the country's interior, regional disparities, and the lack of transparency and individual freedoms."[68]

Much was made of the youth component of the Arab Spring—in Tunisia, for example, 72 percent of the unemployed were under 30 in 2008, and the unemployment of university graduates grew tenfold between 1990 and 2010.[69] The revolt began among working-class youth, spreading to the middle classes as police brutality came in full view. Social networking among youth enabled new spaces of hope and initiative. Over half of the 350 million Arabs are under 30, with dim job prospects, and youth unemployment is as high as 80 percent in some areas. Such conditions nurtured a simmering crisis of the globalization project across the region, coming to a head in 2010 in the Arab Spring.[70] Bread protests recurred in Egypt during the era of the globalization project, as the government encouraged export crops instead of wheat and diverted subsidies toward feed crops and the production of animal protein to provision wealthy consumers—pushing food prices up by 50 percent by the end of the 2000s.[71] The retaking of public space (via sophisticated self-organization in Tahrir Square) laid bare majority deprivations, the savagery of the state apparatus, and the profiteering of the ruling and military elite, who controlled most large Egyptian businesses and contracts.[72] The uprisings were controlled or repressed, with a new dictatorship supported by continuing US military aid cracking down on Egyptian civil rights.

Social inclusion via employment was the central demand. But unemployment is symptomatic of a deeper failing—the disregard of Arab governments for their responsibilities to the social contract, as well as the complicity of the Western powers, particularly the United States, in the long-term security of these regimes, given their proximity to oil and Israel. These regimes have been termed the "Arab exception" insofar as they "remained immune to the great wave of democratization which has swept through Eastern Europe, Latin American, and Africa."[73] The exception perhaps proves the regional rule insofar as persistent authoritarianism within an imperial shell has resulted in predatory states, with continuing emergency laws and persistent human rights violations to control deeply unequal societies.

Because of the centrality of oil, the globalization project rests on question- able foundations. This is even more evident with the subsequent explosion of Sunni/Shia divisions in the region and the formation of the Islamic State (ISIS) in 2014 by Sunnis in the vacuum of a dysfunctional Iraqi state and a retreating Syrian state, mired in a civil war serving as a proxy conflict between the region's major Sunni and Shia powers. This conflict was pre- cipitated by the spread of the Arab Spring to Bahrain (a Shi'ite majority ruled by Sunnis) and Syria (a Sunni majority ruled by a Shia sect).[74] The West, concerned to maintain power in the region, has been caught between containing the key Shi'ite state, Iran, and attempting to "degrade" the forces of ISIS (paradoxically with Iranian collaboration). Former United Nations special rapporteur for human rights, Richard Falk, recalling the conse- quences of US-sponsored "regime change" in Iraq, "as abetted by a pro- Shiite occupation policy," and of historic internal divisions within both Christianity and Judaism, situates the connection between the ISIS emer- gence and Muslim grievances:

> Such grievances include the perception that ISIS was providing the Sunni popu- lation in Iraq with a kind of liberation from Shi'ite and American oppression; as well, recruits to ISIS especially from Europe seem to be drawn from alien- ated youth who are not necessarily strongly religious. The appeal of ISIS is finding a well-paying job that confers a certain kind of dignity. Partaking in the struggle against the West also is an outgrowth of feelings of abuse and discrimination experienced by Muslims living in Europe. In effect, ISIS has flourished in an atmosphere in which it seemed to be addressing widely felt grievances among Muslims, providing an outlet for frustrations and hostile emotions.[75]

One tragic consequence of the destabilization of states like Syria and Iraq (and Afghanistan), and the resulting military brutality, has been a continuing flood of hundreds of thousands of refugees from the east into Europe, over- whelming human rights agencies and states alike, and exposing historic (uneven) divisions between eastern and western European states.

Figure 8.2 Changing of the World-Economic Guard?

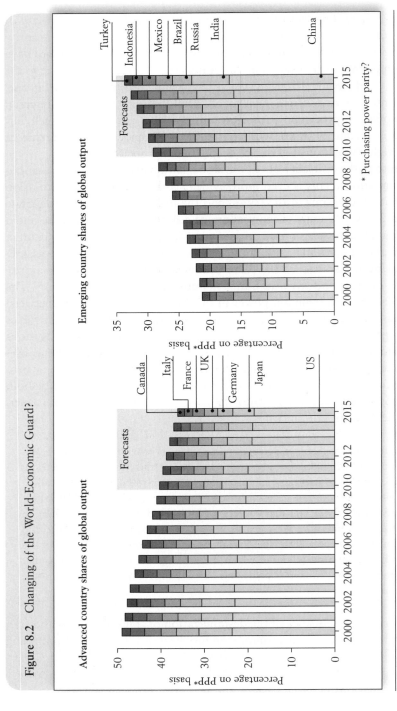

Advanced country shares of global output

Emerging country shares of global output

Sources: IMF, Federal Reserve, and Schroders, via Martin Wolf, "Three Years On, Fault Lines Threaten the World Economy," *Financial Times,* July 14, 2010: 7.

Geopolitical Transitions

The institutional crisis of the globalization project was imminent through the 1990s, taking a turn toward civic unruliness in the new century, as previously mentioned, and also toward geopolitical regrouping. As fallout from the Asian financial crisis of 1997, the **Group of 20 (G20)** formed, combining the original members of the G8 with significant states from the global South, including Argentina, Brazil, China, India, Indonesia, Mexico, Saudi Arabia, South Africa, South Korea, and Turkey (accounting for about 90 percent of the global economy). Meanwhile, key southern states in the G20—Brazil, India, and China—led an effective opposition to northern attempts to retain their unequal economic power through World Trade Organization (WTO) protocols in the Doha "Development Round," which first met in 2001. The southern states objected to the undemocratic procedures of the North, its aggressive attempts to dominate southern markets, and the hypocrisy of continuing farm subsidies in the North while the WTO outlawed them in the South.

The G20's appearance signaled a *turning point in the balance of global forces*. Not only did the politics of the WTO precipitate a solidarity group from the global South, but that solidarity group imprinted its economic rise and recognition in the G20. Their leading edge, the so-called **BRIC** countries (Brazil, Russia, India, China), contribute more than 50 percent to world-economic growth and account for about 15 percent of the world's economy.[76] In 2010, China surpassed Japan as the world's second-largest economic power (although the United States produces two and a half times more). These shifts are portrayed in Figure 8.2. Commenting on the impact of the 2008 financial crisis, *Financial Times* columnist Martin Wolf declared this:

> We already know that the earthquake of the past few years has damaged western economies, while leaving those of emerging countries, particularly Asia, standing. It has also destroyed western prestige. The west has dominated the world economically and intellectually for at least two centuries. That epoch is over. Hitherto, the rulers of emerging countries disliked the west's pretensions, but respected its competence. This is true no longer. Never again will the west have the sole word. The rise of the Group of 20 leading economies reflects new realities of power and authority.[77]

These new realities of power are emerging as increasingly polycentric. Cross-sectional comparison shows the economic dynamism of segments of these rising "middle-income countries" (MICs). As Susan George notes, "A third of all Brazilians are richer than the bottom 5 per cent of Germans; so, more surprisingly, are 200 million Chinese."[78] The first BRIC summit, held in Russia in 2009, raised the question of replacing the US dollar as the world's principal trading currency, as well as reforming international financial institutions to reflect the new balance of economic forces.

In April 2011, South Africa joined the club, rounding out the acronym appropriately—BRICS—and bringing to the table its influence in Africa and in the race to corner mineral and land resources, despite its smaller economy.[79] South Africa also brings its own strategic interests—and official foreign aid agency for conflict resolution—in the African continent. South–South aid programs (notably Chinese and Brazilian) already account for about 10 percent of total aid.[80] South–South aid is matched by South–South alliances, especially among the BRICS. [81]

The new bloc of rising MICs expresses a geopolitical shift of growing significance, challenging the reach of the American empire. Göran Therborn remarked, "Looking backwards from 2010, globalization does not look so much an extension of US capitalism as a delimitation of it, by the rise of China and India."[82]

The rise of China is palpable, with the Chinese currency, the renminbi, emerging as a global reserve currency (alongside the dollar, the euro, the pound, and the yen), and China's state-owned development bank now lending more than the World Bank. China has displaced the United States and Europe as the leading financial power in much of the global South, its foreign investment expanding from $9.5 billion to $86.3 billion between 2005 and 2013, replacing "American imperialism with Chinese imperialism," according to the former energy minister of Ecuador, where China "accounted for more than half of all foreign investment, building oil drilling projects in the Amazon region, power plants and copper mines."[83]

CASE STUDY   Translocal Developments

Development theory has lost its hierarchical national moorings in a global age. The conventional image of national societies with vertical "development ladders" is challenged by horizontal (and selective) markets responsive to shareholder responsibility rather than by states responsive to social contracts. This is a recipe for deepening inequality. India's super-rich—about 50 billionaires in 2010 compared with 10 in France and 35 in Britain—preside over an economic boom stimulated by liberalization. They account for 25 percent of India's GDP but represent just 0.00001 percent of the population. In China—where Lamborghini sales tripled in 2010 and Rolls Royce rose 146 percent to 678 cars, overtaking the UK, and where in

2030 predictions are for more cars than in the whole world in 2000—Jonathan Watts notes a similar segmentation:

> In recent years, the planet's largest corporations have become dependent on the Wangs catching up with the Joneses. The US had shopped until its economy dropped. Sinking in debt, plagued by obesity and increasingly dependent on military might to protect its lifestyle, the world's superconsumer was groaning with indigestion. Europe was too decrepit and conservative to take up the slack, so global manufacturers, retailers and restaurant chains were desperate to stimulate the Chinese appetite. Shanghai was their beachhead.

The Chinese frontier was opened up in the early 1990s by companies such as Mattel, the world's biggest toy company—now with the planet's largest Barbie emporium in Shanghai. More recently, international brands—Louis Vuitton, Gucci, Chanel, and Starbucks—complement retailing giants—America's Walmart, France's Carrefour, Britain's Tesco, and Japan's Ito Yokado. The first KFC opened near Tiananmen Square in 1987, and now the firm has 2,000 outlets in 400 cities as the largest restaurant chain in China; McDonald's has 800 outlets. Unsurprisingly, 15 percent of the population is now overweight, with rising incidences of diabetes and heart disease.

Political scientist Sandra Halperin has for some time argued that development was originally about extending and integrating translocal trade and investment circuits among European aristocracies, understood as a "single transregional elite." The national consequence was a distinctive economic "dualism," expressed in wealthy elites atop impoverished nineteenth-century European working classes. Challenging twentieth-century assumptions of *national* development, Halperin argues that post-colonial elites exploited this nationalist myth as "part of a broad vision that they shared with retreating colonial administrators and with a wide set of transnational elites concerned with maintaining and reproducing the circuit." Given the selectivity of Chinese prosperity (10 percent of the population), Halperin's dualism reappears in the Chinese model, albeit via a band of affluence beyond elites to middle-class consumers hitching their fortunes to the global market.

Ultimately, what does this mean for the concept of "development"? Which nation-state/s now represent the model, or is development now simply the preserve of a relatively narrow transnational class indulging in "high-mass consumption"?

Sources: Chang (2008); Halperin (2005: 42); Ramesh (2009: 17); Watts (2010); Watts (2011b); Wilson (2010: 17).

Alluding to a historical pendulum, Antoine van Agtmael in *The Emerging Markets Century* (2007) predicted that the Third World "will overtake the developed world by around 2030–2035." He extrapolated that prediction from the powerhouse companies: Samsung of South Korea, Infosys of India, Haier of China, and Cemex of Mexico.[84] Whatever "overtaking" means, there is no doubt that the phenomenon of "Chindia" has the attention of the business community—whether as an investment opportunity or a threat to northern businesses or jobs. Goldman Sachs' 2003 *Dreaming With BRICs: The Path to 2050* predicted that by 2050 China would be the world's largest economy, followed by the United States and then India.[85]

India

India is experiencing a palpable shift from producing global services to manufacturing domestic products—an interesting detour from its globalization project path. India has been the center of an offshore service industry, with "dozens of ambitious 20-somethings . . . crammed in like commuters in a subway car, sitting at long banquet tables in front of well-worn computer screens creating websites for companies in the US and around the world." Most of these workers make about $270 a month:

> [It's] enough to pay for a small apartment, a scooter and weekend outings to the food courts at local shopping malls. And they are sufficiently in demand that 40 percent of them move on every year to bigger companies such as Wipro and Infosys, which offer . . . the glamour of working in one of the gleaming new hi-tech parks that have sprung around this Indian industrial center.[86]

However, Indian education is unable to meet the demand for skilled software operatives, a shortage that is inflating wages by 30 percent to 40 percent a year and eroding Indian high-tech cost advantages. Accordingly, policy makers have shifted gears, focusing more on the domestic market of middle-class consumers, requiring expanded employment of lower-skilled labor. While Indian infrastructure is still undeveloped (China invests seven times as much on roads, ports, electricity, and so on), the central government is pursuing an aggressive industrial park program in the "global/satellite cities" of Delhi, Mumbai, Kolkata, Hyderabad, and Chennai.[87]

TNCs such as Renault-Nissan (joining forces with Mahindra & Mahindra of India), Ford, GM, Motorola, Hyundai, Posco of South Korea, and

Mittal Steel of the Netherlands are transforming India from a service to a manufacturing center: Manufactured exports to the United States are rising faster in percentage terms than those from China, and over two-thirds of foreign investment in the mid-2000s entered manufacturing.[88] India itself has emerged as the 11th-largest auto market in the world (China is the most dynamic), and local manufacturers such as Tata and Rajav compete with Renault to build low-cost models for the domestic market.[89] Hyundai, which made a $2-billion investment in Chennai, was attracted to the cheap factory floor labor as well as the abundance of Indian engineers (to manage robotic technology) supplied by the state's technical institutes as they shift their training from computer programmers and engineers to auto production skills—a decisive shift away from its recent IT/software profile.[90]

While two-thirds of Indians are still agrarian, India's rising middle class of some 300 million constitutes a sizable consumer market. And this is symbolized by the supermarket revolution emerging in India. India held the global supermarkets at bay for a few years longer than China, which opened its doors to the behemoths in 2000 and now has half of the top 70 global retailers operating in its prosperous urban markets.[91] In late 2006, India's Reliance Industries Limited opened its first wholly owned supermarket in Hyderabad, with the intention of beating Walmart to the punch. But for most Indians, this was not a cause for nationalist celebration: "At stake is the livelihood security of 12 million small shopkeepers, 40 million hawkers and at least 200 million (of the 600 million) small farmers."[92] Such tension symbolizes the distinct worlds in play—that of small-scale Indian family enterprises versus the reach of the global market as its agents create new, selective high-growth markets. Meanwhile, 90 percent of India's workforce toils in the "informal" sector.[93]

Deep inequalities in India fan class tensions, no less in rural areas where the majority population resides. In 2007, the Indian central government suspended all land acquisition for establishing new special economic zones (SEZs) and industrial parks pursuant to establishing a policy on rehabilitating displaced people. This followed pitched battles between the (Communist) West Bengal government and peasants over plans to acquire 140,000 acres of land for SEZs to be developed by the Tata business group and Indonesia's Salim Group on the outskirts of Kolkata.[94] And in 2010, the Indian Supreme Court expressed concern about development (via land acquisition) and its politically destabilizing effects, given the long-standing popular Naxalite Maoist insurgency centered in mineral-rich forests in 200 of India's 588 districts. The Court observed, "The whole issue of development appears to be so simple, logical and commonsensical. And yet, to millions of Indians, development is a dreadful and hateful word that is aimed at denying them even the source of their sustenance."[95]

Combining Hindu xenophobia (directed at India's minority Muslim population) and populist claims as a "messiah of development" and consumerism, right-wing Bharatiya Janata Party (BJP) candidate Narendra Modi became Prime Minister in 2014. The BJP's preceding neoliberal "Shining India" campaign meant India's former "official rhetoric of egalitarian and shared futures gave way to the media's celebrations of private wealth-creation." Embracing the globalization project exposed India to global finance and "corruption scandals involving the sale of billions of dollars' worth of national resources such as mines, forests, land, water and telecom spectrums have revealed that crony capitalism and rent-seeking were the real engines of India's economy." Consistent with Sandra Halperin's concept of "horizontal development," the Indian beneficiaries "soared into a transnational oligarchy, putting the bulk of their investments abroad and snapping up, together with Chinese and Russian plutocrats, real estate in London, New York and Singapore."[96]

Meanwhile, Indian human development indices remain undisturbed: 43 percent of Indian children under five years old are undernourished, 48 percent of children are stunted, nearly half of Indian women of childbearing age are anaemic, and more than half of all Indians still defecate in the open. With a provocative metaphor, journalist Pankaj Mishra suggests that the majority of citizens long promised "trickle down" development are increasingly "vulnerable to demagogues promising national regeneration. It is this tiger of unfocused fury, spawned by global capitalism in the 'underdeveloped' world, that Modi has sought to ride."[97] As we have seen earlier in this chapter, "market rule" is generating unruly systems, and citizens, everywhere.

China

In China, in spite—and perhaps because—of its authoritarian socialist government, an economic revolution with global economic and ecological implications is underway, and yet despite the omnipresence of the party-regime, labor strikes and rural protests have exploded as the new century has worn on. In Wukan in 2011, 13,000 villagers stormed the town hall and police station, protesting the sale of their land to real estate developers by officials without compensation, forcing party officials and the police to flee the village until agreement was reached for new council elections.[98] In the same year, the number of "incidents" across China increased to 180,000 (from 8,700 in 2005), with workers striking for improved working conditions and higher wages and peasants demonstrating against forced migration.[99] Such displacement characterizes China at present, with 43 percent of Chinese villages having land sold by officials over the last decade and almost four million peasants displaced. From 2000 to 2010, China lost over a million villages—nearly 300 per day. By 2030, 300 million more peasants are to be "urbanized," making one billion city dwellers.[100] The accompanying rising tide of rural resistance is exacerbated by fiscal decentralization, which incentivizes local government collusion with developers as opposed to villagers' lawful rights.[101] In 2007, the government sought to head off rural unrest by repealing agricultural taxation and local fees, providing rural health insurance and increasing compensation for loss of land.[102]

Meanwhile, intensive agriculture has accelerated. Chinese soils are deteriorating from reduced crop rotation, erosion, overfertilization, and the loss of organic content of soils once nourished by manure-based farming. More than 2,000 square kilometers of land turn to desert annually.[103] Millions of Chinese farmers now circulate as a highly exploited reserve army of cheap labor (lacking rights to rural residence: *hukou*), and analysts predict a global grain crisis as China's food dependency grows.[104]

In *Ghost Cities of China*, Wade Shepard details China's reversal of the historic evolution of cities by building cities *before* humans inhabit them, anticipating a continuing process of land-clearing:

> China is an engineer's dream. . . . No other country has ever provided urban designers, civil engineers and architects with so many blank canvases upon which to paint their masterpieces. . . . Obstacles such as evicting tens of thousands of people from their homes, razing entire neighbourhoods and villages, and clearing swathes of development land that extends for hundreds of square kilometres are business-as-usual for the Chinese urbanization machine.[105]

Widespread industrialization (beyond coastal SEZs) is the Chinese goal. Compared with the average Indian, the average Chinese citizen earns two and a half times as much a year.[106] China has been the final assembly station in transnational corporation (TNC) commodity chains, which account for 60 percent of products manufactured in China.[107] In this respect, China's transformation has been a part of the globalization project, as its economic opening coincided with late-1980s deregulation of capital flows, targeting export processing zones consolidated by China's entry into the WTO in 2000. At the same time, China has upgraded from low-value to high-value products, led by electronics and information technology goods; however, it still assembles components designed and made elsewhere or uses copied designs.[108] But this model is in transition as China faces a labor shortage, and energy costs and wages are rising—one consequence being a rush of Chinese investment into cotton textile production in the southern United States, where labor is cheap, land is abundant, and energy is subsidized.[109] Chinese-wage inflation stems from several reasons: escalating labor disputes, enabled by a new Labor Contract Law (2008); new lower-cost production sites in Vietnam, Bangladesh, and India; Chinese government investment in its hinterland as a policy shift in redistributing wealth regionally; and the legacy of China's historic "one child" policy.[110] By 2015, the Chinese government overturned its famous "two-child policy," under pressure from an Internet-linked public desiring more offspring and the rapid ageing of its population (440 million over 60 by 2050).[111]

In broader terms, Chinese development, guided by a strong state, resonates elsewhere (as a post–Washington Consensus model), given the volatility of the neoliberal globalization project. For example, Southeast Asian states are combining authoritarian political systems with market regulation (as opposed to free markets and democracy), in a new **Beijing Consensus:**

> China's stable, if repressive, politics and high-speed economic growth—the "Beijing Consensus"—have impressed elites in places such as Thailand, where democracy seems to have produced only graft, muddled economic planning, and political strife. China encourages this line of thinking by each year training more than 10,000 bureaucrats from other developing countries in economic management and various civil-service skills—in sessions at which China's successes in improving living standards are promoted.[112]

Ecological Crisis

One might say that the globalization project involves an ecological crisis, with most elites and citizens recognizing the necessity to switch tracks to sustainable initiatives, as outlined in the following chapter. The ecological crisis is, of course, a culmination of long-term trends, manifesting in current biodiversity loss, ecosystem deterioration, and climate change. But there are immediate trends, including a global obesity crisis, which reflect more contemporary human-environmental processes with serious health consequence.

Nutrition/Health Crisis

Modern diets stem from the "nutrition transition"—replacing plant-based diets with consumption of animal protein, oils and fats, processed sugars, and processed carbohydrates. This transition is associated with rising affluence, enabling greater dietary diversity and positive health outcomes. However, this scenario remains substantially unrealized at scale because of dietary bifurcation along class lines and the adulteration of food as agro-industrialization proceeds. Food policy analyst Wayne Roberts retorts: "Westerners don't buy food anymore. They buy processed meals assembled from ingredients or inputs" globally sourced.[113] Further, expanded crop yields increase food quantity at the expense of quality (as in nutrient density); for instance, "new varieties of corn, wheat and soy, bred to increase yields, have lower protein and oil content, and high-yield tomatoes are lower in vitamin C, lycopene and beta-carotene." And industrial agriculture deprives soil of organic matter, thereby reducing micronutrients available for crops.[114]

While affluent consumers are more likely to have access to healthy (organic) diets, the structuring of the food regime distributes highly processed high-calorie foods to poorer populations.[115] There is a resulting explosion of malnutrition (associated with obesity), which parallels a persistent undernutrition for a considerable portion of humanity—the WHO estimates over three billion (almost 50 percent of the world's population) suffer from malnutrition.[116] On a positive note, US adult calorie consumption peaked in 2003.[117] Rising obesity is a public health crisis, expressed in rising heart disease, type 2 diabetes, and osteoarthritis. Figure 8.3 indicates obesity distribution across the world—in Australia, for example, while direct health costs of obesity are about $8 billion annually, the overall cost of lost well-being associated with obesity is estimated at more than $58 billion per year.[118]

On the other side of the ledger, with undernutrition disadvantaged populations suffer from stunted growth, vitamin and mineral deficiency, and greater susceptibility to infection. Under these conditions, there is now a techno-fix underway in the food industry called *nutritionalization*. It involves fortification of processed foods (e.g., wheat flour products, baby food) and biofortification via genetically engineered crops (e.g., Golden Rice)—both of which engage a market logic to address dietary deficiency, transforming it into a technical problem and thereby depoliticizing malnutrition.[119] Adulteration of food by overriding its natural elements (depleted soils, processed food) with severe consequence for human bodies is a metabolic crisis of global proportions, with

Figure 8.3   World Obesity, 2013

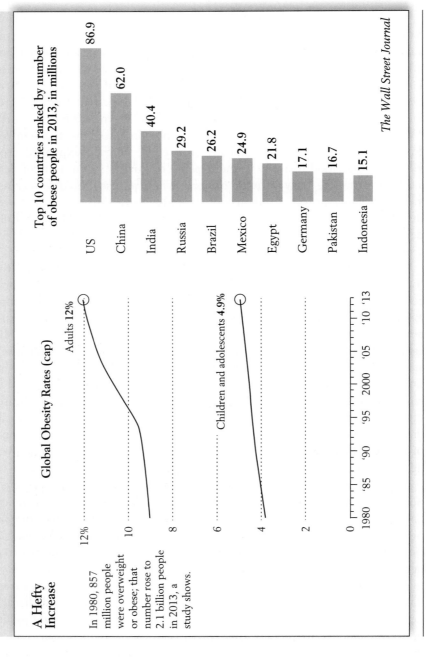

A Hefty Increase

In 1980, 857 million people were overweight or obese; that number rose to 2.1 billion people in 2013, a study shows.

Global Obesity Rates (cap)

Adults 12%

Children and adolescents 4.9%

12%

10

8

6

4

2

0

1980   '85   '90   '95   2000   '05   '10 '13

Top 10 countries ranked by number of obese people in 2013, in millions

US   86.9
China   62.0
India   40.4
Russia   29.2
Brazil   26.2
Mexico   24.9
Egypt   21.8
Germany   17.1
Pakistan   16.7
Indonesia   15.1

The Wall Street Journal

242

Source: Institute for Health Metrics and Evaluation [*The Wall Street Journal*].

ecological foundations. Localization of food systems and agroecology are two mushrooming alternatives.

Human/Nature Separation in the Development Model

Much of environmental degradation is the consequence of a fatal separation over the last two centuries of the natural from the social sciences. Development theory is a prime example—it has been fashioned as if human societies had no ecological basis. And yet it has informed agricultural and industrial practices that fully depend on extractions from nature, and the theory has ignored the environmental impact of development. Until now. This is the crisis—the earth has already lost about one-half of its ecosystems.[120]

While it would be easy to say that the environmental crisis is because of population growth and colonization of the earth, with rapidly diminishing wild spaces (wetlands, forests, grasslands, etc.) to sustain biodiversity, the problem is deeper. In a critical evaluation of conservation efforts, Columbia University ecologist Shahid Naeem makes the point that "almost all aspects of human well-being and prosperity trace back to biodiversity for their foundation":

> The more we relegate wild species to parks, zoos, gardens, and seed banks, and the more we place domestic species [e.g., cattle, commercial plants] in their stead, the more homogenized the world becomes. . . . As the average number of species found in each square of Earth's surface declines, so too will its biomass, its biogeochemistry, and its contribution to a stable, life-supporting biosphere.[121]

We know, for example, that 40 percent of the world's oceans now have been damaged, especially the coral reefs, which constitute the bedrock of oceanic biodiversity, upon which the world's fishing stocks depend.[122] About one-third of the world's fisheries are severely depleted, with complete collapse, for example, of the once-plentiful cod stocks on the Grand Banks off eastern Canada. It is now estimated that given current trends, within half a century there will be no commercially viable marine fisheries.[123]

While the oceans are the last resource frontier, and aquaculture is evolving into the next factory farm complex as wild fish stocks decline, freshwater supplies cannot be taken for granted. Only 3 percent of the world's water supply is freshwater, and two-thirds of that is frozen—so far. The Water Resources Group (WRG), a private sector consortium, predicts a global gap between demand and supply of 40 percent by 2030. The World Business Council for Sustainable Development estimates agriculture uses almost 70 percent of the world's freshwater supplies. China and India, with one-third of the world's population, have less than 10 percent of global water supply. Glacial melting in the Himalaya Mountains poses huge problems for them in the coming decades, as well as for Tibet, Pakistan, and Bangladesh. Agriculture is the flashpoint since it uses 90 percent of India's and 70 percent of China's water. Currently, India uses about 740 billion cubic meters, but by 2030, demand is predicted to reach 53 trillion cubic meters. Rising middle-class diets of meat and sugar are water intensive.[124]

What is key here is that such food products often involve trading "virtual water." This concept measures the amount of water embedded in the production, processing, and trade of commodities: For example, one kilogram of wheat requires 1,000 liters of virtual water, while one kilogram of European or American beef produced with soy imported from the global South requires as much as 15,000 liters of virtual water.[125] As a TNI report on *The Global Water Grab* noted, with respect to the crisis of renewable water resources in the Gulf States over the next 30 years,

> Saudi Arabia, once a net exporter of wheat, intends to phase out domestic production of wheat by 2016 due to the depletion of fresh water reserves in the country. It seeks to compensate for this loss in domestic food production by acquiring farmland abroad, thereby transferring much of the pressure on water resources caused by agricultural production to other countries. This is a strategy likely to be pursued by other water deficit countries as they seek to "lock in" access to water reserves and resolve their own water and food constraints by trading in virtual water.[126]

The virtual water trade is increasingly associated with the "global land grab," which involves appropriations of both "blue water" (freshwater resources: observable surface and ground water—14 percent of available water) and "green water," taken up by plants through soil moisture (and amounting to 86 percent of available water).[127] Freshwater withdrawals across the world have increased nearly sevenfold in the past century, "thereby contributing to an escalating competition for water resources," played out in land grabs and the virtual water trade.[128]

In this scenario, water is predicted to play a similar role to that of oil in geopolitical resource conflict. While agricultural scientists are under pressure to improve cropping and irrigation techniques, resistance to luxury crop production via water-intensive agriculture will grow. For example, there is the "water footprint" of asparagus grown in Peru, its largest exporter. World Bank investments in reclaiming the desert in Ica Valley create 10,000 jobs and increase export revenues, but undermine local aquifers at the expense of local farmers:[129] "In Peru's Ica Valley, the top 0.1% of users—powerful agro exporters—control a third of the total water, while small-scale farmers, 71% of the valley's users, have access to only 9%."[130] The new health food from the Andean region, quinoa, has a similar footprint.

In addition to a looming crisis in water access, conservation of healthy water supplies and wetlands to clean water is threatened by human activity, evident in a large-scale reordering of the planet's hydrology:

> In some places, drought is a result of melt; mountain snowfields and glaciers are the planet's best natural water reservoirs, and they are dramatically receding. That the drought is already beginning is evidenced not by specific events but by a pattern of them: wildfires in Colorado, water woes in northern China, desertification in Spain, food riots in Senegal, and the fact that to describe the recent state of Australia's breadbasket, the Murray-Darling Basin, the term *drought* was discarded in favor of the more permanent-sounding *dryness*.[131]

Largely downplayed in environmental effect by the global media have been oil spills by Shell and Exxon-Mobil over the last half century—spewing 546 million gallons of oil in the Niger Delta (at a rate of 11 million gallons a year): "This ecologically sensitive wetlands region, the source of 10 percent of American oil imports, has most of Africa's mangroves and, like the Louisiana coast, has fed the interior for generations with its abundance of fish, shellfish, wildlife, and crops."[132] Ecosystem depletion includes climatic stress resulting from greenhouse gas emissions. A *Guardian* editorial in 2010 offered a dismal outlook:

> If all nations stopped burning fossil fuels immediately, the planet's oceans would still go on warming, sea levels would continue to rise, windstorms and floods would kill tens of thousands in the tropics. To have prevented the very modest levels of warming the world has seen so far, governments should have taken decisive action 30 years ago. But in 1980 nobody appreciated how swiftly climate might change.[133]

The key issue of our time is the possibility of irreversible global climate change, which *The Economist* has called "a potential time bomb capable of wreaking global havoc."[134] The world has a short time span within which it must learn to transform its energy-use patterns to reduce greenhouse gas emissions by up to 90 percent. Current levels of consumption of goods and services are unsustainable. In addition, they are quite inequitable; not only do Ethiopians emit on average about one-300th of the carbon dioxide generated by the average American, but also low-carbon users are more vulnerable to the impact of climate change: "The effort to tackle climate suffers from the problem of split incentives: those who are least responsible for it are the most likely to suffer its effects."[135]

The prospect of rendering the planet uninhabitable should—and will—be a call to action for the global community. So far, the response is underwhelming, as nations commit to reducing emissions voluntarily but have difficulty with legally binding targets, given the exigencies of the current global development model and uneven responsibilities for greenhouse gas emissions, as depicted in Figure 8.4.

Figure 8.4   Relative Proportion of Global Greenhouse Gas Emissions by Continent

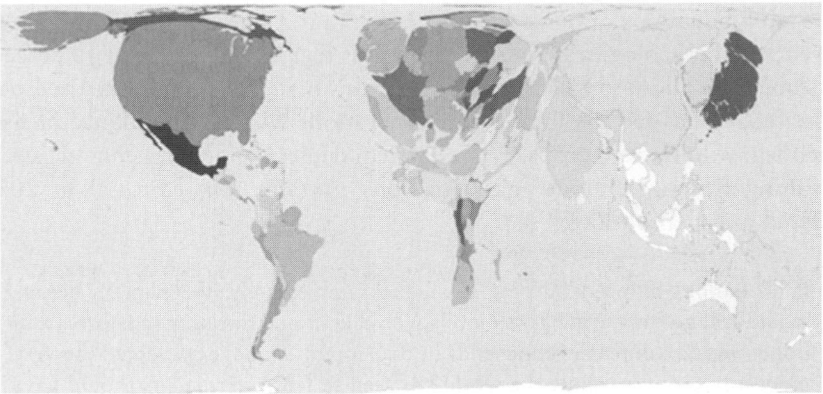

Source: ©Copyright SASI Group (University of Sheffield) and Mark Newman (University of Michigan).

SUMMARY

Is the globalization project over? Not yet. But it appears to be in transition to another project of ordering the world: a sustainability project? The series of crises outlined here are not uniformly coordinated so much as expressing uneven and combined development in global political economy. The political distance between the Latin rebellions (over economic sovereignty), the Arab Spring, and the southern European uprising (over popular sovereignty) is as striking as their combined revolt against neoliberalism's impact (however distinctive to their regions). While some crises are specific to the globalization project (political rebellions and institutional paralysis), other crises are long-term structural crises, such as the ecological crisis—registering an era of fossil fuel dependence.

In the meantime, the general crisis is exposing a tectonic shift underway as the West loses ground to non-Western forces. While this shift is decades in the making, it is already perceptible. In *Losing Control: The Emerging Threats to Western Prosperity*, Stephen King, chief economist at HSBC, argues that Western policymakers suffer from the illusion that they are in control of events. For him, the BRICS challenge the monopolies of the West.[136] It is worth noting here the extraordinary fact that China holds most of the US national debt and that non-Western sovereign wealth funds propped up Western banks during the financial crisis of 2008. As noted, "In the age of globalization, just as the triumph of markets was being widely celebrated, governmental funds—almost always from so-called emerging countries—undertook to rescue the West's largest financial institutions."[137] And yet, perversely, the effect has been to continue market rule, for a time.

FURTHER READING

Arrighi, Giovanni. *Adam Smith in Beijing: Lineages of the Twenty-First Century.* London: Verso, 2007.

Bello, Walden. *The Food Wars.* London: Verso, 2009.

Calhoun, Craig, and Georgi Derluguian, eds. *Aftermath: A New Global Economic Order?* New York: NYU Press, 2011.

Falk, Richard. *Chaos and Counterrevolution: After the Arab Spring.* London: Zed Books, 2015.

Jha, Prem Shankar. *Crouching Dragon, Hidden Tiger: Can China and India Dominate the West?* New York: Soft Skull Press, 2010.

King, Stephen. *Losing Control: The Emerging Threats to Western Prosperity.* New Haven, CT: Yale University Press, 2010.

Parenti, Christian. *Tropic of Chaos: Climate Change and the New Geography of Violence.* New York: Nation Books, 2011.

Roberts, Timmons, and Bradley Parks. *A Climate of Injustice: Global Inequality, North–South Politics, and Climate Policy.* Cambridge, MA: MIT Press, 2007.

Roy, Ananya. *Poverty Capital: Microfinance and the Making of Development.* New York: Routledge, 2010.

Shiva, Vandana. *Soil Not Oil.* Cambridge, MA: South End Press, 2008.

9

Sustainable Development?

The ecological threshold we face today is a stark challenge to a development paradigm with promises of expanding prosperity from an unbridled world market. More than ever before, humanity's survival depends on developing a different set of protocols, ones driven by principles of sufficiency rather than accelerating development along the path of insatiable consumption of dwindling resources. Rostow's *terminal* stage of "high mass consumption" is now perhaps a double entendre. This is the development challenge faced by the global community, and at base, it means giving greater priority—and value—to resources that are not produced for sale—such as biodiversity, habitat, and the global commons (air, water, forests, wetlands, local knowledges, etc.).

A reason for not reducing the value of ecosystems to market prices is that their processes and elements are not independent units. Their value instead lies in their *interdependent* complexity. James Lovelock describes this as the **Gaia hypothesis**, whereby Earth is a "physiological system" that "behaves as if it were alive," maintaining the surface temperature of the planet and recycling nutrients (in soil, water, and forests) with the "unconscious goal of regulating the climate and the chemistry at a comfortable state for life."[1] The age of the **Anthropocene** is so called because of human impact within this system. As Naomi Klein remarks,

> The harnessing of fossil fuel power seemed, for a couple of centuries at least, to have freed large parts of humanity from the need to be in constant dialogue with nature. . . . Coal and oil, precisely because they were fossilized . . . did not behave independently—not like wind, or water, or, for that matter, workers. . . . But what we have learned from atmospheric science is that the

give-and-take that is the essence of all relationships in nature was not eliminated with fossil fuels, it was merely delayed, all the while gaining force and velocity. Now the cumulative effect of those centuries of burned carbon is in the process of unleashing the most ferocious natural tempers of all.[2]

The development paradigm overall has privileged monetary relations and measures often at the cost of nonmonetary resources. Thus, we have seen the conversion of resources such as water and ice shelves (in bottles), air (tradable pollution permits), survival networks of the poor (microcredit), and even maternal love (the global care industry) into commodities.[3] However, nature is now reminding us that to survive we need to revalue what we share as humans, rather than what we consume. Across the world, there are a multitude of experiments in reducing our environmental "impact" that involve "green capitalism," public initiatives to re-embed markets institutionally for socioecological durability, and grassroots initiatives to restore ecological practices as a foundation of social life. There is no single, programmatic path; yet while states, firms, and citizens are exploring forms of sustainable development, there remain powerful interests unwilling and unable (because of "sunken costs") to take the sustainability turn.

This chapter considers these responses to ecological crisis, dividing them into three development tendencies—business as usual, public intervention, and grassroots initiatives—but keeping in mind that they are not mutually exclusive and often overlap. First, we survey the *context* of "climate change emergency."

The Challenge of Climate Change

Undoubtedly, climate change has the potential to swamp all other development challenges in the coming decades. Since "development" has always taken the climate (and environment) for granted, adverse climatic impacts are forcing us all (citizens, development agencies, firms, states) to recognize that the game is changing. We are intensifying the **"environmentalist's paradox,"** where rising well-being is accompanied by deteriorating environments.[4] The Stratigraphy Commission of the Geological Society of London, the world's oldest association of earth scientists, has issued this warning:

> The combination of extinctions, global species migrations and the widespread replacement of natural vegetation with agricultural monocultures is producing a distinctive contemporary biostratigraphic signal. These effects are permanent, as future evolution will take place from surviving (and frequently anthropogenically relocated) stocks.[5]

In other words, we are narrowing our ecological foundations and therefore our ability to survive climatic change.

Bill McKibben, US environmentalist, author of *Eaarth* (2010), and creator of 350.org, echoes, "Global warming is no longer a philosophical threat, no longer a future threat, *no longer a threat at all*. It's our reality. We've changed the planet, changed it in large and fundamental ways."[6] This is a thread spun by Barbara Ward, who wrote in *Only One Earth* (1972), "The relentless pursuit of separate national interests by rich and poor alike can, in a totally interdependent biosphere, produce global disasters of irreversible damage."[7] And it offers a telling perspective on the "development project" in compelling individual nation-states to *compete for economic growth*, with the goal of high-mass consumption but at the expense of the environment. Denial is a characteristic response to this fundamental paradox. This report on air pollution in Beijing (easily matched by Delhi now) states,

> Many Beijingers tend to use the word *wumai* (meaning fog), rather than *wuran* (pollution), to describe the poor air quality—and not just because it's the official Newspeak of weather reports. It's partly because, one local tells me, "If we had to face up to how much we're destroying the environment and our bodies every day it would just be too much." A recent report by researchers in Shanghai described Beijing's atmosphere as almost "uninhabitable for human beings"—not really something you want to be reminded of every day.[8]

The challenge is not only to public health but also to social and political stability. An early report by the US Pentagon (in 2004, before climate change began to register in public discourse), for instance, considered the possibility of megadroughts and mass starvation by 2020, as well as nuclear war resulting from conflict between China, India, and Pakistan over access to water and food. Further, it suggested a tipping point could be reached, where abrupt change in a span of 5 years or less could result in another ice age, freezing northern Europe, converting the American Midwest to a dustbowl, and undermining California's water supply. Five years later the Pentagon and intelligence agencies were conducting exercises and war games in the event that vulnerable regions such as sub-Saharan Africa, the Middle East, and South and Southeast Asia "face the prospect of food shortages, water crises, and catastrophic flooding driven by climate change that could demand an American humanitarian relief or military response."[9] National defense and intelligence agencies are already creating strategic plans for likely outcomes such as hundreds of thousands of refugees, religious conflict, the spread of contagious diseases, and vast infrastructure damage.[10] Climate change security concerns by individual states will not only shape geopolitics, but will be woven into development policy. In the meantime, there is an unequal sharing of the burden of climate change, since northern states—representing 20 percent of the world's population—are responsible for about 70 percent of all greenhouse gas (GHG) pollution, now destabilizing the climate, and southern states (with the least resources) experience the vast majority of natural disasters from hydrometeorological events.[11]

In spite of campaigns of denial, there is no doubt that Earth's climate is in the gear of change, including warming oceans, shrinking ice sheets, declining Arctic sea ice, sea level rise, global temperature rise, glacial retreat, extreme weather events, ocean acidification, and decreased snow cover.[12] Carbon emissions in 2013 were 61 percent higher than they were in 1990, and the atmospheric concentration of carbon dioxide is now 40 percent higher than it has ever been in the last 800,000 years.[13] The "externalization" of GHG emissions means that our shared atmospheric commons has become a free-waste sink for polluters; as the UK *Stern Review on the Economics of Climate Change* (2006) noted, this is "the greatest market failure the world has ever seen."[14]

One component of this market failure concerns the externalities associated with transportation of goods across national borders. Paradoxically, the UN Framework Convention on Climate Change (UNFCCC), signed in 1992, mandated that "measures taken to combat climate change, including unilateral ones, should not constitute . . . a disguised protection on international trade."[15] Three years later the WTO trade regime, unrestricted by climate protections, emerged and intensified the export trade associated with proliferating "world factories" and "world farms." Container shipping has expanded by 400 percent since then, with no international accounting system for shipping emissions that are expected to double or even triple by 2050.[16]

Anticipating Pope Francis's 2015 encyclical, the UNFCCC produced a prescient *Report on Poverty and Climate Change* in 2002, declaring, "Climate change is a serious risk to poverty reduction and threatens to undo decades of development efforts."[17] Five years later, the UN *Human Development Report* declared, "Climate change is the defining human development issue of our generation." And a landmark report appeared in 2012, authored by 21 past winners of the prestigious Blue Planet Prize, issuing this statement:

> In the face of an absolutely unprecedented emergency, society has no choice but to take dramatic action to avert a collapse of civilization. Either we will change our ways and build an entirely new kind of global society, or they will be changed for us.[18]

Responses to the Sustainability Challenge

Business as Usual?

A "business-as-usual" approach to climate change views it as an opportunity, claiming "the world must adapt to what it has become."[19] What it has become combines a growing population of high-mass consumers requiring ever-more unconventional oil exploration and a high-risk environment of deep uncertainty. Unsurprisingly, there are opportunities for windfall profits on both counts. Norway's petroleum and energy minister, for example, remarked, "It's important to recognize that this [Arctic melt] is also an opportunity."[20] The question is, opportunity for whom?

The melting of Arctic sea ice represents a new carbon frontier of oil and gas reserves and 25 percent of the world's known coal reserves. And the oil industry, with its huge sunken costs, is preparing to exploit this opportunity. President Obama's chief of the Alaska gas pipeline project reproduced a rationale for this in reference to Alaska's lucrative oil fields:

> The wealth generated by Prudhoe Bay and the other fields on the North Slope since 1977 is worth more than all the fish ever caught, all the furs ever trapped, all the trees chopped down; throw in all the copper, whalebone, natural gas, tin, silver, platinum, and anything else ever extracted from Alaska, too.[21]

The oil industry exemplifies the nexus between private and public (as in government) interests, with fossil fuel companies receiving up to $1 trillion in annual global subsidies, exploiting government legitimacy needs by maintaining fossil fuel–based economic growth. Sunken costs for business and governments (whose credibility and security depend on an uninterrupted flow of oil) are a powerful combination for maintaining conventional energy supplies even as new energy sources are under consideration.

At a 2000 World Economic Forum meeting at which corporate leaders declared, "Climate change is the greatest threat facing the world," those leaders (from firms such as DuPont, BP, Shell, Suncor, Alcan, Ontario Power, and French aluminum manufacturer Pechiney) joined with US advocacy group Environmental Defense to form the Partnership for Climate Action, announcing, "The primary purpose of the Partnership is to champion market-based mechanisms as a means of achieving early and credible action on reducing greenhouse gas emissions that is efficient and cost-effective." Historian David Noble goes on to remark that in 2004, Goldman Sachs established a Center for Environmental Markets, announcing that it would "aggressively seek market-making and investment opportunities in environmental markets," and "that the management of risks and opportunities arising from climate change and its regulation will be particularly significant and will garner increasing attention from capital market participants."[22]

When *Newsweek* reported that "Wall Street is experiencing a climate change" in recognizing that "the way to get the green is to go green," it reiterated the business-as-usual approach of recycling the (market) problem as solution. An example of the latter is the practice of marketing emissions, institutionalized in the EU's Emissions Trading Scheme (2005), whereby carbon emission permits are assigned, free of charge, to European corporations, subjecting our shared atmosphere to private enclosure.[23] A related initiative involved the establishment of the **Clean Development Mechanism (CDM)**, allowing "countries who cannot meet their promised carbon emissions reductions under the 1997 Kyoto protocol to buy carbon from developing countries by paying for projects like reforestation, power plant energy efficiency, and capturing methane from landfills."[24] In 2007, the Conference of Parties (COP) in Bali established an adaptation fund to be financed (among other sources) through taxing CDM transactions. By 2008, the World Bank was partnering with the COP via a Less Developed Countries Fund (LDCF) to administer **National Adaptation Programmes of Action (NAPA)** through its Global Environmental Facility (GEF). The Commission on Climate Change and Development noted the adaptation fund is "the first example of the use of market-based options to generate substantial financial resources to address climate change. The carbon market . . . has the potential to move huge financial flows to developing countries for mitigation and adaptation."[25] Critics term this *carbon imperialism*, whereby the South is converted to a "carbon dump" while sustaining northern lifestyles.[26]

Applying market metrics to natural processes denies nature's interactive value. A pertinent example is the "pricing of ecosystem services"—as in the UNFCCC-established Reducing Emissions from Deforestation and Forest Degradation (REDD), designed to pay farmers and forest dwellers as well as governments to protect forest capacity. Pricing an ecosystem service is designed to incentivize sustainability. It is a "fictitious commodity" because ecosystem processes are neither singular nor produced for sale. While marketing the environment is an attempt to internalize environmental costs, it is not without hazard since a commodified environment becomes exchangeable. Thus if conditions change, such as a rising price for resources in a forest (oil, timber, minerals), the original conservation purpose may be overridden by a changed financial calculus. And, of course, for forest dwellers, pricing ecosystem services represents the loss of territorial control.[27]

The origins of ecosystem services management stem from the first United Nations Earth Summit in 1992 in Rio de Janeiro. It was here that the idea of "global ecology" emerged, which sociologist Wolfgang Sachs has termed the "rational planning of the planet for Northern Security," when the governments at Rio came around to recognizing the decline of the environment, but insisted on relaunching development. As worn-out development talk prevailed, attention centered on the South and its natural treasures and not on the North and its industrial disorder. There were conventions on biodiversity, climate and forests, but no conventions on agri-business, automobiles or free trade. This indicates that UNCED [United Nations Conference on Environment and Development] attempted to secure the natural resources and waste sinks for economic growth in favour of the global middle class, rather than to embark upon a path towards industrial self-limitation and local regeneration.[28]

Thus, southern forests were understood to provide ecosystem services and to be managed as carbon sinks and for biodiversity preservation—bioregions of intrinsic (ecological) value to a northern-led accumulation drive. At the same time, by classifying the atmosphere and biodiversity as a "global commons," the Bank's GEF overrode protests by the locals, by "effectively assert[ing] that everyone has a right of access to them, that local people have no more claim to them than a corporation based on the other side of the globe."[29] The terms of reference of the current land rush are similar—namely, that global food and ecological security depend on global access to land for offshore food and biofuels (via zoning and capitalization by agencies and corporations). One of the rationales is to engage in "sustainable intensification" of agriculture, which, in regions of the global South, is interpreted as "improving" the land.

Sustainable Intensification

While some view *sustainable intensification* as an oxymoron, it means, in relatively neutral terms, "producing more output from the same area of land while reducing the negative environmental impacts and at the same time increasing contributions to natural capital and the flow of environmental services."[30] The Royal Society makes this claim:

> Food security is one of this century's key global challenges. Producing enough food for the increasing global population must be done in the face of changing consumption patterns, the impacts of climate change and the growing scarcity of water and land.[31]

Under these limiting circumstances, new initiatives with predictable controversy are underway. Thus, for example, while Monsanto's new agricultural technologies (crop-breeding techniques combined with biotechnology) claim to lead to "more production on less land, and collectively reduce the amount of resources needed per unit of production,"[32] Greenpeace claims that the "language of sustainable intensification is essentially an attempt by agribusiness to repackage the same old chemical cocktails under a green veneer."[33] *Nature*'s 2010 editorial advocates a second green revolution:

> Such a revolution will require a wholesale realignment of priorities in agricultural research. There is an urgent need for new crop varieties that offer higher yields but use less water, fertilizers or other inputs . . . and for crops that are more resistant to drought, heat, submersion and pests. Equally crucial is lower-tech research into basics such as crop rotation, mixed farming of animals and plants on smallholder farms, soil management and curbing waste.[34]

How this realignment of priorities is playing out is indicative of the different interpretations of "sustainability." There are two broad approaches, referred to in the *Nature* quote: conservation, meaning high-input agriculture on less land to preserve wilderness biodiversity; and agroecology, where ecoagriculture mimics and restores biodiversity with intercropping, agroforestry, cover crops, and mixed farming.[35] The World Bank interprets the high-input, conservation approach as this:

> Although deforestation associated with the expansion of the agricultural frontier has been a serious problem (and one of the world's largest contributors to greenhouse gas emissions), our analysis shows that the projected increase in the demand for agricultural commodities over the next decade could be met, without cutting down forests, by increasing productivity and farmland expansion in non-forested areas.[36]

The agroecological approach is exemplified in sustainable rice intensification (SRI), which enhances irrigated rice productivity by altering the management of plants, soil, water, and nutrients, raising "yields to about double the present world average without relying on external inputs."[37] That is, SRI attends to the interrelations among various soil biota (from bacteria to earthworms) with extended root systems, rather than applying external inputs (fertilizer, agrochemicals, transgenic seeds). Here, we focus on the former, high-input approach.

The high-input approach starts from the proposition of a "yield gap" between attainable and potential agricultural yields on southern lands. For example, the World Bank claims "none of the African countries of most interest to investors is now achieving more than 30 percent of the potential yield on currently cultivated land."[38] Here, the Bank does not acknowledge the withdrawal of most farming supports over three decades. And the European Commission recommends "secure land tenure and use rights" as "prerequisites for higher productivity of smallholder farmers," encouraging governments to prioritize improving "availability and access to food and stimulate the integration of smallholder farmers in production chains."[39] The G8 is now heavily involved in enabling the new kind of "agriculture for development" advocated in the Bank's *World Development Report* (2007), which reorients agricultural infrastructure for "sustainable intensification," advocating "market smart" subsidies "to stimulate input markets" to capture "the benefits of GMOs for the poor," where "the private sector drives the organization of value chains that bring the market to smallholders and commercial farms."[40] Nobel laureate Wangari Maathai of Kenya's Green Belt Movement avers, "Africa needn't intensify its farming sector so that it takes on the character of the industrial-style agriculture that dominates the West. . . . As we are learning, industrial farming may be efficient, but it has enormous downsides for the environment."[41] In addition, GM crops do not feed the world; rather, they overwhelmingly feed livestock.

CASE STUDY   **The "Meatification" Controversy**

The World Bank modeling for "feeding the world" extrapolates present trends, which include unsustainable and inequitable impacts of dietary "meatification." The *World Development Report* observes, "To meet projected demand, cereal production will have to increase by nearly 50 percent and meat production 85 percent from 2000 to 2030." Geographer Tony Weis claims "meatification" is "normalized in taking the current demand for food as the basis for assessing the overall land-space needed for agriculture, when the current demand for food is not an immutable function of humanity's dietary needs."

For Weis, meat production creates a substantial "ecological hoofprint"—agriculture produces a third of global GHGs, of which livestock (including its feed and transport) accounts for nearly 80 percent. The intensive livestock complex links specialized feed crop regions with proliferating factory farms, with feed crops using 70 percent of agricultural land. Sociologist Mindi Schneider terms this the "meat grab." *Per capita* demand for beef, poultry, and pork in China will double by 2020. Since Chinese intensive meat production is sourced by Brazilian soybeans, and US corn, this single complex produces GHG emissions in multiple ways, from deforestation of the Amazon, fossil fuel-based transport, fertilizer use on intensive grain production, and animal methane.

Meanwhile, climate scientists urge a reversal of livestock production to reduce GHGs, as methane and N_2O (nitrous oxide) contribute more than CO_2 (carbon dioxide) to agriculture's warming effect. Contrarily, conservation

(Continued)

(Continued)

scientist Tim Flannery argues for a "sustainabilitarian diet"—cautioning that meat can be produced more sustainably (but not feedlots). His point is this: "Plant–animal interactions are at the heart of Gaia's self-regulation. Plants capture the sun's energy, and animals, by feeding upon plants, create and swiftly recycle nutrients that plants need in order to grow."

What is it about meat that represents modernity? And why does modernity disfavor mixed farming?

Sources: Flannery (2009: 86–87, 90, 93); Kumar (2011); McMichael et al. (2007); Schneider (2014); Weis (2007: 17, 20, 168, 171); World Bank (2007: 8, 17).

Within this **value chain agriculture** framework (farmers integrated into supply chains organized by global firms and investors), the emphasis is on intensifying agri-inputs (seed, fertilizers, agrochemicals, mechanization). This includes a goal of promoting transgenic seeds. Between 1997 and 2011, the number of acres planted worldwide with genetically modified (GM) crops increased from 25 million to 400 million.[42] Transgenic crops are now referred to as "climate-smart," representing a new profit frontier. Agrochemical and biotechnology firms such as BASF, Monsanto, Syngenta, Bayer, and DuPont have filed over 500 patent documents on "climate-ready genes." This project is represented by a spokesperson for Monsanto, suggesting peasant knowledge is nonadaptive: "I think everyone recognizes that the old traditional ways just aren't able to address these new challenges. The problems in Africa are pretty severe."[43] From this perspective, the premium is now on "improving" the land, with external inputs to raise productivity of commercial, monocultural crops.

In relation to this, at the World Food Security Summit in Rome (2008), the Food and Agriculture Organization (FAO), the International Fund for Agricultural Development (IFAD), and the World Food Programme (WFP) signed a memorandum of understanding (MoU) with the **Alliance for a Green Revolution in Africa (AGRA)**—jointly funded by the Rockefeller Foundation and Bill and Melinda Gates Foundation—to convert Africa's breadbasket regions into a source of food supplies for the continent. While the Rockefeller Foundation sponsored the original Green Revolution using hybrid seeds, the difference now is that the Gates Foundation is allied with Monsanto, a global biotech corporation, and AGRA is committed to introducing imported fertilizers and purchased (some biotech-fortified) seeds.[44] The Gates Foundation does not finance carbon emission reduction (mitigation); rather, as its agricultural strategy states, "We believe the best way for the foundation to address climate change is to help poor farmers adapt."[45]

Adaptation means more than simply coping with climate change; rather, it may portend a transformation of rural life. Dependency on intensifying commercial inputs and volatile export markets substantially alters farming practices, rendering farmers vulnerable to debt and loss of land.[46] This is anticipated in a confidential agricultural development strategy of the Gates Foundation:

> The vision of success involves market-oriented farmers operating profitable farms that generate enough income to sustain their rise out of poverty. Over time, this *will require some degree of land mobility and a lower percentage of total employment involved in direct agricultural production.*[47]

While the jury may still be out regarding the stability, durability, and promise of transgenic technologies (beyond feed crops), their application under current commercial conditions has the drawback of overriding small farmer knowledge of highly variant local ecological conditions and associated seed-sharing networks (discussion later in this chapter).

A more recent commercial initiative is the New Alliance for Food Security and Nutrition (NAFSN) composed of the African Union (AU), its planning body, the New Partnership for Africa's Development (NEPAD), several African governments, and over 100 companies. The NAFSN was launched by the G8 in 2012, with the objective of capitalizing land and labor via value chains under the control of international investors, traders, and retailers.[48] Many of the firms involved provide the entire gamut of the supply chain, including seeds, chemical inputs, production, processing, transport, and commerce with supermarkets. "Agricultural growth corridors" target common lands alienated from millions of small producers, incorporated into value chains as outgrowers. This is the case with the Nacala Corridor in Mozambique, where common lands have been declared abandoned and leased to Brazilian and Japanese investors.[49]

In 2014, the UN launched *The Global Alliance for Climate-Smart Agriculture*, represented as a "voluntary, farmer-led, multi-stakeholder, action-oriented coalition committed to the incorporation of climate-smart approaches within food and agricultural systems."[50] The press release in September 2014 claimed "global efforts to protect 500 million farmers from climate change while increasing agricultural productivity and reducing carbon emissions . . . with commitments pledged by dozens of countries, companies and organizations," such as the World Farmers Organization, the Organic Consumers Association, the Nature Conservancy, and Yara International (the largest global fertilizer corporation). It also noted this:

Walmart, McDonald's and Kellogg Company committed to increase the amount of food in their respective supply chains that are produced with climate-smart approaches. The commitment of these major corporations will greatly expand the use of sustainable agricultural practices and curb carbon emissions from agriculture. . . . McDonald's buys two percent of the world's beef, a major source of agricultural greenhouse gas production. Its commitment to source its beef sustainably is an important step in efforts to curb the food company's contribution to carbon emissions.[51]

An immediate response signed by over 80 civil society organizations (e.g., Institute for Agriculture and Trade Policy, Arab Network for Food Security, World Forum of Fisher People) and farmers' movements (e.g., Campaign for Real Farming [UK], Tamil Nadu Organic Farmer's Federation, Tanzania Organic Agriculture Movement) rejected the initiative, claiming the following:

> The final framework of the Alliance does not contain any criteria or definitions for what can—or cannot—be considered "climate-smart agriculture." Industrial approaches that increase greenhouse gas emissions and farmers' vulnerability by driving deforestation, using genetically modified (GM) seeds, increasing synthetic fertiliser use or intensifying industrial livestock production, are all apparently welcome to use the "climate-smart" label to promote their practices as solutions to climate change.[52]

The civil society argument is that farmers already have the possibility of climate solutions, "based on agroecological practices and the relocalisation of food systems to effectively fight hunger."[53] This is a battle line drawn between opposing models of sustainability: sustainable intensification via commercial inputs versus biodiverse, ecological farming methods. It raises the question of power and rights, but also whether industrial agriculture is sustainable in the long run. Former UN Right to Food Rapporteur, Olivier De Schutter, addressing the UN Commission on Human Rights in March 2011, stated this:

> Agriculture should be fundamentally redirected towards modes of production that are more environmentally sustainable and socially just. . . . [Agroecology] helps small farmers who must be able to farm in ways that are less expensive and more productive. But it benefits all of us, because it decelerates global warming and ecological destruction.[54]

Research has shown small farms are climate friendly, treating soils with organic fertilizer that absorbs and sequesters carbon more effectively than industrial agriculture, such that "the conversion of 10,000 small- to medium-sized farms to organic production would store carbon in the soil equivalent to taking 1,174,400 cars off the road."[55]

Biofuels

Biofuels have always been part of traditional farming practices. As a so-called "transitional fuel" in an age of energy and climate uncertainty, they are now an industrial crop (e.g., corn, oil palm, soy, sugar, jatropha). Biofuels are heavily subsidized by governments—the European Union targets 2020 as a date by which to supply 10 percent of its fuel needs from biofuels. In 2007, the UN reported that biofuels were the fastest growing segment of the world agricultural market,[56] fueled by cross-sectoral investment alliances between energy, agribusiness, trading companies, hedge funds, sovereign funds, states, UN agencies, and universities.[86] In other words, subsidies for this "green fuel" created an expanding market for biofuels such that the competition for food-crop land by biofuels accounted for one third of food price inflation in 2008.[57]

Biofuels meet government and corporate business-as-usual needs (legitimacy/profit) for rising levels of consumption. However, biofuels are controversial. While their burn is cleaner, their *production* is often carbon intensive. For example, one ton of palm oil produces 33 tons of CO_2—10 times more per ton of petroleum.[58] The International Energy Agency estimates that by 2030 biofuels will "barely offset the yearly increase in global oil demand,"[59] and all renewables, including biofuels, will amount to only 9 percent of global energy consumption.[60] Also, they reduce available food supplies—the Bank noted in its 2008 report that the "grain required to fill the tank of a sports utility vehicle with ethanol (240 kilograms of maize for 100 liters of ethanol) could feed one person for a year."[61]

Production decisions depend on a boardroom financial calculus, often with little concern for allocations between crops for food or fuels and/or environmental integrity. Accordingly, the UN Human Rights Rapporteur, Jean Ziegler, charged in 2007 that biofuels are a "crime against humanity."[62] Social movements have renamed biofuels *agrofuels* in recognition of this tradeoff between food and fuel crops, and there have been calls for certification of biofuels to encourage protective socioecological standards.[63] Thus Cargill, for example, in its biofuel plantations in Southeast Asia, claims to avoid disturbing peat soils (which store large amounts of carbon) and to protect biodiversity via a no-burn policy on land clearing.[64] Such initiatives follow sustained civil society pressures on such companies with histories of deforestation in Southeast Asia, West Africa, and Brazil.[65] Even so, a *Biofuelwatch* survey claims a "majority of biofuel industry responses . . . reject any mandatory safeguards. . . . Many responses suggest that not enough is known about life-cycle greenhouse gas emissions from biofuels, but nonetheless demand government support for rapid market expansion."[66]

Such questioning of the precautionary principle has drawbacks—in particular, the longer-term effects of GHGs. Just as carbon emissions from transport have been omitted from the globalization ledger, enabling a false economy, so unregulated biofuels intensify the false economy via the degrading impact of industrial crops on landscapes.[67] A study in *Science* claimed that the conversion of rainforests, peatlands, savannas, or grasslands to produce biofuels in Brazil, Southeast Asia, and the United States "creates a 'biofuel carbon debt' by releasing 17 times to 420 times more CO_2 than the annual greenhouse gas reductions these biofuels provide by displacing fossil fuel."[68] Thus, even as biofuels are viewed as a renewable alternative to fossil fuels, they can contribute to global warming at the same time as they represent a "green fuel" for northerners (who pay in cash and taxes) premised on the "export of sustainability" from southerners (who pay in loss of long-term livelihood and habitat)—as identified by Pope Francis in his 2015 encyclical.

Public Interventions

As a counterpoint to relying on "business as usual," there are a variety of "public interventions" registering concern and proposing pathways into a green future. These divide into publicly oriented reports examining the implications of the Anthropocene age and possible remedies, government-sponsored green technologies and renewable energy programs, and community-based initiatives. The following two paragraphs illustrate quite different forms of public intervention to address climate change effects.

In 2011, 30 health organizations, including the World Medical Association, the International Council of Nurses, and the World Federation of Public Health Associations, met in Durban and, citing "strong evidence" for health benefits from action on climate change (e.g., carbon pollution reduction, smarter transport, healthier diets, clean power), issued a declaration, calling on governments to "recognize the health benefits of climate mitigation and take bold and substantive action to reduce global greenhouse gas emissions in order to protect and promote public health." Their claim is that "climate change is the biggest global health threat of the 21st century. Effects of climate change on health will affect most populations in the next decades and put the lives and well-being of billions of people at increased risk."[69]

Semarang, Indonesia, is a major port city on the low-lying northern coast of the Java Sea, with a population of over five million people, facing the problem of sea level rise, drought, and extreme temperature fluctuations. A 2013 report by the International Institute for Environment and

Development (IIED) offers a model adaptation plan geared to soliciting local input to enhance government responsiveness:

> Using demographic and hazard risk data in conjunction with spatial analyses, we develop a framework for identifying the geographic distribution of potential vulnerabilities. This analysis allows for a community-level, contextualised understanding of vulnerability and can provide a foundation for more effectively fostering adaptive capacity. This localized understanding of needs enhances the capacity of communities to negotiate for resources, and also allows governments to better understand levels of need and more effectively direct resources at the most vulnerable communities and populations.[70]

Urban-Industrial Greening

In 2011, UN-Habitat released a report, *Cities and Climate Change*, warning that cities were the "real battle-ground in the fight against climate change." The Executive Director of UN-Habitat remarked, "Cities are responsible for the majority of our harmful greenhouse gases. But they are also places where the greatest efficiencies can be made." Two small but telling examples of the latter are US urban food systems. First, the Detroit-based Farmed Here enterprise is locally sourcing and is "the first and only US Department of Agriculture Organic Certified and HACCP-certified and audited aquaponic vertical farm in the US . . . [with] a greater than 95% success rate with plants, compared with 70% on traditional farms." And second, Green Spirit Farms near New Buffalo, Michigan, has developed "vertical farms on under-used urban space, yielding 12 harvests per year, compared to around seven harvests per year in California where many of the country's fresh vegetables are grown."[71] Such initiatives are multiplying as northern city administrations develop the incentive and capacity to issue permits to grow food or raise chickens or fish in urban areas, bringing the countryside into the city.

Meanwhile, 3,500 signatory EU cities and towns have committed to reducing emissions by more than 20 percent by 2020, compared to 1990 levels, and New York City reduced its emissions in 2009 by 13 percent below 2005 levels, targeting 30 percent reduction by 2030.[72] The Chinese government is to institute a market for emissions quotas. In an interesting twist in reducing emissions, the English city of Manchester has introduced consumption-based GHG accounting in an effort to reduce the city's ecological footprint, educating employers and homeowners about the benefit (to the city's economy and the planet) of purchasing goods closer to home. Thus, emissions by city residents include the energy needed in the growing and transport of food; the extraction and processing of oil used by the city's automobiles and factories; the emissions generated through the manufacture of electrical devices and appliances; and estimates of aviation emissions by residents flying out of town.[73]

The phenomenon of the "eco-city" is still in its infancy and is a moving target since urban planners need to transform infrastructures and the built environment as much as citizen habits. Intermediate targets such as "zero waste" or "carbon neutrality" are important goals, requiring changed patterns of consumption and transport in addition to renewable energy regimes. The UN recently convened a network among five emerging eco-cities in Southeast Asia—Cebu in the Philippines, Danang in Vietnam, Iskandar in Malaysia, Thailand's Map Ta Phut, and China's Pingtan—to develop a common language of sustainability and set of "best practices" as a longer-term plan.[74] Meanwhile, the UN's GEF has committed to a public–private partnership—the Sustainable Cities Integrated Approach, initially focusing on China,[75] where "almost 300 ecocities are either being built or are in the planning stage," despite the absence of an established standard regarding what constitutes an "eco-city."[76] Ironically, these cities in particular but all cities in general already have a substantial carbon footprint insofar as they are premised on urbanization of the countryside and/or industrial agriculture.

Nevertheless, urban greening is an important new development. In 2013, the inhabitants of Hamburg restored their power, creating a public energy regime whereby electricity, gas, and heating grids were wrested from private control. In the same year, 25 percent of Germany's electricity came from renewables—wind and solar in particular, supplemented by biogas and hydropower (in comparison, wind and solar accounted for just 4 percent of total US electricity generation). As one climate campaigner said, "This marks a clear reversal to the neoliberal policies of the 1990s, when large numbers of German municipalities sold their public services to large corporations as money was needed to prop up city budgets."[77] Munich plans to be the first large city in the world to use all renewable sources to generate electricity by 2025.[78] While energy privatization reversals are spreading, the countries with the strongest commitments to renewable energy are those with strong, publicly owned electricity sectors (the Netherlands, Austria, and Norway), given that private energy monopolies, beholden to shareholders and high quarterly profits, tend not to prioritize emission reductions. Fossil fuel companies, for example, spend no more than 2.5 percent of their overall expenditures on alternative energy, despite BP's rebranding as "Beyond Petroleum."[79] Thus far, the public sector is more likely to improve energy consumption methods.

Renewable Energy and Green Technologies

The potential of low-carbon energy sources and technologies is increasingly attractive in the global South: China has greatly expanded its solar capacity; India plans to reduce emission intensity by 20 percent to 25 percent by 2020, including a low-carbon growth strategy as part of public planning; Colombia has a Green National Development Plan; Ethiopia and Rwanda have low-carbon development plans; and Korea has "adopted a National Strategy and Five-Year Plan for Green Growth, with a budget of US$83.6 billion, around 2% of its GDP."[80]

Publicly managed renewable energy regimes are now entirely possible. The capital cost of solar photovoltaic module prices fell from US$100 per watt in the 1970s to below US$1 per watt in 2015, and in the global South, solar is now an equivalent price to kerosene. Similarly, wind turbine costs have fallen from about US$2.9 million to US$ 1.2 million in 2011, such that new onshore wind turbine electricity has equivalent cost to fossil fuel energy.[81] A 2009 report from a Californian research team (Stanford and UC–Davis) detailed "how 100 percent of the world's energy, for *all* purposes, could be supplied by wind, water and solar resources, by as early as 2030," including power generation as well as transport, heating, and cooling systems. One of the authors told *The New York Times*, "It's absolutely not true that we need natural gas, coal or oil—we think it's a myth."[82] Meanwhile, Australia's University of Melbourne's Energy Institute and the nonprofit Beyond Zero Emissions published "a blueprint for achieving a 60 percent solar and 40 percent wind electricity system in an astonishing ten years," and by 2014, the US National Oceanic and Atmospheric Administration demonstrated that 60 percent of the US electricity system could be powered by cost-effective wind and solar energy as early as 2030.[83]

Green technologies are sprouting everywhere, with the majority focused on energy efficiency and reduction. What is called a "decoupling" between economic growth and energy growth began in the global North following the energy crisis of the 1970s. The EU has achieved a 50 percent reduction in energy consumption since then, and, more recently, since 1990; while China's gross domestic product (GDP) increased nine times, its carbon emissions are only two-and-a-half times greater.[84]

Industrial activity accounts for one-third of global energy demand and almost 40 percent of carbon emissions—centered in materials industries such as chemicals and petrochemicals, iron and steel, cement, pulp and paper, and aluminum. Given current trends, by 2050 the South will account for 80 percent of industrial carbon emissions. Meanwhile, the CDM has slowed green technologies in the North since firms offset their pollution by investing in conservation (reforestation) or pollution abatement (coal scrubbing, carbon capture) initiatives in the South. Greening is nevertheless underway—especially via fuel substitutes, carbon capture and storage, heat loss reduction, and energy recovery from waste capture.[85] In the transport sector, mass transit is the obvious choice, although it is also likely that as energy resources decline, communities, towns, and cities will be redesigned to reduce travel and promote bicycle and pedestrian traffic. Cities across the world are moving in this latter direction and reducing automobile access to inner urban areas.

Alternative power sources are a key target of green technology. About 10 percent of Europe's electricity demand is to be powered by offshore wind projects.[86] Denmark has the largest offshore wind farm, accounting for 20 percent of its electricity. The Danes built a grassroots movement, given that wind is "everyone's business," encouraging a national policy of subsidizing wind farms and guaranteeing community participation in the planning process.[87] Wind power machinery prices are declining as a result of these developments, subsidized by governments.

Europe is planning a renewable power "supergrid" to "connect turbines off the wind-lashed north coast of Scotland with Germany's vast arrays of solar panels, and join the power of waves crashing on to the Belgian and Danish coasts with the hydroelectric dams located in Norway's fjords." The goal is to solve the ultimate criticism of renewable power—namely, that weather is unpredictable and so power delivery is unpredictable. The supergrid combines several different forms of natural energy across a variety of regions, including Germany, France, Belgium, the Netherlands, Luxembourg, Denmark, Sweden, Ireland, and the UK—targeting the EU's pledge to convert 20 percent of its energy to renewable sources by 2020. EU scientists are looking ahead to link solar farms in southern Europe with wind, geothermal, and marine projects elsewhere on the continent and even stray further south to capture just 0.3 percent of sunlight in the Sahara and Middle Eastern deserts to power all of Europe's needs. Concentrated solar power technology would use mirrors to concentrate solar rays on a fluid container, heating the liquid to drive turbines.[88]

For the South, solar thermal energy has enormous potential once costs come down. In the meantime at the household level, plastic solar collectors or cooking stoves are being developed, and in China and Brazil, subsidized solar panels allow water heating and supplementary electricity generation.[89] Meanwhile, the Chinese firm Suntech Power, a global leader in solar energy in over 80 countries, has launched a product called the Solar Home System to serve small, off-grid markets. It is a complete entry-level package for solar electricity generation to power light bulbs and charge cell phones at the household level.[90]

In India, the Bright Green Energy Foundation, set up by a founding member of the Grameen Bank in Bangladesh, has evolved out of Grameen Shakti—a nonprofit organization established to promote and supply renewable energy to millions of rural people, beginning with solar home systems and diversifying into biogas for cooking, electricity, organic fertilizer, and improved cooking stoves to reduce indoor air pollution. Grameen Shakti succeeded by recognizing that women needed to be involved in the adoption of renewable energy and establishing over 40 technology centers to train women in assembly, installation, and maintenance of solar home systems. Founder Dipal Barua claimed, "Women are the main victims of the energy crisis. They are the ones who suffer most from indoor air pollution, drudgery, and a lack of time because of the onerous tasks of wood-gathering and cooking." The Bright Green Energy Foundation is poised to expand its operations so that every household and business in Bangladesh "will have access to environmentally-friendly and pollution-free energy at an affordable cost."[91]

Solar and wind technologies are likely to outlast biofuels. This development is to China's advantage—in 2009 it surpassed the United States and other members of the G20 as the clean energy investment leader.[92] Certainly, one of the first acts of the Obama administration was to commit the United States to $40.75 billion to clean energy initiatives (energy efficiency, weatherizing houses, public transportation, a national electricity grid, postcoal energy, and cleaner cars). But China has committed to almost double that investment per year.[93] China is now the world's leader in clean energy, including compact fluorescent light bulbs, solar water heaters, solar photovoltaic cells, and wind turbines. The executive director of the Environmental Defense Fund observed of the Chinese, "The government realizes green energy technology is the new Industrial Revolution. They say, 'We missed the first one, and we're not going to miss this one.'"[94] This does not mean China will mothball its coal industry and coal-fired plants, as it is at the same time committed to expand its citizen-consumer population. While it is investing in biomass, wind, and solar power at a record pace (to cover 8 percent of its electricity needs by 2020), it is also investing in energy sources offshore, such as hydroelectric power in Burma, oil palm in the Democratic Republic of the Congo, natural gas fields in Texas, and oil fields in Sudan.[95]

Sustainable development initiatives involve widespread green experimentation with a multiplicity of large- and small-scale technologies dedicated to reducing, sequestering, and replacing carbon consumption/emission. But China is taking the lead—with massive government long-term planning and incentives, economies of scale to reduce the cost of solar and wind energy technologies, and more. China leads in carbon capture technology. A report in *The Wall Street Journal* noted, "The so-called China price—the combination of cheap labor and capital that rewrote the rulebook in manufacturing—is spreading to green technology, especially for energy that relies on capital-intensive projects."[96] The goal is to replicate the success of the special economic zones via low-carbon centers with preferential policies to promote low-carbon manufacturing and associated exports.

Whereas in 2004 foreign firms owned 80 percent of China's wind-turbine market, five years later Chinese (state) firms owned 75 percent of the market, with costs one-third cheaper than European producers. Competitors accuse China of subsidizing its own companies from state banks and dumping the excess supply of solar panels and wind turbines overseas. With 30 percent of the global market for photovoltaic solar panels, availability of the whole supply chain now within its borders, and a low-cost regime, China challenges its competitors to relocate to China for the "China price" (combining Chinese and foreign corporate exploitation of labor and environment).[97] Meanwhile, Volkswagen, Nissan, General Motors, and Daimler expect to build electric vehicles in China, where consumers are subsidized to buy such cars.[98]

The International Energy Agency (IEA) predicts China will move from 17 percent of world demand for energy in 2010 to 22 percent by 2035, which will surely sustain the efforts to produce clean energy. As the IEA noted, "One point is certain. The center of gravity of global energy demand growth now lies in the developing world, especially in China and India."[99] Arguably, if the world's future is founded in low-carbon technology—and humanity survives the climate-warming challenge—China is poised to become the dominant power in a global climate regime.

Ecosystem Questions

Beyond green innovation for urban-industrial settings, several public reports have appeared over the last decade or so registering the dilemmas of a development model with "externalities," referring not only to the environmental impacts of fossil fuel-based industrialization but also to those biophysical processes and social activities that remain unaccounted for. Thus, nonmonetized resources such as wild plants and human exchange networks do not appear through a conventional development lens and are thereby easily marginalized; yet these environmental and social resources are central to ecosystem resilience.

The landmark 2005 UN **Millennium Ecosystem Assessment (MEA)**, which addresses threats to the Millennium Development Goals (MDGs) by environmental degradation, states, "Existing national and global institutions are not well designed to deal with the management of common pool resources, a characteristic of many ecosystem services." More than a thousand biological scientists proposed the integration of ecosystem management goals within development planning frameworks at large, noting that "the most important public policy decisions affecting ecosystems are often made by agencies and in policy arenas other than those charged with protecting ecosystems." The MEA points to instances of poverty reduction strategies that shape development priorities, noting, "In general these have not taken into account the importance of ecosystems to improving the basic human capabilities of the poorest."[100] Two important lessons of this report were that the conventional development model has not understood the social and environmental significance of its ecological base (sources and sinks); and the interdependence of common pool resources (ecosystems) are understood and managed by precisely those populations often deemed "poor" by development agencies that then discount these forms of local resilience.

The central paradox identified by the MEA is the "environmentalist's paradox":

> Over the past 50 years, humans have changed ecosystems more rapidly and extensively than in any comparable period of time in human history, largely to meet rapidly growing demands for food, fresh water, timber, fiber, and fuel. This has resulted in a substantial and largely irreversible loss in the diversity of life on Earth. . . . These problems, unless addressed, will substantially diminish the benefits that future generations obtain from ecosystems.[101]

This paradox has not gone unnoticed in the business community, which is sensitive to future profits if not to the environment as such. In 2010, the World Economic Forum (WEF) published a report on *Biodiversity and Business Risk*, with the following leading quotation from the World Resources Institute: "Global warming may dominate headlines today. Ecosystem degradation will do so tomorrow." But given their focus on the "bottom line" and on shareholder loyalty, corporations are not organized to synchronize business with environment cycles. While bio- and geochemical time follow natural rhythms, business is concerned with short-term horizons governed by the velocity of product circulation.[102] It is not in a position to manage ecological crisis adequately. Accordingly, the MEA's goal is to orchestrate multilateral environmental agreements and coordination between environmental agreements and other international social and economic institutions:

> International agreements are indispensable for addressing ecosystem-related concerns that span national boundaries, but numerous obstacles weaken their current effectiveness. Steps are now being taken to increase the coordination

among these mechanisms, and this could help to broaden the focus of the array of instruments. However, coordination is also needed between the multilateral environmental agreements and more politically powerful international institutions, such as economic and trade agreements, to ensure that they are not acting at cross-purposes.[103]

The intent is clear: to champion new development policy frameworks geared to acknowledging and reintegrating human activity with its ecological foundations. Ecological accounting by economists is one thing, but the broader goal is to build environmental impact assessment and restoration into economic activity. The key obstacle for a (minority) world addicted to economic growth is incorporating values other than price into the development equation. Price is convenient in standardizing what is measured and valued as economic activity. But the majority of human activity is local, nonmonetized, and diverse, despite the reach of the universalizing market—hence the sensibility expressed in the MEA in advocating "use of all relevant forms of knowledge and information in assessments and decision-making," women's included. The report suggests that effective ecosystem management requires "place-based" knowledge about the specific dynamics of an ecosystem: "Traditional knowledge or practitioners' knowledge held by local resource managers can often be of considerable value in resource management, but it is too rarely incorporated into decision-making processes and indeed is often inappropriately dismissed."[104]

The *Millennium Ecosystem Assessment* was followed by the 2008 UN and World Bank–sponsored *International Assessment of Agricultural Science and Technology for Development* (IAASTD). This report, prepared by over 400 social and natural scientists and development practitioners of various kinds, advocates a *multifunctional* role for agriculture in reducing poverty and social/gender inequality, stabilizing rural cultures, reversing environmental degradation, and global warming. Stating that "business as usual is not an option," in the face of multiple crises, the IAASTD questions industrial agriculture and transgenic food as solutions since markets fail to adequately value environmental and social harm.[105] With respect to the global food regime, the IAASTD documents its unfavorable impacts on small farmers and recommends switching subsidies from export agriculture to environmental stewardship, as well as allowing national policy flexibility to balance the needs of poor consumers and small farmers (vs. WTO liberalization).[106] Echoing the MEA, the report recommends an integrative view of food, resource, and nutritional security, emphasizing that reinventing agriculture as farming requires scientists (natural, social, and health) to work with local farmers, governments, and civil society organizations.[107] Complementing the substantial literature now on the greater overall productivity—and sustainability—of small-scale farming, an IAASTD contributor noted that a "half-hectare plot in Thailand can grow 70 species of vegetables, fruits, and herbs, providing far better nutrition and feeding more people than a half-hectare plot of high-yielding rice."[108]

To strengthen and secure small farming, IAASTD recommends altering institutional arrangements to ensure **agricultural multifunctionality**, suggesting that the "shift to nonhierarchical development models" must be accompanied by building trust and valuing farmer knowledge and natural and agricultural biodiversity, as well as seed exchange and common resource management systems.[109] IAASTD maps out a general strategy to strengthen food system *resilience* in the face of environmental crises—including promoting agroecological practices with "triple-bottom-line" goals, such as full-cost accounting to incorporate energy, health, and environmental costs, and, as important, a rights-based framework rather than a market-centric organization of the agricultural and food production and delivery system.

The IAASTD report has been largely ignored by a development establishment unable to wean itself from "business as usual." But it stands as a comprehensive, publicly oriented roadmap for recognizing the environmental impact of industrial agriculture and detailing steps toward ecosystem farming that sustains rural communities as well as the land and hydrological cycles. As the High Level Panel of Experts of the FAO's Committee on World Food Security observed in 2013: "Smallholder agriculture is the foundation of food security in many countries and an important part of the social/economic/ecological landscape in all countries."[110]

Grassroots Developments

The third tendency in sustainable development initiatives is grassroots-based, focused on building ecosystem resilience as a social strategy. As noted in Chapter 7, farming systems have been the bedrock of human civilization, yet the development era has progressively lost sight of the ecological relations and impact of modern agriculture. The *Millennium Ecosystem Assessment* underlined the centrality of agriculture to ecosystem management in the following way:

> Agricultural expansion will continue to be one of the major drivers of biodiversity loss well into the twenty-first century. Development, assessment, and diffusion of technologies that could increase the production of food per unit area sustainably without harmful trade-offs related to excessive consumption of water or use of nutrients or pesticides would significantly lessen pressure on other ecosystem services.[111]

Agriculture, once an energy converter and provider, is now a heavy energy consumer—the industrial food system expends 10 or more energy calories to produce one calorie of food. Instead of embracing live/biotic carbon, it burns dead carbon.[112] And it is responsible for one-third of GHG emissions.[113] The reality is that to preserve human civilization and its ecological base, farming the land sustainably means expanding carbon sinks via agroforestry, based on the biodiversity principle, and adopting agroecology as a method of rebuilding soil carbon; both methods reduce carbon in the atmosphere and regenerate nature in the process.

In real time, small producers by necessity must adapt to the effects of climate change, which include drought, flooding, water salination, falling fish catches, and so on. To counterbalance "top-down" adaptation initiatives, NGOs such as the IIED and ActionAid have produced reports of measures used by farmers adapting to climate change—documenting the wealth of grassroots experience of adaptation via resilience. In a report titled *We Know What We Need: South Asian Women Speak Out on Climate Change Adaption*, ActionAid and the Institute for Development Studies (IDS) advocate funding support for women farmers on the front line, who need access to decision-making, rights, resources, and services.[114] A second report, titled *The Time Is NOW: Lessons From Farmers Adapting to Climate Change*, concludes,

> Many poor communities have been adapting to climate change for decades now, and already have ideas for adaptation strategies appropriate to their specific context . . . representatives of affected communities must be meaningfully involved in the governance of multilateral adaptation funds to enhance their effectiveness through transparency, accountability and stakeholder participation.[115]

As we have seen, under the globalization project, *development* means (among other initiatives) the expansion of export agriculture. In Africa, with more land converted to high-value export crops, less is available to accommodate rising farming populations. The International Centre for Soil Fertility and Agricultural Development reports land is overworked as small farmers reduce crop rotation and fallow methods to reproduce crops on the same land—a practice that depletes soil fertility—or encroach on fragile ecosystems—a common, global pattern.[116] While this is inevitable given the constraints some farming communities face, there are many positive cases. Farmers have not only reversed desertification in southern Niger and Kenya, but also, along the edge of the Sahara, in Nigeria, Niger, Senegal, Burkina Faso, and Kenya, they have employed integrated farming, mixed cropping, and traditional soil and water conservation methods that have increased food production substantially ahead of population growth. Population density has proved essential for farming labor needs, especially with cooperative farming practices and developing sustaining social networks to exchange labor, seed, cattle, technology, and cash.[117]

Niger features a success story in the Tahoua region, which has "reclaimed hundreds of hectares of degraded land" and where the president of a women's group remarked on hearing reports claiming degradation of the Sahel, "These experts have never visited us." Following environmental and political crises in the 1980s and 1990s, respectively, 250,000 hectares of strongly degraded land have been rehabilitated since the mid-1980s. In 1980, Niger produced 100,000 tons of dry onions and then 270,000 tons in 2004, a drought year. Further, in those areas where farmers have rehabilitated degraded land, household food security has improved. Overall, farmers in high population parts of Niger have succeeded on at least three million hectares in managing natural regeneration, which is unique for the Sahel.[118]

Such resilient practices are discounted when small farmers are labeled as "traditional," thereby denying their adaptive skills, especially in harnessing the multifunctional role of biodiversity. In the drylands of India's Deccan Plateau—where a variety of rain-fed crops such as sorghum, millets, pulses, and oilseeds are grown—these crops, in combination, solve a wide range of problems faced in Indian agriculture, including soil management, pest control, and minimizing risk and uncertainty. In addition, while biodiversity may allow communities to manage climatic conditions in tenuous environments,

> The many values of uncultivated biodiversity used by people for food, fodder and medicine have generally been unseen and neglected by the official discourse. . . . The number of uncultivated foods that are harvested in Medak district (Andhra Pradesh) greatly exceeds the number of cultivated species. Some 80 species of uncultivated leafy greens are locally used as foods and many dozens more species of uncultivated plants including roots, tubers and fruits. This vast array of "wild" leafy greens, berries and fruits are sources of many nutrients. . . . Most of them are rich sources of calcium, iron, carotene, vitamin C, riboflavin, and folic acid. Therefore they are a boon to pregnant and nursing women as well as to young children. Since they come at no monetary cost at all, they are a blessing for the poor. Dalits know it and have woven these uncultivated foods into their food system.[119]

Native vegetables have greater tolerance to drought and resistance to pests, have shorter growing cycles than cereal crops, and use less space. They also strengthen resilience to price shocks and enable farmers to protect biodiversity and mitigate climate change impacts. Accordingly, researchers with AVRDC/The World Vegetable Center have developed improved varieties of

African eggplant, amaranth, African nightshade, and cowpea.[120] And in Malawi, for example, communities are diversifying farming to increase climate change resilience, embracing methods to improve soil fertility, replacing chemical fertilizers with organic manure.[121] In the Ekwendeni region of northern Malawi, the Soils, Food, and Health Communities project, begun in 2000, responded to the rising cost of fertilizer by developing sustainable farming techniques to improve local food security and child nutrition. The project targeted seven villages, selecting 30 members of a "farmer research team" in a participatory process to learn how "leguminous plant options, such as pigeon pea and groundnut, could be grown to both improve their soils and provide alternative nutritious food sources for their families." The farmers then passed on the knowledge to fellow villagers, and after a decade or so, thousands of farmers in the region are experimenting with different sustainability techniques. And "malnutrition rates have declined substantially in the region, to the extent that the Nutrition Rehabilitation Centre at Ekwendeni Hospital has closed."[122]

CASE STUDY   The Real Cuban Revolution in a Peak-Oil Age

As a consequence of the collapse of the Soviet Union in 1990 and the end of imports of oil, agrochemicals, and farm machinery from the Soviet bloc, Cuba was forced by a US trade embargo to transform its energy and food system. Cuban agriculture developed around organic farming, urban gardens, animal traction, and biological pest control. This was the "Special Period" when Cuba survived a substantial crisis in a hostile international environment, managing to convert its industrial and agricultural economy to increasingly sustainable practices.

A recent study revealed that in less than a decade, depending on the region, 46 to 72 percent of peasant farms use agroecological practices, producing about 60 percent of the vegetables, maize, beans, fruits, and pork meat consumed on the island. Following Hurricane Ike in 2008, it was found that agroecological farms suffered a damage level of 50 percent compared to that of monocultures with levels of 90 to 100 percent. Agroecological farms recovered faster, and about 80 percent of the farms were producing 40 days after the hurricane. Agroecology has proven to be the most efficient, inexpensive, and stable form of food production per unit of land, input, and labor, attracting more small farmers and government land subsidies.

Cuba's urban agricultural achievements are well known: 383,000 urban farms are producing more than 1.5 million tons of vegetables with no synthetic chemicals—enough to supply 40 to 60 percent or more of all the fresh vegetables in Havana, Villa Clara, and other cities. No other country in the world has developed such a form of agriculture that reduces food miles, energy, and input use and integrates production and consumption cycles.

Given the extraordinary conditions driving this agroecological revolution, is it possible to imagine a similar conversion in other countries under future (possibly catastrophic) pressure of climate, food, and energy crises?

Source: Altieri and Toledo (2011).

Feeding the World, Sustainably

Several recent studies have concluded that the relative yields of organic/agroecological versus nonorganic farming are sufficient to provision the current daily average consumption of calories across the world.[123] A 2008 study by the UN Conference on Trade and Development (UNCTAD) and the UN Environment Program (UNEP), *Organic Agriculture and Food Security in Africa,* found that "organic agriculture outperformed conventional production systems based on chemical-intensive farming and is thus more conducive to food security in Africa." Analyzing 114 projects across 24 African countries, the study showed doubling of yields where organic (or near-organic) practices were used. The study also found "strong environmental benefits such as improved soil fertility, better retention of water, and resistance to drought in these areas."[124]

In a related study, Catherine Badgley and colleagues examined 293 cases in a global dataset, finding that on average, organic farming in the global North produces 92 percent of conventional agricultural yields, but in the global South organic farming produces 80 percent *more* than conventional agriculture. Further, the researchers found that sufficient food could be produced organically to feed the world, even without expanding farmland, and that leguminous cover crops could provide sufficient nitrogen to replace current applications of synthetic fertilizers (which, with overuse, undermine soil health). Organic fertilizer is cheap, as it is produced on farms (as compared to chemical fertilizer, which has risen in cost by 300 percent over the last few years). And since most inputs take place directly on farm and replenish soil and watersheds, organic/agroecological farming uses much less energy than industrial agriculture.[125] In 2013, farmers in India's poorest state, Bihar, reported "world record amounts of rice with no GM, and no herbicide" using only farmyard manure and the System of Root Intensification (SRI), deployed in producing

> increased yields with wheat, potatoes, sugar cane, yams, tomatoes, garlic, aubergine and many other crops and is being hailed as one of the most significant developments of the past 50 years for the world's 500 million small farmers and the two billion people who depend on them.[126]

Criticism that agroecological organics are too expensive compared with conventional farming forgets the huge subsidies to industrial agriculture (for energy, conservation, and commodities). Ecologist Ivette Perfecto contests the idea that conventional agriculture is cheap, pointing out that its real costs include the substantial health and environmental costs borne by consumers and further public subsidies.[127] Badgley and Perfecto recognize their research is controversial, but they stress that their study is a claim of sufficiency and that the actuality of a global organic food secure system "depends on policies and prices as much as on yields." Further, "achievements would multiply with additional research on locally suitable cropping systems, fertility methods, and pest management for different agricultural regions."[128]

As suggested, agroecological methods are proliferating, especially via a process of **repeasantization,** as millions of small and family farmers around the world are delinking from agro-inputs (and grinding debt) to refocus on building "ecological capital" on the farm itself. [129] *State of the World 2011* reports that agroecological methods are

> especially important in regions facing high food insecurity and high pressure for agricultural intensification. These methods can not only help farmers in areas with soil degradation and poor water quality, but also provide a sustainable alternative when industrial inputs are unaffordable, unavailable, or economically risky. Slowly but surely, commercial demand is creating attractive market opportunities for eco-certified cropping systems.[130]

Ecologist Miguel Altieri defines *agroecology* as a science and a set of place-specific practices. As science, it consists of the "application of ecological science to the study, design, and management of sustainable agroecosystems," requiring diversification of farms to promote biological interactions to regenerate soil fertility, maintain productivity, and protect crops.[131] Altieri and Toledo summarize this way:

> The core principles of agroecology include recycling nutrients and energy on the farm, rather than introducing external inputs; enhancing soil organic

matter and soil biological activity; diversifying plant species and genetic resources in agroecosystems over time and space; integrating crops and livestock, and optimizing interactions and productivity of the total farming system, rather than the yields of individual species.[132]

CASE STUDY   Seeding the World?

Rural communities have always saved and exchanged their seeds. In research on the dry Deccan Plateau of South India, Carine Pionetti documents the value of women's seed work in forming a "localized seed economy" through seed exchanges with ecological, economic, and sociocultural significance. In contrast to seed commercialization (monopolization under patents, the method favored by the development industry for feeding the world), she notes,

> The continuous exchange of seeds for local crop varieties circulates genetic resources from one field to another within a village territory and beyond. The dynamic management of genetic resources enhances the stability of traditional agrosystems, increases the adaptation potential of local crops to evolving environmental conditions and limits the risk of genetic erosion. Seed transactions also help ensure that land is not left fallow for lack of seeds, thus avoiding soil erosion and increasing the soil's organic matter content and water retention capacity.

Seed saving minimizes risk, increases crop diversity and nutrition, and provides "self-reliance and bargaining power within the household" for women. It also allows women to select seeds to meet specific individual, environmental, and climatic needs; allows planting at appropriate times; and provides assets—seeds constitute a currency, particularly among women with few resources. It constitutes the security of a "knowledge commons." However, once farmers buy or receive agro-industrial seeds, they are "locked into a production chain where the choices of inputs and the use of the harvest are predetermined by agrochemical and food-processing firms" and depend increasingly on "a network of technical information generated by specialists (agricultural scientists, chemists, genetic engineers, nutritionists, etc.)." In short, control over farming practices relocates from the farm to agribusiness complexes: Farming the landscape is converted into an economic sector (agriculture) that is disconnected from ecosystems.

Can we imagine low-input farming (ecosystem reproduction) rather than high-input agriculture (plant production) as the more modern way to manage our future?

Sources: Holt-Giménez (2006: 97); Pionetti (2005: xv, 154, 166).

SUMMARY

Sustainable development initiatives are multifaceted and experimental. In addition to private "green capitalism" initiatives, agencies, governments, and communities are struggling to establish interrelated institutional frameworks and a multitude of practices that reduce or eliminate the "externalities" of the market economy. While these initiatives all count in one way or another, the key question is whether they will be sufficient. Chair of the Copenhagen Climate Council Tim Flannery has stated, "I think that there is now a better than ever risk that, despite our best efforts, in the coming two or three decades Earth's climate system will pass the point of no return."[133] He assigns responsibility for the potential for a "new dark age following the breakdown of our global civilization" entirely with us. His understanding of sustainability is about expanding the Eighth Commandment—namely, "to forbid stealing from future generations."

US environmentalist Bill McKibben's response concerns implementation of sustainable practices and technologies via a Polanyian-style socioecological regulation of the market: "There's only one lever even possibly big enough to make our system move as fast as it needs to, and that's the force of markets."[134] In other words, use the market to raise the price of fossil fuel to radically change ingrained habits of high mass consumption—which has, up to now, been enabled "because fossil fuel doesn't bear the cost of the damage it does to the environment." And the way to "rewrite the economics of carbon in time to prevent the worst catastrophes" is to move governments, and the way to move governments "is to build a real citizen's movement that demands change."[135] In this way, markets can be converted to address social and ecological needs, rather than to serve the unsustainable process of endless accumulation.

FURTHER READING

Borras, Saturnino, Jr., Philip McMichael, and Ian Scoones, eds. *Biofuels, Land and Agrarian Change.* London: Routledge, 2011.

Elliott, Jennifer. *An Introduction to Sustainable Development.* London: Routledge, 2013.

Flannery, Tim. *Atmosphere of Hope. Searching for Solutions to the Climate Crisis.* New York: Atlantic Monthly Press, 2015.

Mol, Arthur, David Sonnenfeld, and Gert Spaargaren, eds. *The Ecological Modernisation Reader: Environmental Reform in Theory and Practice.* London: Routledge, 2009.

Perfecto, Ivette, John Vandermeer, and Angus Wright. *Nature's Matrix: Linking Agriculture, Conservation and Food Sovereignty.* London: Earthscan, 2009.

Taylor, Marcus. *The Political Ecology of Climate Change Adaptation.* London: Earthscan, 2015.

Wittman, Hannah, Annette A. Desmarais, and Nettie Wiebe, eds. *Food Sovereignty: Reconnecting Food, Nature and Community.* Halifax, NS: Fernwood, 2010.

SELECT WEBSITES

IAASTD Report: www.greenfacts.org/en/agriculture-iaastd/

UN Human Settlements Program: www.unhabitat.org

UN Millennium Ecosystem Assessment: www.millenniumassessment.org

UN Sustainable Development Goals: www.sustainabledevelopment.un.org/topics/sustainabledevelopmentgoals

Women Organizing for Change in Agriculture and Natural Resource Management: www.wocan.org

World Bank, *World Development Report (2008)*: www.openknowledge.worldbank.org

WorldWatch Institute: www.blogs.worldwatch.org/nourishingtheplanet

10

Rethinking Development

How the globalization project will evolve, or unravel, toward a new project to order the world is not yet clear. Of course, its internal tensions will condition future possibilities. But this time around, the increasingly evident resource and environmental limits will have a disproportionate effect on the shape of things to come, governed by an emerging climate change regime. Development is already about how to manage the future rather than simply improving on the past. And for a substantial proportion of the world's population this may include simply providing a "bare life," as the "better life" promise of the development vision recedes.

Managing the future means rethinking development. There is no single understanding of what the necessary steps are, even as the UN promotes a new set of sustainable development goals (SDGs) to replace the Millennium Development Goals (MDGs) of 2000.[1] Different social interests envision different development futures, especially when institutions such as the market that have been taken for granted falter. One of the key debates is over whether and to what extent the future can be managed through "business as usual." At a crisis moment, the forces of the *status quo* are most likely to argue for reinvigorating business, whereas those social forces seeking change will view environmental and social crises as a signal to shift course. We saw in the previous chapter how "sustainable development" interpretations inform a variety of responses, reflecting the diversity of social forces across the world. To simplify, we might say that the Polanyian cycle of market versus nonmarket values overlays these responses—both because modernity self-defines through the market institution and because that institution is now facing its greatest material challenge as ecosystems deteriorate. In large part, the struggle for the future concerns this central contradiction. In this closing chapter, we focus on the growing recognition of the limits of conventional development thinking and of the need to imprint sustainable practices in development futures.

Development in the Gear of Social Change

To say development is in crisis has perhaps a double meaning: On the one hand, the pain of northern financial adjustment registers in the widespread rollback of public goods (education, welfare, health care, infrastructure, affordable housing), shrinking employment, and degraded environments, so the development model is unfulfilling; on the other hand, how we understand and measure development (and what we value) is in disarray. Political scientist Lorenzo Fioramonti, critiquing what he terms "the world's most powerful number" (the gross domestic product/GDP), comments:

> The invention of GDP . . . ushered in a new age of market supremacy. . . . As GDP masked the negative externalities of industrial production, all industries (especially the heavy polluters) became champions of progress. Thanks to this statistical Laundromat, their "bads" magically disappeared, as society could only see the money being generated.[2]

Consider also the findings of an official source, the Commission on the Measurement of Economic Performance and Social Progress, whose mandate was to produce "more relevant indicators of social progress." Commenting on the sudden shock of the 2008 financial crisis, the Commission noted, "Our measurement system failed us," alluding to the failure to alert officials that the world economic boom of 2004 to 2007 "may have been achieved at the expense of future growth" and that, had they been available, "metrics which incorporated assessments of sustainability (e.g., measures for increased indebtedness) would have provided a more cautious view of economic performance." In a moment of clarity, the Commission also observed, "The time is ripe for our measurement system to shift emphasis from measuring economic production to measuring people's well-being. And measures of well-being should be put in a context of sustainability."[3]

This observation signals a turning point in public discourse about development—away from the conventional focus on economic growth and consumption targets and toward institutional appreciation for human development, such as health, education, and possibility for enhancement of life experiences.

Nonmarket Values

The Commission's declaration opens the door to taking seriously non-market services (e.g., intergenerational care and community service, health care, environmental and economic security) and even disaggregating averages to document, as the Commission noted, "the diversity of peoples' experiences." Aside from the difficulty of measuring subjective experiences, the report signals a growing recognition that market-driven metrics (such as national income data) are no longer adequate to assess the well-being of citizenries. In 1990, the United Nations *Human Development Report* complemented income measures with a composite of life expectancy and literacy in the **Human Development Index (HDI)**, leading with the premise that "(p)eople are the real wealth of a nation." Identifying human resources (including public health measures) was an important step toward recognition that the well-being of citizens was a holistic conception linked to the 1948 **UN Declaration of Human Rights** and its promotion of a government/citizen **social contract** entitling all to freedom and dignity.

To now suggest citizen "well-being" extends to the diversity of subjective experience is a salutary advance in an age where development has been equated with rising levels of consumption. And diversity extends to development policy insofar as conditions differ across countries and regions. Thus, the 2010 UN *Development Report* states, "The new strands in development thinking recognize that one size does not fit all, that the payoffs to policy reform differ with circumstances and that appropriate strategies need to be identified and developed locally."[4]

For some—such as economist Jean-Paul Fitoussi, a Commission coordinator—a measurement system needs to be standardized—"otherwise it has no validity."[5] However, the emerging **capabilities approach** privileges a diversified commitment to, and attainment for, the equal dignity of all people.[6] Drawing on Nobel laureate Amartya Sen's original formulation of "substantive freedoms—the capabilities to choose a life one has reason to value," Philosopher Martha Nussbaum argues that the new paradigm of capabilities does not assume such choice is equally distributed—rather, it "takes into account that people may need different quantities of resources if they are to come up to the same level of ability to choose and act, particularly if they begin from different social positions."[7]

This line of thinking crystallizes in the concept "shared society," premised on the idea of harnessing difference to build a universally beneficial society, which "is not owned by one section of the community, but belongs to everyone." A summary definition alludes to the multicultural present, given the vast migrations of peoples in the era of "globalization," and the practical need for inclusion:

It is an active form of sharing that goes beyond tolerance and co-existence. If governments and the dominant sectors of society recognize the desire of individuals to belong and fulfill their ambitions even if they seem different from other sectors of society, and if they make spaces for individuals to pursue their personal ambitions in their own way, and at the same time give them the support they need, then there is a strong motivation and incentive to integrate into the rest of society. Those aspects of their identity such as language, religion, clothes, and other cultural practices that mark them out as different do not disappear, but become a matter of personal expression and not a statement of difference.[8]

Politicizing Inequality

In this sense, addressing inequality is a *precondition* for promoting human development. It is one thing to temper the fixation on economic growth, but it is another to acknowledge that this fixation has allowed and legitimized the deepening of material inequalities, experienced mostly by those subject to gender, race, ethnicity, age, and disability discrimination. Indices of global wealth distribution reveal deepening inequalities, which themselves call into question assumptions that development is about improvement on the past. In a recent publication, *Other Worlds Are Possible: Human Progress in an Age of Climate Change*, Oxfam notes that recent research demonstrates "global economic growth is an extremely inefficient way of achieving poverty reduction," especially given that humanity uses more resources and generates more waste than ecosystems around the world can replace and absorb:

> A system has emerged in which the already wealthy become both relatively and absolutely wealthier, receiving the bulk of the benefits of growth. This happens as ownership of everything from property to company shares increases their earning potential. At the same time, the poorest slip further behind, and have their well-being and prospects further undermined by environmental degradation and the fall-out from inequality.[9]

This "system" is now transnational, upending the "stages of growth" scenario. For instance, there has been a divergence between the United States, as standard-bearer of development, and one of its neighbors to the South. In the 1940s, the top 1 percent of the US population controlled about 10 percent of income, compared to 20 percent in Argentina. Since then, these ratios have reversed:

> [The] share controlled by the top 1 percent in Argentina has fallen to a bit more than 15 percent. Meanwhile, inequality in the United States has soared to levels comparable to those in Argentina six decades ago—with 1 percent controlling 24 percent of American income in 2007.[10]

Between 2000 and 2007, the top 1 percent of Americans received over 70 percent of the total income increase, and by 2013, the top 3 percent held more than double the wealth of the poorest 90 percent.[11]

Aside from observing the United States' experience of what has been termed *Latin Americanization*, such trends dramatize the hollowing out of social democracy. In Karl Polanyi's terms, this means the disembedding of the market from society—where privatization and individual market relations trump the kind of social cohesion approached by the mid-twentieth-century development project. That is, class polarization in the United States clearly evidences the reversal of the social model of development, following three decades of neoliberalism. Ironically, while there is much discussion of the decline of the middle class in the United States, a new (global) middle class consolidates across the global South.

New Geography of Inequality

While a global middle class has emerged, centered in the **BRICS** (Brazil, Russia, India, China, and South Africa), there is nevertheless a rising trend in global inequality (if we remove China from consideration). But this inequality is distributed differently now. Whereas 20 years ago 93 percent of poor people lived in low-income countries, now three-fourths of the world's poorest live in middle-income countries, such as the BRICS, Nigeria, Pakistan, and Indonesia.[12] Put another way, over "80% of the world's population lives in countries where income differentials are widening."[13] The World Bank's report of around one billion poor in 2015, concentrated in the middle-income countries and the most difficult to reach, has inspired a new perspective from the University of Sussex's Institute of Development Studies (IDS). Since "poverty may be increasingly turning from an international to a national distribution problem," IDS proposes a new approach to poverty, arguing, "Development policy needs to be about poor *people*, not just about poor *countries*."[14]

Such a condition and policy intervention departs from the Rostovian assumption that development means moving countries up a hierarchy of wealth. What has changed? There are two (related) processes in play here. There is *first* a progressive incorporation of all ("traditional") subcultures into market networks via the globalization project. In World Bank terms, development is about participation in the world market, suggesting that subnational regions and resource complexes, rather than countries, develop. And this occurs through the *second* process: the deepening of global circuits of affluence. These reinforce inequality of access and/or actively exclude populations within nations from a horizontal (transnational) global consumer class.[15] Here, global inequalities no longer appear as geographical divisions; rather, they reappear as social divisions everywhere—with a universal distribution of elites and middle classes across the nation-state system. By 2010, the African Development Bank was claiming an African middle class represented about 34 percent of that continent's population (313 million people, up from 111 million in 1980).[16]

This rising middle class identifies increasingly with access to what the United Nations Department of Economic and Social Affairs (UNDESA) refers to as "largely unregulated global value chains dominated by international companies."[17] The redistribution of the "new bottom billion" to middle-income countries means, for the IDS, a "new focus on relative poverty and supporting the expansion of the tax-paying middle classes . . . to help build the domestic tax system and improve governance and accountability." This generates a new development paradox where such middle classes, given their horizontal affiliation, may be less inclined to redistribute newfound wealth to those fellow citizens experiencing social exclusion. Over the past 25 years of privatization, public assistance has dwindled as social policies have been divorced from development strategy, with the poor excluded from the global marketplace.[18] Political scientists Angus Cameron and Ronen Palan argue "social exclusion" has become a discursive strategy of pathologizing the poor as embodying deficiencies that assign personal and individual—rather than social—responsibility for their condition.[19] Microcredit initiatives reflect this and have sought to fill the void left by shrinking states.

CASE STUDY **The Debt Crisis in the North and the Detroit Revival (Motown Becomes "Growtown")**

Public debt in the global North is excessive. Detroit, home of the US auto industry, much of which has moved offshore, has cut police, lighting, road repairs, and cleaning services, affecting 20 percent of its citizens—25 percent of whom left the city in the first decade of the twenty-first century (the largest percentage drop in history for a US city), leaving 33,000 empty lots and vacant houses. White flight and some black flight to suburbs reduced the tax base of the city, exacerbating an unemployment rate of around 50 percent.

However, drastic urban decay has given way to a revitalization of the inner city, as urban farming has taken over, with about 40 square miles available (acreage the size of San Francisco). Individuals and nonprofit community groups (such as

(Continued)

(Continued)

Urban Farming) farm alongside Hantz Farms, the world's largest urban corporate farm (seen by activists as engaging in an urban "land grab"). For the thousands of people developing urban farming, they are returning Detroit to its preindustrial roots, finding new cooperative ways to make ends meet, and pioneering a template for other declining inner cities in the global North. Urban Farming's founder Taja Sevelle says, "Detroit will be number one in showing people how to pull a city out of a situation like this." Her cooperative serves food banks in Detroit and 25 other cities as part of a general philosophy of food justice.

The food these organizations grow is available free to residents; farms are unfenced, open to all (vandalism is almost unknown), and run by volunteers or charity workers. Patrick Crouch, a farmer for Earthworks (a soup kitchen provider), is skilled in agricultural activism and manages a "model plot," complete with vegetables and beehive, with the potential for replication as a source for a living wage. Urban farms adapt agroecological methods developed in Havana, Cuba, and other Latin American sites. Eight hundred million people worldwide engage in urban agriculture, producing 15 percent to 20 percent of the world's food.

If the northern development model is in decline or moving offshore, what else is there but the possibility of communities rediscovering how to feed themselves—rather than the "world"? Is this the new "stage of growth"?

Sources: Fletcher (2010); Harris (2010); *Nourishing the Planet* (2010); Seelye (2011); Uchitelle, 2011.

Uneven Development

The generalization of social exclusion raises a *key question about the development condition* at large. As suggested, a rising global middle class with weakening ties to national civic purpose indicates transformation of the development frame. Recent development literature represents this as the end of "methodological nationalism" (conceiving of development as a national process). Further, transnational relations unsettle "statecentric" theories that would prioritize the role of the development state. Drawing on global commodity chain analysis, political scientists Anthony Payne and Nicola Phillips argue the focus is "thus on firms rather than states, as the primary drivers of the emerging 'global' (as opposed to international) division of labour."[20] So the rise of China, for example, is not adequately understood via methodological nationalism. Rather, China's emergence is situated in a specific process of the transnationalization of capital via the globalization project. That is, for Payne and Phillips, transnational capital has "landed" in parts of coastal China as a result of particular sets of factor endowments, facilitated by the internal economic reforms undertaken by the Chinese government from the late 1970s onwards. Equally, the growth pattern has been fuelled primarily by the production and investment strategies of companies in the advanced industrialized economies, which in turn are premised largely on demand in these markets. It is consequently misleading to talk about the development of "China" as a national unit—rather, we are seeing the consolidation of a contemporary phase in the evolution of global production networks and value chains, which is manifested in certain spatial sites within the territorial boundaries of the Chinese state.[21]

The project of national development was always a partial (ideological) representation of social reality in the sense that development unfolded within definite international relations. Accordingly, various social patterns (from wage food provisioning to labor skill distributions) could only be explained within a global political-economic framework (food regime, international division of labor, respectively). Deepening of this framework laid the foundations of the globalization project, through which new rules and institutions opened markets and deepened transnational enterprise. As we have seen, northern manufacturing migrated to strategic regions of the global South, spawning world factories and a global labor force supplied by peasant dispossession as industrial agriculture displaced smallholders across the world. In consequence, the world has become a patchwork of uneven development within, and across, nations. The global industrialization of agriculture, for example, generates a rising migrant labor population as well as expanding slumdweller populations. Unemployed manufacturing workers gravitate toward low-paying service work, and new, highly capitalized, urban-industrial corridors migrate to the outskirts of old inner-cities, starved of resources and jobs.

The information revolution in turn has enabled the service sector (e.g., transport, telecommunication and computer services, construction, financial services, wholesale and retail distribution, hotel and catering, insurance, real estate, health and education, professional, marketing, and other business support) to overtake manufacturing and agriculture, contributing two-thirds of world GDP by 2003.[22] Information-based services, as we all know too well, have been transformed by digitization, allowing office functions to be fragmented and relocated to computers or offshore call centers, fashioning a new form of global economy that, for sociologist Manuel Castells, develops "the capacity to work *as a unit in real time* on a planetary scale."[23] As sociologist Ankie Hoogvelt points out, the existence and dynamic of this kind of economic networking in real time allows instantaneous adjustment to competitive relations, such that this twenty-first-century "global economy is highly dynamic, highly exclusionary, and highly unstable in its boundaries." In consequence, "Globalization has rearranged the architecture of world order. Economic, social, and power relations have been recast to resemble *not* a pyramid of rich nations (at the top) and poor nations (at the bottom), but instead a three-tier structure of circles."[24]

The layered structuring of the global population by access to the world economy is represented in Figure 10.1. Hoogvelt's following characterization of such layering preceded the 2008 crisis, which only solidified this hierarchical and centrifugal force:

> All three circles cut across national and regional boundaries. In the core circle, we find the elites of all continents and nations, albeit in different proportions in relation to their respective geographic hinterlands. Very roughly, the figures are 40-30-30 in the rich countries, and 20-30-50 in the poor countries. In Sub-Saharan Africa, where the middle layer is largely missing, the respective proportions are more like 10-20-70 or even 10-10-80. We may count in the core some 20% of the world population who are deemed "bankable" and therefore able to borrow funds. They are encircled by a fluid, larger social layer of between 20% and 30% of the world population (workers and their families) who labour in insecure forms of employment. . . . The third, and largest, circle comprises those who are already effectively excluded from the global system. This does not mean that they are not affected by the global system; on the contrary, they carry more than their fair share of its burdens, of environmental degradation and resource depletion, of war and conflict, of forcible dispossession. But what it means is that they are *expendable*. On a very rough count they comprise the 2.8 billion people who are estimated to be surviving on US$2 per day.[25]

Figure 10.1   Transnational Distribution of Global Population by Relative Inclusion/Exclusion

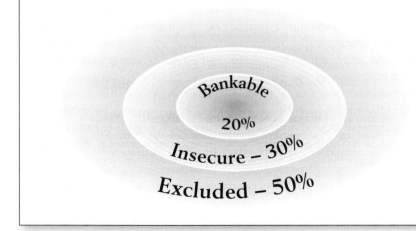

Source: Hoogvelt, 2006: 164.

Paradigm Change

Once we reconfigure the framework of development, the question becomes, how does this alter the meaning and practice, or paradigm, of development? The key point here is that generally development agencies and practitioners are professionally bound to treat the *symptoms*. This means focusing, for example, on the "bottom billion" (e.g., with direct cash transfers to the poor, such as the Brazilian *Bolsa Familia* program), worrying about the appropriate mix of economic and social remedies, and modifying the scope and scale of development interventions. During the period of the neoliberal globalization project, there has been a discernible shift away from targeting states toward targeting subject populations for development and toward participation as the litmus test of "development subject responsibility" (whether of states authoring poverty reduction, individuals embracing microcredit, or NGO-led social mobilization).

Participation may be double-edged, as it confers legitimacy on a policy/development initiative where it is filtered through local hierarchies, without fundamentally altering power relations.[26] It is here that the **development paradox** reappears, insofar as participatory methods still reproduce inequalities, which in turn renew development's legitimacy as poverty adversary. One way out of this paradox is through *self-organizing* democratic participation at the grass roots in determining social need and ecological possibility. There is currently a vast range of such social mobilization and experimentation underway across the world, often under the radar, driven by the shortcomings of development writ large and in anticipation of deteriorating environments. Naturally, the antennae of the development agencies are picking up on these movements, with the goal of appropriation, partnership, or even recognition of a shifting paradigm. In fact, one commentator argues that we are entering a "post-capitalist era":

> We're seeing the spontaneous rise of collaborative production: goods, services and organisations are appearing that no longer respond to the dictates of the market and the managerial hierarchy. The biggest information product in the world—Wikipedia—is made by volunteers for free, abolishing the encyclopedia business and depriving the advertising industry of an estimated $3 billion a year in revenue.
>
> Almost unnoticed, in the niches and hollows of the market system, whole swaths of economic life are beginning to move to a different rhythm. Parallel currencies, time banks, cooperatives and self-managed spaces have proliferated, barely noticed by the economics profession, and often as a direct result of the shattering of the old structures in the post–2008 crisis.[27]

Within the mainstream development community, Oxfam contests the persistent received wisdom that "you can't have development without all that global economic growth entails in terms of its human and environmental costs." Noting that 1987 was the last year when humanity's level of resource use "fell within the means of our life-supporting natural assets," Oxfam calls for a new form of "ecological solidarity," where managing climate change requires a "new development paradigm—a paradigm that has broken free from its carbon chains and its addiction to growth." This would involve "rethinking how to share a finite planet, meeting our collective needs whilst living within environmental limits could not only rescue civilization . . . but be a way to tackle deeply entrenched problems of social injustice, and greatly improve overall human well-being."[28]

Paradigm change thinking is a product of the contradictions of economic growth: from the King of Thailand's articulation of the idea of scaling back to the "sufficiency economy" to the King of Bhutan's notion of *Gross National Happiness* (GNH) as a qualitative benchmark combining material and spiritual development (emphasizing equality, cultural values, environmental sustainability, and good governance) to the index of sustainable economic welfare (ISEW) or the *genuine progress indicator* (GPI). The GPI offers a quantifiable national balance sheet that includes the benefits *and costs* of economic growth—for example, where "GDP counts the value of timber from native forests as a benefit and stops there, the GPI also counts the environmental costs of logging."[29]

An additional dimension of paradigm change concerns the question of world population capacity, conventionally posed as a quantitative issue. There are two qualifiers: first, resource use (and emission) is highly unequal per capita, so the question becomes not are there too many people, but what consumption habits are depleting (renewable) resources (e.g., feed/fuel vs. food crops, industrial agrifoods eroding ecosystem nutrient recycling, car/airplane emissions)? Second is the "population biology" issue—for example, with factory farms "which multiply not only the number of humans but of the beings favoured in agro-food markets, all at the expense of the many beings and relationships in self-organizing ecosystems."[30] We routinely think only of the human population, rather than recognizing we are but one species, and in that sense, our presence—and earthly footprint—is inordinate.

Degrowth Economics

Then there is the concept of "**degrowth economics**." This is a provocative term designed to counter the prevailing economic orthodoxy of unbridled "growth" that translates into "development" today and to create "integrated,

CASE STUDY

Slow Food: An International Movement of Good Taste

The Slow Food movement, originating in Italy in the 1980s but now a global movement, builds on principles of localizing food sheds, retaining local cuisines, and protecting "local" farming in particular and food heritage in general. It seeks to restore direct links between producers and consumers and thereby encourage healthy growing and eating. It proceeds from the premise that progressive social change can be sparked by transformation of attitudes about food and practices of eating. Founder of Slow Food, Carlo Petrini, claims, "The real remedies for the gastronomic ills of the twenty-first century are the assumption of responsibility for the future; the salvation of a heritage of memory, biodiversity, and creative capacity; and the affirmation of a pleasure principle."

The Slow Food Foundation for Biodiversity formed in Italy in 2003 to "know, catalogue and safeguard small quality productions and to guarantee them and economic and commercial future." In relation to this, COOP-Italia, a consortium with over 200 consumer cooperatives, coordinates production and sale of quality food products traceable to their sociospatial origins, within a broader ethical engagement that includes supporting fair-trade initiatives, water provisioning in Africa, and contesting diffusion of genetically modified organisms. Alternative food networks also contribute to the proliferation of new rural development practices, such as agritourism, energy production, and landscape management. These developments, known as "multifunctional," have potential as a new northern agricultural policy paradigm.

The official Slow Food manifesto proclaims, "In the name of productivity, Fast Life has changed our way of being and threatens our environment and our landscapes. So Slow Food is now the only truly progressive answer."

What is the difference between Fast and Slow Food paradigms in development terms?

Sources: Fonte (2006); Petrini (2001: xix, xxiv); Pretty (2002).

self-sufficient and materially responsible societies in both the North and the South." Using a dramatic metaphor to make the point, economist Serge Latouche suggests, "Growth economics, like HIV, destroys societies' immune systems against social ills. And growth needs a constant supply of new markets to survive, so, like a drug dealer, it deliberately creates new needs and dependencies that did not exist before."[31]

Latouche claims the French term *décroissance* (translated as degrowth) actually means "a-growth," and proposes that "we have to change our values. We need to replace egoism with altruism, competition with cooperation and obsessive performance with leisure. But values are systemic . . . without a radical questioning of the system, the value change will remain limited."[32] It is in this context that the phenomenon of "downshifting" has taken hold in the North, as people take leave of the consumer treadmill and pursue a more balanced and rewarding life. In her book *The Overspent American*, Juliet Schor reports that 19 percent of the adult US population has downshifted, "voluntarily switching to lower paid jobs, choosing to reduce their hours of work, and deciding to stay at home and look after their children."[33] The proliferation of alternative conceptions and practices reflects our times, as people rediscover values other than market values in individual and collective attempts to redefine the meaning of development.

According to ecological economist Joan Martinez-Alier, degrowth springs from social movement experiences of cohousing, squatting, neoruralism, reclaiming the streets, alternative energies, waste prevention, and recycling, in addition to activist-led science.[34] Degrowth economics has spawned an originating Paris Conference (2008) and an allied *decrescita* movement in Italy, spreading to Spain, Canada, the UK, Mexico, and South America.

At the Paris Conference, delegates concluded business as usual would result in a "process of involuntary and uncontrolled economic decline or collapse" and called for a "paradigm shift from the general and unlimited pursuit of economic growth to a concept of 'right-sizing' the global and national economies," involving "degrowth in wealthy parts of the world" to preserve environmental space for poorer nations. Practical steps include mainstreaming the concept into public debate and economic institutions and development of policy tools and nonmonetary indicators (including subjective indicators) to assess progress toward economic "right-sizing" (i.e., sustainable ecological footprint)—although it is unclear how capitalist property relations would lose their economic and political sway.[35]

The Second International Conference on Degrowth (2010) in Barcelona deepened the critique, arguing that "an international elite and a 'global middle class' are causing havoc to the environment through conspicuous consumption and the excessive appropriation of human and natural resources," and that the "illusion of debt-fueled growth" will end in social disaster. The conference advanced a series of practical proposals (e.g., local currencies, ecological taxes, establishment of new jurisdictions for a global commons, universal basic income, decommercialization of politics), concluding that degrowth must originate in the rich countries.

At the Barcelona conference, Patricia Perkins put forward a feminist critique of the degrowth movement, centered on the interface between paid and unpaid inputs into the measured economy. She notes much of women's work and nature's services are undervalued and unpaid, generally dwarfing the measured economy in value, yet discounted in policy:

> To the extent that Degrowth is just about—or includes—pushing the frontier between the paid and the unpaid further towards "unpaid," it fails to address these concerns about relative values, undervaluation, and justice—and in fact Degrowth might even exacerbate the exploitation of underpaid workers, and of nature. This is because, as economies become more local and more service-oriented in order to generate less material throughput, there will be shifts in how much work is done and who does it, how much trade takes place and who is put out of work as a result, and whose economic needs are met and unmet.[36]

Two other important practical points raised by Perkins are first, how does degrowth address the point that growth is central to (the possibility of) reducing material inequality? Without growth, "someone must give up resources if others are to gain them"—a question partially answered by the notion of a paradigm shift toward revaluing local resources (especially non-monetized ones such as care work, barter, cooperatives, and resource sharing) in such a way as to redefine what we mean by resources.[37] Second, Perkins introduces a critical point about voice/participation:

> Without growth as the engine, what drives progressive redistribution . . . ? It is fundamentally important for Degrowth theoreticians and activists to seek out assistance from those who already—and generally by default rather than choice—have a great deal of experience with unpaid and low-paid work, with recycling and reusing materials, with living very simply, doing without cars, eating no meat, letting others eat first, using animal or human traction rather than fossil-fuels to accomplish their daily work, fabricating shelter and the other necessities of life from non-industrial materials. These people are all around in this diverse world we inhabit; they are not just in other countries, or in the global South. But are they here at this conference? Why is this? The disenfranchised must be invited to share their views on Degrowth and how to build more equitable societies while living lightly on the earth. They are the experts![38]

From another angle, claiming that degrowth is unpalatable under present circumstances—because of global economic stagnation and high unemployment rates—"zero growth" advocate Tim Jackson, Economics Commissioner for the British Sustainable Development Commission, articulates a profound dilemma: "To resist growth is to risk economic and social collapse. To pursue it relentlessly is to endanger the ecosystems on which we depend for long-term survival." He continues:

In a world of 9 billion people all aspiring to Western lifestyles, the carbon intensity of every dollar of output must be at least 130 times lower in 2050 than it is today. By the end of the century, economic activity will need to be taking carbon out of the atmosphere, not adding to it.[39]

The Jackson study concludes that relying on capitalist efficiency is delusional, given the combination of a profit motive and the grip of consumerism. The principle of decoupling, to reduce material through-out in the economy, *would allow governments to dispense with short-term growth imperatives and refocus on protecting the long term by delivering on social and ecological goals.* A new vision is necessary, based on "rebuilding prosperity from the bottom up," to invest in public/shared goals, assets, and infrastructures. A new, "flourishing"— rather than profit-based—economy should gravitate to service-based activities, ecological/green investment, and a work-time policy to reduce working hours and improve work–life balance. Such a policy suggestion reappears in the literature—for example, a zero-growth model depends on a shorter work year to spread employment around, coupled with the redistribution of productivity gains toward leisure time rather than prof-its and GDP:

[For Canada,] a reduction in the average work year of around 15% by 2035, to 1,500 hours a year, would secure full employment. This work year would still be longer than in some European countries. In Germany, for example, the average paid employee worked 1,430 hours in 2008.[40]

Alongside "degrowth economics" is the current divestment movement, incentivized in part by the economic consequences of climate change. In September of 2015 it was announced that 400 institutions (including the world's biggest sovereign wealth fund in Norway) had committed to dis-investing from fossil fuel companies—including major pension funds, insurance companies, universities, and churches, "all of whom fear the impact of climate change on both the world and the value of their invest-ment portfolios." As the former EU commissioner for climate action remarked, divestment from fossil fuels is "sound economics." Relatedly, there is a trend of major corporations switching to 100 percent renewable energy, with some of them seeing "a 27 percent return on low carbon investments." [41]

Such emergent visions recognize the perceived injustices of a global economy and an environment in crisis. In this sense, it is not so much whether they are immediately practical or popular, but that they antici-pate future needs for inhabiting, collectively, a diminishing material world.

Transition Towns

The **Transition Town** movement is a prime example of this kind of future visioning, emphasizing relocalization. Emerging in the 2000s, it is a movement, or network, by and across communities anticipating peak oil and climate change. As of 2010, there were over 300 official towns, from the United Kingdom and Ireland to Canada, the United States, Australia, New Zealand, Chile, and Italy, engaged in processes to manage "energy descent."[42]

The goal is to build social and ecological resilience into local towns and communities (and their governance) by reducing and eliminating fossil fuel dependence and rebuilding local resources via principles of **permaculture**. Sustainable land use design reintegrates humans with their environment, localizing food systems and restoring and emulating natural cycles to replenish ecological relations and reduce waste. The expectation is that work is reduced by its greater productivity in reproducing community (rather than profits) and biodiversity (rather than products). Local currencies enhance local business and new green jobs and recycle wealth through the community—versus repatriating profits to a corporate offshore brass-plate bank. Local markets encourage environmental stewardship and social connection. Education includes adults and children and is geared to reestablishing generational and bioregional connection and developing grounded skills, local knowledge, and emotional resilience. As the people of the borough of Southend-on-Sea in the United Kingdom claim,

> Climate Change and Peak Oil can cause us to feel confronted by something overwhelmingly huge that we cannot do anything about. The central message of the Transition Movement is that this state of mind is not the place to start from if we want to achieve something, do something, or create something. Indeed, by shifting our mind-set we can actually recognize the coming post-cheap oil era as an opportunity rather than a threat, and design the future low-carbon age to be thriving, resilient, and abundant—somewhere much better to live than our current alienated consumer culture based on greed, war, and the myth of perpetual growth.[43]

Ultimately, the Transition Town movement is a proactive approach to managing the energy- and climate-challenged future—involving mobilization of community resources in such a way as to rediscover local capacity, reduce ecological footprints, and increase resilience. And as a movement, it is about alliances across communities as opposed to a conventional development model that encourages communities and regions to compete with one another.

The Commons

The proliferation of alternative conceptions and practices reflects our times, as people rediscover values other than market values in individual and collective attempts to redefine the meaning of development. One key value concept is the "**commons,**" the source of shared popular livelihoods and cultural meaning enclosed by private property relations during the rise of capitalism; it is currently the target of much of the global land grab primarily in the global South. J. K. Gibson-Graham claims there is today "a revival of interest in reclaiming and enlarging the commons in the industrialized countries and protecting the yet-to-be completely destroyed or expropriated commons in the 'developing' world." Such a revival is at the same time a rejection of the modern ontology of development and the rediscovery of local possibility—exemplified in the Transition Town movement and its variants. Gibson-Graham notes,

> The practice of economic development has been dominated by the naturalized universal of the capitalist economy (as the model of economy, as the only true, viable economy, as something that effaces its particularistic origins in the West, in certain forms of market, in certain types of enterprise). Development discourse centers on the problematic of bringing capitalist economic development to those spaces that are "lacking" its dynamic presence and allure of beneficence. Countless strategies are advocated that will engender (or more proactively "kick start") capitalist industrialization. . . . All strategies are pursued with the promise that increased well-being will trickle down from the capitalist sector and its employees to the wider community. And all are beholden to the conviction that economic growth . . . is unquestionably desirable.[44]

The quest for a new paradigm echoes across the world. For instance, in South Korea, a new desire for a culture of "fairness" confronts its ruthless, ultracompetitive, and increasingly corrupt social system.[45] In West Africa, the concept *Bamtaare* means "harmonious development," integrating community and environment. Ecuador and Bolivia captured the world's imagination in 2008 when their national constitutions reinvented development as "living well" (in Spanish: *buen vivir*, or Quechua: *sumak kawsay*). *Buen vivir*—the fruit of decades of political struggles and alliances between indigenous peoples, peasants, afrodescendants, women, environmentalists, and youth—subordinates economy to ecology, human dignity, and social justice. *Buen vivir* is not dissimilar to Polanyi's re-embedding of the market. It complements legal passage in each state of the rights of nature alongside human rights.[46]

Andean cosmology, placing *Pachamama* (planet earth) at the center of all life, "represents an unprecedented 'biocentric turn' away from the anthropocentrism of modernity."[47] The Bolivian vice president, Alvaro Gardia Linera, claimed, "It makes world history. Earth is the mother of all. It establishes a new relationship between man and nature, the harmony of which must be preserved as a guarantee of its regeneration." Of course, making world history and actually implementing such a relationship are not the same. The Bolivian Law of Mother Earth also redefines the country's mineral deposits as "blessings"—that is, as targets of new conservation measures.[48] As Nicola Bullard of NGO Focus on the Global South observes, "The obstacles to be overcome are tremendous. Bolivia is still deeply embedded in an international division of labor dating back to sixteenth century colonialism, consigned to providing cheap labor, land, and resources to the rest of the world," despite the mobilization of the Bolivian populace for social and environmental justice.[49]

Nevertheless, for anthropologist Arturo Escobar, this "biocentric turn" exemplifies the civilizational transformation imagined by "transition discourses." Such discourses stem from a variety of social movements and the fields of culture, ecology, religion and spirituality, and alternative science (such as living systems and complexity). They invoke a transition, in ecotheologian Thomas Berry's words, "from the period when humans were a disruptive force on the planet Earth to the period when humans become present to the planet in a manner that is mutually enhancing."[50] Further, the essence of transition discourses is the rejection of the one-world view that informs modern ontology and is reproduced in the currency of globalization. Arturo Escobar observes,

> Globalization discourses of all kinds assume that the world is some sort of "global space" that will progressively and inevitably be fully occupied by capitalist modernity. . . . This view of globalization as universal, fully economized, and de-localized is made possible by the immense power of corporations and maintained within manageable levels of dis/order by military might. From its very global conditions are emerging, however, responses and forms of creativity and resistance that make increasingly visible the poverty, perniciousness, and destructiveness of this imaginary.[51]

His point is that the world contains multiple ontologies or worldviews, forming a "pluriverse"—as the Zapatistas claimed, "a world where many worlds fit."

CONCLUSION

So . . . how should we rethink development? In the first place, it is necessary to underline that "development" has been normalized in modern discourse as such a comforting "buzz" word[52] that it is difficult to understand it as anything but natural. We inhabit a world in which our experience of social change pivots on a belief in "development." That is, despite modern catastrophes of one kind or another (chemical contamination, displacements, gender violence, labor exploitation, climate change, forms of malnutrition, and so on), development itself commands positive association. Today, it is symbolized in modern advertising and experienced through consumption—for the planetary minority with the purchasing power to consume.

And here is the rub: Development is thought of and measured only in terms of the positive side of the material ledger. This offers an unrealistic image of development because wealth accumulation has always depended on access to resources to exploit. And so modern accounting depends on, even if it doesn't measure, a negative side of the ledger, whether it is the exploitation of labor or of nature. Just as economic growth measures include clear-cutting forests and oil spill cleanups, they are also enhanced by labor cost reduction. In this sense, "development" is of capitalism, rather than of humans and their relationship with their natural conditions. This does not mean modern capitalism has not brought advances; rather, it means its enumerators and evaluators render only a partial account of its development processes.

While there have always been counterviews and counterpractices, these are bubbling to the surface irrepressibly as humans face their greatest challenge in attempting to sustain their earthly and atmospheric environment equitably—there is, perhaps, an emerging Sustainability Project, which registers a growing recognition of our material and temporal limits—from myriad localization movements all the way up to the United Nations.

Thus, in accounting for a shifting development paradigm, the UN Department of Economic and Social Affairs claims that the Millennium Development Goals "rediscovered the insight that market-based growth strategies were insufficient by themselves to solve the problem of widespread poverty" and that the triple crisis of 2008 exposed the flaws of market deregulation, requiring government intervention, which "dealt a blow to the conventional wisdom underpinning the Washington Consensus" (the globalization project). Related to the market-based neoliberal development paradigm, the "aid architecture fragmented, as aid focused on poverty alleviation and social welfare at the expense of promoting broader, transformative development processes." In consequence of what it terms "systemic failures" exposed by the global economic crisis of 2008 and 2009, the UN Department of Economic and Social Affairs observes, "While the strong desire for quick economic recovery is understandable, getting 'back on track' would mean returning to an unsustainable path of global development. . . . A central concern of the new thinking will be the need for a focus on sustainable development."[53]

Of course, the question is, what does sustainable development look like? How should we think about it? A recent article in *Nature* redefines *sustainable development* as "development that meets the needs of the present while safeguarding Earth's life-support system, on which the welfare of current and future generations depends."[54] Nicola Bullard has a provocative angle:

> Perhaps the greatest challenge we face is not so much how we understand sustainability, but rather how we understand development. . . . Confronted with collapsing ecosystems, toxic environments, soil depletion, climate chaos, disappearing species, and finite fossil fuels, does sustainability even make sense when there is so little left to sustain? Instead, we should be talking about regenerating and restoring what has been destroyed . . . too much human imagination is channeled into "solving" problems the wrong way. What we lack is the imagination to think about how to live differently, how to unravel the power structures that obstruct change, and how to rethink "development."[55]

Rethinking development is already underway, as we have seen, but not in any coordinated fashion. Rethinking may well require a first step of *unthinking* development as we know it, recognizing values routinely discounted in conventional development metrics—from reproductive activity in households and communities to ecological balance—values that are far more resilient and sustaining than monetary relations. There are international bodies and myriad social movements already adopting this perspective.

In sum, development futures will be governed by the tensions between these two concepts: the "one world" ontology, symbolized by the descriptor concept "globalization," and the "pluriverse" world view, symbolized by the alternative descriptor "localization," understood as a globally *situated* process (including connectivity via networks and webs). This is not to reproduce a global/local binary; rather, it is to juxtapose two distinctive organizing principles in which development is either a homogenizing or a diversifying force—with all the democratic and ecological implications. This is the axis around which humans will manage or mismanage the future.

FURTHER READING

Borras, Saturnino M., Jr., Marc Edelman, and Cristóbal Kay, eds. *Transnational Agrarian Movements Confronting Globalization.* Oxford: Wiley-Blackwell, 2008.

Da Costa, Dia. *Development Dramas: Reimagining Rural Political Action in Eastern India.* London: Routledge, 2010.

Escobar, Arturo. *Territories of Difference: Place, Movements, Life, Redes.* Durham, NC: Duke University Press, 2008.

Gibson-Graham, J. K. A *Post-Capitalist Politics.* Minneapolis: University of Minnesota Press, 2006.

Latouche, Serge. *Farewell to Growth*. Cambridge: Polity, 2009.

Patel, Raj. *The Value of Nothing: How to Reshape Market Society and Redefine Democracy.* London: Portobello Books, 2009.

Santos, Boaventura de Sousa, ed. *Another Knowledge Is Possible*. London: Verso, 2007.

Turney, Jon. *The Rough Guide to the Future*. London: Rough Guides, 2010.

Notes

Chapter 1. Development: Theory and Reality

1. Xu (2014).
2. Cowan and Shenton (1996).
3. Mitchell (1991: 68–75, 96).
4. Smith (1776/1904).
5. Polanyi (1944/2001).
6. Rostow (1960).
7. Singer (1950); Prebisch (1950); Lenin (1916/1997).
8. Frank (1970: 5, 7).
9. Wallerstein (1974).
10. Friedman (2005:383). Nonetheless, this sector provides only 0.2 percent of India's jobs.
11. Wallerstein (1988).
12. Huntington (2000: 146).
13. As implied by Sachs (2005).
14. Amin (2003:2).
15. Badgeley et al. (2007); Weis (2007).
16. McMichael (2010); GRAIN (2014).
17. UNDP, 2011a.
18. UNDP, 2011b.
19. *Millennium Ecosystem Assessment* (2005).
20. Raudsepp-Hearne et al. (2010: 579, 576).
21. Cooper (1997: 66–67); Davis (2001); Wolf (1969).
22. Marx (1965).
23. Polanyi (1944/2001).
24. Brecher, Costello, and Smith (2000).
25. Wike (2015).
26. *The Economist* (2010); Sengupta (2009).
27. Barnet and Cavanagh (1994: 383); Crossette (1997).
28. Galeano (2000: 25).
29. "Coltan," Wikipedia (Last modified August 28, 2015).
30. Chan (2011: 19).
31. Lang and Heasman (2004: 240).
32. Ibid., 240–41.
33. Ibid., 241.
34. Lawrence (2011).

Chapter 2. Instituting the Development Project

1. Davidson (1992: 83, 99–101).
2. Quoted in Rist (1997: 58).
3. Bunker (1985).
4. Gupta (1998: 309).
5. Friedmann (1999: 39).
6. Bujra (1992: 146).
7. Quoted in Stavrianos (1981: 247).

8. Day (2010: 25); see also *Better Cotton Initiative*, www. bettercotton.org.
9. McMichael (1985); Tomich (2004).
10. Ali (2002: 168).
11. Chirot (1977: 124).
12. Davis (2001: 26, 299, 315).
13. Ibid., 327.
14. Ibid., 328–29.
15. Ibid., 332–35.
16. Wolf (1982: 369, 377).
17. Mitchell (1991: 175).
18. Cooper and Stoler (1997).
19. James (1963).
20. Memmi (1967: 74).
21. Fanon (1967: 254–55).
22. F. Cooper (1997: 66–67).
23. Stavrianos (1981: 624).
24. Quoted in Clarke and Barlow (1997: 9).
25. Duncan (1996: 120).
26. Adams (1993: 2–3, 6–7).
27. Quoted in Esteva (1992: 6).
28. Quoted in Davidson (1992: 167).
29. Esteva (1992: 7).
30. Rist (1997: 79).
31. Ake (1996: 36).
32. Cited in F. Cooper (1997: 79).
33. See Berger and Weber (2014).
34. Rostow (1960).
35. Sachs (1999: 9).
36. Quoted in Hettne (1990: 3).
37. Quoted in Dube (1988: 16).
38. Bose (1997: 153).
39. Lehman (1990: 5–6).
40. Ibid.
41. Kemp (1989: 162–65).
42. Cardoso and Faletto (1979: 129–31).

Chapter 3. The Development Project: International Framework

1. Block (1977: 76–77).
2. Quoted in Brett (1985: 106–07).
3. Quoted in Kolko (1988: 17).
4. Wood (1986: 38–61).
5. Magdoff (1969: 124).
6. Rich (1994: 72).
7. Woods (2006: 207).
8. Rich (1994: 58); George and Sabelli (1994: 15).
9. Rich (1994: 73).
10. Rich (1994: 75).
11. Adams (1993: 68–69).
12. Quoted in Magdoff (1969: 54).
13. Magdoff (1969: 124); Chirot (1977: 164–65).
14. Quoted in Williams (1981: 6–57).
15. Brett (1985: 209); Wood (1986: 73); Rist (1997: 88).
16. Brett (1985: 209); Wood (1986: 73).
17. Adams (1993: 73).
18. Rich (1994: 84).
19. Harris (1987: 28).
20. The term *newly industrializing countries* (NICs) was coined by the Organisation for Economic Co-Operation and Development in 1979, and it included four southern European countries: Spain, Portugal, Yugoslavia, and Greece. The common attributes of NICs were rapid penetration of the world market with manufactured exports; a rising share of industrial employment; and an increase in real gross domestic product per capita relative to the First World. See Hoogvelt (1987: 25).

21. Brett (1985: 185–86).

22. Brett (1985: 188).

23. Knox and Agnew (1994: 347).

24. Hoogvelt (1987: 64).

25. Knox and Agnew (1994: 331). Between 1975 and 1989, this group enlarged to include China, South Africa, Thailand, and Taiwan; Argentina dropped out.

26. Martin and Schumann (1997: 100–01).

27. Quoted in Brett (1985: 188).

28. Harris (1987: 102).

29. Grigg (1993: 251).

30. Revel and Riboud (1986: 43–44).

31. Grigg (1993: 243–44); Bradley and Carter (1989: 104). Self-sufficiency measures do not necessarily reveal the state of nutrition in a country or region since a country—for example, Japan—may have a low self-sufficiency because its population eats an affluent diet, which depends on imports.

32. Friedmann (1982).

33. Quoted in Magdoff (1969: 135).

34. Dudley and Sandilands (1975).

35. Friedmann (1990: 20).

36. Perkins (1997).

37. Quoted in George (1977: 170).

38. Friedmann (1990: 20); H. Friedmann (1992: 373).

39. McMichael and Raynolds (1994: 322). The terms *peasant foods* and *wage foods* are from de Janvry (1981).

40. Segelken (1995: 5).

41. Quoted in Briscoe (2002: 182–83).

42. Rifkin (1992: 229–30).

43. Wessel (1983: 158).

44. Berlan (1991: 126–27); see also Dixon (2002).

45. Kimbrell (2002: 16); see Weis (2013).

46. Burbach and Flynn (1980: 66); George (1977: 171).

47. Quoted in George (1977: 171–72).

48. H. Friedmann (1992: 377).

49. Gupta (1998: 53, 58–59).

50. Kloppenburg (1988: xiv).

51. Gupta (1998: 54); Busch and Lacy (1983).

52. Gupta (1998: 54–56).

53. Patnaik (2003: 13).

54. Gupta (1998: 50).

55. Patel (2007: 146–47).

56. Cleaver (1977: 17); Walker (2004: 185).

57. Cleaver (1977: 28).

58. Vandana Shiva, quoted in Newman (2006: 2).

59. Quoted in Gupta (1998: 4).

60. Shiva (1997: 50–51); Barndt (2002: 38–39).

61. Newman (2006: 1).

62. Dalrymple (1985: 1069); Andrae and Beckman (1985); Raikes (1988).

63. George (1977: 174–75).

64. Patel (2013).

65. Griffin (1974); Pearse (1980); Byres (1981); Sanderson (1986a); Dhanagare (1988); Raikes (1988); Llambi (1990).

66. Lipton (1977).

67. McMichael and Kim (1994); Araghi (1995).

68. Grigg (1993: 103–04, 185); Araghi (1995).

69. Deere and León (2001: 332).

70. Rich (1994: 95, 155).

71. Rich (1994: 91, 97); Feder (1983: 222).

72. Davis (2006).

Chapter 4. Globalizing Developments

1. Arrighi (1994: 68).

2. Gereffi (1989).

3. Cf. Evans (1995).

4. Cf. Barndt (2002).

5. Hoogvelt (1987: 26–31). At the same time, as a consequence of import-substitution industrialization and the buoyancy of the export-oriented industrialization strategy in the 1970s, the composition of imports mainly from the First World moved from manufactured consumer goods to capital goods.

6. Landsberg (1979: 52, 54).

7. See Gereffi (1994).

8. Quoted in Baird and McCaughan (1979: 130).

9. Baird and McCaughan (1979: 130–32); Bernard (1996). For an excellent and detailed study of the *maquiladora* industry, see Sklair (1989).

10. French (2000: 83–85).

11. Barnet and Cavanagh (1994: 300); Dicken (1998: 131); Ellwood (2001: 68); Boyenge (2007: 1).

12. Fuentes and Ehrenreich (1983).

13. Macdonald (2005: 31); Foster (2005: 215).

14. Fuentes and Ehrenreich (1983).

15. Elson and Pearson (1981: 91).

16. Wick (2010: 27, 30).

17. Perrons (2005: 100); Baird and McCaughan (1979); *Instituto Nacional de Estadística Geografía e Informática* (2004).

18. Perrons (2005: 100).

19. Baird and McCaughan (1979: 135–36).

20. Grossman (1979).

21. Baird and McCaughan (1979: 135).

22. Hobsbawm (1992: 56); Araghi (1999).

23. Davis (2006).

24. *Pacific Basin Reports* (August 1973), quoted in NACLA (1977: 171).

25. Fröbel, Heinrichs, and Kreye (1979: 34–36).

26. Henderson (1991: 54).

27. Korzeniewicz (1994: 261).

28. Henderson (1991).

29. *The Economist* (June 3, 1995: 59); "Slavery in the 21st Century" (2001: 8).

30. Moody (1999: 183, 188).

31. Lang and Hines (1993: 24); Holusha (1996).

32. Woodall (1994: 24); Martin and Schumann (1997: 100–01).

33. Quark (2013: 98).

34. Cited in Lewin (1995: A5).

35. *The Nation* (November 8, 1993: 3).

36. Sanderson (1986b); Raynolds et al. (1993); Raynolds (1994).

37. See Patel (2013).

38. Friedland (1994).

39. *United Nations Population Fund* (www.unfpa.org).

40. Friedmann (1991).

41. P. McMichael (1993a).

42. Watts (1994: 52–53).

43. *The Economist* (June 3, 1995: 59).

44. Reardon and Timmer (2005: 35–37).

45. Collins (1995); Barndt (1997).

46. Strange (1994: 112).

47. Ibid: 107.

48. *New Internationalist* (August 1993: 18); Kolko (1988: 24).

49. Debt Crisis Network (1986: 25).

50. Kolko (1988: 26).

51. Roodman (2001: 21); George (1988: 33).

52. Lissakers (1993: 66).

53. Roodman (2001: 26).

54. Lissakers (1993: 59).

Chapter 5. Instituting the Globalization Project

1. Hoogvelt (1987: 58).

2. Pilger (2002: 28).

3. Pilger (2002: 26–39).

4. Quoted in Magdoff (1969: 53).

5. Quoted in Wood (1986: 197).

6. Quoted in Adams (1993: 123).

7. Rist (1997: 152–53).

8. See Hoogvelt (1987: 87–95).

9. Quoted in Saul (2005: 209).

10. Ruggiero (2000: xiii, xv).

11. Roodman (2001: 21).

12. Lissakers (1993: 67).

13. A. Singh (1992: 141).

14. Ibid., 144.

15. Quoted in Roodman (2001: 30).

16. Barkin (1990:104–05).

17. Quoted in Helleiner (1996: 177).

18. George (1988: 41, 49).

19. Quoted in Roodman (2001: 35).

20. Kohl and Farthing (2006: 62, 72); Graham (1994); Beneria (2003: 55).

21. de la Rocha (1994: 270–71).

22. Barkin (1990: 101, 103).

23. George (1988: 139, 143).

24. Cheru (1989: 24, 27–28, 41–42).

25. Cheru (1989: 24, 27–28, 41–42); Redding (2000).

26. Rich (1994: 186–87).

27. A. Singh (1992: 138–39, 147–48).

28. Bello et al. (1994).

29. George (1992: 97).

30. Cox (1987: 301).

31. Calculated from Crook (1993: 16); Avery (1994: 95); Hoogvelt (1997: 138).

32. Crook (1992: 9).

33. Crook (1993: 16).

34. Canak (1989).

35. Beckman (1992: 99).

36. Sachs (1998: 17).

37. Kagarlitsky (1995); Klein (2007); Kolko (1988: 278–96).

38. Quoted in Saul (2005: 209).

39. Ruggiero (2000: xiii, xv).

40. *The South Centre* (1993: 13), emphasis added.

41. Cahn (1993: 161, 163); Rich (1994); Corbridge (1993: 127).

42. Ricardo (1951).

43. Noreena Hertz, quoted in Collins (2007: 179).

44. Barnet and Cavanagh (1994: 236).

45. Klare (2002: 14–17).

46. George (1992: 11).

47. Nash (1994: C4): Bello et al. (1994: 59).

48. Rich (1994: 188).

49. Quoted in Bello et al. (1994: 63).

50. Rich (1994: 188).

51. Denny (2002: 6).

52. Black (2002: 62).

53. McMichael (1993b).

54. Adams (1993: 196–97).

55. Middleton et al. (1993: 127–29).

56. Quoted in Watkins (1991: 44).

57. Quoted in Ritchie (1993: n. 25).

58. Quoted in Wallach and Sforza (1999: x).

59. Quoted in Ransom (2001a: 27).

60. Quoted in Wallach and Woodall (2004: 219).

61. Quoted in Wallach and Sforza (1999: x).

62. Ritchie (1999).

63. Lehman and Krebs (1996); Gorelick (2000: 28–30); Madeley (2000: 75); Carlsen (2003).

64. McMichael (2005).

65. LeQuesne (1997).

66. Quoted in Bailey (2000); Murphy (1999: 3).

67. Quoted in Madeley (2000: 79).

68. Salmon (2001: 22).

69. Clarke and Barlow (1997: 21).

70. Quoted in Schott (2000: 237).

71. Moran (2000: 235).

72. Ibid., 224–26.

73. Dawkins (2000).

74. Tuxill (1999).

75. ActionAid (2000: 2).

76. Madden and Madeley (1993: 17).

77. Quoted in Weissman (1991: 337).

78. Greenfield (1999).

79. Clarke (2001).

80. Ibid.

81. Wallach (2003).

82. Watkins (2002: 21).

Chapter 6. The Globalization Project in Practice

1. United Nations Development Programme (1997).

2. Quoted in Saul (2005: 157).

3. Therborn (2012: 13).

4. Woods (2006: 168).

5. Wolfensohn (2000).

6. Narayan et al. (2002); Rademacher and Patel (2002).

7. Woods (2006: 168).

8. Fraser (2005: 317).

9. Fraser (2005: 318).

10. Quoted in Weber (2004: 197).

11. Harrison (2004).

12. Weber (2004: 197).

13. Ferguson (2006: 102–03).

14. Quoted in Fraser (2005: 336).

15. Goldman (2005: 229–30).

16. Abrahamsen (2004: 186).

17. Fraser (2005: 332).

18. Elyachar (2005). For an incisive critique of how the development establishment seeks to undermine resistance to destitution via microfinance, see Weber (2010).

19. See www.uncdf.org.

20. Complemented by offshore financial havens—see Palan (2003).

21. Bond (2006: 82–83).

21. Diokno-Pascual (2003).

22. Iriart and Waitzkin (2004).

23. Perrons (2005: 169).

24. Robinson (2004: 18).

25. Woodall (1994: 24); Martin and Schumann (1997: 100–01); Thompson (2005).

26. Friedman (2000: 52); Greenlees (2006).

27. Giridharadas (2007b).

28. Caulkin (2007); Kala (2015).

29. Freeman (2000: 23–48, 65).

30. Harding (2001: 23).

31. Tripathi (2004); Leader (2004); Müller and Patel (2004).

32. Davis (2006: 172).

33. Watkins (2006).

34. Chan (1996).

35. Barboza (2004: C3).

36. Eyferth et al. (2003).

37. Gereffi (1994).

38. Dugger (2004).

39. Busch and Bain (2004).

40. Dolan and Humphrey (2000: 167).

41. Dolan (2004).

42. Marsden (2003: 30, 56–57).

43. Corrado (2011).

44. Greenhouse (2014).

45. Therborn (2012: 12).

46. Silver (2003: 105, 168, 172).

47. Freeman and Li (2013).

48. Beneria (1995: 48); Brecher and Costello (1994: 153–54); Calvo (1997); Dillon (1997, 1998).

49. Evans (2014).

50. Ross and Trachte (1990); Moody (1999, 255–62); Rowling (2001).

51. Raynolds (2000); Ransom (2001b).

52. Bauman (2004).

53. Saul (2005: 146).

54. Kennedy (2001).

55. Davis (2006: 169, 199).

56. Quoted in ActionAid (2004: 11).

57. Parrott and Marsden (2002: 5, 62).

58. *Vía Campesina* (2000).

59. Quoted in Paringaux (2001: 4).

60. Sengupta (2015).

61. Attali (1991: 5, 14).

62. Richburg (2002: 29).

63. Hochschild (2003).

64. Enzenburger (1994: 112); Gündüz (2013).

65. Montalbano (1991: H7); Ride (1998: 9).

66. World Bank Press Release No. 2003/266/S.

67. World Bank (2011, 2014).

68. Thompson (2002b: A3); Perlez (2002: 10); *The Economist* (February 23, 2002: 42); DeParle (2007).

69. DeParle (2007).

70. Tan (1991a).

71. Ball (1990).

72. Tan (1991b).

73. MacShane (1991).

74. Quoted in Perrons (2005: 220).

75. Mize and Swords (2010).

76. Standing (2011).

77. Sadasivam (1997: 636).

78. McDougall (2007).

79. Davis (2006: 23); Vidal (2004: 18).

80. Davis (2006: 1–2).

81. Reich (1991: 42).

82. Boyd (2006: 491, 495, 497).

83. Harvey (2005: 127); Boyd (2006: 493–94).

84. Chen and Wu (2006: 205).

85. ActionAid (2004: 35–36, 40).

86. de Soto (1990: 11).

87. Sharma (2000: 78–79).

88. Menon (2010: 152).

89. Cheru (1989: 8, 19).

90. LaTouche (1993: 130).

91. de la Rocha (1994).

92. Esteva (1992: 21).

93. Weber (2004).

94. Rankin (2001: 32).

95. Quoted in Davis (2006: 184).

96. Davis (2006: 190).

97. Giridharadas (2007a: 3).

98. Davis (2006: 200–01).

99. Harvey (2003).

100. Mamdani (2003).

101. Davidson (1992: 206, 257).

102. Bond (2001: 53); Mamdani (2003).

103. Mamdani (1996: 17–20).

104. Maathai (2010: 184).

105. Ferguson (2006: 41, 12, 101).

106. Ibid., 198–99.

107. Ibid., 204.

108. Berthelot (2005: 10).

109. Arrighi (2002: 5).

110. Hawkins (1998: I); *The Economist* (June 26, 1999: 23–25); Bond (2006: 39, 42, 51, 106).

111. Cited in Makki (2015: 137).

112. Patel (2002b).

113. Bond (2002).

114. Makki (2015: 138).

115. Piot (2010: 4).

116. Dugger (2010).

117. Bond (2006: 58).

118. Ferguson (2006: 194).

119. Harvey (2005: 139); Watts (2005–06: 36).

120. Elliott (2007: 23).

121. McGreal (2006–07: 6); Brautigam (2009).

122. All quoted in French (2010).

123. McGreal (2006–07:6); Muchena (2006: 23).

124. Quoted in Muchena (2006: 23).

125. McGreal (2006–07: 6).

126. Lee (2009: 652).

127. Bond (2006: 60).

128. Muchena (2006: 24–25).

129. Elliott (2007: 23); Smith (2014: 27).

130. Bond (2006: 74); Turner (2007).

131. Renner (2002: 18).

132. World Bank (2007: 16).

133. Provost and Kennard (2015).

134. Scott (2015).

135. UNAC and GRAIN (2015: 3).

136. Quoted in Vidal (2010).

137. Quoted in Daniel (2009: 28).

Chapter 7. Global Countermovements

1. Perrons (2005: 276).

2. Esteva et al. (2013: 27–48).

3. Polanyi (1957).

4. See Hamilton (2003), LaTouche (1993), and McMurtry (2002).

5. Esteva et al. (2013: 38).

6. Francis (2015: n. 52).

7. A. J. McMichael (1993: 51); Carson (1962).

8. *Report of the World Commission on Environment and Development: Our Common Future* (www.un-documents.net/wced-ocf.htm).

9. Brown (2015).

10. Martinez-Alier (2002: 41–42).

11. Francis (2015: n. 21).

12. Harrison (1993: 54).

13. UNMA (2005: 1).

14. Abramovitz (1999: 18–19).

15. Holzman (2012).

16. Martinez-Alier (2002: 47).

17. Ma'anit (2008: 19).

18. Klein (2014: 386).

19. See, e.g., Klein (2014).

20. Kothari and Parajuli (1993: 233).

21. Shashwat (2014).

22. Roy (1999).

23. Quoted in Colchester (1994: 72).

24. Klein (2014: 377).

25. Quoted in Colchester (1994: 78).

26. Colchester (1994: 83, 88).

27. Lohmann (1993: 10).

28. Quoted in Colchester (1994: 89).

29. Rau (1991: 156–57, 160); Gammage (2012).

30. Quoted in George and Sabelli (1994: 170).

31. *TransitionNetwork.org* (www.transitionnetwork.org).

32. Klein (2014: 446).

33. Ibid., 303.

34. Ibid., 346.

35. Ibid., 361.

36. Ibid., 311.

37. Ibid., 347.

38. Quoted in Ibid., 351–52. On air quality, Shepard (2015: 158).

39. Jackson (1993: 1949).

40. Rocheleau (1991).

41. Wacker (1994: 135–39).

42. Van der Gaag (2004: 15).

43. Gita Sen, quoted in Moghadam (2005a: 103).

44. Quoted in Moghadam (2005a: 73).

45. Quoted in Moghadam (2005a: 75–76).

46. Harcourt (1994: 4).

47. Jahan (1995: 13).

48. Razavi and Miller (1995: 3).

49. Razavi and Miller (1995).

50. Sadasivam (1997: 647–48); Derbyshire (2012).

51. Moghadam (2005a: 14–17, 95).

52. Quoted in Moghadam (2005a: 108).

53. Elson (1993: 241).

54. Sadasivam (1997: 636).

55. Quoted in Moghadam (2005a: 112).

56. Harcourt (1994).

57. Sachs (2005: 11–12).

58. Enloe (2004: 59–60).

59. Fussell (2000).

60. Benería (2003: 126).

61. Collins (2003: 164–65).

62. Boyd (1998).

63. "Battle of the Bulge" (1994: 25).

64. Carrington (2014)

65. Krichah et al. (2015).

66. Robey et al., quoted in Stevens (1994: A8).

67. Krichah et al. (2015).

68. Chira (1994: A12).

69. Quoted in Crossette (1994: A8).

70. Bello (1992–1993: 5).

71. Sen (1994: 221).

72. Quoted in Hedges (1994: A10).

73. Krichah et al. (2015).

74. Moghadam et al. (2005b: 401), emphasis added.

75. Green (2015).

76. Bunting (2011: 44).

77. Tsoutsias (June 1, 2014: www.eurogender.eige.europa.eu/news/un-women-launches-first-ever-database-mapping-gender-provisions-constitutions-worldwide).

78. Farooqi (2015).

79. World Assembly of Muslim Youth (2004).

80. "As for sexism, the common law long denied married women any property rights or indeed legal personality apart from their husbands. When the British applied their law to Muslims in place of Shariah, as they did in some colonies, the result was to strip married women of the property that Islamic law had always granted them—hardly progress toward equality of the sexes." Feldman (2008).

81. Coomaraswamy (2001).

82. Geiling (2015).

83. Edelman (1999).

84. Edelman (2014).

85. EZLN (2005).

86. Madeley (2000).

87. "Food and Farming" (2003: 20); Ainger (2003: 10–11).

88. (Desmarais 2007).

89. McKeon (2009, 2015).

90. Wittman et al. (2011); Andreé et al. (2014).

91. IAASTD (2008).

92. Quoted in Claeys (2015, 13).

93. Via Campesina Seattle Declaration (December 3, 1999: retrieved from www.ratical.org/co-globalize/VCdec.txt).

94. Via Campesina: The Right to Produce and Access to Land (November 11–17, 1996: www.voiceoftheturtle.org/library/1996%20Declaration%20of%20Food%20Sovereignty.pdf).

95. Nicholson (2008: 457).

97. ETC (2009); Badgley and

Perfecto (2007).

98. "Food Sovereignty to Answer World Food and Energy Crisis," Speech by Henry Saragih at Swissaid meeting in Berne (May 29, 2008), posted by Zurayk on *Land and People* (June 18, 2008: www.landandpeople. blogspot.com/2008/06/food-security. html).

99. "Food Sovereignty," *P2P Foundation* (www.p2pfoundation.net/ Food_Sovereignty).

100. Cf. Burnett and Murphy (2014).

101. Patel and McMichael (2004: 249).

102. Park et al. (2015); Patel et al. (2015).

103. "Agrarian Reform and Water: Final Declaration," *La Via Campesina: The International Peasant's Voice* (March 9, 2006: http://viacampesina. org/en/index.php/main-issues-mainmenu-27/agrarian-reform-mainmenu-36/165-final-declaration).

104. Ibid.

105. Stedile (2002: 100).

106. Fairbairn (2012: 218); Rose (2012).

107. "Final Declaration"(2006).

108. Via Campesina, "Land Reform: Via Campesina III Int. Conference" (October 2, 2000: http://viacampesina. org/en/index.php/main-issues-main-menu-27/agrarian-reform-mainmenu-36/382-land-reform-via-campesina-iii-int-conference).

Chapter 8. The Globalization Project in Crisis

1. *The Guardian Weekly* (June 26, 2015).

2. Stewart (2015: 14).

3. Weisman (2015).

4. Ibid.

5. Funk (2014: 6).

6. Rasmussen (2015: 42–43); Hutton (2013); Carbon Tracker (2013).

7. Standing (2011: 46–47).

8. Ibid., 61–62.

9. Ibid., 71, 74.

10. Titumir and Kamal (2013: 173, 175).

11. Stancil (2010).

12. Standing (2011: 89).

13. Ibid., 79.

14. Harvey (2011).

15. Bunting (2010b: 21).

16. Allen (2015).

17. George (2010: 100–01).

18. Standing (2011: 49).

19. Ibid., 60.

20. Santos (2015).

21. Savio (2015).

22. Stiglitz (2015: 5).

23. Della Porta (2105a).

24. Iglesias (2015a: 9).

25. Iglesias (2015b: 35).

26. Santos (2015).

27. Beas (2011).

28. Malkin (2015).

29. Heller (2015).

30. Santos (2015).

31. Rasmussen (2015: 74).

32. Wolfensohn (2000).

33. UNDESA (2010b: 11).

34. Payne and Phillips (2010: 161).

35. Titumir and Kamal (2013: 173); Wike (2014).

36. Wike (2014, 2015). *Guardian Weekly*, Editorial (June 26, 2015).

37. Pieterse (2002: 1033).

38. Standing (2015: 77).

39. Sampath (2015).

40. Roy (2010).

41. Quoted in Roy (2010: 31).

42. Yunus (2011: A19).

43. Bunting (2010c).

44. Weber (2004, 2010: 116).

45. Menon (2001); Rankin (2001); Elyachar (2005).

46. Cons and Paprocki (2010: 647).

47. Quoted in Roy (2010: 27).

48. Chonghaile (2014).

49. Bateman (2010).

50. Mitchell (2011: 11).

51. Mankiw (2015: 4).

52. Habermas (2010: 18).

53. Bretton Woods Project (2011).

54. López and Rodríguez (2011: 24).

55. Reich (2015: 5); Davidson (2015).

56. Della Porta (2015b, July 9).

57. Mason (2015a).

58. Della Porta (2015b).

59. Sader (2008: 6).

60. Ibid.

61. Sekler (2009: 63–64).

62. Sader (2009: 178).

63. Harnecker (2010: 37, 58).

64. Eviatar (2006:5).

65. Séréni (2007: 12).

66. Gott (2006: 33).

67. Landsberg (2010).

68. Tran (2011).

69. Tran (2011); Piot (2011).

70. Abderrahim (2011); *Guardian* reporters (2011).

71. Mitchell (1991).

72. Gibson (2011).

73. Gresh (2011: 1).

74. Sergie, et al. (2014).

75. Quoted in Falcone (2015).

76. Rozhnov (2010).

77. Wolf (2010a: 7).

78. George (2010: 84).

79. Hervieu (2011: 11).

80. Glennie (2011: 44).

81. Danglin (2011: 11).

82. Therborn (2011: 52–53).

83. Krauss and Bradsher (2015: 10).

84. Kotkin (2007: 4).

85. Jha (2010: 11).

86. Pearlstein (2011: 20).

87. Bradsher (2006).

88. Ibid.

89. Gow (2007).

90. Bellman (2010b: B1).

91. Ramesh (2006).

92. Sharma (2007).

93. Mishra (2014).

94. Bidwai (2007).

95. *The Economist* (2010: 77); J. Venkatesan (2010).

96. Mishra (2015).

97. Ibid.

98. Rasmussen (2015: 126).

99. Ibid., 121.

100. Shepard (2015: 24, 27, 7).

101. Lee (2008: 15).

102. Jha (2010: 54).

103. Brown (2001: 19).

104. Tyler (1994: D8); Brown (1994: 19).

105. Shepard (2015: 116).

106. Bradsher (2002: A1, A8); Jha (2010: 30).

107. Bobin (2006: 17).

108. Bulard (2006: 6).

109. Tabuchi (2015).

110. Barboza (2006: 1); Rocca (2007: 10); Harvey (2005: 148–49); Wong (2010); Lee (2009).

111. Phillips (2015).

112. Kurlantzick (2014)

113. Roberts (2008: 112).

114. Albritton (2009: 116).

115. McMichael (2013: 103–05).

116. Albritton (2009: 95).

117. Sanger-Katz (2015).

118. Armstrong (2012: 14).
119. Hirata Kimura (2013).
120. Barry (2014).
121. Naeem (2009: 64–67).
122. Jha (2008: 3).
123. Black (2008).
124. Wheatley (2010: 24).
125. Hands Off the Land Alliance (2014: 8).
126. Ibid., 8.
127. Swatuk et al. (2015: 26).
128. Rulli et al. (2012: 892).
129. Lawrence (2010: 29).
130. Hands Off the Land Alliance (2014: 7).
131. Funk (2014: 9).
132. Nossiter (2010: A18).
133. *The Guardian* editorial (August 31, 2010).
134. Quoted in Roberts and Park (2007: 9).
135. Monbiot (2006: 15, 21).
136. Quoted in Wolf (2010b).
137. Warde (2008: 1–2).

Chapter 9. Sustainable Development?

1. Lovelock (2007: 15, 17).
2. Klein (2014: 175).
3. Barlow (1999); Clarke (2001); Elyachar (2005); Hochschild (2003).
4. *UN Development Report* (2011).
5. Quoted in Davis (2010: 31).
6. McKibben (2010: xiii).
7. Quoted in Toulmin (2009: 2).
8. Wainwright (2015: 28).
9. Hertsgard (2004).
10. Broder (2009).
11. Klein (2014: 408); Monbiot (2006: 22).
12. Earth Science Communications Team (2015).
13. Klein (2014: 11, 14); Funk (2014: 5).
14. Quoted in Klein (2014: 70).
15. Quoted in Ibid., 77.
16. Klein (2014: 78–79).
17. Quoted in McMichael (2009a: 248).
18. Quoted in Klein (2014: 22).
19. Funk (2014: 52).
20. Quoted in Funk (2014: 45).
21. Funk (2014: 46).
22. Noble (2007).
23. Monbiot (2006: 46).
24. Hicks et al. (2008: 53).
25. Klein et al. (2008: 4).
26. Storm (2009).
27. McAfee (2012).
28. Sachs (1993: xvi).
29. Hildyard (1993: 34).
30. Pretty (2011).
31. Royal Society (2009).
32. Quoted in Abergel (2011: 267).
33. Oram (2012).
34. *Nature* (2010: 531).
35. Perfecto, Vandermeer, and Wright (2009).
36. World Bank (2011: vii).
37. Uphoff (2003).
38. World Bank (2011: vii).
39. European Commission (2010).
40. World Bank (2007: 8); Mittal (2009: 5).
41. Maathai (2010: 236).
42. Funk (2014: 249).
43. Weiss (2008: 4).
44. Mittal (2009).
45. Quoted in Funk (2014: 247).
46. See, e.g., Graffham et al. (2007).
47. Quoted in Mittal (2009: 4), emphasis added.

48. McKeon (2014).

49. Paul and Steinbrecher (2013: 2, 9).

50. United Nations (2014).

51. "Climate Summit Launches Efforts Toward Food Security for 9 Billion People by 2050," *Climate Summit 2014* (September 23, 2014: http://www.un.org/climatechange/summit/wp-content/uploads/sites/2/2014/05/AGRICULTURE-PR.pdf).

52. "Corporate-Smart Greenwash: Why We Reject the Global Alliance on Climate-Smart Agriculture," *Climate Smart Agricultural Concerns* (September 2014: http://www.climatesmartagconcerns.info/rejection-letter.html).

53. Ibid.

54. De Schutter (2011a).

55. Altieri (2008); and Contiero (2012).

56. ETC (2007: 2).

57. Rainforest Action Network (2007).

58. Ibid.

59. Holt-Giménez (2007).

60. GRAIN (2007: 6).

61. "Biofuels: The Promise and the Risks," *World Bank Policy Brief* (2007).

62. Ferrett (2007).

63. Quoted in Rainforest Action Network (2007).

64. Cargill (2015: 86).

65. Murphy, Burch, and Clapp (2012: 47).

66. Quoted in Rainforest Action Network (2007).

67. Murphy, Burch, and Clapp (2012: 48).

68. Fargione et al. (2008).

69. Armstrong (2012: 7).

70. Mulyana et al. (2013).

71. Thorpe (2015: 19).

72. Rydge and Bassi (2015: 15).

73. Schapiro (2014: 118).

74. Dictus (2015: 21).

75. Ishii (2015).

76. Shepard (2015: 132–33).

77. Quoted in Klein (2014: 97).

78. Rydge and Bassi (2015: 15).

79. Klein (2014: 99–100, 111).

80. Rydge and Bassi (2015: 1, 14).

81. Ibid., 11, 13.

82. Quoted in Klein (2014: 101–02).

83. Klein (2014: 102).

84. Goldemberg and Lucon (2010: 18).

85. Tanaka (2010: 20–21).

86. Jha (2010: 28).

87. D'Armagnac (2010: 31).

88. Jha (2010: 28).

89. Goldemberg and Lucon (2010: 18).

90. Shi (2010: 35).

91. Arthur (2010: 31).

92. Eilperin (2010: 18).

93. Flannery (2009: 57); Eilperin (2010: 18).

94. Dreyfuss (2010: 14).

95. Krauss (2010: D7).

96. Oster (2009).

97. Oster (2009); Harney (2009).

98. Krauss (2010).

99. Quoted in Krauss (2010).

100. UNMA (2005: 20).

101. Ibid., 1.

102. Ibid., 20.

103. Ibid.

104. Ibid., 24.

105. IAASTD (2008: 20).

106. Ibid., 19.

107. Ibid., 17–18.

108. Quoted in Leahy (2008).

109. IAASTD (2008: 5, 7).

110. HLPE (2013: 11).

111. UNMA (2005: 22).

112. Altieri and Toledo (2011: 596).

113. Gilbert (2012).

114. ActionAid (2007: 21).

115. ActionAid (2008: 28).

116. Palmer (2006).

117. Lim (2008).

118. Reij (2006).

119. DDS Community Media Trust et al. (2008: 35).

120. Tenkouano (2011: 29, 36–37).

121. ActionAid (2006: 21).

122. Patel et al. (2015: 33, 38).

123. Stanhill (1990); Pretty and Hine (2001); Pretty, Morison, and Hine (2003): Halberg et al. (2005); Badgley et al. (2007).

124. UNCTAD and UNEP (2008: 236).

125. Badgley et al. (2007).

126. Vidal (2013).

127. Brahic (2007).

128. Badgley and Perfecto (2007: 80, 82).

129. Altieri and Toledo (2011: 606); Van der Ploeg (2009); Isakson (2010).

130. Buck and Scherr (2011: 21).

131. Altieri (2002).

132. Altieri and Toledo (2011: 588).

133. Flannery (2009: 100).

134. Quoted in Flannery (2009: 116).

135. Quoted in Ibid., 117–18.

Chapter 10. Rethinking Development

1. For a critical review of the SDG process, see Sexsmith and McMichael (2015).

2. Fioramonti (2014: 19).

3. The Commission is based in France and represents the United States, France, India, and the United Kingdom. Its principals were Joseph Stiglitz (Columbia University), Amartya Sen (Harvard University), and Jean-Paul Fitoussi (IEP). Quotes from 7–9, 12 of the Executive Summary. Available at www.stiglitz-sen-fitoussi.fr.

4. UNDP (2010: 19).

5. Quoted in Press (2011: 25).

6. See, e.g., Martha Nussbaum (2011a).

7. Nussbaum (2011b: 23).

8. McCartney (2014: 9).

9. Oxfam (2009).

10. Kristoff (2010).

11. Wade (2010); Institute of Policy Studies (2014); "Wealth Inequality" (2013: http://inequality.org/wealth-inequality/).

12. Hale (2011); Sumner (2010).

13. Sundaram (2010).

14. Sumner (2010).

15. Halperin (2005).

16. Smith (2011: 6).

17. UNDESA (2010a: viii).

18. Sundaram (2010: 39).

19. Cameron and Palan (2004).

20. Payne and Phillips (2010: 165–67).

21. Ibid., 168.

22. Hoogvelt (2006: 163).

23. Quoted in Hoogvelt (2006: 163), emphasis added.

24. Ibid., 163.

25. Ibid., 164.

26. See, e.g., Mosse (2004: 649–50, 662); Baviskar (2005).

27. Mason (2015b).

28. Oxfam (2009).

29. Hamilton (2003: 56–58).

30. Friedmann (2006: 464).

31. LaTouche (2004: 15).

32. Quoted in Godoy (2010: 19).

33. Schor (1998: 113).

34. Martinez-Alier (2010).

35. Foster (2011).

36. Perkins (2010).

37. Gibson-Graham (2006).

38. Perkins (2010).

39. Jackson (2009: 187).

40. Victor (2010: 370–71).

41. Jackson (2009: 200–01).

42. Transition Network.org (http://www.transitionnetwork.org/).

43. Southend in Transition (2007).

44. Gibson-Graham (2006: 188, 166).

45. Harlan (2011: 30).

46. Escobar (2011: 138).

47. Ibid.

48. Vidal (2011: 7).

49. Bullard (2011: 141–42).

50. Quoted in Escobar (2011: 138).

51. Escobar (2011: 139).

52. Rist (2007).

53. UNDESA (2010b: ix, xiii, v).

54. Griggs (2013: 307).

55. Bullard (2011: 141–42).

References

Abderrahim, Kader A. "Algeria: North African Perestroika Starts Here." *Le Monde Diplomatique*, February 2011, 6.

Abergel, Elizabeth. "Climate-Ready Crops and Bio-Capitalism: Towards a New Food Regime?" *International Journal of Sociology of Agriculture and Food* 18, no.3 (2011): 260–74.

Abrahamsen, Rita. "Review Essay: Poverty Reduction or Adjustment by Another Name?" *Review of African Political Economy* 31, no. 99 (March 2004): 184–87.

Abramovitz, Janet N. "Nature's Hidden Economy." *World Watch* 11, no. 1 (1999): 10–19.

ActionAid. "Crops and Robbers: Biopiracy and the Patenting of Staple Food Crops." ActionAid International, November 1999. http://stopogm.net/sites/stopogm.net/files/CropsandRobbers.pdf.

———. *Power Hungry: Six Reasons to Regulate Global Food Corporations*. Rome: ActionAid International, 2004.

———. *Hungry for Solutions? Progress Towards Securing the Right to Food Ten Years After the World Food Summit*. Johannesburg: ActionAid International, 2006.

http://allafrica.com/download/resource/main/main/idatcs/00011055:b812889136c5906cdf449b4208ae6687.pdf.

———. *We Know What We Need: South Asian Women Speak Out on Climate Change*. ActionAid International, 2007. http://reliefweb.int/sites/reliefweb.int/files/resources/4B96B48680BB519DC12573A1005007A1-actionaid_nov2007.pdf.

———. *The Time Is NOW: Lessons From Farmers Adapting to Climate Change*. ActionAid International, 2008. http://www.actionaid.org/publications/time-now-lessons-farmers-adapting-climate-change.

Adams, Nassau A. *Worlds Apart: The North–South Divide and the International System*. London: Zed, 1993.

Agarwal, Bina. "Patriarchy and the 'Modernising State': An Introduction." In *Structures of Patriarchy: The State, the Community and the Household*, edited by Bina Agarwal. London: Zed, 1988.

Ainger, Katherine. "The New Peasants' Revolt." *New Internationalist* 353 (January/February 2003): 9–13.

Ake, Claude. *Democracy and Development in Africa*. Washington, DC: Brookings Institute, 1996.

Albritton, Robert. *Let Them Eat Junk: How Capitalism Creates Hunger and Obesity*. Winnipeg: Arbeiter Ring, 2009.

Ali, Tariq. *The Clash of Fundamentalisms: Crusades, Jihads, and Modernity*. London: Verso, 2002.

Allen, Katie. "Global Unemployment to Rise to 212 Million, Says ILO." *The Guardian*, January 19, 2015. http://www.theguardian.com/business/2015/jan/19/global-unemployment-rising-ilo-social-unrest.

Alperovitz, Gar. "Tax the Plutocrats!" *The Nation,* January 27, 2003, 15–18.

Altieri, Miguel. "Agroecology: The Science of Natural Resource Management for Poor Farmers in Marginal Environments." *Agriculture, Eco-Systems, and Environment* 93 (2002): 1–24.

———. "Small Farms as a Planetary Ecological Asset: Five Key Reasons Why We Should Support the Revitalization of Small Farms in the Global South." *Food First* (January 2008). http://www.researchgate.net/publication/237427498_Small_Farms_as_a_Planetary_Ecological_Asset_Five_Key_Reasons_Why_We_Should_Support_the_Revitalisation_of_Small_Farms_in_the_Global_South.

Altieri, Miguel A., and Clara I. Nicholls. "Scaling Up Agroecological Approaches for Food Sovereignty in Latin America." *Development* 51, no. 4 (2008): 472–80.

Altieri, Miguel A., and Victor Manuel Toledo. "The Agroecological Revolution in Latin America: Rescuing Nature, Ensuring Food Sovereignty, and Empowering Peasants." *Journal of Peasant Studies* 38, no. 3 (2011): 587–612.

Amar, Paul. "Egypt After Mubarak." *The Nation*, May 23, 2011, 11–15.

Amenga-Etego, Rudolf. "Stalling the Big Steal." *New Internationalist* 354 (2003): 20–21.

Amin, Samir. *Capitalism in the Age of Globalization*. London: Zed, 1997.

———. "World Poverty: Pauperization and Capital Accumulation." *Monthly Review* 55, no. 5 (2003): 1–9.

Amin, Samir, Giovanni Arrighi, Andre Gunder Frank, and Immanuel Wallerstein. *Transforming the Revolution: Social Movements and the World System*. New York: Monthly Review Press, 1990.

Andrée, Peter, Jeffrey Ayres, Michael J. Bosia, and Marie-Josée Massicotte, eds. *Globalization and Food Sovereignty: Global and Local Change in the New Politics of Food*. Toronto: University of Toronto Press, 2014.

"Arab Youth Anger in the Ascendancy." *Guardian Weekly*, February 25, 2011, 28.

Araghi, Farshad. "Global Depeasantization, 1945–1990." *Sociological Quarterly* 36, no. 2 (1995): 337–68.

———. "The Great Global Enclosure of Our Times: Peasants and the Agrarian Question at the End of the Twentieth Century." In *Hungry for Profit: The Agribusiness Threat to Farmers, Food, and the Environment,* edited by Fred Magdoff, John Bellamy Foster, and Frederick H. Buttel. New York: Monthly Review Press, 1999.

Armstrong, Fiona. *Our Uncashed Dividend: The Health Benefits of Climate Action*. Sydney: Climate

& Health Alliance/The Climate Institute, 2012.

Arrighi, Giovanni. *The Long Twentieth Century: Money, Power, and the Origins of Our Times.* London: Verso, 1994.

———. "The African Crisis." *New Left Review* 15 (2002): 5–38.

———. *Adam Smith in Beijing: Lineages of the Twenty-First Century.* London: Verso, 2007.

Arthur, Charles. "Women Entrepreneurs Transforming Bangladesh." *Making It* 2 (April 2010): 30–31.

Attali, Jacques. *Millennium: Winners and Losers in the Coming World Order.* New York: Times Books, 1991.

Avery, Natalie. "Stealing From the State." In *50 Years Is Enough: The Case Against the World Bank and the IMF,* edited by Kevin Danaher and Muhammad Yunus. Boston: South End, 1994.

Ayittey, George. "AIDS Scourge Saps Africa's Vitality." *Financial Gazette,* April 18, 2002. www.fingaz.co.zw.

Badgley, C., J. Moghtader, E. Quintero, E. Zakem, M. J. Chappell, K. Aviles-Vazquez, A. Samulon, and I. Perfecto. "Organic Agriculture and the Global Food Supply." *Renewable Agriculture and Food Systems* 22, no. 2 (2007): 86–108.

Badgley, Catherine, and Ivette Perfecto. "Can Organic Agriculture Feed the World?" *Renewable Agriculture and Food Systems* 22, no. 2 (2007): 80–85.

Bailey, Mark. "Agricultural Trade and the Livelihoods of Small Farmers." Oxfam GB Discussion Paper No. 3/00, Oxfam, GB Policy Department Oxford, UK, 2000. www.oxfam.org.uk/policy/papers/agricultural_trade/agric.htm.

Baird, Peter, and Ed McCaughan. *Beyond the Border: Mexico & the U.S. Today.* New York: North American Congress on Latin America, 1979.

Baird, Vanessa. "Fear Eats the Soul." *New Internationalist,* October 2002: 9–12.

Ball, Rochelle. "The Process of International Contract Labor Migration from the Philippines: The Case of Filipino Nurses." PhD dissertation, Department of Geography, University of Sydney, Australia, 1990.

Barboza, David. "In Roaring China, Sweaters Are West of Socks City," *New York Times,* December 24, 2004, C1, C3.

———. "Labor Shortage in China May Lead to Trade Shift," *New York Times,* April 3, 2006, 1.

Barkin, David. *Distorted Development: Mexico in the World Economy.* Boulder, CO: Westview, 1990.

Barlow, Maude. *Blue Gold.* San Francisco: International Forum on Globalization, 1999.

Barndt, Deborah. "Bio/Cultural Diversity and Equity in Post–NAFTA Mexico (or: Tomasita Comes North While Big Mac Goes South)." In *Global Justice, Global Democracy,* edited by Jay Drydyk and Peter Penz. Winnipeg: Fernwood, 1997.

———. *Tangled Routes: Women, Work, and Globalization on the Tomato Trail.* New York: Rowman & Littlefield, 2002.

Barnet, Richard J., and John Cavanagh. *Global Dreams: Imperial Corporations and the New World Order.* New York: Touchstone, 1994.

Barry, Glen. "Terrestrial Ecosystem Loss and Biosphere Collapse."

Management of Environmental Quality 25, no. 5 (2014): 542–63.

Bateman, Milford. "The Power of the Community." *Making It*, November 12, 2010. http://www.makingitmagazine.net/?p=2397.

"Battle of the Bulge." *The Economist*, September 3, 1994, 25.

Bauman, Zygmut. *Wasted Lives: Modernity and Its Outcasts*. Cambridge: Polity, 2004.

Baviskar, Amita. "The Dream Machine: The Model Development Project and the Remaking of the State." In *Waterscapes: The Cultural Politics of a Natural Resource*, edited by Amita Baviskar. New Delhi: Oxford University Press, 2005.

Beams, Nick. "UN Figures Show: International Production System Developing." *World Socialist Web Site*, 1999. http://www.wsws.org/en/articles/1999/.

Beas, Diego. "How Spain's 15-M Movement Is Redefining Politics." *The Guardian*, October 15, 2011. http://www.theguardian.com/commentisfree/2011/oct/15/spain-15-m-movement-activism.

Becker, Elizabeth. "U.S. Unilateralism Worries Trade Officials." *New York Times*, March 17, 2003.

Beckman, Björn. "Empowerment or Repression? The World Bank and the Politics of African Adjustment." In *Authoritarianism, Democracy and Adjustment: The Politics of Economic Reform in Africa*, edited by Peter Gibbon, Yusuf Bangura, and Arve Ofstad. Uppsala, Sweden: Nordiska Afrikainstitutet, 1992.

Bellman, Eric. "Japan's Exporters Eye Every Rupee." *Wall Street Journal*, July 7, 2010a: B1.

———. "A New Detroit Rises in India's South." *Wall Street Journal*, July 9, 2010b: B1.

Bello, Walden. "Population and the Environment." *Food First Action Alert*, Winter 1992/1993, 5.

Bello, Walden, with Shea Cunningham and Bill Rau. *Dark Victory: The United States, Structural Adjustment and Global Poverty*. London: Pluto Press, with Food First and Transnational Institute, 1994.

Benería, Lourdes. "Accounting for Women's Work: The Progress of Two Decades." *World Development* 20, no. 11 (1992): 1547–60.

———. "Response: The Dynamics of Globalization" (Scholarly Controversy: Global Flows of Labor and Capital). *International Labor and Working-Class History* 47 (1995): 45–52.

———. *Gender, Development, and Globalization: Economics As If All People Mattered*. New York: Routledge, 2003.

Benería, Lourdes, and Shelley Feldman, eds. *Unequal Burden: Economic Crises, Persistent Poverty, and Women's Work*. Boulder, CO: Westview, 1992.

Benin, Joel. "Egypt's Workers Rise Up." *The Nation*, March 7–14, 2011, 8.

Berlan, Jean-Pierre. "The Historical Roots of the Present Agricultural Crisis." In *Towards a New Political Economy of Agriculture*, edited by W. Friedland, L. Busch, F. Buttel, and A. Rudy. Boulder, CO: Westview, 1991.

Bernard, Mitchell. "Beyond the Local–Global Divide in the Formation of the Eastern Asian Region." *New Political Economy* 1, no. 3 (1996): 335–53.

Berthelot, Jacques. "The WTO: Food for Thought?" *Le Monde Diplomatique,* December 2005, 10–11.

Bidwai, Praful. "India: Special Economic Zones on the Backburner." *Inter Press Service,* February 12, 2007.

Black, Maggie. *The No-Nonsense Guide to International Development.* London: Verso, 2002.

Black, Richard. "Fisheries Waste 'Costs Billions.'" Available at *BBC News,* October 8, 2008. http://news.bbc.co.uk/2/hi/science/nature/7660011.stm.

Block, Fred L. *The Origins of International Economic Disorder: A Study of United States International Monetary Policy from World War II to the Present.* Berkeley: University of California Press, 1977.

Bobin, Frédéric. "Mutually Assured Dependence." *Guardian Weekly,* July 14–20, 2006, 17.

Bond, Patrick. "Radical Rhetoric and the Working Class During Zimbabwean Nationalism's Dying Days." *Journal of World-Systems Research* 7, no. 1 (2001): 52–89.

———. "NEPAD." June 20, 2002. http://adelinotorres.com/africa/NEPAD%20by%20Patrick%20Bond.htm.

———. *Gender, Development, and Globalization: Economics As If All People Mattered.* New York: Routledge, 2003.

———. *Looting Africa: The Economics of Exploitation.* Pietermaritzburg: University of Kwa-Zulu Natal Press, 2006.

Booth, Karen. "National Mother, Global Whore, and Transnational Femocrats: The Politics of AIDS and the Construction of Women at the World Health Organization." *Feminist Studies* 24, no. 1 (1998): 115–39.

Bose, Sugata. "Instruments and Idioms of Colonial and National Development: India's Historical Experience in Comparative Perspective." In *International Development and the Social Sciences,* edited by Frederick Cooper and Randall Packard. Berkeley: University of California Press, 1997.

Boseley, Sarah. "Scientists Find Way to Bring Cheap Drugs to Poor Nations." *Guardian Weekly,* January 5–11, 2007, 1.

Boyd, Rosalind. "Labour's Response to the Informalization of Work in the Current Restructuring of Global Capitalism: China, South Korea and South Africa." *Canadian Journal of Development Studies* 27, no. 4 (2006): 487–502.

Boyd, Stephanie. "Secrets and Lies." *New Internationalist* 303 (1998): 16–17.

Boyenge, Jean-Pierre Singa. *ILO Database on Export Processing Zones.* Geneva: International Labor Office, 2007.

Bradley, P. N., and S. E. Carter. "Food Production and Distribution—and Hunger." In *A World in Crisis? Geographical Perspectives,* edited by R. J. Johnston and P. J. Taylor. Oxford, UK: Blackwell, 1989.

Bradsher, Keith. "White House Moves to Increase Aid to Mexico." *New York Times,* January 12, 1995, D6.

———. "India Slips Far Behind China, Once Its Closest Rival." *New York Times,* November 29, 2002, A1, A8.

———. "A Younger India Is Flexing Its Industrial Brawn." *New York Times,* September 1, 2006, 1, C4.

Brahic, Catherine. "Organic Farming Could Feed the World." *New Scientist,* July 12, 2007. http://www.newscientist.com/article/dn12245.

Branigan, Tania. "China 'Ready to Export Factories,'" *Guardian Weekly,* December 11, 2009, 17.

Brautigam, Deborah. *The Dragon's Gift: The Real Story of China in Africa.* Oxford: Oxford University Press, 2009.

Brecher, Jeremy, and Tim Costello. *Global Village or Global Pillage? Economic Reconstruction from the Bottom Up.* Boston: South End, 1994.

Brecher, Jeremy, Tim Costello, and Brendan Smith. *Globalization From Below: The Power of Solidarity.* Cambridge, MA: South End, 2000.

Breman, Jan. "Myth of the Global Safety Net." *New Left Review 59* (2009): 29–36.

Brett, E. A. *The World Economy Since the War: The Politics of Uneven Development.* London: Macmillan, 1985.

Bretton Woods Project. "IMF's Austerity Drive Goes On Despite Failures and Protests." June 13, 2011. http://www.brettonwoodsproject.org/.

Briscoe, Mark. "Water: The Untapped Resource." In *The Fatal Harvest Reader: The Tragedy of Industrial Agriculture,* edited by Andrew Kimball. Washington, DC: Island Press, 2002.

Broder, John M. "Climate Change Seen as Threat to U.S. Security." *New York Times,* August 8, 2009.

Brown, Chip. "Kayapo Courage." *National Geographic,* July 2015. http://ngm.nationalgeographic.com/2014/01/kayapo/brown-text.

Brown, Lester R. "Who Will Feed China?" *World Watch* 7, no. 5 (1994): 10–19.

———. "Bad Tidings on the Wind for Chinese." *Guardian Weekly,* June 7–13, 2001, 19.

Brown, Michael Barratt. *Fair Trade.* London: Zed, 1993.

Buck, Louis E., and Sara J. Scherr. "Moving Ecoagriculture into the Mainstream." In *State of the World 2011: Innovations That Nourish the Planet.* New York: Norton, 2011.

Bujra, Janet. "Diversity in Pre-Capitalist Societies." In *Poverty and Development in the 1990s,* edited by Tim Allen and Allan Thomas. Oxford, UK: Oxford University Press, 1992.

Bulard, Martine. "China Breaks the Iron Rice Bowl." *Guardian Weekly,* January 6, 2006.

Bulatlat. "Foreign Land Deals: Global Land Grabbing?" *Food Crisis and the Global Land Grab,* June 16, 2011. http://farmlandgrab.org/post/view/18813.

Bullard, Nicola. "It's Too Late for Sustainability: What We Need Is System Change." *Development* 54, no. 2 (2011): 141–42.

Bunker, Stephen. *Underdeveloping the Amazon: Extraction, Unequal Exchange and the Failure of the Modern State.* Urbana: University of Illinois Press, 1985.

Bunker, Stephen G., and Paul S. Ciccantell. *Globalization and the Race for Resources.* Baltimore: Johns Hopkins University Press, 2005.

Bunsha, D. "Rural Resistance." *Frontline* 23, no. 20 (October 2006): 1.

Bunting, Madeleine. "Promoting Happiness and Cutting Welfare: What a Devious Combination." *The Guardian,* November 28, 2010a.

———. "Cameron's Myth of Happiness." *Guardian Weekly,* December 3, 2010b, 21.

———. "Microfinance: Development Panacea, or Exorbitant, Ineffective Poverty Trap?" *The Guardian,* December 22, 2010c. http://www.guardian.co.uk/global-development/poverty-matters/2010/dec/22/micro finance-india-sector-regulated.

———. "Justice for Women: A Work in Progress." *Guardian Weekly,* July 15, 2011, 44.

Burbach, Roger, and Patricia Flynn. *Agribusiness in the Americas.* New York: Monthly Review Press, 1980.

Busch, L., and C. Bain. "New! Improved? The Transformation of the Global Agrifood System." *Rural Sociology* 69, no. 3 (2004): 321–46.

Busch, Lawrence, and William B. Lacy. *Science, Agriculture, and the Politics of Research.* Boulder, CO: Westview, 1983.

Byres, Terry J. "The New Technology, Class Formation and Class Action in the Indian Countryside." *Journal of Peasant Studies* 8, no. 4 (1981): 405–54.

Cahn, Jonathan. "Challenging the New Imperial Authority: The World Bank and the Democratization of Development." *Harvard Human Rights Journal* 6 (1993): 159–94.

Calvo, Dana. "Tijuana Workers Win Labor Battle." 1997. tw-list@essential.org.

Cameron, Angus, and Ronen Palan. *The Imagined Economies of Globalization.* London: Sage, 2004.

Canak, William L. "Debt, Austerity, and Latin America in the New International Division of Labor." In *Lost Promises: Debt, Austerity, and Development in Latin America,* edited by William L. Canak. Boulder, CO: Westview, 1989.

Carbon Tracker. "Unburnable Carbon 2013: Wasted Capital and Stranded Assets." 2013. http://carbontracker.live.kiln.it/Unburnable-Carbon-2-Web-Version.pdf.

Cardoso, Fernando H., and Enzo Faletto. *Dependency and Development in Latin America.* Berkeley: University of California Press, 1979.

Cargill. "150 Years of Helping the World Thrive." *Sky Delta,* August 2015, 79–86.

Carlsen, Laura. "The Mexican Farmers' Movement: Exposing the Myths of Free Trade." *Americas Program Policy Report.* Silver City, NM: Interhemispheric Resource Center, 2003.

Carrington, Damian. "World Population to Hit 11 Billion in 2100—With 70% Chance of Continuous Rise." *The Guardian,* September 18, 2014. http://www.theguardian.com/environment/2014/sep/18/world-population-new-study-11bn-2100ved.

Carrington, Damian, and Emma Howard. "Institutions Worth $2.6 Trillion Have Now Pulled Investments Out of Fossil Fuels." *The Guardian,* September 22, 2015. http://www.theguardian.com/environment/2015/sep/22/leonardo-dicaprio-joins-26tn-fossil-fuel-divestment-movement.

Carson, Rachel. *Silent Spring.* Boston: Houghton Mifflin, 1962.

Caulkin, Simon. "If Everything Can Be Outsourced, What Is Left?" *Observer,* April 1, 2007.

Central Intelligence Agency. "The Global Infectious Disease Threat and Its Implications for the United States." 2000. www.cia.gov/cia/publications/nie/report/nie99–17d.html.

Chan, Anita. "Boot Camp at the Shoe Factory." *Guardian Weekly,* November 17, 1996, 20–21.

Chan, Jenny. "iSlave." *New Internationalist* 441 (2011). http://www.newint.org/features/2011/04/01/islave-foxconn-suicides-workers/.

Chang, Leslie T. "Gilded Age, Gilded Cage." *National Geographic,* May 2008.

Chatterjee, Partha. *Nationalist Thought and the Colonial World.* Minneapolis: University of Minnesota Press, 2001.

Cheru, Fantu. *The Silent Revolution in Africa: Debt, Development and Democracy.* London: Zed, 1989.

Chira, Susan. "Women Campaign for New Plan to Curb the World's Population." *New York Times,* April 13, 1994, A12.

Chirot, Daniel. *Social Change in the Twentieth Century.* New York: Harcourt Brace Jovanovich, 1977.

Chomsky, Noam. *World Orders Old and New.* New York: Columbia University Press, 1994.

Chonghaile, Clar Ni. "Microfinance's Future Up in the Air." *Guardian Weekly,* November 14, 2014, 33.

Chossudovsky, Michel. *The Globalisation of Poverty and the New World Order.* Shanty Bay, ON: Global Outlook, 2003.

Chung, Youg-Il. "The Agricultural Foundation for Korean Industrial Development." In *The Economic Development of Japan and Korea,* edited by Chung Lee and Ippei Yamazawa. New York: Praeger, 1990.

Claeys, Priscilla. *Human Rights and the Food Sovereignty Movement: Reclaiming Control.* London: Routledge (Earthscan), 2015.

Clarke, T., and M. Barlow. *MAI: The Multilateral Agreement on Investment and the Threat to Canadian Sovereignty.* Toronto: Stoddart, 1997.

Clarke, Tony. "Serving Up the Commons." *Multinational Monitor* 22, no. 4 (2001). www.essential.org/monitor/mm2001/01april/corp2.html.

Cleaver, Harry. "Food, Famine and the International Crisis." *Zerowork* 2 (1977): 7–70.

Colchester, Marcus. "Sustaining the Forests: The Community-Based Approach in South and Southeast Asia." In *Development & Environment: Sustaining People and Nature,* edited by Dharam Ghai. Oxford, UK: Blackwell, 1994.

Colchester, Marcus, Wee Aik Pang, Wong Meng Chuo, and Thomas Jalong. *Land Is Life: Land Rights and Oil Palm Development in Sarawak.* Moreton-in-Marsh, UK: Forest Peoples' Programme and Perkumpulan Saxit Watch, 2007.

Collins, Elizabeth Fuller. *Indonesia Betrayed: How Development Fails.* Honolulu: University of Hawaii Press, 2007.

Collins, Jane. "Gender and Cheap Labor in Agriculture." In *Food and Agrarian Orders in the World-Economy,* edited by Philip McMichael. Westport, CT: Praeger, 1995.

———. *Threads: Gender, Labor, and Power in the Global Apparel Industry.* Chicago: University of Chicago Press, 2003.

Collins, Joseph, and John Lear. *Chile's Free Market Miracle: A Second*

Look. Oakland, CA: Food First Books, 1996.

Cons, Jason, and Kasia Paprocki. "Contested Credit Landscapes: Microcredit, Self-Help and Self-Determination in Rural Bangladesh." *Third World Quarterly* 31, no. 4 (2010): 637–54.

Contiero, Marco. "Outreach on Climate Change and Sustainable Development." *Stakeholder Forum,* 2012. http://www.stakeholderforum.org/sf/outreach/index.php/cop17day9home/532-cop17day-9item3).

Coomaraswamy, Radhika. "Different but Free: Cultural Relativism and Women's Rights as Human Rights." In *Religious Fundamentalisms and the Human Rights of Women,* edited by Courtney W. Howland. New York: Palgrave, 2001.

Cooper, Frederick. "Modernizing Bureaucrats, Backward Africans, and the Development Concept." In *International Development and the Social Sciences,* edited by Frederick Cooper and Randall Packard. Berkeley: University of California Press, 1997.

Cooper, Frederick, and Ann Laura Stoler, eds. *Tensions of Empire: Colonial Cultures in a Bourgeois World.* Berkeley: University of California Press, 1997.

Corbridge, Stuart. "Ethics in Development Studies: The Example of Debt." In *Beyond the Impasse: New Directions in Development Theory,* edited by Frans J. Schuurman. London: Zed, 1993.

Coronil, Fernando. *The Magical State: Nature, Money and Modernity in Venezuela.* Chicago: University of Chicago Press, 1997.

Cowan, M. P., and R. W. Shenton. *Doctrines of Development.* London: Routledge & Kegan Paul, 1996.

Cox, Robert W. *Production, Power, and World Order: Social Forces in the Making of History.* New York: Columbia University Press, 1987.

Crook, Clive. "New Ways to Grow: A Survey of World Finance." *The Economist,* Special Supplement, September 25, 1993: 3–22.

Crossette, Barbara. "A Third-World Effort on Family Planning." *New York Times,* September 7, 1994, A8.

———. "Kofi Annan's Astonishing Facts!" In *Human Development Report 1997.* New York: United Nations Development Program, 1997.

Crutzen, P. J., A. R. Mosier, K. A. Smith, and W. Winiwarter. "N20 Release from Agro-Biofuel Production Negates Global Warming Reduction by Replacing Fossil Fuels." *Atmospheric Chemical Physics Discussion* 7 (2007): 11191–205.

D'Armagnac, Bertrand. "Lesson in Wind Power." *Guardian Weekly,* August 13, 2010, 31.

Dalrymple, D. "The Development and Adoption of High-Yielding Varieties of Wheat and Rice in Developing Countries." *American Journal of Agricultural Economics* 67 (1985): 1067–73.

Daly, Herman. "Sustainable Growth: An Impossibility Theorem." *Development* 3–4 (1990): 45–47.

Danglin, François. "A Model for South-South Alliances." *Le Monde Diplomatique,* March 2011, 11.

Daniel, Shepard. *The Great Land Grab: Rush for World's Farmland Threatens*

Food Security for the Poor. The Oakland Institute, 2009.

Davidson, Adam. "On Money." *New York Times Magazine*, August 2, 2015, 14–17.

Davidson, Basil. *The Black Man's Burden: Africa and the Curse of the Nation-State.* New York: Times Books, 1992.

Davis, Mike. *Late Victorian Holocausts: El Nino Famines and the Making of the Third World.* London: Verso, 2001.

———. *The Monster at Our Door: The Global Threat of Avian Flu.* New York: The New Press, 2005.

———. *Planet of Slums.* London: Verso, 2006.

———. "Who Will Build the Ark?" *New Left Review* 61 (2010): 29–46.

Dawkins, Kristin. "Battle Royale of the 21st Century." *Seedling* 17, no. 1 (2000): 2–8.

Dawson, Alexander S. *Third World Dreams: Mexico Since 1989.* Halifax, NS: Fernwood, 2006.

Day, Elizabeth. "Cotton-Pickin' Trade." *Guardian Weekly*, December 10, 2010, 25–27.

DDS Community Media Trust, P. V. Satheesh, and Michel Pimbert. *Affirming Life and Diversity: Rural Images and Voices on Food Sovereignty in South India.* London: International Institute for Environment and Development, and the Deccan Development Society, 2009.

de Castro, Josué. "Introduction: Not One Latin America." In *Latin American Radicalism*, edited by Irving Louis Horowitz, Josué de Castro, and John Gerassi. New York: Vintage, 1969.

de Janvry, Alain. *The Agrarian Question and Reformism in Latin America.* Baltimore: Johns Hopkins University Press, 1981.

de la Rocha, Mercedes Gonzaléz. *The Resources of Poverty: Women and Survival in a Mexican City.* Cambridge, MA: Blackwell, 1994.

De Schutter, Olivier. "Responsibly Destroying the World's Peasantry." *Project Syndicate*, 2010. http://www.project-syndicate.org/commentary/deschutter1/English.

de Soto, Hernando. *The Other Path: The Invisible Revolution in the Third World.* New York: Harper & Row, 1990. Deere, Carmen Diana, and Magdalena León. *Empowering Women: Land and Property Rights in Latin America.* Pittsburgh: University of Pittsburgh Press, 2001.

De Waal, Alex. "What AIDS Means in a Famine." *New York Times*, November 19, 2002, 25.

Della Porta, Donatella. "A 12-Step Guide to the EU's Crisis of Political Responsibility." *openDemocracy*, July 8, 2015a.

———. "The European Union's Crisis of Legitimacy and the Greek Referendum." *The Bullet*, July 9, 2015b, 1138.

Denny, Charlotte. "Poor Always the Losers in Trade Game." *Guardian Weekly: Earth*, August 2002, 6.

DeParle, Jason. "Jobs Abroad Underwriting 'Model State.'" *New York Times*, September 7, 2007, A1, A16.

Derbyshire, Helen. "Gender Mainstreaming: Recognizing and Building on Progress. Views From the UK Gender and Development

Network." *Gender & Development* 20, no. 3 (2012): 405–18.

Desmarais, Annette Aurélie. *La Vía Campesina: Globalization and the Power of Peasants.* Halifax, NS: Fernwood, 2007.

Dhanagare, D. N. "The Green Revolution and Social Inequalities in Rural India." *Bulletin of Concerned Asian Scholars* 20, no. 2 (1988): 2–13.

Dias Martins, Monica. "The MST Challenge to Neoliberalism." *Latin American Perspectives* 27, no. 5 (2000): 33–45.

Dicken, Peter. *Global Shift: Transforming the World Economy.* New York: Guilford, 1998.

Dictus, Jan. "Eco-Cities: Creating a Common Language." *Making It* 18 (2015): 20–21.

Dillon, Sam. "After 4 Years of NAFTA, Labor Is Forging Cross-Border Ties." *New York Times,* December 20, 1997, A1, A7.

———. "U.S. Labor Leader Seeks Union Support in Mexico." *New York Times,* January 23, 1998, A3.

Diokno-Pascual, Maitet. "Power Splurge." *New Internationalist* 355 (April 2003): 25.

Dixon, Jane. *The Changing Chicken: Chooks, Cooks, and Culinary Culture.* Sydney: UNSW Press, 2002.

Dolan, C., and J. Humphrey. "Governance and Trade in Fresh Vegetables: The Impact of UK Supermarkets on the African Horticulture Industry." *Journal of Development Studies* 37 (2000): 147–76.

Dolan, C. S. "On Farm and Packhouse: Employment at the Bottom of a Global Value Chain." *Rural Sociology* 69, no. 1 (2004): 99–126.

Dreyfuss, Robert. "The Greening of China." *The Nation,* September 20, 2010, 14.

Dube, S. C. *Modernization and Development: The Search for Alternative Paradigms.* London: Zed, 1988.

Dudley, Leonard, and Roger Sandilands. "The Side Effects of Foreign Aid: The Case of Public Law 480, Wheat in Colombia." *Economic Development and Cultural Change* 23, no. 2 (1975): 325–36.

Dugger, Celia W. "Supermarket Giants Crush Central American Farmers." *New York Times,* December 28, 2004, A1, A10.

———. "Clinton Foundation Announces a Bargain on Generic AIDS Drugs." *New York Times,* May 9, 2007, 6.

———. "Report Optimistic on African Economies." *New York Times,* June 23, 2010.

Duncan, Colin. *The Centrality of Agriculture: Between Humankind and the Rest of Nature.* Montreal: McGill-Queen's University Press, 1996.

Earth Science Communications Team. "Global Climate Change." *NASA's Jet Propulsion Laboratory.* California Institute of Technology, 2015. http://climate.nasa.gov/evidence/.

Economist, The. "A Bumpier but Freer Road." *Briefing,* October 2, 2010, 75–77.

———. "India's Surprising Economic Miracle." *Leaders,* October 2, 2011, 11.

Edelman, Mark. *Peasants Against Globalization: Rural Social Movements in Costa Rica.* Stanford: Stanford University Press, 1999.

———. "Food Sovereignty: Forgotten Genealogies and Future Regulatory Challenges." *Journal of Peasant Studies* 41, no. 6 (2014): 959–98.

Editorial. "Climate Change: The Facts of life." *The Guardian,* August 31, 2010.

Editorial. "A Moral Solution to Climate Change." *Guardian Weekly,* June 26, 2015.

Elliott, Larry. "Evil Triumphs in a Disease-Ridden World." *Guardian Weekly,* February 14–21, 2001, 12.

———. "When Austerity Is Not Enough." *Guardian Weekly,* September 10, 2010, 18.

Elliott, Michael. "The Chinese Century." *Time,* January 22, 2007, 19–27.

Ellwood, Wayne. "Multinationals and the Subversion of Sovereignty." *New Internationalist* 246 (1993): 4–7.

———. *The No-Nonsense Guide to Globalization.* Oxford, UK: New Internationalist, 2001.

Elson, Diane, ed. *Male Bias in the Development Process.* Manchester: Manchester University Press, 1991.

———. "Gender-Aware Analysis and Development Economics." *Journal of International Development* 5, no. 2 (1993): 237–47.

Elson, Diane, and Ruth Pearson. "Nimble Fingers Make Cheap Workers: An Analysis of Women's Employment in Third World Export Manufacturing." *Feminist Review* 7 (1981): 87–101.

Elyachar, Julia. *Markets of Dispossession: NGOs, Economic Development, and the State in Cairo.* Durham, NC: Duke University Press, 2005.

Enloe, Cynthia. *The Curious Feminist: Searching for Women in a New Age of Empire.* Berkeley: University of California Press, 2004.

Enzenburger, Hans Magnus. *Civil Wars: From L.A. to Bosnia.* New York: New Press, 1994.

Erlanger, Steven. "Europeans Fear Crisis Threatens Liberal Benefits." *New York Times,* May 23, 2010.

Escobar, Arturo. *Encountering Development: The Making and Unmaking of the Third World.* Princeton, NJ: Princeton University Press, 1995.

———. "Sustainability: Design for the Pluriverse." *Development* 54, no. 2 (2011): 137–40.

Esteva, Gustavo. "Development." In *The Development Dictionary,* edited by Wolfgang Sachs. London: Zed, 1992.

ETC Group. "Peak Soil + Peak Oil = Peak Spoils." *ETC Group Communiqué,* 96. November/December 2007, 1–14.

———. "Patenting the 'Climate Genes' . . . and Capturing the Climate Agenda." *ETC Group Communiqué,* 99, 2008.

———. "Who Will Feed Us?" *ETC Group Communiqué,* 102, November 2009.

European Commission. "An EU Policy Framework to Assist Developing Countries in Addressing Food Security Challenges." SEC (2010): 379 http://eur-lex.europa.eu/legal-content/EN/TXT/?uri=celex:52010DC0127.

Evans, Alex. *The Feeding of the Nine Billion: Global Food Security for the 21st Century.* Chatham House Report, 2009. www.chathamhouse.org.uk/files/13179_r0109.

Evans, Peter. *Dependent Development*. Princeton, NJ: Princeton University Press, 1979.

———. *Embedded Autonomy: States and Industrial Transformation*. Princeton, NJ: Princeton University Press, 1995.

———. "National Labor Movements and Transnational Connections: Global Labor's Evolving Architecture Under Neoliberalism." *Global Labour Journal* 5, no. 3 (2014): 258–82.

Eviatar, Daphne. "Latin Left Turn." *The Nation*, December 25, 2006, 5–6.

Eyferth, J., P. Ho, and E. B. Vermeer. "Introduction: The Opening Up of China's Countryside." *Journal of Peasant Studies* 30, no. 3–4 (2003): 1–17.

Fairbairn, Madeleine. "Framing Transformation: The Counter-Hegemonic Potential of Food Sovereignty in the US Context." *Agriculture and Human Values* 29 (2012): 217–30.

Faison, Seth. "Detours Behind It: The Giant Follows Asian's Growth Path." *New York Times*, March 4, 1997, A1, D4.

Falcone, Dan. "Richard Falk on ISIS and Islamic 'Essentialism.'" *Truthout*, March 19, 2015. http://www.truth-out.org/news/item/29609-richard-falk-on-isis-and-islamic-essentialism.

Fanon, Frantz. *The Wretched of the Earth*. Harmondsworth, UK: Penguin, 1967.

Fargione, J., J. Hill, D. Tilman, S. Polasky, and P. Hawthorne. "Land Clearing and the Biofuel Carbon Debt." *Science*, February 7, 2008.

Farooqi, Sadaf. "Muslim Women: Productive and Positive in Every Role." *On Islam*, March 3, 2015. http://www.onislam.net/english/reading-islam/understanding-islam/women-in-islam/471193-muslim-women-productive-a-positive-in-every-role.html.

Feder, Ernst. *Perverse Development*. Quezon City, Philippines: Foundation for Nationalist Studies, 1983.

Feldman, Noah. "Why Shariah?" *New York Times*, March 16, 2008. http://www.nytimes.com/2008/03/16/magazine/16Shariah-t.html?pagewanted=all&_r=0.16.:http://www.nytimes.com/2008/03/16/magazine/16Shariah-t.html?pagewanted=all&_r=0

Ferguson, James. *Global Shadows: Africa in the Neoliberal World Order*. Durham, NC: Duke University Press, 2006.

Fernandez Kelly, Patricia. *For We Are Sold, I and My People: Women and Industry in Mexico's Frontier*. Albany, NY: SUNY Press, 1983.

Ferrett. Grant. "Biofuels 'Crime Against Humanity.'" *BBC News*, October 27, 2007.

Fioramonti, Lorenzo. "The World's Most Powerful Number." *Anthropology Today* 30, no. 2 (2014): 16–19.

Flannery, Tim. *Now or Never: Why We Must Act Now to End Climate Change and Create a Sustainable Future*. New York: Atlantic Monthly Press, 2009.

Flavio de Almeida, Lucio, and Felix Ruiz Sanchez. "The Landless Workers' Movement and Social Struggles Against Neoliberalism." *Latin American Perspectives* 22, no. 5 (2000): 11–32.

Fletcher, Michael A. "Politicians 'Look Away' as One in Seven Americans Fall Into Poverty." *Guardian Weekly*, September 24, 2010, 3.

Flynn, Matthew. "Cocktails and Carnival." *New Internationalist* 346 (2002): 16–17.

Food and Agriculture Organization of the United Nations. *The State of Food Insecurity in the World 2008: High Food Prices and Food Security— Threats and Opportunities*. http://www.fao.org/docrep/fao/011/i0291_e/i0291e00a.htm.

"Food and Farming: The Facts." *New Internationalist* 353 (2003): 20–21.

Fonte, Maria. "Slow Foods Presidia: What Do Small Producers Do With Big Retailers?" In *Between the Local and the Global: Confronting Complexity in the Contemporary Agri-Food Sector*, edited by Terry Marsden and Jonathan Murdoch. Oxford: Elsevier, 2006.

Foster, John Bellamy. "Capitalism and Degrowth: An Impossibility." *Monthly Review* 62, no. 8 (2011): 26–33.

Foster, John W. "The Trinational Alliance Against NAFTA: Sinews of Solidarity." In *Coalitions Across Borders: Transnational Protest and the Neoliberal Order*, edited by Joe Bandy and Jackie Smith. New York: Rowman & Littlefield, 2005.

Fox, Jonathan. "The Challenge of Democracy: Rebellion as Catalyst." *Akwekon* 11, no. 2 (1994): 13–19.

Francis, (Pope). "Laudato Si'." 2015. file:///Users/pdm1/Desktop/Laudato%20si'%20(24%20May%202015).html.

Frank, Andre Gunder. "The Development of Underdevelopment." In *Imperialism and Underdevelopment,* edited by Robert H. Rhodes. New York: Monthly Review Press, 1970.

Fraser, Alistair. "Poverty Reduction Strategy Papers: Now Who Calls the Shots?" *Review of African Political Economy*, 104/5 (2005): 317–40.

Freeman, Carla. *High Tech and High Heels in the Global Economy: Women, Work, and Pink-Collar Identities in the Caribbean*. Durham, NC: Duke University Press, 2000.

Freeman, Richard B., and Ziaoying Li. "Has China's New Labour Contract Law Worked?" *VOX. CEPR's Policy Portal*, December 22, 2013. http://www.voxeu.org/article/has-china-s-new-labour-contract-law-worked.

French, Hilary. *Vanishing Borders: Protecting the Planet in the Age of Globalization*. New York: Norton, 2000.

French, Howard W. "The Next Empire." *The Atlantic*, May 2010.

Friedland, William H. "The Global Fresh Fruit and Vegetable System: An Industrial Organization Analysis." In *The Global Restructuring of Agro-Food Systems*, edited by Philip McMichael. Ithaca, NY: Cornell University Press, 1994.

Friedman, Thomas. *The Lexus and the Olive Tree: Understanding Globalization*. New York: Anchor, 2000.

———. *The World Is Flat: A Brief History of the Twentieth Century*. New York: Farrar, Straus, & Giroux, 2005.

Friedmann, Harriet. "The Political Economy of Food: The Rise and

Fall of the Postwar International Food Order." *American Journal of Sociology* 88S (1982): 248–86.

———. "The Origins of Third World Food Dependence." In *The Food Question: Profits Versus People?* edited by Henry Bernstein, Ben Crow, Maureen Mackintosh, and Charlotte Martin. New York: Monthly Review Press, 1990.

———. "Changes in the International Division of Labor: Agri-Food Complexes and Export Agriculture." In *Towards a New Political Economy of Agriculture,* edited by William Friedland, Lawrence Busch, Frederick H. Buttel, and Alan P. Rudy. Boulder, CO: Westview, 1991.

———. "Distance and Durability: Shaky Foundations of the World Food Economy." *Third World Quarterly* 13, no. 2 (1992): 371–83.

———. "Remaking 'Traditions': How We Eat, What We Eat, and the Changing Political Economy of Food." In *Women Working the NAFTA Food Chain,* edited by Deborah Barndt. Toronto: Second Story, 1999.

———. "Focusing on Agriculture: A Comment on Henry Bernstein's 'Is There an Agrarian Question in the 21st Century?'" *Canadian Journal of Development Studies* 27, no. 4 (2006): 461–65.

Friedmann, John. *Empowerment: The Politics of Alternative Development.* Cambridge, UK: Blackwell, 1992.

Fröbel, Folker, Jürgen Heinrichs, and Otto Kreye. *The New International Division of Labor.* New York: Cambridge University Press, 1979.

Fuentes, Anna, and Barbara Ehrenreich. "The New Factory Girls." *Multinational Monitor* 4, no. 8 (1983).

Fussell, M. E. "Making Labor Flexible: The Recomposition of Tijuana's *Maquiladora* Female Labor Force." *Feminist Economics* 6, no. 3 (2000): 59–80.

Gaia Foundation. *Agrofuels and the Myth of the Marginal Land.* Briefing, 2008. http://www.gaiafoundation.org/documents/Agrofuels&MarginalMyth.pdf.

Galeano, Eduardo. *Upside Down: A Primer for the Looking Glass World.* New York: Picador, 2000.

Gammage, Bill. *The Biggest Estate on Earth: How Aborigines Made Australia.* Sydney: Allen & Unwin, 2012.

Gardner, Gary, and Brian Halweil. "Underfed and Overfed: The Global Epidemic of Malnutrition." *Worldwatch* Paper No. 150, Washington, DC: Worldwatch Institute, 2000.

Geiling, Natasha. "Why Climate Change Is a Women's Rights Issue." *Climate Progress,* June 24, 2015. http://thinkprogress.org/climate/2015/06/24/3672960/climate-change-womens-rights-united-nations/.

George, Susan. *How the Other Half Dies: The Real Reasons for World Hunger.* Montclair, NJ: Allenheld, Osmun, 1977.

———. *A Fate Worse Than Debt: The World Financial Crisis and the Poor.* New York: Grove, 1988.

————. *The Debt Boomerang: How Third World Debt Harms Us All.* Boulder, CO: Westview, 1992.

————. *Whose Crisis? Whose Future? Towards a Greener, Fairer, Richer World.* Cambridge: Polity, 2010.

George, Susan, and Fabrizio Sabelli. *Faith and Credit: The World Bank's Secular Empire.* Boulder, CO: Westview, 1994.

Gereffi, Gary. "Rethinking Development Theory: Insights From East Asia and Latin America." *Sociological Forum* 4, no. 4 (1989): 505–33.

————. "The Organization of Buyer-Driven Global Commodity Chains: How U.S. Retailers Shape Overseas Production Networks." In *Commodity Chains and Global Capitalism,* edited by Gary Gereffi and Miguel Korzeniewicz. Westport, CT: Praeger, 1994.

Gevisser, Mark. "AIDS: The New Apartheid." *The Nation,* May 14, 2001, 5–6.

Gibson, Nigel C. "Egypt and the Revolution in Our Minds." *Pambazuka News,* February 17, 2011. http://pambazuka.org/en/category/features/70972.

Gibson-Graham, J. K. *A Postcapitalist Politics.* Minneapolis: University of Minnesota Press, 2006.

Gilbert, Natasha. "One-Third of Our Greenhouse Gas Emissions Come From Agriculture." *Nature,* October 31, 2012. http://www.nature.com/news/one-third-of-our-greenhouse-gas-emissions-come-from-agriculture-1.11708.

Giridharadas, Anand. "'Second Tier' City to Rise Fast under India's Urban Plan." *New York Times,* May 13, 2007a, 3.

————. "Outsourcing Works, So India Is Exporting Jobs." *New York Times,* September 25, 2007b.

Glennie, Jonathan. "The Rise of the 'South–South' Aid Agencies." *Guardian Weekly,* March 4, 2011, 44.

Godoy, Julio. "Vive La Décroissance." *New Internationalist* 434 (2010): 19.

Godrej, Dinyar. "Precious Fluid." *New Internationalist* 354 (2003): 9–12.

Goldemberg, J., and O. Lucon. "Renewable Energy Options in Developing Countries." *Making It* 2 (2010): 16–18. http://www.makingitmagazine.net.

Goldman, Michael. *Imperial Nature: The World Bank and Struggles for Social Justice in the Age of Globalization.* New Haven: Yale University Press, 2005.

Goldsmith, James. *The Trap.* New York: Carroll & Graf, 1994.

Gorelick, Sherry. "Facing the Farm Crisis." *The Ecologist* 30, no. 4 (2000): 28–32.

Goss, Jasper, David Burch, and Roy E. Rickson. "Agri-Food Restructuring and Third World Transnationals: Thailand, the CP Group and the Global Shrimp Industry." *World Development* 28, no. 3 (2000): 513–30.

Gott, Richard. "Latin America Is Preparing to Settle Accounts With Its White Settler Elite." *The Guardian,* November 15, 2006, 33.

Gow, David. "India Gets a Brand New Carmaker—As It Runs Out of Roads to Drive On." *The Guardian,* March 30, 2007, 8.

Gowan, Peter. "The American Campaign for Global Sovereignty."

In *Fighting Identities: Socialist Register,* edited by Leo Panitch and Colin Leys. London: Merlin, 2003.

Graffham, A., J. Cooper, H. Wainwright, and J. MacGregor. *Small-Scale Farmers Who Withdraw From GlobalGAP: Results of a Survey in Kenya.* London: DFID, 2008.

Graham, Carol. *Safety Nets, Politics, and the Poor: Transitions to Market Economies.* Washington, DC: Brookings Institution, 1994.

GRAIN. "Agrofuels." *Seedling,* July 2007. www.grain.org/seedling/?type=68&1=0.

———. "The World Bank in the Hot Seat." *Seedling,* May 8, 2010. www.grain.org/articles/?id=64.

———. *Hungry for Land.* Report, May 2014. www.grain.org/article/entries/4929.

Green, Shannon N. "Human Rights and Gender Equality in the Sustainable Development Goals." *Center for Strategic and International Studies,* June 19, 2015. http://csis.org/publication/human-rights-and-gender-equality-sustainable-development-goals.

Greenfield, Gerard. "The WTO, the World Food System, and the Politics of Harmonised Destruction." 1999. www.labournet.org/discuss/global/wto/html.

Greenhouse, Steven. "In Florida Tomato Fields, a Penny Buys Progress." *New York Times,* April 24, 2014. http://www.nytimes.com/2014/04/25/business/in-florida-tomato-fields-a-penny-buys-progress.html?_r=0.

Greenlees, Donald. "Outsourcing Drifts to the Philippines After India Matures." *International Herald Tribune,* November 11, 2006, 1.

Greenpeace. "Eating Up the Amazon." 2006.

Greider, William. "A New Giant Sucking Sound." *The Nation,* December 31, 2001, 22–24.

———. "The Establishment Rethinks Globalization." *The Nation,* April 30, 2007, 11–14.

Gresh, Alain. "Freedom Makes You Giddy." *Le Monde Diplomatique,* February 2011, 1.

Griffin, K. B. *The Political Economy of Agrarian Change: An Essay on the Green Revolution.* Cambridge, MA: Harvard University Press, 1974.

Grigg, David. *The World Food Problem.* Oxford, UK: Blackwell, 1993.

Griggs, David. "Sustainable Development Goals for People and Planet." *Nature* 495, no. 21 (2013): 305–07.

Grossman, Raquel. "Globalization, Commodity Chains and Fruit Exporting Regions in Chile." *Tijdschrift voor Economische en Sociale Geographie* 90, no. 2 (1979): 211–25.

Gündüz, Zuhal Yeşilyurt. "The Feminization of Migration." *Monthly Review* 65, no. 7 (2013): 32–43.

Gupta. Akhil. *Postcolonial Developments: Agriculture in the Making of Modern India.* Durham, NC: Duke University Press, 1998.

Habermas, Jürgen. "Germany and the Euro-Crisis." *The Nation,* June 28, 2010, 18–22.

Halberg, N., H. F. Alroe, M. T. Knudsen, and E. S. Kristensen, eds. *Global Development of Organic Agriculture: Challenges and Promises.* Wallingford, UK: CAB International, 2005.

Hale, Stephen. "Global Campaigning to Tackle Poverty and Injustice Is No

Longer North v. South." *The Guardian,* February 14, 2011.

Halperin, Sandra. "Trans-Local and Trans-Regional Socio-Economic Structures in Global Development: A 'Horizontal' Perspective." In *New Directions in the Sociology of Global Development,* edited by Frederick H. Buttel and Philip McMichael, 19–56. Oxford: Elsevier, 2005.

Hamilton, Clive. *Growth Fetish.* Sydney: Allen & Unwin, 2003.

Hands Off the Land Alliance. *The Global Water Grab.* Amsterdam: TNI, 2014.

Harcourt, Wendy. "Introduction." In *Feminist Perspectives on Sustainable Development,* edited by Wendy Harcourt. London: Zed, 1994.

———. *Body Politics in Development: Critical Debates in Gender and Development.* London: Zed, 2009.

Harding, Luke. "Delhi Calling." *Guardian Weekly,* March 15–21, 2001, 23.

Harlan, Chico. "All Together Now." *Guardian Weekly,* July 15, 2011, 30.

Harnecker, Marta. "Latin America & Twenty-First Century Socialism." *Monthly Review* 62, no. 3 (2010): 3–83.

Harney, Alexandra. *The China Price: The True Cost of Chinese Competitive Advantage.* New York: Penguin Books, 2009.

Harris, Nigel. *The End of the Third World: Newly Industrializing Countries and the Decline of an Ideology.* Harmondsworth, UK: Penguin, 1987.

Harris, Paul. "Detroit Gets Growing." *The Observer,* July 11, 2010.

Harrison, Graham. *The World Bank and Africa: The Construction of Governance States.* London: Routledge, 2004.

Harrison, Paul. *The Third Revolution: Population, Environment and a Sustainable World.* Harmondsworth, UK: Penguin, 1993.

Harvey, David. *The New Imperialism.* Oxford: Oxford University Press, 2003.

———. *A Brief History of Neoliberalism.* Oxford: Oxford University Press, 2005.

———. *The Enigma of Capital.* Oxford: Oxford University Press, 2011.

Hawkins, Tony. "At the Heart of Further Progress." *Financial Times,* June 2, 1998, I–VI.

Hedges, Chris. "Key Panel at Cairo Talks Agrees on Population Plan." *New York Times,* September 13, 1994, A10.

Held, David. *Democracy and the Global Order: From the Modern State to Cosmopolitan Governance.* Stanford, CA: Stanford University Press, 1995.

Held, David, and Aysa Kaya, eds. *Global Inequality.* New York: Polity Press, 2007.

Helleiner, Eric. *States and the Reemergence of Global Finance: From Bretton Woods to the 1990s.* Ithaca, NY: Cornell University Press, 1996.

Heller, Patrick. "BRICS From Below: Counterpower Movements in Brazil, India and South Africa." *openDemocracy,* April 30, 2015. https://www.opendemocracy.net/patrick-heller/brics-from-below-countepower-movements-in-brazil-india-and-south-africa.

Henderson, Jeffrey. *The Globalisation of High Technology Production.*

London: Routledge & Kegan Paul, 1991.

Henriques, Diana. "Food Is Gold, So Billions Invested in Farming." *New York Times,* June 5, 2008.

Hertsgard, Mark. "Who's Afraid of Climate Change Now? The Pentagon." *The Nation,* July 2004.

Hervieu, Sébastien. "South Africa Gains Entry to BRIC Club." *Guardian Weekly,* April 22, 2011, 11.

Hettne, Björn. *Development Theory and the Three Worlds.* White Plains, NY: Longman, 1990.

Hicks, R. L., B. C. Parks, J. T. Roberts, and M. J. Tierney. *Greening Aid? Understanding the Environmental Impact of Development Assistance.* Oxford: Oxford University Press, 2008.

Hightower, Jim. "How Wal-Mart Is Remaking Our World." Pamphlet #7, Ithaca, NY, 2002.

Hildyard, Nicholas. "Foxes in Charge of Chickens." In *Global Ecology: A New Arena of Political Conflict,* edited by Wolfgang Sachs. London: Zed, 1993.

Hirata Kimura, Aya. *Hidden Hunger: Gender and the Politics of Smarter Foods.* Ithaca, NY: Cornell University Press, 2013.

Hobsbawm, Eric J. "The Crisis of Today's Ideologies." *New Left Review* 192 (1992): 55–64.

Hochschild, Arlie Russell. "Love and Gold." In *Global Woman: Nannies, Maids, and Sex Workers in the New Economy.* New York: Metropolitan Books, 2003.

Hodal, Kate, Chris Kelly, and Felicity Lawrence. "Revealed: Asian Slave Labour Producing Prawns for Supermarkets in US, UK." *The Guardian,* June 10, 2014. http://www.theguardian.com/global-development/2014/jun/10/supermarket-prawns-thailand-produced-slave-labour.

Holt-Giménez, Eric. *Campesino a Campesino: Voices From Latin America's Farmer to Farmer Movement for Sustainable Agriculture.* Oakland: FoodFirst, 2006.

———. "Exploding the Biofuel Myths." *Le Monde Diplomatique,* July 2007, 10–11.

Holt-Giménez, Eric, and Isabella Kenfield. "When 'Renewable' Isn't Sustainable: Agrofuels and the Inconvenient Truths Behind the 2007 U.S. Energy Independence and Security Act." *Policy Brief No. 13.* Oakland: Institute for Food and Development Policy, 2008.

Holtzman, David C. "Accounting for Nature's Benefits: The Dollar Value of Ecosystem Services." *Environmental Health Perspectives* 120, no. 4 (2012): 152–57. http://www.ncbi.nlm.nih.gov/pmc/articles/PMC3339477/.

Holusha, John. "Squeezing the Textile Workers." *New York Times,* February 21, 1996, D1, D20.

Hoogvelt, Ankie M. M. *The Third World in Global Development.* London: Macmillan, 1987.

———. *Globalization and the Postcolonial World: The New Political Economy of Development.* London: Macmillan, 1997.

———. "Globalization and Post-Modern Imperialism." *Globalizations* 3, no. 2 (2006): 159–74.

Huang, Yasheng. "Change to Change: Modernization, Development and Politics." In *From Modernization to Globalization: Perspectives on Development and Social Change,* edited by J. Timmons Roberts and Amy Hite. London: Blackwell, 2000.

Huntington, Samuel P. "Rethinking the Beijing Consensus." *Asia Policy* 11 (2011): 1–26.

Hutton, Will. "Burn Our Planet or Face Financial Meltdown: Not Much of a Choice." *The Guardian*, April 20, 2013. http://www.theguardian.com/commentisfree/2013/apr/21/carbon-problems-financial-crisis-hutton.

Iglesias, Pablo. "Understanding Podemos." *New Left Review* 93 (2015a): 7–22.

———. "Spain on Edge." *New Left Review* 93 (2015b): 23–42.

Instituto Nacional de Estadíscita, Geografía e Informática. 2004. www.inegi.gob.mx/ inegi/default.asp.

International Assessment of Agricultural Knowledge, Science and Technology for Development. *Executive Summary of the Synthesis Report, 2008.* www.agassessment.org/docs/SR_Exec_Sum_280508_English.pdf.

International Confederation of Free Trade Unions. 1995. www.cftu.org.

International Fund for Agriculture. "As Threat of a Renewed Food Crisis Looms, UN Food Agencies to Join G8 Agricultural Ministers in Treviso." *ReliefWeb*, April 19, 2009. www.reliefweb.int/rw/rwb.nsf/db900sid/MYAI-7R98NJ?OpenDocument.

International Labor Organization. 1995. www.ilo.org.

International Labor Organization. 2003. www.ilo.org.

Iriart, Celia, and Howard Waitzkin. "Managed Care Goes Global." *Multinational Monitor* 25, no. 10 (2004).

Isakson, S. Ryan. "No hay ganancia en la milpa: The Agrarian Question, Food Sovereignty, and the On-Farm Conservation of Agrobiodiversity in the Guatemalan Highlands." *Journal of Peasant Studies* 36, no. 4 (2010): 725–60.

Ishii, Naoko. "From Problem to Solution: Working With Industry for the Global Environment." *Making It* 16 (2014): 28–31.

Jackson, Cecile. "Doing What Comes Naturally? Women and Environment in Development." *World Development* 21, no. 12 (1993): 1947–63.

Jackson, Tim. *Prosperity Without Growth: Economics for a Finite Planet.* London: Earthscan, 2009.

Jaffee, Daniel. *Brewing Justice: Fair Trade Coffee, Sustainability, and Survival.* Berkeley: University of California Press, 2007.

Jahan, Rounaq. *The Elusive Agenda: Mainstreaming Women in Development.* London: Zed, 1995.

James, C. L. R. *The Black Jacobins: Toussaint L'Ouverture and the San Domingo Revolution.* New York: Vintage, 1963.

Jha, Alok. "Huge study Gives Wake-Up Call on State of World's Oceans." *Guardian Weekly,* March 22, 2008, 3.

Jha, Prem Shankar. *Crouching Dragon, Hidden Tiger: Can China and India Dominate the West?* New York: Soft Skull Press, 2010.

Jordan, Mary, and Kevin Sullivan. "Trade Brings Riches, but Not to Mexico's Poor." *Guardian Weekly,* April 3, 2003, 33.

Jowit, Juliette. "Trillion-Dollar Cost of Global Pollution." *Guardian Weekly,* February 26, 2010, 17.

Kagarlitsky, Boris. *The Mirage of Modernization.* New York: Monthly Review Press, 1995.

Kala, Anant Vijay. "India's Services Expansion Quickest in 8 Months in February." *Wall Street Journal,* March 4, 2015. http://www.wsj.com/articles/indias-services-expansion-quickest-in-8-months-in-february-1425451528.

Karliner, Joshua. *The Corporate Planet: Ecology and Politics in the Age of Globalization.* San Francisco: Sierra Club Books, 1997.

Kemp, Tom. *Industrialization in the Non-Western World.* London: Longman, 1989.

Kennedy, Bruce. "China's Three Gorges Dam." *CNN.* 2001. http://www.cnn.com/SPECIALS/1999/china.50/asian.superpower/three.gorges/.

Kernaghan, Charles. *Zoned for Slavery: The Child Behind the Label* [Videotape]. New York: National Labor Committee, 1995.

Kidron, Michael, and Ronald Segal. *The State of the World Atlas.* London: Pan, 1981.

Kimbrell, Andrew. *The Fatal Harvest Reader: The Tragedy of Industrial Agriculture.* Washington, DC: Island Press, 2002.

Kinver, Mark. "UN Report: Cities Ignore Climate Change at Their Peril." *BBC News,* March 29, 2011. http://www.bbc.co.uk/news/science-environment-12881779.

Klare, Michael T. *Resource Wars: The New Landscape of Global Conflict.* New York: Henry Holt, 2002.

Klein, Naomi. *The Shock Doctrine. The Rise of Disaster Capitalism.* New York: Metropolitan Books, 2007.

———. *This Changes Everything: Capitalism vs. the Climate.* London: Allen Lane, 2014.

Klein, R., T. Banuri, S. Kartha, and L. Schipper. "International Climate Policy." *Commission on Climate Change and Development,* March 2008.

Kloppenburg, Jack R., Jr. *First the Seed: The Political Economy of Plant Biotechnology, 1492–2000.* Cambridge, MA: Cambridge University Press, 1988.

Knox, Paul, and John Agnew. *The Geography of the World Economy.* London: Edward Arnold, 1994.

Kohl, Benjamin, and Linda Farthing. *Impasse in Bolivia: Neoliberal Hegemony & Popular Resistance.* London: Zed, 2006.

Kolko, Joyce. *Restructuring the World Economy.* New York: Pantheon, 1988.

Korten, David. *When Corporations Rule the World.* New York: Kumarian, 1995.

Korzeniewicz, Miguel. "Commodity Chains and Marketing Strategies: Nike and the Global Athletic Footwear Industry." In *Commodity Chains and Global Capitalism,* edited by Gary Gereffi and Miguel Korzeniewicz. Westport, CT: Praeger, 1994.

Kothari, Smitu, and Pramod Parajuli. "No Nature Without Social Justice: A Plea for Cultural and Ecological Pluralism in India." In *Global Ecology: A New Arena of Political*

Conflict, edited by Wolfgang Sachs. London: Zed, 1993.

Kotkin, Stephen. "First World, Third World (Maybe Not in That Order)." *New York Times,* May 6, 2007, 4.

Krauss, Clifford. "In Global Forecast, China Looms Large as Energy User and Maker of Green Power." *New York Times,* November 10, 2010, D7.

Krauss, Clifford, and Keith Bradsher. "China's Global Ambitions, Cash and Strings Attached." *New York Times,* July 26, 2015, 1, 10.

Krichah, Samah, Nzira Deus, Natasha Sajjad, Mariana Mancilla, Diakhoumba Gassama, and Sarah Gold. "Women Need the Same Rights as Men, Because Development Needs Equality." *The Guardian,* April 17, 2015. http://www.theguardian.com/global-development/2015/apr/17/commission-population-development-new-york-young-feminists.

Kristoff, Nicholas D. "A Hedge Fund Republic?" *New York Times,* November 18, 2010.

Kumar, Karthick. "Organic Farming—Can It Feed the World?" *EcoWalk the Talk,* March 11, 2011.

Kurlantzik, Joshua. "The Rise of Elected Autocrats Threatens Democracy." *Bloomberg Business,* January 23, 2014. http://www.bloomberg.com/bw/articles/2014-01-23/the-rise-of-elected-autocrats-threatens-democracy.

Landsberg, Martin. "ALBA and the Promise of Cooperative Development." *Monthly Review* 62, no. 7 (2010): 1–17.

———. "Export-Led Industrialization in the Third World: Manufacturing Imperialism." *Review of Radical Political Economics* 2, no. 4 (1979): 50–63.

Lang, Tim, and Colin Hines. *The New Protectionism: Protecting the Future Against Free Trade.* New York: The New Press, 1993.

Lang, Tim, and Michael Heasman. *Food Wars: The Global Battle for Mouths, Minds and Markets.* London: Earthscan, 2004.

Lapēna, Carmena. "Women Around the World Unite Versus Landgrabbing." *Food Crisis and the Global Land Grab,* July 7, 2011. http://farmlandgrab.org/post/view/18917.

Lappé, Frances Moore, and Anna Lappé. *Hope's Edge.* New York: Tarcher/Putnam, 2002.

LaTouche, Serge. *In the Wake of the Affluent Society: An Exploration of Post-Development.* London: Zed, 1993.

———. "Degrowth Economics." *Le Monde Diplomatique,* November 2004, 15.

Lawrence, Felicity. "Sucked Dry by Asparagus." *Guardian Weekly,* October 24, 2010, 24.

———. "Guatemala Pays a High Price for Global Food System Failings." *The Guardian,* June 1, 2011.

Le Carre, John. "In Place of Nations." *The Nation,* April 9, 2001, 11–13.

Leader. "Shining Example." *The Guardian,* April 23, 2004, 3.

Leahy, Stephen. "Reinventing Agriculture." *Inter Press Service,* April 15, 2008.

Lee, Ching Kwan. "Rights Activism in China." *Contexts.* 2008.

———. "Raw Encounters, Chinese Managers, African Workers and the Politics of Casualization in Africa's Chinese Enclaves." *The China Quarterly* 199 (2009): 647–99.

Lehman, David. *Democracy and Development in Latin America.* Philadelphia: Temple University Press, 1990.

Lehman, K., and A. Krebs. "Control of the World's Food Supply." In *The Case against the Global Economy, and for a Turn Toward the Local,* edited by J. Mander and E. Goldsmith. San Francisco: Sierra Club Books, 1996.

Lenin, Vladimir Ilych. *Imperialism: The Highest Stage of Capitalism.* New York: International Publishers, 1997. (Original work published 1916)

LeQuesne, C. "The World Trade Organization and Food Security." Talk to UK Food Group, July 15, 1997, London.

Leslie, Jacques. "The Last Empire." *Mother Jones,* January/February 2008, 28–39, 83.

Lewin, Tamar. "Family Decay Global, Study Says." *New York Times,* May 30, 1995, A5.

Lewis, Paul. "IMF Seeks Argentine Deal Linking Credit to Governing." *New York Times,* July 15, 1997, D1, D19.

Li, Tania Murray. "Centering Labor in the Land Grab Debate." *Journal of Peasant Studies* 38, no. 2 (2011): 281–98.

Lim, L. C. "Sustainable Agriculture Pushing Back the Desert." *Institute of Science in Society.* 2008. isis.org.uk/desertification.php.

Lipton, Michael. *Why Poor People Stay Poor: Urban Bias in World Development.* London: Temple Smith, 1977.

Lissakers, Karin. *Banks, Borrowers, and the Establishment: A Revisionist Account of the International Debt Crisis.* New York: Basic Books, 1993.

Llambi, Luis. "Transitions To and Within Capitalism: Agrarian Transitions in Latin America." *Sociologia Ruralis* 30, no. 2 (1990): 174–96.

Lohmann, Larry. "Resisting Green Globalism." In *Global Ecology: A New Arena of Political Conflict,* edited by Wolfgang Sachs. London: Zed, 1993.

López, Isidro, and Emmanuel Rodríguez. "The Spanish Model." *New Left Review* 69 (2011): 5–29.

Lovelock, James. *The Revenge of Gaia: Earth's Climate Crisis and the Fate of Humanity.* New York: Basic Books, 2007.

Lütkenhorst, Manfried. "A Changing Climate for Industrial Policy." *Making It* 3 (July 2010): 16–19.

Ma'anit, Adam. "Costing the Earth." *New Internationalist* 413 (2008): 17–19.

Maathai, Wangari. *The Challenge for Africa.* New York: Anchor Books, 2010.

Macdonald, Laura. "Gendering Transnational Social Movement Analysis: Women's Groups Contest Free Trade in the Americas." In *Coalitions Across Borders. Transnational Protest and the Neoliberal Order,* edited by Joe Bandy and Jackie Smith. New York: Rowman & Littlefield, 2005.

MacShane, Denis. "Working in Virtual Slavery: Gulf Migrant Labor." *The Nation,* March 18, 1991, 325, 343–44.

Madden, Peter, and John Madeley. "Winners and Losers: The Impact of the GATT Uruguay Round in Developing Countries." *Christian Aid,* December 1993, 17.

Madeley, John. *Hungry for Trade.* London: Zed, 2000.

Magdoff, Harry. *The Age of Imperialism.* New York: Monthly Review Press, 1969.

Makki, Fouad. "Post-Colonial Africa and the World Economy: The Long Waves of Uneven Development." *Journal of World-Systems Research* 21, no. 1 (2015): 124–46.

Malkin, Elizabeth. "Wave of Protests Spreads to Scandal-Weary Honduras and Guatemala." *New York Times,* June 14, 2015, 9.

Mamdani, Mahmood. *Citizen and Subject: Contemporary Africa and the Legacy of Late Colonialism.* Princeton, NJ: Princeton University Press, 1996.

———. "Making Sense of Political Violence in Post-Colonial Africa." In *Fighting Identities: Race, Religion and Ethno-Nationalism: Socialist Register 2003,* edited by Leo Panitch and Colin Leys. London: Merlin, 2003.

Mankiw, Gregory N. "History Echoes Through Greek Debt Crisis." *New York Times,* July 19, 2015, Sunday Business, 4.

Mann, Alana. *Global Activism in Food Politics. Power Shift.* New York: Palgrave MacMillan, 2014.

Mark, Jason. "Brazil's MST: Taking Back the Land." *Multinational Monitor* 22 (2001): 10–12.

Marsden, Terry K. *The Condition of Rural Sustainability.* Wageningen: Van Gorcum, 2003.

Marsden, Terry, and Jonathan Murdoch, eds. *Between the Local and the Global: Confronting Complexity in the Contemporary Agri-Food Sector.* Oxford: Elsevier, 2006.

Martin, Hans-Peter, and Harold Schumann. *The Global Trap: Globalisation and the Assault on Democracy and Prosperity.* London: Zed, 1997.

Martinez-Alier, Joan. *The Environmentalism of the Poor: A Study of Ecological Conflicts and Valuation.* Cheltenham, UK: Edward Elgar, 2002.

———. "Beyond GDP Lies Economic Degrowth." *European Alternatives,* March 2010. http://www.euroalter .com/2010/beyond-gdp-lies-economic-degrowth/.

Marx, Karl. *Das Kapital.* Moscow: Progress, 1965.

Mason, Paul. "'Hope Begins Today': The Inside Story of Syriza's Rise to Power." *The Guardian,* January 28, 2015a. http://www.theguardian .com/world/2015/jan/28/greek-people-wrote-history-how-syriza-rose-to-power.

———. "The End of Capitalism Has Begun." *The Guardian,* July 17, 2015b. http://www.theguard-ian.com/books/2015/jul/17/postcapitalism-end-of-capitalism-begun.

Maybarduk, Peter. "A People's Health System." *Multinational Monitor* 25, no. 10 (2004).

McAfee, Kathy. "The Contradictory Logic of Global Ecosystems Services Markets." *Development and Change* 43, no. 1 (2012): 105–32.

McBride, Stephen. "Reconfiguring Sovereignty: NAFTA Chapter 11 Dispute Settlement Procedures and the Issue of Public-Private Authority." *Canadian Journal of Political Science/Revue canadienne de science politique* 39, no. 4 (2006): 1–21.

McCartney, Clem. "Interrogating Shared Societies Through Practice and Theory." *Development* 57, no. 1 (2014): 8–14.

McDougall, Dan. "Success in a Slum." *Guardian Weekly,* March 16–22, 2007, 29.

McGreal, Chris. "Continent Waits to See Cost of Lavish Embrace." *Guardian Weekly,* December 22–January 4, 2006–07, 6.

McKeon, Nora. *The United Nations and Civil Society: Legitimating Global Governance—Whose Voice?* London: Zed, 2009.

———. *The New Alliance for Food Security and Nutrition: A Coup for Corporate Capital?* TNI Agrarian Justice Programme, Policy Paper, May 2014. Amsterdam: Transnational Institute.

———. *Food Security Governance. Empowering Communities, Regulating Corporations.* London: Routledge, 2015.

McKibben, Bill. *Eaarth: Making a Life on a Tough New Planet.* New York: Times, 2010.

McMichael, A. J. *Planetary Overload: Global Environmental Change and the Health of the Human Species.* Cambridge, UK: Cambridge University Press, 1993.

McMichael, A. J., J. W. Powles, C. D. Butler, and R. Uauy. "Food, Livestock Production, Energy, Climate Change and Health." *Lancet,* September 13, 2007.

McMichael, Philip. *Settlers and the Agrarian Question: Foundations of Capitalism in Colonial Australia.* Cambridge: Cambridge University Press, 1985.

———. "Agro-Food Restructuring in the Pacific Rim: A Comparative-International Perspective on Japan, South Korea, the United States, Australia, and Thailand." In *Pacific-Asia and the Future of the World-System,* edited by Ravi Palat. Westport, CT: Greenwood, 1993.

———. "World Food System Restructuring under a GATT Regime." *Political Geography* 12, no. 3 (1993): 198–214.

———. "Global Development and the Corporate Food Regime." In *New Directions in the Sociology of Global Development,* edited by Frederick H. Buttel and Philip McMichael. Amsterdam: Elsevier, 2005.

———. "Contemporary Contradictions of the Global Development Project: Geopolitics, Global Ecology, and the 'Development Climate.'" *Third World Quarterly* 30, no. 1 (2009a): 247–62.

———. "A Food Regime Analysis of the 'World Food Crisis.'" *Agriculture and Human Values* 4 (2009b): 281–95.

———. "Banking on Agriculture: A Review of the World Development

Report 2008." *Journal of Agrarian Change* 9, no. 2 (2009c): 235–46.

———. "The Agrofuels Project at Large." *Critical Sociology* 35, no. 6 (2009d): 825–39.

———. "Agrofuels in the Food Regime." *Journal of Peasant Studies* 37, no. 4 (2010): 609–29.

———. *Food Regimes and Agrarian Questions.* Halifax, NS: Fernwood, 2013.

McMichael, Philip, and Chul-Kyoo Kim. "Japanese and South Korean Agricultural Restructuring in Comparative and Global Perspective." In *The Global Restructuring of Agro-Food Systems,* edited by Philip McMichael. Ithaca, NY: Cornell University Press, 1994.

McMichael, Philip, and Laura T. Raynolds. "Capitalism, Agriculture, and World Economy." In *Capitalism and Development,* edited by Leslie Sklair. London: Routledge & Kegan Paul, 1994.

Memmi, Albert. *The Colonizer and the Colonized.* Boston: Beacon, 1967.

Menon, Gayatri A. *The Multivalency of Microcredit: The Cultural Politics of Credit and Citizenship in India.* Unpublished Master's Thesis, Development Sociology, Cornell University, New York, 2001.

———. "Recoveries of Space and Subjectivity in the Shadow of Violence: The Clandestine Politics of Pavement Dwellers in Mumbai." In *Contesting Development: Critical Struggles for Social Change,* edited by Philip McMichael, 151–64. New York: Routledge, 2010.

Middleton, Neil, Phil O'Keefe, and Sam Moyo. *Tears of the Crocodile: From Rio to Reality in the Developing World.* Boulder, CO: Pluto, 1993.

Mies, Maria. *Patriarchy and Accumulation on a World Scale: Women in the International Division of Labor.* London: Zed, 1991.

Millennium Ecosystem Assessment. *Ecosystems and Human Well-Being.* Washington, DC: World Resources, Institute, 2005. http://www.millenniumassessment.org/documents/document.358.aspx.pdf

Miroff, Nick. "Commodity boom Extracts a Heavy Toll on Amazon Forests." *Guardian Weekly,* January 9, 2015, 12.

Mishra, Pankaj. "Narendra Modi and the New Face of India." *The Guardian,* May 16, 2015.

Mitchell, Timothy. *Colonizing Egypt.* Berkeley: University of California Press, 1991.

Mitchell, William. "Deficit Mania Is Built on a Series of Destructive Neoliberal Myths." *The Nation,* April 4, 2011, 12.

Mittal, Anuradha. "Introduction." In *Voices from Africa: African Farmers and Environmentalists Speak Out Against a New Green Revolution in Africa,* edited by Anuradha Mittal with Melissa Moore. The Oakland Institute, 2009.

Mize, Ronald L., and Alicia C. S. Swords. *Consuming Mexican Labor. From the Bracero Program to NAFTA.* Toronto: University of Toronto Press, 2010.

Moghadam, Valentine M. *Modernizing Women: Gender and Social Change in the Middle East.* Boulder, CO: Lynne Rienner, 1993.

———. *Globalization Women: Transnational Feminist Networks.*

Baltimore: Johns Hopkins University Press, 2005a.

———. "Editorial." *International Social Science Journal*, 184 (2005b): 203–06.

Monbiot, George. *Heat: How to Stop the Planet Burning*. London: Allen Lane, 2006.

Montalbano, William D. "A Global Pursuit of Happiness." *Los Angeles Times*, October 1, 1991, F1.

Mooallem, Jon. "The Afterlife of Cellphones." *New York Times*, January 13, 2008.

Moody, Kim. *Workers in a Lean World: Unions in the International Economy*. London: Verso, 1999.

Moran, Theodore H. "Investment Issues." In *The WTO After Seattle*, edited by Jeffrey J. Schott. Washington, DC: Institute for International Economics, 2000.

Morrow, Adrian. "Big Problems in Little Bahrain." *The Global and Mail*, March 18, 2011, A10.

Mosse, David. "Is Good Policy Unimplementable? Reflections on the Ethnography of Aid Policy and Practice." *Development and Change 35*, no. 4 (2004): 639–71.

Muchena, D. T. "The China Factor in Southern Africa." *Openspace* 1, no. 4 (2006): 22–26.

Müller, Anders Riel, and Raj Patel. "Shining India? Economic Liberalization and Rural Poverty in the 1990s." *Food First Policy Brief No. 10, 2004.*

Mulyana, Wahyu, Ivo Setiono, Amy Kracker Selzer, Sainan Zhang, David Dodman, and Daniel Schensul. *Urbanisation, Demographics and Adaptation to Climate Change in Semarang, Indonesia*. London: International Institute for Environment and Development, 2013.

Murphy, Sophia. "WTO, Agricultural Deregulation, and Food Security." Paper presented at the Globalization Challenge Initiative, December 1999. www.foreignpolicyinfocus. org/briefs/v0114n34wto_body. html.

Murphy, Sophia, David Burch, and Jennifer Clapp. *Cereal Secrets. The World's Largest Grain Traders and Global Agriculture*. Oxfam Research Reports, August 2012. https://www .oxfam.org/sites/www.oxfam.org/ files/rr-cereal-secrets-grain-traders- agriculture-30082012-en.pdf.

Myers, N., and J. Kent. "New Consumers: The Influence of Affluence on the Environment." *Proceedings of the National Academy of Sciences of the USA* 100, no. 8 (2003): 4963–68.

Myerson, Allen R. "In Principle, a Case for More 'Sweatshops.'" *New York Times*, June 22, 1997, 5.

Naeem, Shahid. "Lessons from the Reverse Engineering of Nature." *Miller-McCune* 2, no. 3 (2009): 56–71.

Narayan, Deepa, with Raj Patel, Kai Schaft, Anne Rademacher, and Sarah Koch-Schulte. *Can Anyone Hear Us? Voices of the Poor*. New York: Oxford, 2002.

Nash, Nathaniel C. "Vast Areas of Rain Forest Are Being Destroyed in Chile." *New York Times*, May 31, 1994, C4.

Newman, Bryan. "Indian Farmer Suicides: A Lesson for Africa's Farmers." *Food First Backgrounder* 12, no. 4 (2006): 2.

Nicholson, Paul. "Vía Campesina: Responding to Global Systemic Crisis." *Development* 51, no. 4 (2008): 456–59.

Noble, David. "The Corporate Climate Coup." *GlobalResearch*, May 4, 2007. www.globalresearch .ca/the-corporate-climate-coup/ 5568

North American Congress on Latin America. "A Run for Their Money." *North American Congress on Latin America* 11, no. 4 (1977): 168–75.

Nossiter, Adam. "Half a World From the Gulf, a Spill Scourge 5 Decades Old." *New York Times,* June 17, 2010, A1, A18.

Nourishing the Planet. "Farming the Cities, Feeding an Urban Future." *World Watch Institute*, 2010. http://blogs.worldwatch.org/ nourishingtheplanet/.

Nussbaum, Martha. *Creating Capabilities: The Human Development Approach.* Cambridge: Harvard University Press, 2011a.

———. "What Makes Life Good?" *The Nation,* May 2, 2011b, 23.

Ong, Aihwa. "The Gender and Labor Politics of Postmodernity." In *The Politics of Culture in the Shadow of Capital,* edited by Lisa Lowe and David Lloyd. Durham, NC: Duke University Press, 1997.

Oram, Julian. "Sustainable Intensification in Africa Feeds Greedy Agribusiness, Not People." Greenpeace International, May 4, 2012. http:// www.greenpeace.org/international/ en/news/Blogs/makingwaves/sustainable-intensification-in-africafeeds-t/blog/40270/.

Orlanda Pinnasi, Maria, Fatima Cabral, and Mirian Claudia Lourencao. "An Interview With Joao Pedro Stedile." *Latin American Perspectives* 27, no. 5 (2000): 46–62.

Orth, Sheri. *Subsistence Foods to Export Goods: The Impact of an Oil Palm Plantation on Local Food Sovereignty, North Bariot, Central Kalimantan, Indonesia.* Sawit Watch, Wagenigen: Van Hall Larenstein, 2007.

Oster, Shai. "World's Top Polluter Emerges as Green-Technology Leader." *Wall Street Journal,* December 15, 2009.

Oxfam. *Other Worlds Are Possible: Human Progress in an Age of Climate Change,* 2009. http://www .oxfam.org.uk/resources/policy/climate_change/other-worlds-are-possible.html.

Palan, Ronen. *The Offshore World. Sovereign Markets, Virtual Places, and Nomad Millionaires.* Ithaca, NY: Cornell University Press, 2003.

Palmer, Karen. "Africa Faces Barren Future." *The Star,* March 31, 2006.

Paranagua, Paulo A. "Caracas Runs on Easy Money." *Guardian Weekly,* February 9–15, 2007, 27.

Parenti, Christian. "Hugo Chávez and Petro Populism." *The Nation,* April 11, 2005, 15–21.

Paringaux, R.-P. "The Deliberate Destruction of Agriculture: India: Free Markets, Empty Bellies." *Le Monde Diplomatique,* September 2001, 1–9.

Park, Clara Mi Young, and Julia Ben White. "We Are Not All the Same: Taking Gender Seriously in Food Sovereignty Discourse." *Third World Quarterly* 36, no. 3 (2015): 584–99.

Parrott, Nicholas, and Terry Marsden. *The Real Green Revolution: Organic and Agroecological Farming in the South*. London: Greenpeace Environmental Trust, 2002.

Patel, Raj. "What Does NEPAD Stand For?" *Voice of the Turtle*, 2002b. http://voiceoftheturtle.org/show_article.php?aid=97.

———. *Stuffed and Starved: Markets, Power and the Hidden Battle for the World Food System*. London: Portobello, 2007.

———. "The Long Green Revolution." *Journal of Peasant Studies* 40, no. 1 (2013): 1–63.

Patel, Raj, Rachel Bezner Kerr, Lizzie Shumba, and Oaifolo Dakishoni. "Cook, Eat, Man, Woman: Understanding the New Alliance for Food Security and Nutrition; Nutritionism and Its Alternatives From Malawi. *Journal of Peasant Studies* 42, no. 1–2 (2015): 21–44.

Patel, Raj, with A. Delwiche. "The Profits of Famine: Southern Africa's Long Decade of Hunger." *Backgrounder, Food First* 8, no. 4 (2002a). www.foodfirst.org/pubs/backgrdrs/ 2002/f02v8n4.html.

Patnaik, Probat. "The Accumulation Process in the Period of Globalization." *Economic & Political Weekly* 28 (2008): 108–13.

Patnaik, Utsa. "Global Capitalism, Deflation and Agrarian Crisis in Developing Countries." *Social Policy and Development Programme Paper Number 15*. Geneva: UNRISD, 2003.

Paul, Helena, and Ricarda Steinbrecher. "African Agricultural Growth Corridors and the New Alliance for Food Security and Nutrition: Who Benefits, Who Loses?" EcoNexus, 2013. www.econexus.inof/sites/econexus/files/African_Agricultural_Growth_Corridors_&_New_Alliance_-_EcoNexus_June_2013.pdf.

Payne, Anthony, and Nicola Phillips. *Development*. Cambridge: Polity, 2010.

Pearlstein, Steven. "What's Retarding India's Growth?" *Guardian Weekly*, April 22, 2011, 20.

Pearse, A. *Seeds of Plenty, Seeds of Want*. Oxford, UK: Clarendon, 1980.

Perfecto, Ivette, John Vandermeer, and Angus Wright. *Nature's Matrix: Linking Agriculture, Conservation and Food Sovereignty*. London: Earthscan, 2009.

Perkins, John H. *Geopolitics and the Green Revolution: Wheat, Genes and the Cold War*. New York: Oxford University Press, 1997.

Perkins, Patricia E. "Equitable, Ecological Degrowth: Feminist Contributions." Presented at 2nd Conference on Economic Degrowth, Barcelona, March 26–29, 2010. http://www.barcelona.degrowth.org/fileadmin/content/documents/Proceedings/Perkins.pdf.

Perlez, Jane. "U.N. Chief Calls on U.S. Companies to Donate to AIDS Fund." *New York Times*, June 2, 2001, A1.

———. "For Some Indonesians, Echoes of 'Coolie' Nation." *New York Times*, August 18, 2002, 10.

Perrons, Diane. *Globalization and Social Change: People and Places in a Divided World*. London: Routledge, 2005.

Petrini, Carlo. *Slow Food: The Case for Taste.* New York: Columbia University Press, 2001.

Phillips, Tom. "China May Adopt 'Two-Child Policy' This Year as Demographic Time Bomb Looms." *The Guardian,* July 23, 2015.

Pieterse, Jan Niederveen. "Global Inequality: Bringing Politics Back In." *Third World Quarterly* 23, no. 6 (2002):1023–46.

Pilger, John. *The New Rulers of the World.* London: Verso, 2002.

Pionetti, Carine. *Sowing Autonomy: Gender and Seed Politics in Semi-Arid India.* London: IIED, 2005.

Piot, Olivier. "Tunisia: Diary of a Revolution." *Le Monde Diplomatique,* February, 2011, 4.

Piot, Charles. *Nostalgia for the Future: West Africa After the Cold War.* Chicago: University of Chicago Press, 2010.

Polanyi, Karl. *The Great Transformation.* Boston: Beacon Press. 1944/2001.

Polgreen, Lydia. "Africa's Storied Colleges, Jammed and Crumbling." *New York Times,* May 20, 2007, A1, 4.

Prebisch, Raúl. "The Economic Development of Latin America and its Principal Problems." Reprinted in *Economic Bulletin for Latin America* 7, no. 1 (1962): 1–22.

Press, Eyal. "Beyond GDP." *The Nation,* May 2, 2011, 25.

Pretty, J., and R. Hine. "Reducing Food Poverty With Sustainable Agriculture: A Summary of New Evidence." Final report from the "SAFE World" Research Project, University of Essex, 2001. www2.essex.ac.uk/ces/ Fresearch Programmes/SAFEWexecsumm finalreport.htm.

Pretty, J., C. Toulmin, and S. Williams. "Sustainable Intensification in African Agriculture." *International Journal of Agricultural Sustainability* 9, no. 1 (2011): 1–241. http://www.julespretty.com/ wp-content/uploads/2013/09/17.-IJAS-Africa-Sust-Intensification-Pretty-et-al-2011.pdf.

Pretty, J. N., J. J. L. Morison, and R. E. Hine. "Reducing Food Poverty by Increasing Agricultural Sustainability in Developing Countries." *Agriculture, Ecosystems, & Environment,* 95 (2003): 217–34.

Pretty, Jules. *Agri-Culture: Reconnecting People, Land and Nature.* London: Earthscan, 2002.

Provost, Claire, and Matt Kennard. "Ukraine Agribusiness Firms in 'Quiet Land Grab' With Development Finance." *The Guardian,* July 30, 2015.

Public Citizen. "Down on the Farm: NAFTA's Seven-Year War on Farmers and Ranchers in the U.S., Canada and Mexico." *Report for Public Citizen's Global Trade Watch,* 2001. http://www.publiccitizen.org/documents/ACF18B. PDF

Quark, Amy A. *Global Rivalries: Standards, Wars, & the Transnational Cotton Trade.* Chicago: University of Chicago Press, 2013.

Rademacher, Anne, and Raj Patel. "Retelling Worlds of Poverty: Reflections on Transforming Participatory Research for a Global Narrative." In *Knowing Poverty: Critical Reflections on Participatory Research and Policy,* edited by

K. Brock and R. McGee. London: Earthscan, 2002.

Raikes, Philip. *Modernising Hunger: Famine, Food Surplus & Farm Policy in the EC and Africa.* London: Catholic Institute for International Affairs, 1988.

Rainforest Action Network. "Getting Real About Biofuels." 2007. http://www.ran.org/getting-real-about-biofuels#main-content.

Ramesh, Randeep. "Indians Get First Taste of Supermarket Shopping, but Wal-Mart Is Kept at Bay." *Guardian Weekly,* June 9–15, 2006, 16.

———. "India Grows Its Crop of Billionaires." *Guardian Weekly,* November 27, 2009, 17.

Rankin, Kathy. "Governing Development: Neoliberalism, Microcredit, and Rational Economic Woman." *Economy and Society* 30, no. 1 (2001): 18–37.

Ransom, David. "A World Turned Upside Down." *New Internationalist* 334 (2001a): 9–11.

———. *The No-Nonsense Guide to Fair Trade.* London: Verso, 2001b.

Rasmussen, Mikkel Bolt. *Crisis to Insurrection: Notes on the Ongoing Collapse.* Wivenhoe: Minor Compositions, 2015. http://www.historicalmaterialism.org/news/distributed/new-book-crisis-to-insurrection.-notes-on-the-ongoing-collapse.

Rau, Bill. *From Feast to Famine: Official Cures and Grassroots Remedies to Africa's Food Crisis.* London: Zed, 1991.

Raudsepp-Hearne, Ciara, Garry D. Peterson, Maria Tengö, Elena M. Bennett, Tim Holland, Karina Benessaiah, Graham K. MacDonald,

and Laura Pfeifer. "Untangling the Environmentalist's Paradox: Why Is Human Well-Being Increasing as Ecosystem Services Degrade?" *BioScience,* September 2010.

Raynolds, Laura T. "The Restructuring of Export Agriculture in the Dominican Republic: Changing Agrarian Relations and the State." In *The Global Restructuring of Agro-Food Systems,* edited by Philip McMichael. Ithaca, NY: Cornell University Press, 1994.

———. "Re-Embedding Global Agriculture: The International Organic and Fair Trade Movements." *Agriculture and Human Values* 17 (2000): 297–309.

———. "New Plantations, New Workers: Gender and Production Politics in the Dominican Republic." *Gender & Society* 15, no. 1 (2001): 7–28.

Raynolds, Laura T., David Myhre, Philip McMichael, Viviana Carro-Figueroa, and Frederick H. Buttel. "The 'New' Internationalization of Agriculture: A Reformulation." *World Development* 21, no. 7 (1993): 1101–21.

Razavi, Shahrashoub, and Carol Miller. *From WID to GAD: Conceptual Shifts in the Women and Development Discourse.* Occasional Paper 1. Geneva: UN Research Institute for Social Development, UNDP, 1995.

Reardon, Tom, and C. P. Timmer. "Transformation of Markets for Agricultural Output in Developing Countries Since 1950: How Has Thinking Changed?" In *Handbook of Agricultural Economics,* edited by R. E. Evenson, P. Pingali, and T. P. Schultz. Oxford: Elsevier, 2005.

Redding, Sean. "Structural Adjustment and the Decline of Subsistence Agriculture in Africa." 2000. http://women crossing.org/redding.html.

Reich, Robert B. "Secession of the Successful." *New York Times Magazine*, January 20, 1991, 42.

———. *The Work of Nations: Preparing Ourselves for 21st Century Capitalism*. New York: Vintage, 1992.

———. "Waterboarding Greece." *The Nation*, August 3–10, 2015, 4–5, 8.

Reij, Chris. "More Success Stories in Africa's Drylands Than Often Assumed." *ROPPA* (The Network of Peasant Organizations and Producers in West Africa), 2006. http://roppa.info/?IMG/pdf/More_success_stories_in_Africa-Reij_Chris.pdf.

Renner, Michael. *The Anatomy of Resource Wars*. Worldwatch Paper No. 162. Washington, DC: Worldwatch, 2002.

Revel, Alain, and Christophe Riboud. *American Green Power*. Baltimore: Johns Hopkins University Press, 1986.

Ricardo, David. *On the Principles of Political Economy and Taxation*, 3rd ed. In *The Works and Correspondence of David Ricardo*, Vol. 1, edited by P. Sraffe with the collaboration of M. M. Dobb. Cambridge, UK: Cambridge University Press, 1951. (Originally published 1817)

Rice, A. "Is There Such a Thing as Agro-Imperialism?" *New York Times*, November 22, 2009.

Rice, Xan. "Ethiopia—Country of the Silver Sickle—Offers Land Dirt Cheap to Farming Giants." *The Guardian*, January 15, 2010.

Rich, Bruce. *Mortgaging the Earth: The World Bank, Environmental Impoverishment, and the Crisis of Development*. Boston: Beacon, 1994.

Richburg, Keith B. "Illegal Workers Do Europe's Dirty Work." *Guardian Weekly*, August 15–21, 2002, 29.

Ride, Anouk. "Maps, Myths, and Migrants." *New Internationalist* 305 (1998): 9.

Rifkin, Jeremy. *Beyond Beef: The Rise and Fall of the Cattle Culture*. New York: Penguin, 1992.

———. *The Biotech Century: Harnessing the Gene and Remaking the World*. New York: Tarcher/Putnam, 1998.

Rist, Gilbert. *The History of Development: From Western Origins to Global Faith*. London: Zed, 1997.

———. "Development as Buzzword." *Development in Practice* 17, no. 4–5 (2007).

Ritchie, Mark. *Breaking the Deadlock: The United States and Agriculture Policy in the Uruguay Round*. Minneapolis: Institute for Agriculture and Trade Policy, 1993.

———. "The World Trade Organization and the Human Right to Food Security." Paper presented at the International Cooperative Agriculture Organization General Assembly, August 29, 1999, Quebec City, Canada. www.agricoop.org/activities/mark_ritchie.htm.

Roberts, Timmons J., and Bradley C. Park. *A Climate of Injustice. Global Inequality, North–South Politics, and Climate Policy*. Cambridge, MA: MIT Press, 2007.

Roberts, Wayne. *The No-Nonsense Guide to World Food*. Oxford: The New Internationalist, 2008.

Robinson, William I. "Remapping Development in Light of Globalization: From a Territorial to a Social Cartography." *Third World Quarterly* 23, no. 6 (2002): 1047–71.

———. *A Theory of Global Capitalism: Production, Class, and State in a Transnational World*. Baltimore: Johns Hopkins University Press, 2004.

Rocca, Jean-Louis. "The Flaws in the Chinese Economic Miracle." *Le Monde Diplomatique,* May 2007, 10.

Rocheleau, Dianne E. "Gender, Ecology, and the Science of Survival: Stories and Lessons from Kenya." In *Feminist Perspectives on Sustainable Development,* edited by Wendy Harcourt. London: Zed, 1991.

Roodman, David Malin. "Still Waiting for the Jubilee: Pragmatic Solutions for the Third World Debt Crisis." Worldwatch Paper No. 155. Washington, DC: Worldwatch, 2001.

Rose, Nicholas J. *Optimism of the Will: Food Sovereignty as Transformative Counter-Hegemony in the 21st Century*. PhD Thesis, School of Global Studies, RMIT University, Australia. 2012.

Ross, Robert J. S., and Kent C. Trachte. *Global Capitalism: The New Leviathan*. Albany, NY: SUNY Press, 1990.

Rostow, Walt W. *The Stages of Economic Growth: A Non-Communist Manifesto*. Cambridge, UK: Cambridge University Press, 1960.

Rowley, C. D. *The Destruction of Aboriginal Society*. Ringwood, Australia: Penguin, 1974.

Rowling, Megan. "Sea Change." *New Internationalist* 341 (2001): 23–24.

Roy, Ananya. *Poverty Capital: Microfinance and the Making of Development*. New York: Routledge, 2010.

Roy, Arundhati. "The Greater Common Good." *Friends of River Narmada,* 1999. http://www.narmada.org/gcg/gcg.html.

Royal Society. *Reaping the Benefits: Science and the Sustainable Intensification of Global Agriculture*. London: The Royal Society, 2009.

Rozhnov, Konstantin. "BRIC Tries to Shift Power Balance." *BBC News,* July 16, 2010.

Ruggiero, Renato. "Reflections From Seattle." In *The WTO After Seattle,* edited by Jeffrey Schott. Washington, DC: Institute for International Economics, 2000.

Rulli, Maria Cristina, Antonio Saviori, and Paolo D'Odorico. "Global Land and Water Grabbing." *PNAS* 110, no. 3 (2012): 892–97.

Rydgem, James, and Samuela Bassi. "Global Cooperation and Understanding to Accelerate Climate Action." In *The Global Development of Policy Regimes to Combat Climate Change,* edited by Nicholas Stern, Alex Bowen, and John Whalley. London: World Scientific, 2015.

Sachs, Jeffrey. "The IMF and the Asian Flu." *The American Prospect,* March–April, 1998, 16–21.

———. *The End of Poverty: Economic Possibilities for Our Time*. New York: Penguin, 2005.

Sachs, Wolfgang. "One World." In *The Development Dictionary*, edited by Wolfgang Sachs. London: Zed, 1992.

———. *Planet Dialectics: Explorations in Environment and Development*. London: Zed, 1999.

Sadasivam, Bharati. "The Impact of Structural Adjustment on Women: A Governance and Human Rights Agenda." *Human Rights Quarterly* 19, no. 3 (1997): 630–65.

Sader, Emir. "The Weakest Link? Neoliberalism in Latin America." *New Left Review* 52 (2008): 5–32.

———. "Postneoliberalism in Latin America." *Development Dialogue* 51 (2009): 171–80.

Salehabadi, Djahane. "*Der Kampf um den Abfallstrom*: Conflict and Contestation in Re-Valuing E-Waste in Germany." *Re/Cycling Histories* Conference, Rachel Carson Center, Munich, Germany, May 27–29, 2011.

Salmon, Katy. "Where There Are No Subsidies." *New Internationalist* 334 (2001): 22.

Sammy, Wambua. "Water Privatization in Kenya." Heinrich Böll Stiftung, Global Issue Papers, No. 8, 2004. https://www.boell.de/sites/default/files/assets/boell.de/images/download_de/internationalepolitik/GIP8.pdf.

Sampath, G. "Teaching the Poor to Behave." *The Hindu*, June 30, 2015. http://www.thehindu.com/opinion/op-ed/teaching-the-poor-to-behave/article7368130.ece.

Sanderson, Steven. *The Transformation of Mexican Agriculture: International Structure and the Politics of Rural Change*. Princeton, NJ: Princeton University Press, 1986a.

———. "The Emergence of the 'World Steer': Internationalization and Foreign Domination in Latin American Cattle Production." In *Food, the State, and International Political Economy*, edited by F. L. Tullis and W. L. Hollist. Lincoln: University of Nebraska Press, 1986b.

Sanger, David E. "Dissension Erupts at Talks on World Financial Crisis." *New York Times*, October 7, 1998, A6.

Sanger-Katz, Margot. "America Starts to Push Away From the Plate." *New York Times*, July 26, 2015, 15.

Santos, Boaventura de Sousa. *Towards a New Legal Common Sense*. London: Butterworths, 2002.

———. "The Podemas Wave." *openDemocracy*, March 16, 2015.

Saul, John Ralston. *The Collapse of Globalism and the Reinvention of the World*. New York: Penguin, 2005.

Savio, Roberto. "The Hidden Truths Behind the Greek Drama." *The Forum*, SID, 2015. http://www.sidint.net/content/hidden-truths-behind-greek-drama.

Schaar, J. "Overview of Adaptation Mainstreaming Initiatives." *Commission on Climate Change and Development*, March 2008.

Schapiro, Mark. *Carbon Shock. How Carbon Is Changing the Cost of Everything*. White River Junction, VT: Chelsea Green, 2014.

Schneider, Cathy Lisa. *Shantytown Protest in Pinochet's Chile*. Philadelphia: Temple University Press, 1995.

Schneider, Howard. "Arab World Needs an Economic Revolution." *Guardian Weekly,* March 4, 2011, 17.

Schneider, Mindi. "Developing the Meat Grab." *Journal of Peasant Studies* 41, no. 3–4 (2014): 613–34.

Schor, Juliet. *The Overspent American.* New York: Harper Collins, 1998.

Schott, Jeffrey J. "The WTO After Seattle." In *The WTO After Seattle,* edited by Jeffrey J. Schott. Washington, DC: Institute for International Economics, 2000.

Schwarzer, S., A. De Bono, G. Guiliani, S. Kluser, and P. Peduzzi. "E-Waste: The Hidden Side of IT Equipment's Manufacturing and Use." In *Environment Alert Bulletin,* edited by UNEP/GRID-Europe. Geneva: United Nations Environment Programme DEWA/GRID, 2005.

Scott, Jason. "Chinese Eye Australian Outback in $43 Billion Foreign Farming Policy." *Bloomberg Business,* August 4, 2015.

Seelye, Katherine Q. "Detroit Census Figures Confirm a Grim Desertion Like No Other." *New York Times,* March 23, 2011, A1, A20.

Segelken, Roger. "Fewer Foods Predicted for Crowded Future Meals." *Cornell Chronicle,* February 23, 1995, 5.

Seidman, Gay. *Manufacturing Militance: Workers' Movements in Brazil and South Africa, 1970–1985.* Berkeley: University of California Press, 1994.

Sekler, Nicola. "Postneoliberalism From and As a Counter-Hegemonic Perspective." *Development Dialogue,* January 2009: 59–71.

Sen, Gita. "Women, Poverty, and Population: Issues for the Concerned Environmentalist." In *Feminist Perspectives on Sustainable Development,* edited by Wendy Harcourt. London: Zed, 1994.

Sengupta, Somini. "As Indian Growth Soars, Child Hunger Persists." *New York Times,* July 17, 2009.

———. "60 Million People Fleeing Chaotic Lands, U.N. Says." *New York Times,* June 18, 2015. http://nyti.ms/1fixgP7.

Séréni, Jean-Pierre. "Hydrocarbon Nationalism." *Le Monde Diplomatique,* March 2007, 12.

Sergie, Mohamad Aly, Robert McMahon, Jeremy Sherlick, and Hagit Ariav. "The Sunni–Shia Divide." *Foreign Affairs,* 2014. http://www.cfr.org/peace-conflict-and-human-rights/sunni-shia-divide/p33176#!/.

Sexsmith, Kathleen, and Philip McMichael. "Formulating the SDGs: Reproducing or Reimagining State-Centered Development?" *Globalizations* 12, no. 4 (2015): 581–96.

Sharma, Devinder. "Big Box Retail Will Boost Poverty." *India Together,* February 16, 2007.

Sharma, Kalpana. *Rediscovering Dharavi: Stories From Asia's Largest Slum.* New Delhi: Penguin, 2000.

Shashwat, D.C. "Green Concerns on the Rise of Saffron Modi." *Sustainabilityzero,* 2014. http://sustainabilityzero.com/modienvironment/.

Shattuck, Annie. "The Financial Crisis and the Food Crisis: Two Sides of the Same Coin." *FoodFirst,* September 2008.

Sheller, Mimi. *Consuming the Caribbean.* New York: Routledge, 2003.

Shenker, Jack. "Cairo Strikes $3 Billion IMF Deal." *Guardian Weekly,* June 10, 2011, 18.

Shepard, Wade. *Ghost Cities of China.* London: Zed, 2014.

Shi, Zhengrong. "Everywhere Under the Sun." *Making It* 2 (April 2010): 32–35.

Shiva, Vandana. *The Violence of the Green Revolution.* London: Zed, 1991/2000.

———. *Biopiracy: The Plunder of Nature and Knowledge.* Boston: South End, 1997.

———. *Soil Not Oil: Environmental Justice in an Age of Climate Crisis.* Cambridge, Mass: South End Press, 2008.

Silver, Beverly. *Forces of Labor: Worker's Movements and Globalization Since 1870.* Cambridge, UK: Cambridge University Press, 2003.

Singer, Hans W. "U.S. Foreign Investment in Underdeveloped Areas: The Distribution of Gains Between Investing and Borrowing Countries." *American Economic Review, Papers and Proceedings* 40 (1950): 473–85.

Singh, Ajit. "The Lost Decade: The Economic Crisis of the Third World in the 1980s—How the North Caused the South's Crisis." *Contention* 2 (1992): 58–80.

Sklair, Leslie. *Assembling for Development: The Maquila Industry in Mexico and the United States.* Boston: Unwin Hyman, 1989.

———. *Globalization: Capitalism & Its Alternatives.* Oxford, UK: Oxford University Press, 2002.

Smith, Adam. *An Inquiry Into the Nature and Causes of the Wealth of Nations,* 2 Vols. London: Dent & Sons, 1776/1904.

Smith, David. "One in Three Africans 'Now Middle-Class.'" *Guardian Weekly,* May 13, 2011, 6.

———. "Ethiopia's Road to Affluence Bypasses Democratic Rule." *Guardian Weekly,* November 14, 2014, 27.

Smith, Jeremy. "An Unappealing Industry." *The Ecologist* 32, no. 3 (2002): 40–41.

South Centre, The. *Facing the Challenge: Responses to the Report of the South Commission.* London: Zed, 1993.

Southend-of-the-Sea in Transition. 2007. https://westclifftransition.wordpress.com/.

Stancil, Jordan. "Europe's Voodoo Economics." *The Nation,* June 28, 2010.

Standing, Guy. *The Precariat: The New Dangerous Class.* London and New York: Bloomsbury Academic, 2011.

Stanhill, G. "The Comparative Productivity of Organic Agriculture." *Agriculture, Ecosystems and Environment* 30 (1990): 1–26.

Starr, Amory. *Naming the Enemy: Anti-Corporate Movements Confront Globalization.* London: Zed, 2000.

Stavrianos, L. S. *Global Rift: The Third World Comes of Age.* New York: William Morrow, 1981.

Stern, Nicholas. *The Economics of Climate Change: The Stern Review.* Cambridge: Cambridge University Press, 2006.

Stevens, William K. "Poor Lands' Success in Cutting Birth Rate Upsets Old Theories." *New York Times,* January 2, 1994, A8.

Stewart, Heather. "Has Globalization Hit the Wall?" *Guardian Weekly,* May 29, 2015, 1, 14.

Stiglitz, Joseph. "Greece, the Sacrificial Lamb." *New York Times*, July 26, 2015, Sunday Review, 5.

Strange, Susan. *States and Markets.* London: Pinter, 1994.

Stuart, Liz. "Journey's End for Trafficked Humans." *Guardian Weekly,* February 13–19, 2003, 21.

Subcomandante Marcos. "First Declaration of the Lacandon Jungle." *AVA* 42, no. 31 (1994): 1.

Sumner, Andy. "The New Bottom Billion and the MDGs—A Plan of Action." *IDS in Focus Policy Briefing,* October 2010.

Sundaram, Jomo K. "Rethinking Poverty Reduction." *Making It* 3 (2010): 38–39.

Swatuk, Larry, Meghan McMorris, Charmaine Leung, and Yuyan Zu. "Seeing 'Invisible Water': Challenging Conceptions of Water for Agriculture, Food and Human Security." *Canadian Journal of Development Studies* 36, no. 1 (2015): 24–37.

Swing, William Lacy. "Migration Comes of Age." *Strategic Review*, July 6, 2015.

Tabuchi, Hiroko. "Chinese Textile Mills Are Now Hiring in Places Where Cotton Was King." *New York Times*, August 2, 2015. http://www.nytimes.com/2015/08/03/business/chinese-textile-mills-are-now-hiring-in-places-where-cotton-was-king.html?smid=nytcore-iphone-share&smprod=nytcore-iphone&_r=0.

Tan, Abby. "Paychecks Sent Home May Not Cover Human Losses." *Los Angeles Times,* October 1, 1991a, H2–H3.

———. "The Labor Brokers: For a Price, There's a Job Abroad—Maybe." *Los Angeles Times,* October 1, 1991b, H1.

Tanaka, Nobuo. "The Next Industrial Revolution." *Making It* 2 (April 2010): 19–21.

Tenkouano, Abdou. "The Nutritional and Economic Potential of Vegetables." In *State of the World 2011: Innovations That Nourish the Planet.* New York: Norton, 2011.

Therborn, Göran. *The World: A Beginner's Guide.* Cambridge: Polity, 2011.

———. "Class in the 21st Century." *New Left Review* 78 (2012): 5–29.

Thomas, Alan, and Ben Crow, eds. *Third World Atlas.* 2nd ed. Washington, DC: Taylor & Francis, 1994.

Thompson, Ginger. "Big Mexican Breadwinner: The Migrant Worker." *New York Times,* March 25, 2002, A3.

Thompson, Tony. "All Work and No Play in 'Virtual Sweatshop.'" *Guardian Weekly,* March 25–31, 2005, 17.

Thorpe, David. "Can Cities Feed Their Inhabitants?" *Making It* 18 (2015): 17–19.

Titumir, Rashed Al Mahmud, and Mustafa Kamal. "Growing Together Sustainably: A Zero-Poverty Post–2015 Development Framework." *Development* 56, no. 2 (2013): 172–84.

Tomich, Dale. *Through the Prism of Slavery: Labor, Capital and World Economy.* Boulder: Rowman & Littlefield, 2004.

Toulmin, Camilla. *Climate Change in Africa.* London: Zed, 2009.

Tran, Mark. "Tunisia Offers Wake-Up Call for Development." *Guardian,* June 9, 2011.

Tripathi, Salil. "Shine On." *Guardian Unlimited,* May 13, 2004.

Turner, Mandy. "Scramble for Africa." *The Guardian,* May 2, 2007.

Tuxill, John. "Nature's Cornucopia: Our Stake in Plant Diversity." Worldwatch Paper No. 148. Washington, DC: Worldwatch, 1999.

Tyler, Patrick E. "China Planning People's Car to Put Masses Behind Wheel." *New York Times,* September 22, 1994, A1, D8.

Uchitelle, Louis. "NAFTA Should Have Stopped Illegal Immigration, Right?" *New York Times,* February 18, 2007, 4.

———. "From Two Breadwinners to One." *The Nation,* May 23, 2011, 17–19.

UNAC and GRAIN. *The Land Grabbers of the Nacala Corridor: A New Era of Struggle Against Colonial Plantations in Northern Mozambique,* February 2015. http://viacampesina.org/en/images/stories/pdf/2015-grain-5137-the-land-grabbers-of-the-nacala-corridor.pdf.

United Nations. *Human Development Report.* New York: Oxford University Press, 1997.

United Nations Conference on Trade and Development. *Trade and Development Report 1996.* Geneva: Author, 1996.

United Nations Conference on Trade and Development and United Nations Environment Programme. *Organic Agriculture and Food Security in Africa.* New York: United Nations, 2008.

United Nations Department of Economic and Social Affairs. "Retooling Global Development." *World Economic and Social Survey.* New York: United Nations, 2010a.

———. *The Millennium Development Goals Report.* New York: United Nations, 2010b. http://www.unfpa.org/public/site/global/lang/en/pid/6090.

United Nations Development Programme. *United Nations Development Report.* New York: Oxford University Press, 1997.

———. *Human Development Report.* New York: Oxford University Press, 2010.

———. *Human Development Report.* New York: United Nations, 2011a. http://hdr.undp.org/en/statistics/indices/.

———. *Human Development Report.* New York: United Nations, 2011b. http://hdr.undp.org/en/reports/global/hdr2011/.

———. Global Alliance for Climate-Smart Agriculture Action Plan. *Climate Summit,* 2014. http://www.un.org/climatechange/summit/wp-content/uploads/sites/2/2014/09/AGRICULTURE-Action-Plan.pdf.

UN-HABITAT. *The Challenge of Slums*: *Global Report on Human Settlements.* London: Earthscan, 2003.

United Nations Framework Convention on Climate Change. *Report of the 7th Conference of Parties.* New York: United Nations, 2001. http://unfccc.int/national_reports/napa/items/2719.php.

Uphoff, Norman. "Higher Yields With Fewer External Inputs? The System of Rice Intensification and Potential Contributions to Agricultural

Sustainability." *International Journal of Agricultural Sustainability* 1 (2003): 38–50.

Van der Gaag, Nikki. *The No-Nonsense Guide to Women's Rights*. London: Verso, 2004.

Van der Ploeg, J.D. *The New Peasantries: New Struggles for Autonomy and Sustainability in an Era of Empire and Globalization*. London: Earthscan, 2009.

Venkatesan, J. "Supreme Court Report." *The Hindu,* July 22, 2010. www.thehindu.com/2010/07/22/stories/2010072 261200300.htm.

Vía Campesina. "Bangalore Declaration." October 6, 2000. http://viacampesina.org/main_en/index.php?option=com_content&task=view&id=53&Itemid=28.

Victor, Peter. "Questioning Economic Growth." *Nature* 468 (2010): 370–71.

Vidal, John. "All Dried Up." *Guardian Weekly,* March 27–April 2, 2003, 24.

———. "Beyond the City Limits." *The Guardian,* September 8, 2004, 18.

———. "Climate Change and Shortages of Fuel Signal Global Food Crisis." *Guardian Weekly,* September 11, 2007, 3.

———. "Climate Change to Force Mass Migration." *The Guardian,* May 14, 2007.

———. "Billions Wasted on UN Climate Programme." *Guardian Weekly,* May 30–June 5, 2008: 1.

———. "How Food and Water Are Driving a 21st-Century African Land Grab." *The Observer,* March 7, 2010.

———. "Bolivia Enshrines Rights of Mother Nature." *Guardian Weekly,* April 15, 2011, 7.

———. "India's rice revolution." *The Guardian,* February 16. http://www.theguardian.com/global-development/2013/feb/16/india-rice-farmers-revolution.

Wacker, Corinne. "Sustainable Development Through Women's Groups: A Cultural Approach to Sustainable Development." In *Feminist Perspectives on Sustainable Development,* edited by Wendy Harcourt. London: Zed, 1994.

Wade, Robert. "Reply to Martin Wolf." *Financial Times,* July 26, 2010.

Wainwright, Oliver. "Life in China Can Be Perfectly Fine—If You Have a Dome." *Guardian Weekly,* January 16, 2015, 27–28.

Walker, Richard. *The Conquest of Bread: 150 Years of Agribusiness in California*. New York: New Press, 2004.

Wallach, Lori. "What the WTO Didn't Want You to Know." March 7, 2003. http://www.dissidentvoice.org/Articles2/Wallach_WTO.htm

Wallach, Lori, and Michelle Sforza. *Whose Trade Organization? Corporate Globalization and the Erosion of Democracy*. Washington, DC: Public Citizen, 1999.

Wallach, Lori, and Patrick Woodall. *Whose Trade Organization? A Comprehensive Guide to the WTO*. New York: New Press, 2004.

Wallerstein, Immanuel. "Development: Lodestar or Illusion?" *Economic and Political Weekly* 23, no. 39 (1988): 2017–23.

———. *The Modern World-System*. New York: Academic Press, 1974.

Walton, John, and David Seddon. *Free Markets & Food Riots: The Politics of Global Adjustment.* Oxford, UK: Blackwell, 1994.

Warde, Ibrahim. "Are They Saviours, Predators or Dupes?" *Le Monde Diplomatique,* May 2008, 1–2.

Waring, Marilyn. *If Women Counted: A New Feminist Economics.* San Francisco: Harper & Row, 1988.

Watkins, Kevin. "Agriculture and Food Security in the GATT Uruguay Round." *Review of African Political Economy* 50 (1991): 38–50.

———. "Money Talks." *Guardian Weekly,* May 9–15, 2002, 21.

———. "The Forgotten Other India." *The Guardian,* October 3, 2006.

Watts, Jonathan. "Rivals Awake to a Giant in Their Midst." *Guardian Weekly,* December 23–January 5, 2005/2006, 36.

———. "Greatest Shoppers Ever?" *Guardian Weekly,* July 16, 2010, 25–27.

———. "China Counts Cost of Breakneck Growth." *Guardian Weekly,* January 7, 2011a, 10.

———. "Rich in China Get Richer Only Faster." *Guardian Weekly,* July 11, 2011b.

Watts, Michael. "Life Under Contract: Contract Farming, Agrarian Restructuring, and Flexible Accumulation." In *Living Under Contract: Contract Farming and Agrarian Transformation in Sub-Saharan Africa,* edited by Peter D. Little and Michael J. Watts. Madison: University of Wisconsin Press, 1994.

Weber, Heloise. "The 'New Economy' and Social Risk: Banking on the Poor?" *Review of International Political Economy* 11, no. 2 (2004): 356–86.

———. "Politics of Global Social Relations: Organizing 'Everyday Lived Experiences' of Development and Destitution." *Australian Journal of International Affairs* 64, no. 1 (2010): 105–22.

Weis, Tony. *The Global Food Economy.* London: Zed, 2007.

———. *The Ecological Hoofprint: The Global Burden of Industrial Livestock.* London: Zed, 2013.

Weisman, Jonathan. "At Global Economic Gathering, U.S. Primacy Is Seen as Ebbing." *New York Times,* April 17, 2015a. http://www.nytimes.com/2015/04/18/business/international/at-global-economic-gathering-concerns-that-us-is-ceding-its-leadership-role.html?_r=0.

———. "U.S. Shifts Stance on Drug Pricing in Pacific Trade Pact Talks, Document Reveals." *New York Times,* June 10, 2015b. http://www.nytimes.com/2015/06/11/business/international/us-shifts-stance-on-drug-pricing-in-pacific-trade-pact-talks-document-reveals.html?_r=0.

Weiss, R. "Firms Seek Patents on 'Climate Ready' Altered Crops." *Washington Post,* May 13, 2008.

Weissman, Robert. "Prelude to a New Colonialism: The Real Purpose of GATT." *The Nation,* March 18, 1991, 337.

Wessel, James. *Trading the Future: Farm Exports and the Concentration of Economic Power in Our Food System.* San Francisco: Institute for Food and Development Policy, 1983.

Wheatley, Alan. "Water Crisis Threatens Asia's Rise." *International Herald Tribune,* October 12, 2010, 24.

White, Richard E., and Gloria Eugenia González Marino. "Las Gaviotas: Sustainability in the Tropics." *World Watch* 20, no. 3 (2007): 18–23.

Wick, Ingeborg. *Women Working in the Shadows: The Informal Economy and Export Processing Zones.* March 22, 2010. http://digitalcommons.ilr.cornell.edu/globaldocs/334/.

Widmer, Rolf, Heidi Oswald-Krapf, Deepali Sinha-Khetriwal, Max Schnellmann, and Heinz Böni. "Global Perspectives on E-Waste." *Environmental Impact Assessment Review* 25 (2005): 436–58.

Wike, Richard. "With 41% of Global Wealth in the Hands of Less Than 1%, Elites and Citizens Agree Inequality Is a Top Priority." *Pew Research*, November 8, 2014. http://www.pewresearch.org/fact-tank/2014/11/08/with-41-of-global-wealth-in-the-hands-of-less-than-1-elites-and-citizens-agree-inequality-is-a-top-priority/.

———. "Inequality Is at Top of the Agenda as Global Elites Gather in Davos." *Pew Research*, January 21, 2015. http://www.pewresearch.org/fact-tank/2015/01/21/inequality-is-at-top-of-the-agenda-as-global-elites-gather-in-davos/.

Williams, Gwyneth. *Third-World Political Organizations: A Review of Developments.* Montclair, NJ: Allenheld, Osmun, 1981.

Wilson, Elliot. "Billions Pour In for India's Superclass." *Guardian Weekly,* May 14, 2010, 17.

Wittman, Hannah. "Reworking the Metabolic Rift: La Vía Campesina, Agrarian Citizenship and Food Sovereignty." *Journal of Peasant Studies* 36, no. 4 (2009): 805–26.

Wittman, Hannah, Annette Aurélie Desmarais, and Nettie Wiebe, eds. *Food Sovereignty: Reconnecting Food, Nature and Community.* Halifax, NS: Fernwood Press, 2010.

Wolf, Eric. *Peasant Wars of the Twentieth Century.* New York: HarperCollins Paperbacks, 1969.

———. *Europe and the People Without History.* Berkeley: University of California Press, 1982.

Wolf, Martin. "Three Years On, Fault Lines Threaten the World Economy." *Financial Times,* July 14, 2010a, 7.

———. "Why the West Faces a Harsher Future." *Financial Times,* July 12, 2010b.

Wolfensohn, James. "Rethinking Development—Challenges and Opportunities." *UNCTAD* Meeting, Bangkok, February 16, 2000.

Wolford, Wendy. *This Land Is Ours Now: Social Mobilization and the Meanings of Land in Brazil.* Durham, NC: Duke University Press, 2010.

Wong, Edward. "As China Aids Labor, Unrest Is Still Rising." *New York Times,* June 21, 2010.

Wood, Robert E. *From Marshall Plan to Debt Crisis: Foreign Aid and Development Choices in the World Economy.* Berkeley: University of California Press, 1986.

Woodall, Pam. "War of the Worlds: A Survey of the Global Economy." *The Economist,* October 1, 1994, Special Supplement, 24.

Woods, Ngaire. *The Globalizers: The IMF, the World Bank, and Their*

Borrowers. Ithaca, NY: Cornell University Press, 2006.

World Assembly of Muslim Youth. "Women in Islam: Beyond the Stereotypes." *Discover Islam.* 2004. http://discover.islamway.net/articles.php?article_id=16.

World Bank. *World Development Report.* Washington, DC: World Bank, 1998–1999.

———. *Voices of the Poor.* New York: Oxford University Press, 2000.

———. *World Development Report.* Washington, DC: World Bank, 2000.

———. Press Release. Foreign Investment, Remittances Outpace Debt as Sources of Finance for Developing Countries: World Bank No. 2003/266/S, 2003. http://go.worldbank.org/1RE2A DYFF0.

———. *World Development Report.* Washington, DC: World Bank, 2007.

———. *Rising Global Interest in Farmland: Can It Yield Sustainable and Equitable Benefits?* Washington, DC: World Bank, 2011.

———. *Benchmarking the Business of Agriculture.* 2014.

———. *Migration and Development Brief 23.* October 6, 2014.

———. *The Practice of Responsible Investment Principles in Larger-Scale Agricultural Investment: Implications for Corporate Performance and Impact on Local Communities.* Report No 86175-GLB. Washington, DC: World Bank, 2014.

World Institute for Development Economics Research. *The World Distribution of Household Wealth.* Helsinki, 2006.

Wu, Beina. "China's Environmental Crisis." Council on Foreign Relations, Backgrounder, April 25, 2014. http://www.cfr.org/china/chinas-environmental-crisis/p12608.

Yumkella, Kandeh K., and Leena Srivastava. "Energy for All." *Making It* 2 (April 2010): 23–29.

Yunus, Muhammad. "Sacrificing Microcredit for Megaprofits." *New York Times,* January 15, 2011, A19.

Zapatista Army of National Liberation. "How We See the World." *EZLN Communiqué,* June 30, 2005. http://www.anarkismo.net/newswire.php?story_id=805.

Index